AMERICA THROUGH WOMEN'S EYES

AMERICA
THROUGH WOMEN'S EYES

Edited by

MARY R. BEARD

GREENWOOD PRESS, PUBLISHERS
NEW YORK

Beard, Mary (Ritter) 1876–1958, *ed.*
America through women's eyes. New York, Greenwood
Press ₍1969, °1933₎

558 p. 23 cm.

Bibliography : p. 549–552.

1. Women in the United States. 2. U. S.—Social conditions.
3. U. S.—History. ɪ. Title.

E161.B42   1969   301.41′2′0973   68–54772
                                                          MARC

Library of Congress   ₍5₎

Reprinted with the permission of William Beard and Miriam
B. Vagts

Reprinted by Greenwood Press, Inc.

First Greenwood reprinting 1969
Paperback edition 1976

Library of Congress Catalog Card Number 68-54772

ISBN 0-8371-0301-0 Cloth edition
ISBN 0-8371-8951-9 Paper edition

Printed in the United States of America

PREFATORY NOTE

MARY R. BEARD, our mother and the editor of this collection of women's writings, was a life-long student of American history who had a deep appreciation of the rôle women had played in it. Seeking to win for them greater recognition, she gave them careful attention in the two school texts she wrote with her husbands, the noted historian Charles A. Beard—*History of the United States* (1921, last revised 1932) and *The Making of American Civilization* (1937). Her interest in their work and ideas found further expression in the two major histories they wrote for the general public—*The Rise of American Civilization* (1927) and *A Basic History of the United States* (1944).

Through the volume reprinted here, she rendered American women still another service. She let them tell their own story in greater detail and in their own words; then she did her best to secure for them a wider audience.

In a brief acknowledgment appearing in the original edition (published by the Macmillan Company in 1933), she credited her husband for his assistance "in framing the conception of American history" that she had illustrated with her selections. Finally, she left behind, on her death, a personal copy of the original edition in which she had noted a few minor errors. We checked all of these notations and made the necessary corrections before this reprinting was begun.

—WILLIAM BEARD and MRS. MIRIAM B. VAGTS
Scottsdale, Arizona; Sherman, Connecticut—1968

CONTENTS

AMERICA THROUGH WOMEN'S EYES

INTRODUCTION

THE most striking and significant tendency of contemporary social thought is in the direction of integrating all the aspects of life. That thought is widening the range of interest to the very borders of culture and deepening its roots in the substance of history. "The "economic man" and the "political man" are disappearing as "causal factors" and efforts to comprehend the movement of society which we call contemporary history become increasingly catholic in their reaches. So marked has been this recent trend of social thought that it is scarcely too much to say that we are now in the very midst of an intellectual revolution, perhaps the most fundamental in the long course of civilization—that we are today passing over the threshold of a period even more re-constructive than the Renaissance which flowered in the sixteenth century.

Illustrations of this statement are to be found everywhere in the thinking of the Western World. In Europe it is manifest in the writings of Benedetto Croce, particularly in his *History: Its Theory and Practice,* and in the works of cultural anthropologists in Germany. The founding of the Social Science Research Council in the United States offers evidence that American intellectualism has recognized the limitations of specialism and is seeking to advance by an integration of knowledge. Officially this same movement in ideas has been made manifest in the report on *Recent Social Trends,* by President Hoover's Committee, where an effort is made to bring the several divisions of social thought to a focus on a central problem—that of American civilization itself. And a recognition of this drift in thinking is also revealed in the call of the National Council of Women, representing a membership of five million women in the component organizations, for the conference at Chicago in 1933 on "Our Common Cause—Civilization." In these and many other tendencies is found the warrant for saying that the revolution in social thought is already in process and that the alignment of interests to harmonize with it has begun.

In the light of this wider and deeper understanding of the course of culture and civilization, all the divisions of thought, so assiduously cultivated by specialists—such as economics, politics, war, art, literature, education and feminism—are being dissolved as independent entities. They are no longer regarded as isolated departments of life, open to special observation, self-contained, each running under its own momentum according to its own laws or characteristics. All conceptions of culture or civilization as collections of commodities in a basket called history are being definitely abandoned by contemporary thinkers. They are rejected because they do not correspond with the reality of society in development. They are even regarded as hindrances to the understanding of civilization and to the formulation of social policies designed to conserve and promote it. By no possible exercise of the imagination can we turn the clock back and restore the intellectual climate of the nineteenth century. That age has passed and the new epoch has opened, although a few may fail to note it while they continue to dwell in their memories.

It is now recognized that what seemed to be eternal in the age of Victoria was a transient phase—a pause of peace—in the long and turbulent history of mankind. For a brief moment in the development of the Western World, when statecraft and high finance appeared to be firmly established, it was assumed that politicians and businessmen were making the wheels of society turn and the sun rise in the east. Then historians and "rigorous" thinkers concentrated on politics and economics, of the capitalist type. Since the titular directors of politics and economics were men, women dropped out of the historical thought which was concerned with the outward and the obvious. Practical statesmen, professional diplomats, and competent businessmen seemed to be the primordial forces actually running society; and the golden stream of profits pouring into the purses of their wives and daughters presumably proved the point. Women of the leisure class trained in colleges accepted this thesis of "the man's world" at face value and their highest aspiration was to win "equality" in the world so conceived. Having once occupied a place of power and action in the economy of agriculture and handicrafts, without the exercise of much sex consciousness, they now waged a conscious battle for a foothold in the apparently solid structure of the new economics and politics with their professional appendages; and after they had won a large measure of equality with legal safeguards, they showed an inclination to settle back in its illusory security and to forget about women, that is about society as an organism in process of evolution.

It was generally agreed, to be sure, that this new social structure was occasionally shaken from foundation to turret by wars and panics, but these phenomena were commonly regarded as fleeting clouds drifting over the sun of normalcy. Normalcy was deemed to be truly "normal" and social earthquakes merely incidents. After all, had not the United States in the "long" course of a hundred years ridden safely through many such calamities? The hundred years, admittedly, was only a brief span in the thousands of years between the dawn of civilization and the latest hour, but that meant little to busy politicians and businessmen and to the economists, historians, and other specialists engaged in describing, praising and advising. For them, it seemed, the making of history had come to an end and the absolute and unconditioned had been reached—if not in the age of McKinley, at least in the age of Coolidge.

But when the panic that opened in 1929 spread with devastating sweep over the nation supposedly secure, the question was raised whether a civilization based on profit-making industry and spoils-dividing politics, so enriching for women of the leisure class and so generous in opportunities for higher employments offered to women of the lower middle class, was not after all a transitory phase of history, notwithstanding its duration of a century or more. That "man's world," in which women had secured a foothold, had been more of a nightmare than a dreamland for millions of working women. This they knew from bitter experience. And when the mirage dissolved in the crash which began in 1929, when the claims of propertied women to a life divorced from labor became, to an amazing degree, worthless paper, when emancipated professional women lost their clients and pupils, and the proletariat was turned into the streets, then the social thought, that had been slowly developing before the crisis, came into its own. Once more bewildered humanity began to ponder on the foundations and primary functions of life, with reference to economy, the family, the community and the nation. And since that social thought embraced all culture and civilization, the time arrived for a reconsideration of women's rôle in the world, especially as the guardians and disintegrators of the processes necessary for the very existence and perdurance of society. Henry Adams had prophesied that the awakening would come before 1940. He missed the year by a trifle. His historic sense was sound.

Since it is now widely recognized by social thinkers that politicians and financiers cannot, with the sole aid of their implements, guarantee the existence of civilization or keep it running smoothly, that the sources of conservation and destruction lie deep in culture, the age of superficial thought about women— an age marked by pedantry and sentiment on the one side and sex perversion on the other—draws to a close. It is now believed, and perhaps actually known, that the continuance of political and economic structures depends upon cultural resources and powers. Hence the place of women in the evolution of society, that is, in activities and thought, will of necessity receive a new and more realistic treatment. The conception of woman as man will disappear with the conception of woman as child-wife, drudge, or plaything. It will then be found by social and historical exploration that woman is woman, whether or not she is history as Spengler declares; that woman has always been acting and thinking, intuitively and rationally, for weal or for woe, at the center of life—where operations are carried on efficiently for the care and protection of life, or where this fundamental cultural responsibility is discarded in the pursuit of self-interest.

This new social and historical philosophy does not condemn the feminism of the nineteenth century but describes the conditions which brought it into being and reveals its relative character—absorbs it in the coming synthesis. When the domestic system of industry which revolved around the care of life—woman's prime concern—was demolished by the factory system, the very exigencies of survival forced millions of women to think in terms of competition for place, income, and power. Their clamor for equal opportunity at acquisition in the madness of the market place naturally followed their loss of opportunity in domestic production and management. A sound economy in which they shared as workers, directors, and beneficiaries gave place to the feverish economy of capitalism, dependent upon the vicissitudes of trade, in which they had to battle as individuals for a foothold, handicapped by the continued necessity of maternal duties now unrelated to vocation.

To secure that foothold and to achieve a reputation for prowess and competence on the new basis, women often had to pay the price of celibacy. Whatever the price, they were inclined to pay it; indeed they were usually compelled to pay it. And when legal equality to scramble for place in a competitive economy was achieved, it was generally supposed that a new and permanent order of freedom for women had been established. Women were no longer women; they were competing units in a society of competing units called "human beings"—the abstractions of labor power celebrated by the economists and political theorists—competing in industry, in education, in politics, in law, medicine, and theology. They had no distinct function as women. They were not to think and work as women but presumably as human abstractions; actually as men. In this situation they lightly assumed that men were really thinkers when they thought of themselves as the makers of State and Economy.

But with the widening of social thought to include all culture and with the renewed search for fundamentals, the limitations and relativity of this feminism become apparent, along with the limitations and relativity of the masculinism of politics and economics. Cultural sociology, the larger view, reveals in elaborate studies how, from primitive times to the modern era, societies have been organized with reference to the supreme functions of life—its continuance, care, and protection. Societies that are not so organized, it shows, are robber bands exploiting other societies until inevitable degeneration sets in. In the work of continuing and protecting life, instinct, thought and action are all involved; industry and the arts are functional; this operation is called "culture." Here all women are engaged in primordial functions—continuing and protecting life—without which history ceases and all philosophy becomes futile. And as they develop these functions, men are more or less subdued to the requirements of the situation.

When, however, the men of such a culture turn to fighting, of their own motion or spurred on by woman [1] or in defense, and conquer other cultures, civilization begins, wealth is accumulated, leisure is made possible for the few, and arrangements, ceremonial and decorative, that is "artificial," become objects of interest for men and women. If the civilization becomes highly complex, as it develops, women tend to over-refinement, while men dedicate an ever-larger share of their energies to the acquisition of commodities and the erection of institutions which, as the old Romans remarked, "tend to effeminacy of the spirit," [2] that is to the over-coddling of life. Here women, as always, still near the center interest, aid in tearing down as they once aided in building up, destroying by inanity, individualism, and abdication what they once assisted in erecting by personal vigor, by coöperative community discipline, and by functional art. Here strength of race declines, the arts become meretricious, and individualism veering to anarchy pulls the establishment over.

[1] Tacitus, *Germania*.
[2] Caesar, *Gallic War*, Book I, "ea quae ad effeminandos animos pertinent."

But when great societies, such as the Roman Empire, crumble through the failure of centralized political and military authority to draw sufficient vitality from culture, communal organization is renewed from the ground up through a surviving concern for primordial realities, largely among the working orders, concern for the care and protection of life—the primary interests of women. Thus in periods of dissolution, as leisure classes sink down into the elemental struggle for existence, the domestic arts indispensable to the maintenance of society, originated by women, are fostered by the mothers, wives and daughters of men. So it would seem, if there is in all history any primordial force, that force is woman—continuer, protector, preserver of life, instinctive, active, thoughtful, ever bringing thought back from sterile speculation to the center of life and work. She is primordial in the making of culture and the destruction of civilization, if there is any primordial force in the world, anything but the ever-flowing stream of events, causeless and timeless.

No less dynamic in history than woman as force is woman's conception of herself and her rôle in the processes of culture and civilization, for, as many writers correctly insist, ideas are also forces in social evolution. As thinker and student, woman, like every thinker and student, borrows with more or less understanding from the heritage of thought in which she finds herself; thus she may accept ready-made views of her personality and the world as she now accepts ready-made clothing in the stores. Or aware of her functional emotions, she may challenge, break, or transform borrowed conceptions, in the alembic of her intuition, with respect to the basic realities of life. What woman conceives her rôle to be, if any at all, and how she regards civilization become as important to the continuance and quality of civilization as are her activities in every department of society and economy. Here as everywhere a divorce of thought from action leads to a decline in creative intelligence.

While this view of social evolution seems warranted by contemporary historical thought, we must be on our guard against the cyclical theory which Spengler has recently revived and employed to startle mankind. History does not exactly repeat itself. Modern mechanical economy, nation-wide, even world-wide in its sweep, is a novel experiment. If civilization—the great society of today—is to continue, then the problem becomes one of making the huge superstructure of economics and politics function for the essential purposes of life and at the same time of maintaining a sound and creative community life at the basis. In this effort, which engages the best talent of the time, women are sure to be involved from beginning to end, in thought and in action. And in the trembling balance of things, the decision of a few may mark the turning point in history. It is too early to know what will be the outcome of the revolt against Hitlerism in Germany, led by Frau Katherina von Oheim-Kardorff, president of the National Women's Association and former Reichstag deputy, in the spring of 1933. But this feminist rebellion against a State conceived mainly in the ancient terms of fighting men and breeding women is a vigorous expression of the twentieth-century social outlook.

In the current reconsideration of social thought and woman's place in the evolution of society, the methods of cultural anthropology are being applied to all history as well as to the description of primitive societies. When dealing with the early stages of social evolution, anthropology does not look through a medium of abstractions created by so-called philosophers, but actually observes primitive societies wherever they may still be found and employs the realistic data of primitive records. Hence in dealing with cultural origins, social thought already gives to woman the position and functions which belonged to her in fact—functions of the highest value. But the long gap between knowledge of early societies and thought about contemporary society remains at present a chaos. So far the intervening space is filled with history conceived as political, military, and economic occurrences or abstractions, divorced from life as a unit and thus taking no account of woman as woman. However there is ground for believing that the methods of cultural anthropology will soon be applied to all phases of history, from primitive times onward, disclosing woman's function and rôle in the clear light of research and understanding.

For this revolutionary work of social thought, much ground, hitherto uncultivated, must be tilled. The materials have not been prepared by the collection, editing, sifting and cataloguing of sources dealing with women's work and thought in the making of civilization. Students concerned with these intellectual operations may work in many directions. There is room for the collector and the investigator who inquire into local, regional, temporal and special phases of women's rôle in social development. There is room for the person with a coördinating turn of mind who ponders the materials thus collected, sifted, and ordered in detail.

The pages which follow are designed to serve a modest purpose in the new exploration: to illustrate, if in a fragmentary way, the share of women in the development of American society —their activity, their thought about their labor, and their thought about the history they have helped to make or have observed in the making. If this volume suggests new plowings and garnerings, then the hopes of the editor will be abundantly gratified.

CHAPTER I

OPENING UP THE WILDERNESS

THE traditional history of American colonization was long concentrated on the religious and political aspects of the complex movement which brought the new society into being. This was natural enough. The leading men among the early colonists were usually theologians or persons who had taken part in the political conflicts of the Old World. However practical they were in economic affairs, their journals and other writings reflected their interest in religion and government and did not portray the multitudinous activities and purposes which entered into the cultural foundations for American society. The historians, too, who came after them, usually emphasized the formalisms of religious and political development. It was a long time before any serious consideration was given to the basic concerns of the colonists which conditioned the manifestations of religious and political history. And it is only recently that the borders of history have been widened to take in the whole of colonial culture and deepened to include the total cultural heritage which was sifted and carried forward in the process of colonization. The completion of this task waits on the advancement of cultural anthropology.

The outlines of this wider cultural picture are dimly discernible and beginnings have been made at filling in the details. In the new view the migration to the New World was another manifestation of the continuous efforts of men and women to subdue the earth to the purposes of life. It was not an attempt to escape from responsibility. On the contrary it meant the assumption of heavier obligations in many directions. Hence the capacity to carry physical and intellectual burdens was essential to the success of the movement.

Starting at the bottom, on the soil, the first settlements rested squarely on the labor, skill and intelligence of both the sexes. The women who took part in colonization, as a rule, came from those classes of English women whose initiative, competence, and managerial capacities are described by Alice Clark in her "Working Life of Women in the Seventeenth Century." They were efficient in all departments of economy and shared in the intellectual concerns of their time. Interested in achievement more than approbation, they took little time from their work to set down directly their impressions of their own deeds and the common adventure in its entirety, but wherever colonial records deal with life and thought about life—with culture in short—the ideas, activities and interests of women stand out in the social scene.

Since colonial women did not vie with Cotton Mather in voluminous writing, they did not leave behind them many bulky journals from which pictures may be drawn of America in the making. They did leave sketches but it has been necessary for modern women, trained in historical scholarship, to search far and wide in colonial sources for the materials with which to reconstruct the society of the colonial age. For example, it is to the work of modern students, such as Annie Marble and Ethel Noyes, that we must turn for a systematic knowledge of the pilgrim mothers who accompanied the pilgrim fathers to America. These students show us that imprisonment had been meted out to both sexes for their religious opinions and that it was spiritual conviction as well as affection for their mates which led women to board the *Mayflower* and sail across the seas amid the hazards of the time. They were used to hazards. Twelve years before, some of them on the way from England to Holland had been searched and cruelly treated by the ship's master at Boston. "Later they were abandoned by the Dutchman at Hull to wait for fourteen days of frightful storm while their husbands and protectors were carried far away in a ship toward the coast of Norway, 'their little ones hanging about them and quaking with cold. " Solicitude about the future of their children as well as religious conviction and marital affection led the pilgrim mothers to undertake the migration over the sea. And once in the New World, in spite of its hardships, not a woman of the band accepted the captain's offer to return to England at his expense if she would cook and nurse the crew in case of need.

In part through the eyes of twentieth century women we get realistic impressions of what actually happened in the American wilderness as it was conquered, just as we form our conceptions of ancient Greece and Rome from the findings of those who have mastered the archaeological and documentary remains. Indeed there are few periods of history, perhaps none at all, which are comprehensively presented to us by a contemporary observer.

Men without women, who had made the original landing at Jamestown, had miserably failed to find the clue to prosperity. But this error was soon rectified, as we may learn by reading Alice Morse Earle's COLONIAL DAMES AND GOOD-WIVES.[1]

In the early days of the colony of Massachusetts Bay, careful lists were sent back to old England by the magistrates, telling what "to provide to send to New England" in order to ensure the successful planting and tender nourishing of the new settlement. The earliest list includes such homely items as "benes and pese," tame turkeys, copper kettles, all kinds of useful apparel and wholesome food; but the list is headed with a most significant, a typically Puritan item, *Ministers.* The list sent to the Emigration Society by the Virginian colonists might equally well have been headed, to show their most crying need, with the word *Wives.*

[1] Reprint obtained through the courtesy of The Macmillan Company.

The settlement of Virginia bore an entirely different aspect from that of New England. It was a community of men who planted Jamestown. There were few women among the early Virginians. In 1608 one Mistress Forrest came over with a maid. . . . But wives were few, save squaw wives; therefore the colony did not thrive. Sir Edwin Sandys, at a meeting of the Emigration Society in London, in November, 1619, said that "though the colonists are seated there in their persons some four years, they are not settled in their minds to make it their place of rest and continuance." They all longed to gather gold and to return to England as speedily as possible, to leave that state of "solitary uncouthness," as one planter called it. Sandys and that delightful gentleman, the friend and patron of Shakespeare, the Earl of Southampton, planned, as an anchor in the new land, to send out a cargo of wives for these planters, that the plantation might "grow in generations and not be pieced out from without." In 1620 the *Jonathan* and the *London Merchant* brought ninety maids to Virginia on a venture, and a most successful venture it proved.

There are some scenes in colonial life which stand out of the past with much clearness of outline, which seem, though no details survive, to present to us a vivid picture. One is this landing of ninety possible wives—ninety homesick, seasick but timidly inquisitive English girls—on Jamestown beach, where pressed forward, eagerly and amorously waiting, about four hundred lonely emigrant bachelors—bronzed, sturdy men, in leather doublets and breeches and cavalier hats, with glittering swords and bandoleers and fowling pieces, without doubt in their finest holiday array, to choose and secure one of these fair maids as a wife. . . . But whosoever he won was indeed a prize, for all were asserted to be "young, handsome, honestly educated maids, of honest life and carriage." What more could any man desire? Gladly did the husband pay to the Emigration Company the one hundred and twenty pounds of leaf tobacco, which formed, in one sense, the purchase money for the wife. This was then valued at about eighty dollars; certainly a man in that matrimonial market got his money's worth; and the complaining colonial chronicler who asserted that ministers and milk were the only cheap things in New England, might have added—and wives the only cheap things in Virginia.

It was said by old writers that some of these maids were seized by fraud, were trapanned in England, that unprincipled spirits "took up rich yeomen's daughters to serve his Majesty as breeders in Virginia unless they paid money for their release." This trapanning was one of the crying abuses of the day, but in this case it seems scarcely present. For the girls appear to have been given a perfectly fair showing in all this barter. They were allowed to marry no irresponsible man, to go nowhere as servants, and, indeed were not pressed to marry at all if against their wills. They were to be "housed, lodged and provided for of diet" until they decided to accept a husband. Naturally nearly all did marry, and from the unions with these young, handsome, and godly-carriaged maids sprang many of our respected Virginian families. . . .

Other shiploads of maids followed, and with the establishment of these Virginian families was dealt, as is everywhere else that the family exists, a fatal blow at a community of property and interests, but the colony flourished, and the civilization of the new world was begun. For the unit of society may be the individual, but the molecule of civilization is the family. When men had wives and homes and children they "sett down satysfied" and no longer sighed for England. Others followed quickly and eagerly; in three years thirty-five hundred emigrants had gone from England to Virginia, a marked contrast to the previous years of uncertainty and dissatisfaction.

Virginia was not the only colony to import wives for its colonists. In 1706 His Majesty Louis XIV sent a company of twenty young girls to the Governor of Louisiana, Sieur de Bienville, in order to consolidate his colony. They were to be given good homes, and to be well married, and it was thought they would soon teach the Indian squaws many useful domestic employments. These young girls were of unspotted reputation, and upright lives, but they did not love their new homes; a dispatch to the Governor says:

The men in the colony begin through habit to use corn as an article of food, but the women, who are mostly Parisians, have for this kind of food a dogged aversion which has not been subdued. Hence they inveigh bitterly against his Grace the Bishop of Quebec who they say has enticed them away from home under pretext of sending them to enjoy the milk and honey of the land of promise.

They rebelled and threatened to run away—whither I cannot guess, nor what they would eat save Indian corn if they did run away—and they stirred up such a dissatisfaction that the imbroglio was known as the Petticoat Rebellion, and the governor was much jeered at for his unsuccessful wardship and his attempted matrimonial agency.

In 1721 eighty young girls were landed in Louisiana as wives, but these were not godly-carriaged young maids; they had been taken from Houses of Correction, especially from Paris. In 1728 came another company known as *filles à la cassette,* or casket girls, for each was given by the French government a casket of clothing to carry to the new home; and in later years it became a matter of much pride to Louisianians that their descent was from the casket-girls, rather than from the correction-girls.

Another wife-market for the poorer class of wifeless colonists was afforded through the white bond-servants who came in such numbers to the colonies. They were of three classes: convicts, free-willers or redemptioners, and "kids" who had been stolen and sent to the new world, and sold often for a ten years' term of service.

Maryland, under the Baltimores, was the sole colony that not only admitted convicts, but welcomed them. The labor of the branded hand of the malefactor, the education and accomplishments of the social outcast, the acquirements and skill of the intemperate or over-competed tradesman, all were welcome to the Maryland tobacco-planters; and the possibilities of rehabilitation of fortune, health, reputation, or reëstablishment of rectitude, made the custom not unwelcome to the convict or to the redemptioner. Were the indentured servant no rogue, but an

honest tradesman, crimped in English coast-towns and haled off
to Chesapeake tobacco fields, he did not travel or sojourn, perforce, in low company. He might find himself in as choice companionship, with ladies and gentlemen of as high quality, albeit
of the same character, as graced those other English harbors of
ne'er-do-wells, Newgate or the Fleet Prison. Convicts came
to other colonies, but not so openly nor with so much welcome
as to Maryland.

All the convicts who came to the colonies were not rogues,
though they might be condemned persons. The first record in
Talbot County, Maryland, of the sale of a convict, was in September, 1716, "in the third Yeare of the Reign of our Sovereign
Lord King George." And it was for rebellion and treason against
his Majesty that this convict, Alexander MacQueen, was taken
in Lancashire and transported to America, and sold to Mr.
Daniel Sherwood for seven years of service. With him were
transported two shiploads of fellow-culprits, Jacobites, on the
Friendship and *Goodspeed*. The London Public Record Office
(on American and West India matters, No. 27) records this
transportation and says the men were "Scotts Rebells." Earlier
still, many of the rebels of Monmouth's rebellion had been sold
for transportation, and the ladies of the court of James had
eagerly snatched at the profits of the sale. Even William Penn
begged for twenty of these rebels for the Philadelphia market.
Perhaps he was shrewd enough to see in them good stock for
successful citizens. Were the convict a condemned criminal, it
did not necessarily follow that he or she was thoroughly vicious.
One English husband is found petitioning on behalf of his wife,
sentenced to death for stealing but three shillings and sixpence,
that her sentence be changed to transportation to Virginia.

The redemptioners were willing immigrants, who contracted to
serve for a period of time to pay the cost of their passage, which
usually had been prepaid to the master of the ship on which they
came across-seas. At first the state of these free-willers was not
unbearable. Alsop, who was a redemptioner, has left on record
that the work required was not excessive:

Five dayes and a halfe in the summer is the allotted time that they worke, and for two months, when the Sun is predominate in the highest pitch of his heat, they claim an antient and customary Priviledge to repose themselves three hours in the day within the house. In Winter they do little but hunt and build fires . . . the four years I served there were not to me so slavish as a two-year's servitude of a handicraft apprenticeship in London.

Many examples can be given where these redemptioners rose to respected social positions. In 1654, in the Virginia Assembly were two members and one Burgess who had been bond-servants. Many women-servants married into the family of their employers. Alsop said it was the rule for them to marry well. The niece of Daniel Defoe ran away to escape a marriage entanglement in England, sold herself on board ship as a redemptioner when but eighteen years old, was bought by a Mr. Job of Cecil County, Maryland, and soon married her employer's son. Defoe himself said that so many good maid-servants were sold to America that there was a lack for domestic service in England.

Through the stealing of children and youths to sell in the plantations, it can plainly be seen that many a wife of respectable birth was furnished to the colonists. This trade, by which, as Lionel Gatford wrote in 1657, young people were "cheatingly deckoyed by Poestigeous Plagiaries," grew to a vast extent, and in it, emulating the noble ladies of the court, women of lower rank sought a degrading profit.

In 1655, in Middlesex, England, one Christian Sacrett was called to answer the complaint of Dorothy Perkins:—

She accuseth her of a spirit, one that takes upp men, women and children, and sells them a-shipp to be conveyed beyond the sea, having inticed and inveigled one Edward Furnifall and Anna his wife with her infant to the waterside, and putt them aboard the ship called the Planter to be conveied to Virginia.

Sarah Sharp was also asserted to be a "common taker of children and setter to Betray young men and maydens to be conveyed to ships.". . .

In the *Sot-Weed Factor* are found some very coarse but graphic pictures of the women emigrants of the day. When the factor asks the name of "one who passed for chambermaid" in one planter's house in "Mary-Land," she answered with an affected blush and simper:

> In better Times, ere to this Land
> I was unhappily Trapanned,
> Perchance as well I did appear
> As any lord or lady here.
> Not then a slave for twice two year.
> My cloaths were fashionably new,
> Nor were my shifts of Linnen blue;
> But things are changed, now at the Hoe
> I daily work, and barefoot go.
> In weeding corn, or feeding swine,
> I spend my melancholy time.
> Kidnap'd and fool'd I hither fled,
> To shun a hated Nuptial Bed.
> And to my cost already find
> Worse Plagues than those I left behind.

Another time, being disturbed in his sleep, the factor finds that in an adjoining room,—

> . . . a jolly Female Crew
> Were Deep engaged in Lanctie Loo.

Soon quarreling over their cards, the planters' wives fall into abuse, and one says scornfully to the other:—

> . . . tho now so brave,
> I knew you late a Four Years Slave,
> What if for planters wife you go,
> Nature designed you for the Hoe.

Still we must not give the *Sot-Weed Factor* as sole or indeed as entirely unbiased authority. The testimony to the housewifely virtues of the Maryland women by other writers is almost universal. . . .

Wives were just as eagerly desired in New England as in Virginia, and a married estate was just as essential to a man of dig-

nity. As a rule, emigration thereto was in families, but when
New England men came to the New World, leaving their
families behind them until they had prepared a suitable home
for their reception, the husbands were most impatient to send
speedily for their consorts. . . .

Occasionally, though rarely, there was found a wife who did
not long for a New England home. . . . Even the ministers'
wives did not all sigh for the New World. The removal of Rev.
Mr. Wilson to New England "was rendered difficult by the indisposition of his dearest consort thereto." He very shrewdly interpreted a dream to her in favor of emigration, with but scant
and fleeting influence upon her, and he sent over to her from
America encouraging accounts of the new home, and he finally
returned to England for her, and after much fasting and prayer
she consented to "accompany him over an ocean to a wilderness." . . .

We truly cannot from our point of view "marvayle" that these
consorts did not long to come to the strange, sad, foreign shore,
but wonder that they were any of them ever willing to come;
for to the loneliness of an unknown world was added the dread
horror of encounter with a new and almost mysterious race, the
blood-thirsty Indians, and if the poor dames turned from the
woods to the shore, they were menaced by "murthering
pyrates." . . .

All women did not run at the approach of the foe. . . . Most
famous and fierce of all women fighters was Hannah Dustin,
who, in 1697, with another woman and a boy, killed ten Indians
at midnight, and started for home; but, calling to mind a thought
that no one at home, without corroborative evidence, would
believe this extraordinary tale, they returned, scalped their victims, and brought home the bloody trophies safely to Haver-
hill. . . .

A very exciting and singular experience befell four dignified
Virginian wives in Bacon's Rebellion, not through the Indians
but at the hands of their erstwhile friends. It is evident that the
women of that colony were universally and deeply stirred by

the romance of this insurrection and war. We hear of their dramatic protests against the tyranny of the government. Sarah Drummond vowed she feared the power of England no more than a broken straw, and contemptuously broke a stick of wood to illustrate her words. Major Chriesman's wife, "the honor of her sex," when her husband was about to be put to death as a rebel, begged Governor Berkeley to kill her instead, as he had joined Bacon wholly at her solicitation. One Ann Cotton was moved by the war to drop into literary composition, an extraordinary ebullition for a woman in her day, and to write an account of the Rebellion, as she deemed "too wordishly," but which does not now read very wordishly to us. But for these four dames, the wives of men prominent in the army under Governor Berkeley—prime men, Ann Cotton calls them—was decreed a more stirring participation in the excitements of war. The brilliant and erratic young rebel, Bacon, pressed them into active service . . . he brought them to the scene of battle, and heartlessly placed them—with still further and more acute indisposition—on the "fore-front" of the breastworks as a shield against the attacks of the four distracted husbands with their soldiers. . . . And this hiding of soldiers behind women was done by the order of one who was called the most accomplished gentleman in Virginia, but whom we might dub otherwise if we wished, to quote the contemporary account, to "oppose him further with pertinances and violent perstringes."

I wish I could truthfully say that one most odious and degrading eighteenth century English custom was wholly unknown in America—the custom of wife-trading, the selling by a husband of his wife to another man. . . . But just as I was "setting down satysfyed" at the superiority in social ethics and morality of our New England ancestors, I chanced, while searching in the *Boston Evening Post* of March 15, 1736, for the advertisement of a sermon on the virtues of our forebears . . . to find instead, by a malicious and contrary fate unwelcome and mortifying news not about Old England but about New England's "dolours and horrours."

Being a wife was not the sole justification for existence how-ever. Nor did it satisfy the creative energies of women. With a wilderness to open up and a new society to create, they all had productive and distributive tasks to perform connected with that operation. It was a time of extraordinary opportunities for women of which they seem to have taken full advantage, as we discover in part from Elisabeth Dexter's COLONIAL WOMEN OF AFFAIRS.[2]

Wealth and position in the New World, as in most other places, were based on the ownership of land, and from a very early date women shared in this, not only by favor of their men-folk, but in their own right. There are several instances where women served as leaders of groups of settlers. Probably the earliest case is that of Margaret and Mary Brent, who came to Maryland in 1638, bringing nine colonists with them. The sisters took up manors—that is, plantations of a thousand acres or more—and sent back to England for more settlers. The lord of a manor had the right of holding so-called "courts-baron," but only two instances have been found where this right was exercised. One of these was in 1659 at St. Gabriel's manor, the property of Mistress Mary Brent.

A tenant appeared, did fealty to the lady, and took seisin of a messuage of thirty-seven acres by delivery of a rod, "according to the custom of the manor," engaging to pay yearly "fifteen pecks of good Indian corn and one fat capon or a hen and a half; and for a heriot half a barrel of like corn or the value thereof."

The record does not state what was to become of the other half hen.

Margaret Brent exercised still greater influence. Before his death in 1647, Governor Leonard Calvert appointed Thomas Greene as his successor in office, but made Mistress Brent his sole executor, with the laconic instruction: "Take all and pay all." The historian of Maryland [W. H. Browne] remarks:

[2] Reprint obtained through the courtesy of Houghton Mifflin Company.

"In view of subsequent occurrences one is tempted to think that if he had reversed his testamentary dispositions and made Greene his executor and Mistress Brent governor, it would have been, on the whole, a better arrangement."

Leonard Calvert had been attorney for his brother, Lord Baltimore, and with the approval of the court she succeeded to this responsibility. A crisis soon arose, which she met vigorously. The times were troublous, and in order to drive out marauders, Governor Calvert had been obliged to hire quite a body of soldiers for whose payment he had pledged his own and his brother's estates. He died before he could fulfill his contract, and the soldiers threatened mutiny. Mistress Brent succeeded in calming them, and took enough of Lord Baltimore's cattle to make up the necessary sum. His lordship, who had had nothing to say about her appointment as his attorney, was not well pleased by her action; but the Assembly wrote him that she had obtained from the soldiers a respect they would have shown to none other, and that without her prompt interference, the colony would have been ruined.

One tribute alone the Assembly withheld. The Archives of Maryland state that on January 21, 1647/48

came Mrs. Margarett Brent and requested to have vote in the house for herselfe and voyce allso, for that att the last Court 3d Jan. it was ordered that the said Mrs. Brent was to be looked upon and received as his Lps. Attorney. The Govr, denyed that the sd. Mrs. Brent should have any vote in the Howse. And the sd. Mrs. Brent protested against all proceedings in this present Assembly unless shee may be present and have vote as aforesd.

A surprisingly modern sentiment! "Mrs." in those days was used as a title of respect, without regard to marital status. Apparently Margaret Brent never married. Her last recorded appearance was about some property, left her by the will of a distinguished suitor.

Another woman colonizer was Elizabeth Haddon. Her father, John Haddon, a Quaker of Surrey, England, had acquired title to some land in New Jersey. In 1701, when Elizabeth was only nineteen years old, she crossed the water alone to look after her father's property. After staying awhile with co-religionists in Philadelphia, she moved into a house which she had had built for her on her father's land, and named the region Haddonfield. The following year she married John Estaugh, a minister among the Friends whom she had met in England and again in Philadelphia. Tradition says that she was obliged to imitate Priscilla Alden's method of bringing him to the point. Mrs. Estaugh had no children of her own, but she adopted one of her sister's. Throughout her long life, she exercised a leading influence in the community. She died in 1762, about eighty years old.

In Pennsylvania also a woman figures as one of the early proprietors. Mary Warenbuer and her husband John (or Daniel?) Ferree, a silk weaver, had lived in Lindau, France. Suffering persecution as Huguenots, they fled with their six children to Strassburg. Here the husband soon died, and the management of affairs devolved upon the wife. When her children were grown, she put through plans for transporting the whole family and some friends to America. First they went to England, where she obtained an interview with William Penn. He was much interested in her, and not only promised his assistance, but took her to see Queen Anne. After six months in London, the little company joined some French and German settlers who were going to New York. In 1711, Madame Ferree took out a warrant for two thousand acres of land in New Strassburg, Lancaster County, Pennsylvania. This warrant was afterwards confirmed to her son Daniel and her son-in-law, Isaac Le Fevre. Madame Ferree died at Conestoga in 1716.

In the same year that Margaret Brent went to Maryland, Anne Hutchinson was the moving spirit (in more senses than one) of a group who journeyed from the comparative security of Massachusetts Bay to the wilderness of Rhode Island, where they established the little town of Portsmouth, from which later sprang Newport. A far cry, it seems, from the inspired Puritan woman to the social leaders of modern Newport! Almost a century and a half later, another inspired woman, Ann Lee, led a company of her disciples from England to western New York. These women, however, were colonizers only incidentally; their real significance is as religious leaders. This little company purchased land in Watervliet, New York, where they established a community of believers.

In all the colonies, women seem to have owned land on exactly the same terms as men. Women who possessed large tracts were naturally less common in New England than elsewhere. Elizabeth Poole, one of the rare "old maidens" of early days, is mentioned as the founder of Taunton, Massachusetts, and Abigail Bromfield was one of the proprietors, along with John Hancock, Samuel Adams, and other men, of the undivided land in Maine. And in 1771, the remarkably named Marcy Cheese advertised for sale "the small island of Chopoquidic, adjoining Martha's Vineyard."

It is farther south, however, that the great estate flourished. Many are the women of New Netherland who owned and increased valuable properties. An advertisement in the "New York Gazette" for July 20, 1730, calls to mind a family in which unusual ability made itself manifest from mother to daughter for three generations. This notice is in regard to the sale at auction of the real estate of the late Cornelia DePeyster, and it enumerates the following:

A House and Lot in Broad Street, joyning to the House now building by Mr. Scott,
A House and Lot, joyning the former, in which Mr. Annis lives,
A House and Lot joyning thereunto, wherein Mrs. DePeyster lives,
A House and Lot adjoyning, wherein John Anthony lives,
A Lot on Mill Street, near the Jews' Synagogue,
A House and Lot on Beaver Street, which reaches back to Petticoat Lane,
A Lot on Queen street.

Not a bad bit of property, even if real estate in New York was worth less then than now. Mrs. DePeyster, as Cornelia Lubbetse, had come to New Amsterdam in 1651, to join her betrothed, Johannes DePeyster; and she had died in 1725, over ninety years of age. Throughout her long life she had played a prominent part in the town. She is credited with responsibility for the first cargo of salt brought to the colony—an important article—before local methods of production had been discovered.

Mrs. DePeyster's elder daughter, Maria, married a young merchant named Schrick, who owned property in Hartford and Flushing as well as in New York. He died shortly after the marriage, and the youthful widow carried on his business in her own name. She soon remarried, the second husband being a Scotchman named Spratt. After ten years he died also, leaving her again a widow, this time with four young children. Her mother and sister aided her to carry on her double business inheritance but three years later she married her third husband, a widower with many children. It is hardly surprising that the much-married lady died herself in the following year, 1700, at the age of forty-one.

The Spratt children were brought up by their Grandmother DePeyster. The daughter, Mary Spratt, was married when only about seventeen to Samuel Provoost, a successful young importer. The "Dictionary of National Biography" says he had made a fortune by smuggling. Mary's money was partly invested in the business—whatever it was—and she assisted in the management. This was fortunate, for after a few years she was left a widow, with two young children. Thereupon, according to the dictionary aforesaid, "the lady began a provision business of a lawful kind." She had a row of offices built in front of her house. Her counting-house was on a side street, and, in order to encourage business, she had flat stones laid along her property, and up to the streets on either side. This was the first sidewalk in New York, and it is said to have attracted visitors from far and wide. It may have been one reason why the business flourished, for flourish it did, and was continued after her second marriage, in 1722, to James Alexander. On one occasion during the French and Indian wars Mrs. Alexander received the contract to supply provisions for the King's troops. Mr. and Mrs. Alexander were people of great influence in the colony.

After a few years, Mrs. Alexander bought a country place at Perth Amboy, which a writer of the times tells us could be reached in "a short voyage of less than three days from New York." Here Mrs. Alexander took great interest in the welfare of her Indian neighbors, among whom she gained fame as a medicine-woman. James Alexander died in 1756, and his wife in 1760. Their son William asserted his title as sixth Earl of Stirling; nevertheless, he continued his mother's business in his native land. During the Revolution, he took an active and useful part on the American side, and became a general.

An advertisement in Zenger's Journal for March 10, 1735, announced that two houses, one large and one small, and seventeen acres of land, belonging to the estate of the late Catharina Philipse, would be sold at auction by her executors, Philip and Frederick Van Cortland. This was undoubtedly the widow Catharina Duval, born Van Cortland, who married Frederick Philipse in 1694. Mrs. Philipse had been intensely interested in the welfare of the Indians, and she provided a school for them, and had a church built near her manor-house. It is said that she personally superintended its construction, riding over every day on her gray mare. She endowed these charitable projects with a considerable part of her fortune.

Frederick Philipse was a widower when he married Catharina Van Cortland, and his first wife, Margaret Hardenbroeck, has been called "perhaps the most enterprising of all the Dutch colonists, male or female." She came to the New World when quite young, with her first husband, Peter De Vries; they bought a plantation on Staten Island and began a settlement there. After the death of De Vries, his widow sold this property and invested the money in ships, with which she established what was probably the first packet line between Europe and America. Mrs. De Vries went repeatedly as supercargo, in order to superintend the buying and selling. She fell in love with Frederick Philipse on one of these trips when he was a passenger taking a stock of furs to be sold in Europe. After her remarriage in 1661, Mrs. Philipse continued her business. The combined industry of husband and wife made them the richest couple in New Amsterdam, and they bought large holdings around what is now Yonkers, which was erected into "The Philipse Manor," besides considerable property in Manhattan. Margaret Philipse died about 1690.

A diary kept by the Labbadist missionaries, who came to America in 1679, gives a not wholly flattering side-light on Mrs. Philipse's industry. These men sailed from Holland "in a small flute ship, of which Thomas Singleton was master, but the superior authority over both ship and cargo was in Margaret Philipse, who was the owner of both, and with whom we agreed for our passage from Amsterdam to New York, in New Netherland, at 75 guelders for each person, payable in Holland." Mrs. Philipse was not on the ship when it sailed, but she overtook it in her own yacht, and came on board with her husband and daughter, and two servants. Unfortunately, according to the diarists, the passengers suffered greatly from overcrowding and filth, and they accuse the owner of avarice.

Another Dutchwoman of affairs was Mrs. Cornelia Schuyler, the mother of General Philip Schuyler of Revolutionary fame. Her father was Stephanus Van Cortland. In the division of the manor estate, her share came to more than seven thousand acres. This amount she increased; on one occasion, after the death of her husband, she took out a patent for thirteen hundred acres.

Women in the Southern States also owned and managed huge plantations. Mrs. Elizabeth Digges possessed one hundred and eight negro slaves, apparently the greatest number held by any one person in seventeenth-century Virginia; according to current prices, these must have been worth about twenty-four hundred pounds. The inventory of Mrs. Digges's estate, presented in 1699, shows her to have had a lavishly furnished house, according to the standards of the day. One chest, for instance, contained one hundred and twenty-six napkins, and sixty tablecloths. Her silver plate amounted to two hundred and sixty-one ounces. Her hall parlor contained five tables, twenty chairs, two couches, two pairs of brass andirons, and one clock. To set off this magnificence, hung on the walls were five pictures, valued at one shilling apiece! Throughout the mansion, the contents of which are meticulously itemized, not a single book is mentioned. [But one must not judge from this that no Southern home had a library.]

Plenty of women dealt in land on a smaller scale. Rebecca Wells, of Philadelphia, was apparently an early real estate agent; for instance, on January 20, 1757, she advertises two lots of land for sale and a house for rent.

For over twenty years, Mrs. Sarah Boylston, of Boston, inserts occasional advertisements of property to rent. The location noted in most of them is "near Faneuil Hall," and it may be that the "large brick dwelling-house," the "convenient dwelling-house," and so forth, were all the same, and that for some reason her tenants changed often. On her last appearance, however, in the "Boston Evening Post" for January 28, 1765, she is advertising as to let "a very Convenient Dwelling-House and Gardens, together with about 15 acres of land, near Col Joseph Williams's in Roxbury," and this time she gives her address "near Faneuil Hall." Perhaps she had given the large brick house up for renting purposes, and had gone to live in it herself.

Some methods of stimulating business appear to have been in good and regular standing in colonial days, which would hardly be smiled upon in our own time. The "Pennsylvania Gazette" for April 25, 1745, has the following notice:

> To be set up by way of Lottery, by Nicholas Bishop and Hester his Wife, 70 odd Lots in Wilmington; each subscriber paying 4 shillings in Hand, and 2 shillings a year Ground-Rent. There are no blanks, but all Prizes. The Lottery will be drawn the 16th of May in this City.

No need, evidently, to look the ground over beforehand. These colonial Bishops hardly require points from Babbit.

Women worked the land, as well as traded in it—and perhaps worked their customers. The records of the Quarterly Courts of Essex County give numerous glimpses of women about Salem who were wresting a livelihood from the land. In September, 1648, Widow Luce Waite sued Samuel Greenfield for debt, for 1460 pipe-staves which she had furnished him, at three pounds per thousand. The defendant appealed. Pipe-staves were the cause of controversy again in 1653, when Thomas King sued Edward Colcord for not having delivered 1400 to the Widow Chase; defendant acknowledged judgment to the plaintiff. The next year widow Chase appeared in her own behalf, charging Christopher Palmer with running a ditch through her meadow; judgment for the plaintiff. In 1658, Widow Margaret Scott accused Richard Shatswell of trespass, for ploughing up her land and felling trees and causing trees to be felled on her ground. In 1664, Widow Susan Rogers received a verdict against Mr. Philip Nelson, for having interfered with her meadow of forty acres, taking away ten loads of hay which she had had cut.

Mrs. John Davenport, wife of the minister of New Haven, looked after the extensive property interests of John Winthrop, the younger, when political business kept him in England. The correspondence between Governor Winthrop and Mr. Davenport is filled with messages in regard to the management of the iron-works, payments for supplies, receipts for produce, employment of workmen, and so forth, all attended to by Mrs. Davenport. She had some amusing difficulties, not unknown in other times; her husband, in a letter to Winthrop dated "Newhaven, this 22 of the 9th, 1655," wrote:

My wife had a man in pursuite that would be very fitt to manage your Island, if a marriage, which he is about, doth not hinder.

It is rather astonishing to discover a Puritan divine conniving at his wife's pursuit of another man; but the object here was laudable. Governor Winthrop was in need of a competent manager for Fisher's Island, "against the mouth of the Pequot River," which had been granted to him in 1640.

Farmers or plantation owners naturally did not advertise their wares like merchants or tavern-keepers; but they used the papers constantly to announce the dereliction of an indentured servant, slave, or horse, or now and then the finding of a stray animal. The servants and live stock of New England seem a little less migratory than elsewhere, but even here they were open to reproach. In many of the journals from farther south, the bulk of the advertising is of this nature, and these brief items give glimpses of many women who managed plantations, and sometimes indicate the variety of home industries which they conducted. Thus, Mrs. Christine Eltington, of Somerset County, East New Jersey, advertised in the "New York Gazette" for November 10, 1729, the loss of two servant men, one a weaver and one a cooper; she would pay four pounds reward for the return of both.

Four years later, in the same paper, Judith Vincent, at Mount Pleasant, Monmouth County, East New Jersey, advertised that her "Indian Fellow named Stoffil" had run away; he was cooper and carpenter by trade. She offered three pounds reward and charges. Coopers seemed to be particularly elusive, but horses were almost as bad. In one issue of the "Providence Gazette," November 29, 1771, Alice Philbrook, of Cumberland, offered five dollars reward for the return of a stolen mare—ten dollars if the thief be caught; and Marcy Dexter, of North Providence, offered three dollars and six dollars for a horse, ditto. Notices of this sort are legion.

Several women owned and managed wharves. The "Essex County Gazette" for August 30, 1768, gave notice of the sale of a schooner of 120 tons, "now laying at Mrs. Hodges's Wharf." Wharves frequently served as the prototype of our employment bureaus, although under an unpleasant aspect. Thus, the "American Mercury" in the fall of 1725 announced:

A Choice Parcel of Men Servants and one Woman to be sold, on Board the Ship Lovely, now lying at the Wharf of the Widow Allen, at 12 to 14 pounds per head, also very good Gloucester Cheese, at Eightpence a Pound.

In 1730, the same paper mentioned Widow Hun's wharf in a similar connection. In the "Boston Evening Post" for November

28, 1763, Mrs. Knox at Bull Wharf advertised seven indented maids to dispose of.

Some of the women mentioned in these brief newspaper advertisements may have been merely carrying on the farm work of a dead husband or father, without any real initiative in the matter; the information is usually too brief to settle this point. There are not a few women, however, about whom more knowledge is available, and who certainly showed a commendable degree of enterprise. Such a woman was Hannah Dubre (or Dubrey, or Duberry, for the records allow a choice), who thus first addressed the public through the "Pennsylvania Gazette" in the fall of 1753:

To be sold by Hannah Dubre, living in the Northern Liberties, next plantation to Capt Peal's, within two miles of Philadelphia, . . . All sorts of seeds either wholesale or retail, at very reasonable rates.

By the next issue, the distance had grown to two miles and a half; otherwise the statement was practically the same, and it was inserted several times nearly every autumn for the next fifteen years, and occasionally in the spring. Sometimes shops in town were named where the seeds might be bought, if would-be purchasers were discouraged by the two and one half miles. Numerous women shopkeepers sold imported seeds, but this is the only woman noted who sold seeds which she herself grew. In February, 1770, Mrs. Dubre advertised her plantation for sale, thirty-three acres with fruit orchard, kitchen garden, asparagus beds, and a house with good kitchen, and a pump before the door. This, no doubt, was "modern conveniences" at that time.

Mrs. Grant, of Laggan, a Scotchwoman who lived in the colonies, chiefly New York State, from 1760 to 1768, says that "not only the training of children but of plants . . . was the female province."

I think I yet see, what I have so often beheld in town and country, a respectable mistress of a family going out to her garden, in an April morning, with her great calash, her little painted basket of seed, and her rake over her shoulder, to her garden labors. These were by no means figurative.

From morn till noon, from noon till dewy eve,

A woman in very easy circumstances, and abundantly gentle in form and manners, would sow, and plant, and rake, incessantly.

Another Scotchwoman, Janet Schaw, who spent some time in the Southern States shortly before the Revolution, pictures such a woman who put her skill to good use. Writing in Wilmington, North Carolina, in the spring of 1775, she speaks of a particularly attractive estate which she had seen, and continues:

They tell me, however, that the Mrs. of this place is a pattern of industry, and that the house and everything in it was the product of her labors. She has (it seems) a garden, from which she supplies the town with what vegetables they use, also with mellons and fruits. She even descends to make minced pies, tarts, and cheese-cakes, and little biscuits, which she sends down to town once or twice a day, beside her eggs, poultry, and butter, and she is the only one who continues to have Milk. They tell me she is an agreeable woman, and I am sure that she has good sense, from one circumstance,—all her little commodities are contrived so as not to exceed one penny a piece, and her customers know she will not run tick, which were they to run by the length of sixpence, must be the case, as that is a sum not in everybody's power, and she must be paid by some other articles, whereas the two coppers (that is, half pence) are ready money. I am sure I would be happy in such an acquaintance. But this is impossible; her husband is at best a brute by all accounts and is beside the president of the committee and the instigator of the cruel and unjust treatment the friends of government are experiencing at present.

A note states that this was Mary, the wife of Cornelius Harnet, who owned a big plantation named Hilton, near Wilmington. Mrs. Harnet died in New York City, April 19, 1792. Her husband was a prominent patriot. He may not have been a brute— Miss Schaw was prejudiced against patriots anyway—but the editor inclines to the opinion that he was not a particularly estimable man.

A good many people nowadays would have a fellow-feeling on financial matters with the natives of Wilmington; but a place where one could get a "minced pie" or an egg, not to mention poultry, which perhaps Miss Schaw overlooked, for two coppers, sounds like Eldorado.

Several colonial women attained distinction as botanists. Foremost among these is Jane Colden, the daughter of Cadwalader Colden, Lieutenant-Governor of New York. He had had an excellent education in Europe, and was a man of high scientific attainments. He taught his daughter the recently published system of Linnæus, and both she and her father corresponded with the Swedish naturalist. . . .

A more intimate glimpse of her is given in a letter written by a young Scotchman, William Rutherford, describing a visit to Dr. Colden's home:

His daughter Jenny is a Florist, and a Botanist. She has discovered a great number of plants never before described, and has given them Properties and Virtues, many of which are found useful in Medicine and she draws and colors them with great beauty.

N.B. She makes the best cheese I ever ate in America. . . .

The notes and letters of ELIZA LUCAS PINCKNEY,[8] *edited by Harriot Horry Ravenel, are one important source of contemporary description. In these records made by a woman of Carolina, born in England but beginning in 1739, in her teens, to manage plantations in the New World, the culture may be observed from many angles. Eliza was an economist, a loyal subject of the Crown as long as her interests were not invaded, an educated person enlarging her mind by classical and other literature, a mother concerned about the training of her children, a stanch patriot when the battle lines were drawn, a reconciler when independence was established, thinking of the future instead of dwelling to excess on the past.*

[*1739*] Dear Madam (Mrs. Boddicott),—I flatter myself it will be a satisfaction to you to hear I like this part of the world as my lott has fallen here, which I really do. I prefer England to it 'tis

[8] Reprint obtained through the courtesy of Charles Scribner's Sons.

true, but think Carolina greatly preferable to the West Indies, and was my Papa here I should be very happy. We have a very good acquaintance from whom we have received much friendship and Civility. Charles Town the principal one in this province is a polite agreeable place, the people live very Gentile and very much in the English taste. The Country is in general fertile and abounds with Venson and wild fowl. The Venson is much higher flavoured than in England but 'tis seldom fatt.

My Papa and Mama's great indulgence to mee leaves it to mee to chuse our place of residence either in town or country, but I think it more prudent as well as most agreeable to my Mama and selfe to be in the Country during my father's absence. Wee are 17 miles by land, and 6 by water from Charles Town where wee have about 6 agreeable families around us with whom wee live in great harmony. I have a little library well furnished (for my Papa has left mee most of his books) in wch I spend part of my time. My Musick and the Garden wch I am very fond of take yp the rest that is not imployed in business, of wch my father has left me a pretty good share, and indeed 'twas unavoidable, as my Mama's bad state of health prevents her going thro' any fatigue.

I have the business of 3 plantations to transact, wch requires much writing and more business and fatigue of other sorts than you can imagine, but least you should imagine it too burthensom to a girl at my early time of life, give mee leave to assure you I think myself happy that I can be useful to so good a father. By rising very early I find I can go through with much business, but least you should think I shall be quite moaped with this way of life, I am to inform you there is two worthy Ladies in C^{rs} Town, Mrs. Pinckney and Mrs. Cleland who are partial enough to mee to wish to have mee with them, and insist upon my making theor houses my hom when in Town, and press mee to relax a little much oftener than 'tis in my power to accept of their obliging intreaties, but I am sometimes with one or the other for three weeks or a month at a time, and then enjoy all the pleasures C^{rs} Town affords. But nothing gives mee more than subscribing myself. . . .

[*Memorandum in 1739*] I wrote my father a very long letter on his plantation affairs . . . on the pains I had taken to bring the Indigo, Ginger, Cotton, Lucern, and Cassada to perfection, and had greater hopes from the Indigo—if I could have the seed earlier the next year from the East Indies—than any of ye things I had tryd . . . also concerning pitch and tarr and lime and other plantation affairs.

[*1742*] Hon^d Sir.—. . . I sympathize most sincerely with ye Inhabitance of Antigua in so great a calamity as the scarcity of provisions, and the want of ye Necessarys of life to ye poorer sort. We shall send all we can get of provisions, I wrote this day to Starrat for a bar^l of butter.

The Cotton, Guiney corn and most of the Ginger planted here was cutt off by a frost.

I wrote you in former letter we had a fine crop of Indigo Seed upon the ground and since informed you the frost took it before it was dry. I picked out the best of it and had it planted but there is not more than a hundred bushes of it come up, wch proves the more unlucky as you have sent a man to make it. I make no doubt Indigo will prove a very valueable commodity in time, if we could have the seed from the East Indies time enough to plant the latter end of March, that the seed might be dry enough to gather before our frost. I am sorry we lost this season we can do nothing towards it now but make the works ready for next year. The Lucern is yet but dwindling, but Mr Hunt tells mee 'tis always so here the first year. I am very much obliged to you for the present you were so good to send me of the fifty-pound bill. . . .

> My Dear Papa
> Your ob^t and ever Devoted Daughter
>
> E Lucas

[*To my father*] The crop at Garden Hill turned out ill (but a hundred and sixty bar^ls (of rice) and at Wappoo only forty-three, the price is so low as thirty shillings p^r hundred, we have sent very little to town yet, for that reason. People differ very much in sentiment about the number of ships we are still to have. We have not heard from England for more than two months, what can keep the shipping? We conjecture 'tis an imbargo. In my letter of Feby 3rd I desired to know if you approved of setting a plantation to the North near Major Pawly. Please let me know in your next if it has your approbation and it shall be done in the Fall.

We expect a vizit from the Spainiards this summer. Mr. Oglethorpe harasses them much at their forts at St Augustine. He has lately killed some and took two prisoners. . . .

[*Memorandum 1741–1742*] Wrote to my Father an account of a large ship, the "Balticke Merchant," from hence, being taken and carried into St Sebastien. The Capt, a Quaker, would not fight— poor Col^l Braithwait undertook to fight the ship, they had not powder enough—the Spaniards boarded her, and upon inquiring and being told Col^l B fought the ship, he went in to the Cabbin where he found him comforting his wife who was greatly frighted, and shot him dead in her sight—but as soon as he arrived at St Sebastien's the Govr of that place hanged him. Acknowledged the Re^{ct} of things sent by my father to us in sev^l vessels lately. Ac^t of Mr Whitfield and the Ecclesiastical Court here. Ac^t of my cousen Fayweathers going to Boston to endeavour to recover her fortune. Old Mr Devereux, very kind in Instructing me in planting affairs—Shall Endeavour to get some Curiositys for the Duke of Marlborough.

O! I had like to forgot the last thing I have done a great while. I have planted a large figg orchard, with design to dry them, and export them. I have recond my expence and the prophets to arise from those figgs, but was I to tell you how great an Estate I am to make this way, and how 'tis to be laid out, you would think me far gone in romance. Y^r good Uncle I know has long thought I have a fertile brain at schemeing, I only confirm him in his oppinion; but I own I love the vegitable world extreamly. I think it an innocent and useful amusement, and pray tell him if he laughs much at my projects, I never intend to have any hand in a silver mine, and he will understand as well as you, what I mean! . . .

[*1742*] Dear Miss Bartlett . . . Wont you laugh at me if I tell you I am so busy in providing for Posterity I hardly allow myself time to Eat or sleep, and can but just snatch a minuet to write to you and a friend or two more.

I am making a large plantation of oaks wch I look upon as my own property, whether my father gives me the land or not, and therefore I design many years hence when oaks are more valuable than they are now, wch you know they will be when we come to build fleets, I intend I say, 2 thirds of the produce of my oaks for a charrity (I'll let you know my scheme another time) and the other 3^d for those that shall have the trouble of puting my design in Execution; I sopose according to custom you will show this to y^r Uncle and Aunt. "She is a good girl" says Mrs Pinckney, "she is never Idle and always means well"—"tell the little Visionary" says your Uncle, "to come to town and partake of some of the amusements suitable to her time of life," pray tell him I think these so, and what he may now think, whims and projects may turn out well by and by—out of many surely one may hitt.

I promised to tell you when the mocking bird began to sing, the little warbler has done wonders; the first time he opend his soft pipe this spring he inspired me with the spirrit of Rymeing and produced the 3 following lines while I was laceing my Stays.

> Sing on thou charming mimick of the featherd kind
> And let the rational a lesson learn from thee
> To mimick (not defects) but harmony.

If you let any mortal besides your self see this exquisite peice of poetry, you shall never have a line more than this specimen, and how great will be your loss you who have seen the above may judge as well as

Your most Obed^t Servt

[*To her father, 1744*] Out of a small patch of Indigo growing at Wappoo, (which Mama made a present to Mr P:) the Brother of Nicholas Cromwell besides saving a quantity of Seed, made us 17 pounds of very good Indigo, so different from N–C's, that we are convinced he was a mere bungler at it. Mr. Deveaux has made some likewise, and the people in gen^l very sanguine about it. Mr P. sent to England by the last man of warr 6 pounds to try how t'is aproved of there. If it is I hope we shall have a bounty from home, we have already a bounty of 5^s currency from this province upon it. We please ourselves with the prospect of exporting in a few years a good quantity from hence, and supplying our Mother Country with a manifacture for wch she has so great a demand, and which she is now supplyd with from the French Collonys, and many thousand pounds per annum thereby lost to the nation.

[*1759*] The beginning of this year there was such a fine prospect on our plantations of a great crop y^t I was hopeful of clearing all that was due upon the estate, but the great drought in most parts of ye Country, such as I never remembered here, disapointed these expectations so much, y^t all that we make from ye planting interest will hardly defray ye charges of ye plantations; and upon our arrival here we found they wanted but every thing, and every way in bad order, with ignorant and dishonest overseers.

My Nephew had no management of ye planting interest, and my Brother who had it, by a stroke of the palsy had been long incapable of all business. I thank God there is now a prospect of things being differently conducted. I have prevailed upon a conspicuous good man . . . to undertake the direction and inspection of the overseers. He is an excellent planter, a dutchman, originally Servant and overseer to Mr Golightly, who has been much solicited to undertake for many Gentlemen, but as he has no family but a wife, and is comfortable in his circumstances, refuses to do for any but women & children, who are not able to do for themselves. So if it pleases God to prosper us and send good Seasons I hope to Clear all next year. I find it requires great care and attention to attend to a Carolina Estate, tho' but a moderate one, and to do one's duty, and make all turn to acc^t. I have as

much business of one kind & another as I can go through; perhaps 'tis better for me, and I believe it is, had there not been a
necessity for it I might have sunk to the grave by this time, in
that Lethargy of stupidity wch had seized me. . . .

[*1742–1744*] I have got no further than the first vol^m of Virgil, but
was most agreably disapointed to find myself instructed in agriculture as well as entertained by his charming penn, for I am
persuaded tho' he wrote for Italy it will in many Instances suit
Carolina. I had never perused these books before, and imagined
I should immediately enter upon battles, storms and tempests,
that put mee in a maze, and make mee shudder while I read.
But the calm and pleasing diction of pastoral and gardening
agreably presented themselves not unsuitably to this charming
season of the year, with wch I am so delighted that had I butt the
fine soft Language of our Poet to paint it properly, I should give
you but little respite 'till you came into the country, and attended
to the beauties of pure Nature unassisted by Art. . . .

instead of the Easy and agreeable conversation of our Friends,
I am engaged with the rudiments of the Law, to wch I am yett
but a stranger, and what adds to my mortification I soon discovered that Doc^{tr} Wood (a law book) wants the consideration
of y^r good Uncle, who with a graceful ease and good nature
peculiar to himself, is always ready to instruct the ignorant. But
this rustic seems by no means to court my acquaintance for he
often treats me with such cramp phrases, I am unable to understand him.

However I hope in a short time with the help of Dictionary's
french and English, we shall be better friends; nor shall I grudge
a little pains and application, if that will make me useful to any
of my poor Neighbours, we have Some in this Neighbourhood,
who have a little Land a few Slaves and Cattle to give their Children, that never think of making a will 'till they come upon a
sick bed, and find it too Expensive to send to town for a Lawyer.

I have made two wills already! . . .

A widow hereabouts with a pretty little fortune, teazed me

intolerable to draw her a marriage settlement, but it was out of my depth and I absolutely refused it, so she got an abler hand to do it, indeed she could afford it, but I could not gett off from being one of the Trustees to her Settlement, and an old gentleman the other. . . .

[*To her son, being educated in England, 1761*] 'Tis with the greatest satisfaction my dear Charles that I acknowledge the receipt of y^r letter. . . . I, and some of our friends here that I have consulted think it high time you were fitted for the University; of all the Publick schools Westminster I think is to be preferred, and therefore should choose you go there. Master Tomm Evance's going to Warrington would be a great inducement to y^r going there also, but I think the distance you must then be from your dear brothers will be too great; besides I am informed the Business of that school is to fitt young Gent^n for the Ministry, and as you are not to be brought up to the Church, it will not do so well for you. Harrow, I think can hardly be called a publick school, and as Doct^r Thackeray is dead I don't think of that; others advise rather to a private Tutor than any publick school. There is indeed an objection to all publick schools, and a great one if 'tis true that the Morrals of Youth are taken little care of; but I have soo good an oppinion of your sobriety and modesty, and flatter myself you have rather a serious than a wild turn of mind, that I hope I may venture to trust you to Westminster, without running any risk of what must be fatal to me as well as to yourself, vizt corrupt principles; for be asured my dear Child, I would not hesitate a moment were it in my choice whether I would have you a learned man with every accomplishment, or a good man, without any; but as I hope you will be both I commit you to the Divine Protection and guidance . . . it will require your utmost vigilance to watch over your passions as well as your constant attendance at the Throne of Grace; be particularly watchful against heat of temper, it makes constant work for repentance and chagrine, and is so often productive of the greatest mischiefs and misfortunes. . . .

[*To Mr. Keate, a "literary man," 1762*] If you won't think me romantick I will communicate a scheme I have if I live a few years longer; not merely for the pleasure of scribbling a long letter, but because I really want your opinion and advice upon it; as your residence in Geneva must make you more capable of judging of the matter, than those that never were there.

Upon a Peace, (for I can't think of crossing the great Atlantic before that desirable time), I intend to see England again, and after Charles has been two years at Oxford to go with my two boys to finish their studies at Geneva. . . . Harriott pays her Comp^{ts}; she is much engaged just now with Geography and Musick. . . .

[*To her mother-in-law, 1780*] I am much obliged to you for your good wishes relative to the small-pox.—It will be almost impossible for our family to escape as it is on every plantation within 15 Miles around us. A Doctor from the Northward innoculates up here with great success, upward of a Thousand Blacks and Whites, and not one died amongst the number.

For many reasons the colonial Puritan, religionist and economist, is still a center of discussion both in Europe and America. Special mirrors are turned upon him by Protestants, Catholics, Socialists, Skeptics, and Feminists and, by the lens with which culture thus examines culture, various values are placed upon his theories of state and his social controls. Agnes Repplier, in UNDER DISPUTE,[4] brings the mind of a Catholic to bear upon the theme.

When William Chillingworth preaching at Oxford in the first year of England's Civil War, defined the Cavaliers as publicans and sinners, and the Puritans as Scribes and Pharisees, he expressed the reasonable irritation of a scholar who had no taste

---

[4] Reprint obtained through the courtesy of Houghton Mifflin Company.

or aptitude for polemics, yet who had been blown about all his life by every wind of doctrine. Those were uneasy years for men who loved moderation in everything, and who found it in nothing. It is not from such that we can hope for insight into emotions from which they were exempt, and purposes to which they held no clue.

In our day it is generously conceded that the Puritans made admirable ancestors. We pay them this handsome compliment in after-dinner speeches at all commemorative meetings. Just what they would have thought of their descendants is an unprofitable speculation. Three hundred years divide us from those stern enthusiasts who, coveting lofty things, found no price too high to pay for them. "It is not with us as with men whom small matters can discourage, or small discontentments cause to wish themselves at home again," wrote William Brewster, when one half of the Mayflower Pilgrims had died in the first terrible year, and no gleam of hope shone on the survivors. To perish of hunger and cold is not what we should now call a "small discontentment." To most of us it would seem a good and sufficient reason for abandoning any enterprise whatsoever. Perhaps if we would fix our attention upon a single detail—the fact that for four years the Plymouth colonists did not own a cow—we should better understand what life was like in that harsh wilderness, where children who could not get along without milk had but one alternative—to die.

Men as strong as were the Puritan pioneers ask for no apologies at our hands. Their conduct was shaped by principles and convictions which would be insupportable to us, but which are none the less worthy of regard. Matthew Arnold summed up our modern disparagement of their standards when he pictured Virgil and Shakespeare crossing on the Mayflower, and finding the Pilgrim fathers "intolerable company." I am not sure that this would have been the case. Neither Virgil nor Shakespeare could have survived Plymouth. That much is plain. But three months on the Mayflower might not have been so "intolerable" as Mr. Arnold fancied. The Roman and the Elizabethan were strong-stomached observers of humanity. They knew a man when they saw one, and they measured his qualities largely.

Even if we make haste to admit that two great humanizers of society, art and letters, played but a sorry part in the Puritan colonies, we know they were less missed than if these colonies had been worldly ventures, established solely in the interest of agriculture or of trade. Sir Andrew Macphail tersely reminds us that the colonists possessed ideals of their own, "which so far transcended the things of this world that art and literature were not worth bothering about in comparison with them." Men who believe that, through some exceptional grace or good fortune, they have found God, feel little need of culture. If they believe that they share God with all races, all nations, and all ages, culture comes in the wake of religion. But the Puritan's God was a somewhat exclusive possession. "Christ died for a select company that was known to Him, by name, from eternity," wrote the Reverend Samuel Willard, pastor of the South Church, Boston, and author of that famous theological folio, "A Compleat Body of Divinity." "The bulk of mankind is reserved for burning," said Jonathan Edwards genially; and his Northampton congregation took his word for it. That these gentlemen knew no more about Hell and its inmates than did Dante is a circumstance which does not seem to have occurred to any one. A preacher has some advantages over a poet.

If the Puritans never succeeded in welding together Church and State, which was the desire of their hearts, they had human nature to thank for their failure. There is nothing so abhorrent— or so perilous—to the soul of man as to be ruled in temporal things by clerical authority. Yet inasmuch as the colony of Massachusetts Bay had for its purpose the establishment of a state in which all citizens should be of the same faith, and church membership should be essential to freemen, it was inevitable that the preacher and the elder should for a time dominate public counsels. "Are you, sir, the person who serves here?" asked a stranger of a minister whom he met in the streets of Rowley. "I am, sir, the person who rules here," was the swift and apt response.

Men whose position was thus firmly established resented the unauthorized intrusion of malcontents. Being reformers themselves, they naturally did not want to be reformed. Alone among New England colonists, the Pilgrims of Plymouth, who were Separatists or Independents, mistrusted the blending of civil and religious functions, and this mistrust had deepened during the sojourn of their leaders in Holland. Moreover, unlike their Boston neighbors, the Pilgrims were plain, simple people; "not acquainted," wrote Governor Bradford, "with trades nor traffique, but used to a countrie life, and the innocente trade of husbandry." They even tried the experiment of farming their land on a communal system, and, as a result, came perilously close to starvation. . . .

To the courage and intelligence of the Pilgrim and Puritan leaders, Governor Bradford and Governor Winthrop, the settlers owed their safety and survival. The instinct of self-government was strong in these men, their measures were practical measures, their wisdom was the wisdom of the world. If Bradford had not made friends with the great sachem, Massasoit, and clinched the friendship by sending Edward Winslow to doctor him with "a confection of many comfortable conserves" when he was ill, the Plymouth colonists would have lost the trade with the Indians which tided them over the first crucial years. If Winthrop had not by force of argument and persuasion obtained the lifting of duties from goods sent to England, and induced the British creditors to grant favorable terms, the Boston colony would have been bankrupt. The keen desire of both Plymouth and Boston to pay their debts is pleasant to record, and contrasts curiously with the reluctance of wealthy States to accept the Constitution in 1789, lest it should involve a similar course of integrity.

It is hardly worth while to censure communities which were establishing, or seeking to establish, "a strong religious state" because they were intolerant. Tolerance is not, and never has been, compatible with strong religious states. The Puritans of New England did not endeavor to force their convictions upon unwilling Christendom. They asked only to be left in peaceful possession of a singularly unprolific corner of the earth, which they were civilizing after a formula of their own. Settlers to whom this formula was antipathetic were asked to go elsewhere. If they did not go, they were sent, and sometimes whipped into the bargain—which was harsh, but not unreasonable.

Moreover, the "persecution" of Quakers and Antinomians was not primarily religious. Few persecutions recorded in history have been. For most of them theology has merely afforded a pious excuse. Whatever motives may have underlain the persistent persecution of the Jews, hostility to their ancient creed has had little or nothing to do with it. To us it seems well-nigh incredible that Puritan Boston should have vexed its soul because Anne Hutchinson maintained that those who were in the covenant of grace were freed from the covenant of works—which sounds like a cinch. But when we remember that she preached against the preachers, affirming on her own authority that they had not the "seal of the Spirit"; and that she "gave vent to revelations," prophesying evil for the harassed and anxious colonists, we can understand their eagerness to be rid of her. She was an able and intelligent woman, and her opponents were not always able and intelligent men. When the turmoil which followed in her wake destroyed the peace of the community, Governor Winthrop banished her from Boston. "It was," says Fiske, "an odious act of persecution."

A vast deal of sympathy has been lavished upon the Puritan settlers because of the rigors of their religion, the austerity of their lives, their lack of intellectual stimulus, the comprehensive absence of anything like amusement. It has even been said that their sexual infirmities were due to the dearth of pastimes; a point of view which is in entire accord with modern sentiment, even if it falls short of the facts. Impartial historians might be disposed to think that the vices of the Puritans are apparent to us because they were so industriously dragged to light. When all moral offenses are civil offenses, and when every man is under the close scrutiny of his neighbors, the "find" in sin is bound to be heavy. Captain Kemble, a Boston citizen of some weight and fortune, sat two hours in the stocks on a wintry afternoon, 1656, doing penance for "lewd and unseemly behaviour"; which behaviour consisted in kissing his wife "publiquely" at his own front door on the Lord's day. The fact that he had just returned from a long voyage, and was moved to the deed by some excess of emotion, failed to win him pardon. Neighbors were not lightly flouted in a virtuous community.

That there were souls unfit to bear the weight of Puritanism, and unable to escape from it, is a tragic truth. People have been born out of time and out of place since the Garden of Eden ceased to be a human habitation. When Judge Sewall read to his household a sermon on the text, "Ye shall seek me and shall not find me," the household doubtless protected itself by inattention, that refuge from admonition which is Nature's kindliest gift. But there was one listener, a terrified child of ten, who had no such bulwark, and who brooded over her unforgiven sins until her heart was bursting. Then suddenly, when the rest of the family had forgotten all about the sermon, she broke into "an amazing cry," sobbing out her agonized dread of Hell. And the pitiful part of the tale is that neither father nor mother could comfort her, having themselves no assurance of her safety. "I answered her Fears as well as I could," wrote Judge Sewall in his diary, "and prayed with many Tears on either part. Hope God heard us."

The incident was not altogether uncommon. A woman of Boston, driven to desperation by the uncertainty of salvation, settled the point for herself by drowning her baby in a well, thus ensuring damnation,- and freeing her mind of doubts. Methodism, though gentler than Calvinism, accomplished similar results. In Wesley's journal there is an account of William Taverner, a boy of fourteen, who was a fellow passenger on the voyage to Georgia; and who, between heavy weather and continuous exhortation, went mad with fear, and saw an indescribable horror at the foot of his bed, "which looked at him all the time unless he was saying his prayers."

Our sympathy for a suffering minority need not, however,

blind us to the fact that the vast majority of men hold on to a creed because it suits them, and because their souls are strengthened by its ministrations. "It is sweet to believe even in Hell," says that arch-mocker, Anatole France; and to no article of faith have believers clung more tenaciously. Frederick Locker tells us the engaging story of a dignitary of the Greek Church who ventured, in the early years of his faith, to question this popular tenet; whereupon "his congregation, justly incensed, tore their bishop to pieces."

No Puritan divine stood in danger of suffering this particular form of martyrdom. The religion preached in New England was a cruel religion, from which the figure of Christ, living mercifully with men, was eliminated. John Evelyn noted down in his diary that he heard the Puritan magistrates of London "speak spiteful things of our Lord's Nativity." William Brewster was proud to record that in Plymouth "no man rested" on the first Christmas day. As with Bethlehem, so with Calvary. Governor Endicott slashed with his sword the red cross of Saint George from the banner of England. The emblem of Christianity was anathema to these Christians, as was the Mother who bore Christ, and who saw Him die. The children whom He blessed became to Jonathan Edwards "young vipers, and infinitely more hateful than vipers." The sweetness of religion, which had solaced a suffering world, was wiped out. "The Puritans," wrote Henry Adams pithily, "abandoned the New Testament and the Virgin in order to go back to the beginning, and renew the quarrel with Eve."

It took strong men to live and thrive under such a ministration, wrestling with a sullen earth for subsistence, and with an angry Heaven for salvation. Braced to endurance by the long frozen winters, plainly fed and plainly clad, in peril, like Saint Paul, of sea and wilderness, narrow of vision but steadfast to principles, they confronted life resolutely, honoring and illustrating the supreme worth of freedom.

That they had compensations, other than religious, is apparent to all but the most superficial observer. The languid indifference to our neighbor's moral and spiritual welfare, which we dignify by the name of tolerance, has curtailed our interest in life. There must have been something invigorating in the iron determination that neighbors should walk a straight path, that they should be watched at every step, and punished for every fall. The Puritan who said, "I will not. Thou shalt not!" enjoyed his authority to the uttermost. The prohibitionist who repeats his words to-day is probably the only man who is having a thoroughly good time in our fretful land and century. It is hard, I know, to reconcile "I will not. Thou shalt not!" with freedom. But the early settlers of New England were controlled by the weight of popular opinion. A strong majority forced a wavering minority along the road of rectitude. Standards were then as clearly defined as were boundaries, and the uncompromising individualism of the day permitted no juggling with responsibility.

It is not possible to read the second chapter of "The Scarlet Letter," and fail to perceive one animating principle of the Puritan's life. The townspeople who watch Hester Prynne stand in the pillory are moved by no common emotions. They savor the spectacle, as churchgoers of an earlier age savored the spectacle of a penitent in sackcloth at the portal; but they have also a sense of personal participation in the dragging of frailty to light. Hawthorne endeavors to make this clear, when, in answer to Roger Chillingworth's questions, a bystander congratulates him upon the timeliness of his arrival on the scene. "It must gladden your heart, after your troubles and sojourn in the wilderness, to find yourself at length in a land where iniquity is searched out, and punished in the sight of rulers and people." An unfortunate speech to make to the husband of the culprit (Hawthorne is seldom so ironic), but a cordial admission of content.

There was a picturesque quality about the laws of New England, and a nicety of administration, which made them a source of genuine pleasure to all who were not being judged. A lie, like an oath, was an offense to be punished; but all lies were not equally punishable. Alice Morse Earle quotes three penalties, imposed for three falsehoods, which show how much pains a magistrate took to discriminate. George Crispe's wife who "told a lie, not a pernicious lie, but inadvisedly," was simply admonished. Will Randall who told a "plain lie" was fined ten shillings. Ralph Smith who "lied about seeing a whale" was fined twenty shillings and excommunicated—which must have rejoiced his suffering neighbors' souls.

The rank of a gentleman, being a recognized attribute in those days, was liable to be forfeited for a disgraceful deed. In 1631, Josias Plastowe of Boston was fined five pounds for stealing corn from the Indians; and it was likewise ordered by the Court that he should be called in the future plain Josias, and not Mr. Plastowe as formerly. Here was a chance for the community to take a hand in punishing a somewhat contemptible malefactor. It would have been more or less than human if it had not enjoyed the privilege.

By far the neatest instance of making the punishment fit the crime is recorded in Governor Bradford's "Diary of Occurrences." The carpenter employed to construct the stocks for the Plymouth colonists thought fit to charge an excessive rate for the job; whereupon he was speedily clapped into his own instrument, "being the first to suffer the penalty." And *we* profess to pity the Puritans for the hardness and dullness of their lives! Why, if we could but see a single profiteer sitting in the stocks, one man out of the thousands who impudently oppress the public punished in this admirable and satisfactory manner, we should be willing to listen to sermons two hours long for the rest of our earthly days.

And the Puritans relished their sermons, which were masterful like themselves. Dogma and denunciation were dear to their souls, and they could bear an intolerable deal of both. An hourglass stood on the preacher's desk, and youthful eyes strayed wistfully to the slender thread of sand. But if the discourse continued after the last grain had run out, a tithingman who sat by the desk turned the glass, and the congregation settled down for a fresh hearing. A three-hour sermon was a possibility in those iron days, while an eloquent parson, like Samuel Torrey of Weymouth, could and did pray for two hours at a stretch. The Reverend John Cotton, grandfather of the redoubtable Cotton Mather, and the only minister in Boston who was acknowledged by Anne Hutchinson to possess the mysterious "seal of the Spirit," had a reprehensible habit of preaching for two hours on Sunday in the meeting-house (his family and servants of course attending), and at night, after supper, repeating this sermon to the sleepy household who had heard it in the morning.

For a hundred and fifty years the New England churches were unheated, and every effort to erect stoves was vigorously opposed. This at least could not have been a reaction against Popery, inasmuch as the churches of Catholic Christendom were at that time equally cold. That the descendants of men who tore the noble old organs out of English cathedrals, and sold them for scrap metal, should have been chary of accepting even a "pitch-pipe" to start their unmelodious singing was natural enough; but stoves played no part in the service. The congregations must have been either impervious to discomfort, or very much afraid of fires. The South Church of Boston was first heated in the winter of 1783. There was much criticism of such indulgence, and the "Evening Post," January 25th, burst into denunciatory verse:

> Extinct the sacred fires of love,
>   Our zeal grown cold and dead;
> In the house of God we fix a stove
>   To warm us in their stead.

Three blots on the Puritans' escutcheon (they were men, not seraphs) have been dealt with waveringly by historians. Witchcraft, slavery and Indian warfare loom darkly against a shining background of righteousness. Much has been made of the fleeting phase, and little of the more permanent conditions—which proves the historic value of the picturesque. That Salem should today sell witch spoons and trinkets, trafficking upon memories she might be reasonably supposed to regret, is a triumph of commercialism. The brief and dire obsession of witchcraft was in strict accord with times and circumstances. It bred fear, horror, and a tense excitement which lifted from Massachusetts all reproach of dullness. The walls between the known and the unknown world were battered savagely, and the men and women who thronged from house to house to see the "Afflicted Children" writhe in convulsions had a fearful appreciation of the spectacle. That terrible child, Ann Putnam, who at twelve years of age was instrumental in bringing to the scaffold some of the most respected citizens of Salem, is a unique figure in history. The apprehensive interest she inspired in her townspeople may be readily conceived. It brought her to ignominy in the end.

The Plymouth colonists kept on good terms with their Indian neighbors for half a century. The Bay colonists had more aggressive neighbors, and dealt with them accordingly. It was an unequal combat. The malignancy of the red men lacked concentration and thoroughness. They were only savages, and accustomed to episodic warfare. The white men knew the value of finality. When Massachusetts planned with Connecticut to exterminate the Pequots, less than a dozen men escaped extermination. It was a very complete killing, and no settler slept less soundly for having had a hand in it. Mr. Fiske says that the measures employed in King Philip's War "did not lack harshness," which is a euphemism. The flinging of the child Astyanax over the walls of Troy was less barbarous than the selling of King Philip's little son into slavery. Hundreds of adult captives were sent at the same time to Barbados. It would have been more merciful, though less profitable, to have butchered them at home.

The New England settlers were not indifferent to the Indians' souls. They forbade them, when they could, to hunt or fish on the Lord's day. John Eliot, Jonathan Edwards, and other famous divines preached to them earnestly, and gave them a fair chance of salvation. But, like all savages, they had a trick of melting into the forest just when their conversion seemed at hand. Cotton Mather, in his "Magnalia," speculates ruthlessly upon their condition and prospects. "We know not," he writes, "when or how these Indians first became inhabitants of this mighty continent; yet we may guess that probably the Devil decoyed these miserable savages hither, in hopes that the Gospel of the Lord would never come to destroy or disturb his absolute Empire over them."

Naturally, no one felt well disposed towards a race which was under the dominion of Satan. Just as the Celt and the Latin have small compunction in ill-treating animals, because they have no souls, so the Puritan had small compunction in ill-treating heathens, because their souls were lost.

Slavery struck no deep roots in New England soil, perhaps because the nobler half of the New England conscience never condoned it, perhaps because circumstances were unfavorable to its development. The Negroes died of the climate, the Indians of bondage. But traders, in whom conscience was not uppermost, trafficked in slaves as in any other class of merchandise, and stoutly refused to abandon a profitable line of business. Moreover, the deep discordance between slavery as an institution and Puritanism as an institution made such slave-holding more than ordinarily odious. Agnes Edwards, in an engaging little volume on Cape Cod, quotes a clause from the will of John Bacon of Barnstable, who bequeathed to his wife for her life time the "use and improvement" of a slave-woman, Dinah. "If, at the death of my wife, Dinah be still living, I desire my executors to sell her, and to use and improve the money for which she is sold in the purchase of Bibles, and distribute them equally among my said wife's and my grandchildren."

There are fashions in goodness and badness as in all things else; but the selling of a worn-out woman for Bibles goes a step beyond Mrs. Stowe's most vivid imaginings.

These are heavy indictments to bring against the stern forebears whom we are wont to praise and patronize. But Pilgrim and Puritan can bear the weight of their misdeeds as well as the glory of their achievements. Of their good old English birthright, "truth, pitie, freedom and hardiness," they cherished all but pitie. No price was too high for them to pay for the dignity of their manhood, or for the supreme privilege of dwelling on their own soil. They scorned the line of least resistance. Their religion was never a cloak for avarice, and labor was not with them another name for idleness and greed. Eight hours a day they held to be long enough for an artisan to work; but the principle of giving little and getting much, which rules our industrial world today, they deemed unworthy of freemen. No swollen fortunes corrupted their communities; no base envy of wealth turned them into prowling wolves. If they slew hostile Indians without compunction, they permitted none to rob those who were friendly and weak. If they endeavored to exclude immigrants of alien creeds, they would have thought it shame to bar them out because they were harder workers or better farmers than themselves. On the whole, a comparison between their methods and our own leaves us little room for self-congratulation.

From that great mother country which sends her roving sons over land and sea, the settlers of New England brought undimmed the sacred fire of liberty. If they were not akin to Shakespeare, they shared the inspiration of Milton. "No nobler heroism than theirs," says Carlyle, "ever transacted itself on this earth." Their laws were made for the strong, and commanded respect and obedience. In Plymouth, few public employments carried any salary; but no man might refuse office when it was tendered to him. The Pilgrim, like the Roman, was expected to serve the state, not batten on it. What wonder that a few drops of his blood carries with it even now some measure of devotion and restraint. These were men who understood that life is neither a pleasure nor a calamity. "It is a grave affair with which we are charged, and which we must conduct and terminate with honour."

CHAPTER II

MAKING THE REVOLUTION

WHEN colonial society came to maturity, a conflict opened with Great Britain all along the line—political, religious, and cultural, including under the last head all those social and democratic habits and ideas which gave distinction to American life. A revolution was the outcome, a wide-reaching revolution which awakened echoes in all parts of Europe, speeding up the French Revolution, ushering in an age of storms.

In all such upheavals women have been activists and thinkers. This was true of the Puritan uprising in the seventeenth century which sent Charles I to the scaffold. More than a hundred years later, hungry women of Paris led the march to Versailles and committed there the overt act which started the avalanche to republicanism. Then, after a lapse of more than another century, the hungry women of Petrograd—the low-paid textile workers—declared that they had borne pain and misery long enough and called upon soldiers, peasants, and proletarians to proclaim the end of the old régime.

The American Revolution was no exception to this apparent law of history. In its early stages women organized Daughters of Liberty to parallel the Sons of Liberty; they boycotted British goods with unrelenting vigor; they spun and wove to supply the markets thus closed to importations; they wrote letters and spoke hot words to spur on the laggards; they edited and published flaming newspapers; they cheered the crowds which tore down royal insignia; and added their swelling passions to the tumult.

When this excitement broke in open revolt, women's bravery entered into the operation. Among the "classes," they declared for independence, shared in the outlawry which befell Signers of the Declaration, brought social machinery to bear against obstructionists, gave private fortunes to the patriot cause, upheld through advice and public correspondence the morale of men at the political helm, and then turning to the issues of self-government considered the best policies for the future.

The "masses" supplied both brawn and ingenuity. Expert with horses that they could tame and swim as well as ride, slayers of bears and panthers, companions of hunters and sharp-shooters, trained to outwit native savages or slay them in self-defense, accustomed to managing industrial enterprise, physically strong and mentally alert, the women of '76 were daunted by no problems of rebellion.

Colonial women could fire guns and make munitions. "Handy Betsy the Blacksmith" was the peer of the most skilled in her work on cannon and other arms. Mrs. Proctor of Salem, who owned a tool factory at the opening of the war, was a boon to Joseph Swain placed in charge of collecting a rebel arsenal. Several women found the artillery service so irresistible that they joined husbands and sweethearts in manipulating that branch of fighting.

Torture could not intimidate, bribes could not beguile, danger could not awe, nor wiles beguile women "with the devil in them," as the Indians sometimes styled the white newcomers to their hunting-grounds. The women collected funds for soldier equipment or relief; nursed the sick and wounded; piled up supplies of clothing for the army, at their spinning wheels and looms; and kept the farms producing while the regular ploughmen were at the front.

Dorcas Richardson of South Carolina, who had urged her husband to withstand the allurements of pardon and promotion, offered for loyalism, lived to be ninety-three—in her last years one of a large group of old ladies surviving the terrors of warfare. Sarah Dickinson of North Carolina, a mother of nine children, tarried until she was ninety-six, remembering how her plantation had been laid waste in revenge for her capture of five Tories. "Moll O' the Pitcher," whose real name was Mary Ludwig Hays, died at ninety having been honored by Washington and pensioned by Congress and her State for her services. Sarah Bradlee Fulton, "Mother of the Boston Tea-party," lived to be ninety-four. But Ruth Cole lingered until she was one hundred and one, her mind clear to the end, endeavoring to be benevolent as well as patriotic.

Notwithstanding the rôle of the hearth in the Revolution, when its history came to be written, politics generally took charge of the selection and arrangement of "facts." The wide and deep social movement, which conditioned it, was usually left out of account. Particularly in school histories has the political aspect been emphasized. Nevertheless Mrs. Elizabeth Ellet in 1848 wrote the domestic history of the Revolution in an effort to restore the balance. And when the Daughters of the American Revolution entered the lists of national societies in 1890 they began to collect, edit and arrange the materials discovered by research into old records and documents; many excellent biographies were the outcome. On such sources Harry Clinton Green mainly relied for his three-volume treatise, "The Pioneer Mothers of America," published in 1912.

Mercy Warren, the sister of James Otis, jurist and orator of the Revolution, is often called its "penwoman." When she was not producing poems, plays, and direct arguments for the patriots, letters would pour in urging her to keep her flame burning. Strong claims are advanced relative to her priority as an advocate of independence but there can be no doubt about her influence on public opinion. Jefferson was one of her correspondents.

In 1775 at the request of John Adams, Mrs. Warren composed

*the following poem in commemoration of the Boston Tea
Party, using the language of mythology as he had suggested.
She calls it THE SQUABBLE OF THE SEA NYMPHS; OR
THE SACRIFICE OF THE TUSCARAROES.*

"Bright Phœbus drove his rapid car amain,
And plung'd his steeds beyond the western plain,
Behind a golden skirted cloud to rest.
Ere ebon night had spread her sable vest,
And drawn her curtain o'er the fragrant vale,
Or Cynthia's shadows dress'd the lonely dale,
The heroes of the Tuscararo tribe,
Who scorn'd alike a fetter or a bribe,
In order rang'd and waited freedom's nod,
To make an offering to the wat'ry god.

Grey Neptune rose, and from his sea green bed,
He wav'd his trident o'er his oozy head;
He stretch'd, from shore to shore, his regal wand,
And bade the river deities attend;
Triton's hoarse clarion summon'd them by name,
And from old ocean call'd each wat'ry dame.

In council met to regulate the state,
Among their godships rose a warm debate.
What luscious draught they next should substitute,
That might the palates of celestials suit,
As Nectar's stream no more meandering rolls,
The food ambrosial of their social bowls
Profusely spent;—nor, can Scamander's shore,
Yield the fair sea nymphs one short banquet more.

The Titans all with one accord arous'd,
To travel round Columbia's coast propos'd;
To rob and plunder every neighb'ring vine,
(Regardless of Nemesis' sacred shrine;)
Nor leave untouch'd the peasant's little store,
Or think of right, while demi gods have power. . .

'Till fair Salacia perch'd upon the rocks,
The rival goddess wav'd her yellow locks,
Proclaim'd, hysonia shall assuage their grief,
With choice souchong, and the imperial leaf.

The champions of the Tuscararan race,
(Who neither hold, nor even wish a place,
While faction reigns, and tyranny presides,
And base oppression o'er the virtues rides;
While venal measures dance in silken sails,
And avaraice o'er earth and sea prevails;
While luxury creates such mighty feuds,
E'en in the bosom of the demi gods;)
Lent their strong arm in pity to the fair,
To aid the bright Salacia's generous care;
Pour'd a profusion of delicious teas,
Which, wafted by a soft favonian breeze,
Supply'd the wat'ry deities, in spite
Of all the rage of jealous Amphytrite.

The fair Salacia, victory, victory, sings,
In spite of heroes, demi gods, or kings;
She bids defiance to the servile train,
The pimps and sycophants of George's reign."

Until recent times it was deemed irreverent in the United States to attribute economic motives to the framers of the American Constitution. But an examination of Mercy Warren's correspondence shows that even the female of the species was a realist in the eighteenth century. The first of the following messages to her husband was written on May 3, 1775; the second in 1776.

The important question you mentioned as preventing your leaving Congress yesterday leads me to offer my thoughts on the perplexed state of affairs—I think such a question should not be agitated untill you have a new Choice of Delegates—if anything of that nature is done it ought to be in full assembly—in an assembly of men of judgment, integrity & fortune—for nothing permanent or that will give general satisfaction can be done with regard to that matter unless there are a considerable number of men of property to give consequence to the measure. Men of this description ought not to sit still at home when every thing is afloat—do you not think as Congress has been weakened by calling of several of its active members to other departments it would be best to supply their places by a speedy appointment of fresh hands—for if by a little too much precipitation in so great an affair—or if by making an effort when you have not sufficient strength to carry it through: and the movement should thereby prove unsuccessful it would have been better never to have attempted it—but believe all will agree that it ought to be postponed no longer than the thirty first instant. . . .

I am very glad to hear the provincial Congress is so full—and that you are not apprehensive of immediate danger from the king's troops—yet I cannot say I am altogether so well pleased with the expression *that you are all very easy* without mentioning anything energetic that you are about to do. it appears to me there has been a hesitance full long enough and if on the whole it is thought most expedient your body should not act with more decission and vigor would it not be most for the honour of individual Gentlemen to make some plausible excuse and retreat homeward?

Committees of Correspondence were the agency for diffusing insurrectionary ideas and their origin is sometimes traced to the letter-writing practices of Mercy Warren and Abigail Adams. These two women were in the habit of discussing events not only with each other by correspondence but also with a wide circle of men at the head of the protest. Their remarks and questions received serious comments and replies which they read to groups of people assembled to discuss them.

For this and other reasons it is a gross mistake to regard colonial women as ignorant and illiterate. Part of the misunderstanding comes from Abigail Adams' lament that her sex had inadequate facilities for education but her standards required nothing less than the best collegiate training of her time. Though the institutions of learning were closed to them, women were

*taught to read and write and often had private tutors to carry
them on into the higher ranges of discipline. Given the fundamentals, they frequently had the will to educate themselves. And
in the FAMILIAR LETTERS OF JOHN ADAMS AND HIS
WIFE, ABIGAIL ADAMS edited by Charles Francis Adams,
we see how Abigail belied her statements relative to women's
ignorance. Writing to her husband, during his service in the
Continental Congress, she covers all the ground pertinent to the
revolt, including profiteering, the will to independence, the problems raised by the arms requirements, recruiting, financing, har-
vesting, and the desire of her sex for consideration in the new
government to be formed.*

[*1774*] Did ever any kingdom or state regain its liberty,
when once it was invaded, without bloodshed? I cannot think
of it without horror. Yet we are told that all the misfortunes of
Sparta were occasioned by their too great solicitude for peasant
tranquillity, and, from an excessive love of peace, they neglected
the means of making it sure and lasting. They ought to have
reflected, says Polybius, that, "as there is nothing more desirable
or advantageous than peace, when founded in justice and honor,
so there is nothing more shameful, and at the same time more
pernicious, when attained by bad measures and purchased at the
price of liberty." I have received a most charming letter from
our friend, Mrs. Warren. She desires me to tell you that her
best wishes attend you through your journey, both as a friend
and a patriot—hopes you will have no uncommon difficulties to
surmount, or hostile movements to impede you, but, if the
Locrians should interrupt you, she hopes that you will beware,
that no future annals may say you chose an ambitious Philip for
your leader, who subverted the noble order of the American
Amphictyons, and built up a monarchy on the ruins of the
happy institution. . . .

[*1774*] I judge you reached Philadelphia last Saturday night.
I cannot but felicitate you upon your absence a little while from

this scene of perturbation, anxiety, and distress. I own I feel not a little agitated with the accounts I have this day received from town: great commotions have arisen in consequence of a discovery of a traitorous plot of Colonel Brattle's—his advice to Gage to break every commissioned officer and to seize the province's and town's stock of gunpowder. This has so enraged and exasperated the people that there is great apprehension of an immediate rupture. They have been all in flames ever since the new-fangled counselors have taken their oaths. The importance, of which they consider the meeting of the Congress, and the result thereof to the community withholds the arms of vengeance already lifted. . . .

[*September 2, 1774*] Since the news of the Quebec bill arrived, all the Church people here have hung their heads and will not converse upon politics, though ever so much provoked by the opposite party. Before that, parties ran very high, and very hard words and threats of blows upon both sides were given out. They have had their town-meeting here, which was full as usual, chose their committee for the county meeting, and did business without once regarding or fearing for the consequences. . . .

[*September 14, 1774*] The Governor is making all kinds of warlike preparations, such as mounting cannon upon Beacon Hill, digging entrenchments upon the Neck, placing cannon there, encamping a regiment there, throwing up breast-works, etc. The people are much alarmed, and the selectmen have waited upon him in consequence of it. The County Congress have also sent a committee; all of which proceedings you will have a more particular account of than I am able to give you, from the public papers. But as to the movements of this town, perhaps you may not hear them from any other person.

In consequence of the powder being taken from Charlestown, a general alarm spread through many towns and was caught pretty soon here. . . . This town appears as high as you can well imagine, and, if necessary, would soon be in arms. Not a Tory but hides his head. The church parson thought they were coming after him, and ran up garret; they say another jumped out of his window and hid among the corn, while a third crept under his board fence and told his beads. . . .

[*September 24, 1774*] The maxim, "In time of peace prepare for war" (if this may be called a time of peace) resounds throughout the country. Next Tuesday they are warned at Braintree, all above fifteen and under sixty, to attend with their arms; and to train once a fortnight from that time is a scheme which lies much at heart with many. . . .

[*October 16, 1774*] We have too many high-sounding words, and too few actions that correspond with them. I have spent one Sabbath in town since you left. I saw no difference in respect to ornament, etc.; but in the country you must look for that virtue, of which you find but small glimmerings in the metropolis. Indeed, they have not the advantages, nor the resolution, to encourage our own manufactories, which people in the country have. To the mercantile part, it is considered as throwing away their own bread; but they must retrench their expenses, and be content with a small share of gain, for they will find but few who will wear their livery. As for me, I will seek wool and flax, and work willingly with my hands; and indeed there is occasion for all our industry and economy. . . .

The people in the country begin to be very anxious for the Congress to rise; they have no idea of the weighty business you have to transact, and their blood boils with indignation at the hostile preparations they are constant witnesses of. . . .

[*May 7, 1775*] I received by the Deacon two letters from you, this day, from Hartford. I feel a recruit of spirits upon the reception of them, and the comfortable news which they contain. We had not heard anything from North Carolina before, and we could not help feeling anxious lest we should find a defection there, arising more from their ancient feuds and animosities than from any settled ill-will in the present contest; but the confirmation of their delegates by their Assembly leaves not a doubt of their firmness. . . . Great events are most certainly in the womb of futurity; and, if the present chastisements which we experience have a proper influence upon our conduct, the event will certainly be in our favor. The distresses of the inhabitants of Boston are beyond the power of language to describe; there are but very few who are permitted to come out in a day; they delay giving passes, make them wait from hour to hour, and their counsels are not two hours together alike. One day, they shall come out with their effects; the next day, merchandise is not effects. One day, their household furniture is to come out; the next, only wearing apparel; the next, Pharoah's heart is hardened, and he refuseth to hearken to them, and will not let the people go. May their deliverance be wrought out for them, as it was for the children of Israel. I do not mean by miracles, but by the interposition of Heaven in their favor. They have taken a list of all those who they suppose were concerned in watching the tea, and every other person whom they call obnoxious, and they and their effects are to suffer destruction. . . .

[*May 24, 1775*] We wait, with longing expectation, in hopes to hear the best accounts from you, with regard to union and harmony, etc. We rejoice greatly on the arrival of Dr. Franklin, as he must certainly be able to inform you very particularly of the situation of affairs in England. I wish you would, if you can get time, be as particular as you may, when you write. Everyone hereabouts comes to me, to hear what accounts I have. . . .

Our house has been, upon this alarm, in the same scene of confusion that it was upon the former. Soldiers coming in for a lodging, for breakfast, for supper, for drink, etc. Sometimes refugees from Boston, tired and fatigued, seek an asylum for a day, a night, a week. You can hardly imagine how we live. . . . My best wishes attend you, both for your health and happiness, and that you may be directed into the wisest and best measures for our safety and the security of our posterity. . . . Hitherto

I have been able to maintain a calmness and presence of mind, and hope I shall, let the exigency of the time be what it will. Adieu, breakfast calls. . . .

[*June 15, 1775*] We now expect our seacoast ravaged; perhaps the very next letter I write will inform you that I am driven away from our yet quiet cottage. Necessity will oblige Gage to take some desperate steps. We are told for truth that he is now eight thousand strong. We live in continual expectation of alarms. Courage I know we have in abundance; conduct I hope we shall not want; but powder—where shall we get a sufficient supply? . . .

[*June 22, 1775*] We hear that the troops destined for New York are all expected here; but we have got to that pass that a whole legion of them would not intimidate us. I think I am very brave, upon the whole. If danger comes near my dwelling, I suppose I shall shudder. We want powder, but, with the blessing of Heaven, we fear them not. Write every opportunity you can. . . .

[*July 5, 1775*] I hope we shall not now have famine added to war. Grain, grain is what we want here. Meat we have enough, and to spare. Pray don't let Bass forget my pins. Hardwick has applied to me for Mr. Bass to get him a hundred of needles, number six, to carry on his stocking weaving. We shall very soon have no coffee, nor sugar, nor pepper, here; but whortleberries and milk we are not obliged to commerce for. . . .

I was struck with General Washington. You had prepared me to entertain a favorable opinion of him, but I thought the half was not told me. Dignity with ease and complacency, the gentleman and soldier, look agreeably blended in him. Modesty marks every line and feature of his face. . . .

General Lee looks like a careless, hardy veteran, and by his appearance brought to my mind his namesake, Charles the Twelfth, of Sweden. The elegance of his pen far exceeds that of his person. . . .

You used to be more communicative on Sundays. I always loved a Sabbath day's letter, for then you had a greater command of your time; but hush to all complaints. . . .

[*July 25, 1775*] An order has been given out in town that no person shall be seen to wipe his face with a white handkerchief. The reason I hear is that it is a signal of mutiny. General Burgoyne lives in Mr. Sam Quincy's house. A lady, who lived opposite, says she saw raw meat cut and hacked upon her mahogany tables, and her superb damask curtain and cushions exposed to the rain, as if they were of no value. How much better do the Tories fare than the Whigs?

[*September 8, 1775*] And such is the distress of the neighborhood, that I can scarcely find a well person to assist in looking after the sick. . . . So sickly and so mortal a time the oldest man does not remember. . . . By the first safe conveyance be kind enough to send me one ounce of Turkey rhubarb, the root, and to procure me one quarter of a pound of nutmegs, for which here I have to give 2s.8d. lawful; one ounce of cloves, two of cinnamon. I should be glad of one ounce of Indian root. So much sickness has occasioned a scarcity of medicines. . . . The small-pox in the natural way was not more mortal than this distemper has proved in this and neighboring towns. . . .

[*September 16, 1775*] As to politics, there seems to be a dead calm on all sides. Some of the Tories have been sending out their children. Colonel Chandler has sent out his, and Mr. Winslow has sent out his daughter. People appear to be gratified with the Remonstrance, Address, and Petition, and most earnestly long for further intelligence. . . .

[*October 21, 1775*] Haskins says no language can paint the distress of the inhabitants (of Boston); most of them destitute of wood and of provisions of every kind. The bakers say, unless they have a new supply of wood they cannot bake above one fortnight longer; their biscuit are not above one half the former size; the soldiers are obliged to do very hard duty, and are uneasy to a great degree, many of them declaring they will not continue much longer in such a state, but at all hazards will escape. The inhabitants are desperate, and contriving means of escape. A floating battery of ours went out two nights ago, and rowed near the town, and then discharged their guns. Some of the balls went into the workhouse, some through the tents in the Common, men, women, and children screaming, and threw them into the utmost distress; but, very unhappily for us, in the discharge of one of the cannon, the ball not being properly rammed down, it split and killed two men, and wounded seven more, upon which they were obliged to return. . . .

In the course of the last week, several persons have found means to escape. One of them says it is talked in town that Howe will issue a proclamation, giving liberty to all who will not take up arms, to depart the town, and making it death to have any intercourse with the country afterwards. . . .

[*November 5, 1775*] It seems human nature is the same in all ages and countries. Ambition and avarice reign everywhere, and where they predominate, there will be bickerings after places of honor and profit. . . .

I inclose to you the paper you sent for. Your business in collecting facts will be very difficult, and the sufferings of this people cannot be described with pen, ink, and paper. . . .

[*November 12, 1775*] The intelligence you will receive before this reaches you will, I should think, make a plain path, though a dangerous one, for you. I could not join today in the petition of our worthy pastor, for a reconciliation between our no longer parent state, but tyrant state, and these colonies. Let us separate; they are unworthy to be our brethren. Let us renounce them; and instead of supplications, as formerly, for their prosperity and happiness, let us beseech the Almighty to blast their counsels. . . .

[*November 27, 1775*] I wish I knew what mighty things were fabricating. If a form of government is to be established here, what one will be assumed, Will it be left to our Assemblies to choose one? And will not many men have many minds?

I am more and more convinced that man is a dangerous creature; and that power, whether vested in many or a few, is ever grasping, and, like the grave, cries, "Give, give!" The great fish swallow up the small; and he who is most strenuous for the rights of the people, when vested with power, is as eager after the prerogatives of government. You tell me of degrees of perfection to which human nature is capable of arriving, and I believe it, but at the same time lament that our admiration should arise from the scarcity of the instances.

The building up a great empire, which was only hinted at by my correspondent, may now, I suppose, be realized even by the unbelievers. Yet, will not ten thousand difficulties arise in the formation of it? The reins of government have been so long slackened, that I fear the people will not quietly submit to those restraints which are necessary for the peace and security of the community. If we separate from Britain, what code of laws will be established? How shall we be governed so as to retain our liberties? Can any government be free which is not administered by general stated laws? Who shall frame these laws? Who will give them force and energy? It is true, your resolutions, as a body, have hitherto had the force of laws; but will they continue to have?

When I consider these things, and the prejudices of people in favor of ancient customs and regulations, I feel anxious for the fate of our monarchy, or democracy, or whatever is to take place. I soon get lost in a labyrinth of perplexities; but, whatever occurs, may justice and righteousness be the stability of our times, and order arise out of confusion. Great difficulties may be surmounted by patience and perseverance. . . .

[*March 2, 1776*] I am charmed with the sentiments of "Common Sense," and wonder how an honest heart, one who wishes the welfare of his country and the happiness of posterity, can hesitate one moment at adopting them. I want to know how these sentiments are received in Congress. I dare say there would be no difficulty in procuring a vote and instructions from all the Assemblies in New England for Independency. I most sincerely wish that now, in the lucky moment, it might be done. . . .

[*April 14, 1776*] The officers and Tories have lived a life of dissipation. Inclosed is a prologue of Burgoyne's, with a parody written in Boston, soon after it was acted. Burgoyne is a better poet than soldier. . . .

[*April 21, 1776*] I heard yesterday that a number of gentlemen who were together at Cambridge thought it highly proper that a committee of ladies should be chosen to examine the Tory ladies, and proceeded to the choice of three—Mrs. Winthrop, Mrs. Warren, and your humble servant. . . .

[*July 21, 1776*] Last Thursday, after hearing a very good sermon, I went with the multitude into King Street [Boston] to hear the proclamation for Independence read and proclaimed. Some field-pieces with the train were brought there. The troops appeared under arms, and all the inhabitants assembled there (the small-pox prevented many thousands from the country), when Colonel Crafts read from the balcony of the State House the proclamation. Great attention was given to every word. As soon as he ended, the cry from the balcony was, "God save our American States," and then three cheers rent the air. The bells rang, the privateers fired, the cannon were discharged, the platoons followed, and every face appeared joyful. Mr. Bowdoin then gave a sentiment, "Stability and perpetuity to American independence." After dinner, the King's Arms were taken down from the State House, and every vestige of him from every place in which it appeared, and burnt in King Street. Thus ends royal authority in this State. And all the people shall say Amen. . . .

[*September 9, 1776*] But if we should be defeated, I think we shall not be conquered. A people fired like the Romans with love of their country and of liberty, a zeal for the public good, and a noble emulation of glory, will not be disheartened or dispirited by a succession of unfortunate events. But like them may we learn by defeat the power of becoming invincible! . . .

[*September 29, 1776*] The rage for privateering is as great here as anywhere. Vast numbers are employed in that way. If it is necessary to make any more drafts upon us, the women must reap the harvests. I am willing to do my part. I believe I could gather corn, and husk it; but I should make a poor figure at digging potatoes. . . .

[*April 2, 1777*] 'Tis said here that General Washington has but eight thousand troops with him. Can it be true? That we have but twelve hundred at Ticonderoga? I know not who has the care of raising them here, but this I know, we are very dilatory about it. All the troops which were stationed upon Nantasket and at Boston are dismissed this week, so that we are now very fit to receive an enemy. I have heard some talk of routing the enemy at Newport; but if anything was designed against them, believe me 'tis wholly laid aside. Nobody seems to consider them as dangerous, or indeed to care anything about them. Where is General Gates? We hear nothing of him.

The Church doors were shut up last Sunday in consequence of a presentiment; a farewell sermon preached and much weeping and wailing; persecuted, be sure, but not for righteousness' sake. The conscientious parson had taken an oath upon the Holy Evangelists to pray for his most gracious Majesty as his sovereign lord, and having no father confessor to absolve him, he could not omit it without breaking his oath. . . .

[*April 20, 1777*] I believe we shall be the last State to assume government. Whilst we harbor such a number of designing Tories amongst us, we shall find government disregarded and every measure brought into contempt by secretly undermining and openly contemning them. We abound with designing Tories and ignorant, avaricious Whigs. . . .

[*May 9, 1777*] I must add a little more. A most horrid plot has been discovered of a band of villains counterfeiting the Hampshire currency to a great amount. No person scarcely but what has more or less of these bills. I am unlucky enough to have about five pounds L.M. of it, but this is not the worst of it. One Colonel Farrington, who has been concerned in the plot, was taken sick, and has confessed not only the counterfeiting, but says they had engaged and enlisted near two thousand men, who, upon the troops' coming to Boston, were to fall upon the people and make a general havoc. . . . The Hampshire people have been stupid enough to let one of the principal plotters, Colonel Holland, out upon bail, and he has made his escape. . . .

[*July 31, 1777*] I have nothing new to entertain you with, unless it be an account of a new set of mobility, which has lately taken the lead in Boston. You must know that there is a great scarcity of sugar and coffee, articles which the female part of the State is very loath to give up, especially whilst they consider the scarcity occasioned by the merchants having secreted a large quantity. There had been much rout and noise in the town for several weeks. Some stores had been opened by a number of people, and the coffee and sugar carried into the market and dealt out by pounds. It was rumored that an eminent, wealthy, stingy merchant (who is a bachelor) had a hogshead of coffee in his store, which he refused to sell to the committee under six shillings per pound. A number of females, some say a hundred, some say more, assembled with a cart and trucks, marched down to the warehouse, and demanded the keys, which he refused to deliver. Upon which one of them seized him by his neck, and tossed him into the cart. Upon his finding no quarter, he delivered the keys, when they tipped up the cart and discharged him; then opened the warehouse, hoisted out the coffee themselves, put it into the trucks, and drove off.

It was reported that he had personal chastisement among them; but this, I believe, was not true. A large concourse of men stood amazed, silent spectators of the whole transaction. . . .

[*August 5, 1777*] It is almost thirteen years since we were united, but not more than half that time have we had the happiness of living together. The unfeeling world may consider it in what light they please. I consider it as a sacrifice to my country, and one of my greatest misfortunes for you to be separated from my children, at a time of life when the joint instructions and admonitions of parents sink deeper than in maturer years. . . .

[*September 24, 1777*] The loss of Ticonderoga has awakened the sleeping genius of America, and called forth all her martial fire. May it never again be lulled to rest till crowned with victory and peace. Good officers will make good soldiers. . . .

Thus you see we go from step to step in our improvement. We can live much better than we deserve within ourselves. Why should we borrow foreign luxuries? Why should we wish to bring ruin upon ourselves? I feel as contented when I have breakfasted upon milk as ever I did with Hyson or Souchong. Coffee and sugar I use only as a rarity. There are none of these things but I could totally renounce. My dear friend knows that I could always conform to times and circumstances. My children have never cried for bread nor been destitute of clothing. Nor have the poor and needy gone empty from my door, whenever it was in my power to assist them. . . .

[*October 20, 1777*] I was greatly surprised when I heard that the enemy was in possession of Philadelphia, without any engagement on our part. If men will not fight and defend their own particular spot, if they will not drive the enemy from their doors, they deserve the slavery and subjection which awaits them. . . .

[*June 8, 1779*] I cannot say that I think our affairs go very well here. Our currency seems to be the source of all our evils. We cannot fill up our Continental army by means of it. No bounty will prevail with them. What can be done with it? It will sink in less than a year. The advantage the enemy daily gains over us is owing to this. . . .

[*July 16, 1780*] What shall I say of our political affairs? Shall I exclaim at measures now impossible to remedy? No. I will hope all from the generous aid of our allies, in concert with our own exertions. I am not suddenly elated or depressed. I know America capable of anything she undertakes with spirit and vigor. "Brave in distress, serene in conquest, drowsy when at rest" is her true characteristic. Yet I deprecate a failure in our present effort. The efforts are great, and we give, this campaign, more than half our property to defend the other. He who tarries from the field cannot possibly earn sufficient at home to reward him who takes it. Yet, should Heaven bless our endeavors, and crown this year with the blessings of peace, no exertion will be thought too great, no price of property too dear. My whole soul is absorbed in the idea. The honor of my dearest friend, the welfare and happiness of this wide-extended country, ages yet unborn, depend for their happiness and security upon the able and skillful, the honest and upright, discharge of the important trust committed to him.

[*December 23, 1782*] If I had known, sir, that Mr. Adams could have effected what he has done, I would not only have submitted to the absence I have endured, painful as it has been, but I would not have opposed it, even though three years more should be added to the number (which Heaven avert!) I feel a pleasure in being able to sacrifice my selfish passions to the general good, and in imitating the example which has taught me to consider myself and family but as the small dust of the balance, when compared with the great community.

The following letter by Deborah Champion (later Mrs. Samuel Gilbert) [1] *is remarkable for its classical style no less than for the amazing performance it reports. Deborah was born at New London, Connecticut, in 1753, the daughter of Colonel Henry Champion of French and Indian War fame who was made Com-*

[1] Reprint obtained through the courtesy of Deborah Champion Chapter, Daughters of the American Revolution, Adams, New York.

*missary General of the Revolutionary army soon after it was
organized. The story she tells concerned an important mission
which she undertook at the age of twenty-two, in the year 1775,
for the purpose of penetrating British lines with dispatches for
General Washington.*

MY DEAR PATIENCE:

I know that you will think it a weary long time since I have
written to you, and indeed I would have answered your last
sweet letter long before now, but I have been away from home.
Think of it! I know that you will hardly believe that such a
stay-at-home as I should go and all alone too, to where do you
think? To Boston! Really and truly to Boston. Before you
suffer too much with amazement and curiosity, I will hasten to
tell you all about it. About a week after receiving your letter
I had settled with myself to spend a long day with my spinning,
being anxious to prepare for some cloth which my mother needed
to make some small clothes for father. Just as I was busily engaged I noticed a horseman enter the yard and, knocking on
the door with the handle of his whip, he asked for General
Champion, and after a brief converse he entered the house with
father. Whereat mother presently asked me to go to the store
in town and get her spices and condiments, which I was very
sure were already in the storeroom. However, as I was to be
sent out of the way there was nothing left for me but to go, which
I accordingly did, not hurrying myself, you may be sure. When
I returned, the visitor was gone, but my father was walking up
and down the long hall with hasty steps, and worried and per-
turbed aspect. You know father has always been kind and good
to me, but none know better than you the stern self-repression
our New England character engenders, and he would not have
thought seemly that a child of his should question him, so I
passed on to find mother and deliver my purchases. "My father
is troubled, Mother, is aught amiss?" "I cannot say, Deborah;
you know he has many cares, and the public business presses
heavily at times; it may be he will tell us." Just then my father

stood in the doorway. "Wife, I would speak with you." Mother hastily joined him in the keeping room, and they seemed to have long and anxious converse. Finally, to my astonishment, I was called to attend them. Father laid his hand on my shoulder (a most unusual caress with him) and said solemnly: "Deborah, I have need of thee; hast thou the heart and the courage to go out in the dark and in the night and ride as fast as may be until thou comest to Boston town?" "Surely, my Father, if it is thy wish, and will please thee."

"I do not believe, Deborah, that there will be actual danger to threaten thee, else I would not ask it of thee, but the way is long and the business urgent. The horseman that was here awhile back brought dispatches which it is desperately necessary that General Washington should receive as soon as possible. I cannot go, the wants of the army call me at once to Hartford, and I have no one to send but my daughter. Dare you go?"

"Dare! father, and I your daughter—and the chance to do my country and General Washington a service. I am glad to go."

So, dear Patience, it was finally settled that I should start in the early morning and Aristarchus should go with me. He has been devoted to me since I made a huge cake to grace his wedding with Glory and found a name for the dusky baby which we call Sophronista. For a slave, he has his fair share of wits, also. Early in the morning, before it was fairly light, mother called me, though I had seemed to have hardly slept at all. I found a nice hot breakfast ready, and a pair of saddle-bags packed with such things as mother thought might be needed. Father told me again of the haste with which I must ride and the care to use for the safety of the dispatches, and I set forth on my journey with a light heart and my father's blessing. The British were at Providence, in Rhode Island, so it was thought best I should ride due north to the Massachusetts line, and then east, as best I could to Boston. The weather was perfect, but the roads none too good as there had been recent rains, but we made fairly good time going through Norwich, then up the valley of the Quinebaug to Canterbury, where we rested our horses for an hour, then pushed on, hoping to get to Pomfret before dark. At father's desire I was to stay the night with Uncle Jirey, and, if needful, get a change of horses. All went as well as I could expect. We met few people on the road, almost all the men being with the army and only the very old men and the women at work in the villages and farms. Dear heart, but war is a cruel thing! but I was glad, so glad that I could do even so little to help! Uncle Jirey thought we had better take fresh horses in the morning, and sun found us on our way again. I heard that it would be almost impossible to avoid the British unless by going so far out of the way that too much time would be lost, so I plucked up what courage I could and secreting my papers in a small pocket in the saddle-bags, under all the eatables mother had filled them with, I rode on, determined to ride all night. It was late at night, or rather very early in the morning, that I heard the call of the sentry and knew that now, if at all, the danger point was reached, but pulling my calash still farther over my face, I went on with what boldness I could muster. Suddenly, I was ordered to halt; as I couldn't help myself I did so. I could almost hear Aristarchus' teeth rattle in his mouth, but I knew he would obey my instructions and if I was detained, would try to find the way alone. A soldier in a red coat proceeded to take me to headquarters, but I told him it was early to wake the captain, and to please to let me pass for I had been sent in urgent haste to see a friend in need, which was true if ambiguous. To my joy, he let me go on, saying: "Well, you are only an old woman anyway," evidently as glad to get rid of me as I of him. Will you believe me, that is the only bit of adventure that befell me in the whole long ride. When I arrived in Boston, I was so very fortunate as to find friends who took me at once to General Washington and I gave him the papers, which proved to be of the utmost importance, and was pleased to compliment me most highly both as to what he was pleased to call the courage I had displayed and my patriotism. Oh, Patience, what a man he is, so grand, so kind, so noble, I am sure we will not look to him in vain to save our fair country to us.

On the appointment of Robert Morris of Philadelphia to the post of financier for the Revolution, his wife received from Mrs. John Jay, then in Spain, a letter of congratulation which was more than a formal courtesy shown by a friend to a friend.

Mrs. Jay was the daughter of William Livingston, scion of a powerful Whig family of New York, whose country-place in New Jersey was known as "Liberty Hall." She was married to John Jay the year that the first Continental Congress assembled and protest reached the form of organization. When she wrote to Mrs. Morris, as follows, her husband was in Madrid serving as the representative of the American Confederation.

No circumstance of a public nature since my absence from America has given me greater satisfaction than Mr. Morris's acceptance of that important office which he at present holds; nor would you, my dear madam, even regret being so frequently obliged to dispense with his company, if you could be witness to the universal satisfaction it has diffused among the friends of our country, but w'd (were you as malicious as myself) even enjoy the confusion of our enemies upon the occasion. Besides the public utility which must arise from the measure, I have a peculiar pleasure, which results from the more frequent mention of the person, from whose abilities and integrity so much is expected, in terms the most grateful to friendship. Your fears for Mr. Morris's health are, I own, too well founded, and I think a little address to draw him into the country, at least of evenings, would be patriotic.

While Trumbull was painting revolutionary scenes, Mercy Warren was writing the account of what had taken place. She completed a history of the Revolution before the eighteenth century closed but it was not published until 1805, when she was seventy-seven years old. Since her generation was familiar with the social nature of the struggle, popular interest in her history at the time centered in her interpretation of such patriots as John

Hancock and Samuel Adams and hence she inadvertently helped to fix the political approach to the study of the Revolution for the generations to come. John Adams was incensed by her portrait of himself which seemed to imply that beneath his zeal for a strong central government lurked the desire for a monarchy, and the two friends had a prolonged quarrel over the objectives of the war, Mrs. Warren arguing that luxury, wealth and titles had no place in the new régime.

Nearly half a century later, Mrs. Elizabeth Ellet, in living contact with the insurgence of Jacksonian Democracy and the ferments of Europe then hovering on the verge of another cataclysm, as she pondered on the American Revolution, brought back into its history the social side of the struggle, calling her volume THE WOMEN OF THE AMERICAN REVOLUTION. From this work the following pages are taken.

All Americans are accustomed to view with interest and admiration the events of the Revolution. Its scenes are vivid in their memory, and its prominent actors are regarded with the deepest veneration. But while the leading spirits are thus honored, attention should be directed to the source whence their power was derived—to the sentiment pervading the mass of the people. The force of this sentiment, working in the public heart, cannot be measured; because, amidst the abundance of materials for the history of action, there is little for that of the feeling of those times. And, as years pass on, the investigation becomes more and more difficult. Yet it is both interesting and important to trace its operation. It gave statesmen their influence, and armed heroes for victory. What could they have done but for the home-sentiment to which they appealed, and which sustained them in the hour of trial and success? They were thus aided to the eminence they gained through toils and perils. Others may claim a share in the merit, if not the fame, of their illustrious deeds. The unfading laurels that wreathe their brows had their root in the hearts of the people, and were nourished with their life-blood.

The feeling which wrought thus powerfully in the community depended, in great part, upon the women. It is always thus in times of popular excitement. Who can estimate, moreover, the controlling influence of early culture? During the years of the progress of British encroachment and colonial discontent, when the sagacious politician could discern the portentous shadows of events yet far distant, there was time for the nurture, in the domestic sanctuary, of that love of civil liberty, which afterwards kindled into a flame, and shed light on the world. The talk of matrons, in American homes, was of the people's wrongs, and the tyranny that oppressed them, till the sons who had grown to manhood, with strengthened aspirations toward a better state of things, and views enlarged to comprehend their invaded rights, stood up prepared to defend them to the utmost. Patriotic mothers nursed the infancy of freedom. Their counsels and their prayers mingled with the deliberations that resulted in a nation's assertion of its independence. They animated the courage, and confirmed the self-devotion of those who ventured all in the common cause. They frowned upon instances of coldness or backwardness; and in the period of deepest gloom, cheered and urged on the desponding. They willingly shared inevitable dangers and privations, relinquished without regret prospects of advantage to themselves, and parted with those they loved better than life, not knowing when they were to meet again. It is almost impossible now to appreciate the vast influence of woman's patriotism upon the destinies of the infant republic. We have no means of showing the important part she bore in maintaining the struggle, and in laying the foundations on which so mighty and majestic a structure has arisen. History can do it no justice; for history deals with the workings of the head, rather than the heart. And the knowledge received by tradition, of the domestic manners, and social character of the times, is too imperfect to furnish a sure index. We can only dwell upon individual instances of magnanimity, fortitude, self-sacrifice, and heroism, bearing the impress of the feeling of Revolutionary days, indicative of the spirit which animated all, and to which, in its various and multiform exhibitions, we are not less indebted for national freedom, than to the swords of the patriots who poured out their blood. . . .

Their patriotic sacrifices were made with an enthusiasm that showed the earnest spirit ready on every occasion to appear in generous acts. Some gave their own property, and went from house to house to solicit contributions for the army. Colors were embroidered by fair hands, and presented with the charge never to desert them; and arms and ammunition were provided by the same liberal zeal. They formed themselves into associations renouncing the use of teas, and other imported luxuries, and engaging to card, spin, and weave their own clothing. In Mecklenburgh and Rowan counties, North Carolina, young ladies of the most respectable families pledged themselves not to receive the addresses of any suitors who had not obeyed the country's call for military service.

The needy shared the fruit of their industry and economy. They visited hospitals daily; sought the dungeons of the provost, and the crowded holds of prison ships; and provisions were carried from their stores to the captives whose only means of recompense was the blessing of those who were ready to perish. Many raised grain, gathered it, made bread, and carried it to their relatives in the army, or in prisons, accompanying the supply with exhortations never to abandon the cause of their country. The burial of friends slain in battle, or chance-encounters, often devolved upon them; and even enemies would not have received sepulture without the service of their hands.

When the resources of the country scarcely allowed the scantiest supply of clothing and provisions, and British cruisers on the coast destroyed every hope of aid from merchant vessels; when, to the distressed troops, their cup of misfortune seemed full to overflowing, and there appeared no prospect of relief, except from the benevolence of their fellow-citizens; when even the ability of these was almost exhausted by repeated applications— then it was that the women of Pennsylvania and New Jersey, by their zealous exertions and willing sacrifices, accomplished what had been thought impossible. Not only was the pressure of want removed, but the sympathy and favor of the fair daughters of America, says one of the journals, "operated like a charm on the soldier's heart—gave vigor to exertion, confidence to his hopes of success, and the ultimate certainty of victory and peace." General Washington, in his letter of acknowledgement to the committee of ladies, says, "The army ought not to regret its sacrifices or its sufferings, when they meet with so flattering a reward, as in the sympathy of your sex; nor can it fear that its interests will be neglected, when espoused by advocates as powerful as they are amiable." An officer in camp writes, in June, 1780: "The patriotism of the women of your city is a subject of conversation with the army. Had I poetical genius, I would sit down and write an ode in praise of it. Bourgoyne, who, on his first coming to America, boasted that he would dance with the ladies, and coax the men to submission, must now have a better understanding of the good sense and public spirit of our females, as he has already heard of the fortitude and inflexible temper of our men." Another observes: "We cannot appeal in vain for what is good, to that sanctuary where all that is good has its proper home—the female bosom."

How the influence of women was estimated by John Adams, appears from one of his letters to his wife: " . . . I believe the two Howes have not very great women for wives. If they had, we should suffer more from their exertions than we do. This is our good fortune. A smart wife would have put Howe in possession of Philadelphia a long time ago." . . .

The sentiments of the women towards the brave defenders of their native land were expressed in an address widely circulated at the time, and read in the churches of Virginia. "We know," it says—"that at a distance from the theatre of war, if we enjoy any tranquillity, it is the fruit of your watchings, your labors, your dangers. . . . And shall we hesitate to evince to you our gratitude? Shall we hesitate to wear clothing more simple, and dress less elegant, while at the price of this small privation, we shall deserve your benedictions?"

The same spirit appears in a letter found among some papers belonging to a lady of Philadelphia. It was addressed to a British officer in Boston, and written before the Declaration of Independence. The following extract will show its character:

"I will tell you what I have done. My only brother I have sent to the camp with my prayers and my blessings. I hope he will not disgrace me: I am confident he will behave with honor, and emulate the great examples he has before him; and had I twenty sons and brothers they should go. I have retrenched every superfluous expense in my table and family; tea I have not drunk since last Christmas, nor bought a new cap or gown since your defeat at Lexington; and what I never did before, have learned to knit, and am now making stockings of American wool for my servants; and this way do I throw in my mite to the public good. I know this—that as free I can die but once; but as a slave I shall not be worthy of life. I have the pleasure to assure you that these are the sentiments of all my sister Americans. They have sacrificed assemblies, parties of pleasure, tea drinking and finery, to that great spirit of patriotism that actuates all degrees of people throughout this extensive continent. If these are the sentiments of females, what must glow in the breasts of our husbands, brothers, and sons! They are as with one heart determined to die or be free. It is not a quibble in politics, a science which few understand, that we are contending for; it is this plain truth, which the most ignorant peasant knows, and is clear to the weakest capacity —that no man has a right to take their money without their consent. You say you are no politician. Oh, sir, it requires no Machiavellian head to discover this tyranny and oppression. It is written with a sunbeam. Every one will see and know it, because it will make every one feel; and we shall be unworthy of the blessings of Heaven if we ever submit to it. . . .
Heaven seems to smile on us; for in the memory of man, never were known such quantities of flax, and sheep without number. We are making powder fast, and do not want for ammunition."

From all portions of the country thus rose the expression of woman's ardent zeal. Under accumulated evils, the manly spirit that alone could secure success might have sunk but for the firmness and intrepidity of the weaker sex. It supplied every persuasion that could animate to perseverance, and secure fidelity.

The noble deeds in which this irrepressible spirit breathed itself were not unrewarded by persecution. The case of the quakeress Deborah Franklin, who was banished from New York by the British commandant for her liberality in relieving the sufferings of the American prisoners, was one among many. . . . The alarms of war—the roar of the strife itself, could not silence the voice of woman, lifted in encouragement or in prayer. The horrors of battle or massacre could not drive her from the post of duty. . . . The heroism of the Revolutionary women has passed from remembrance with the generation who witnessed it; or is seen only by faint and occasional glimpses, through the gathering obscurity of tradition.

To render a measure of justice—inadequate it must be—to a few of the American matrons, whose names deserve to live in remembrance—and to exhibit something of the domestic side of the Revolutionary picture—is the object of this work. As we recede from the realities of that struggle, it is regarded with increasing interest by those who enjoy its results; while the elements which were its life-giving principle, too subtle to be retained by the grave historian, are fleeting fast from apprehension. Yet without some conception of them, the Revolution cannot be appreciated. We must enter into the spirit, as well as master the letter.

While attempting to pay a tribute but too long withheld, to the memory of women who did and endured so much in the cause of liberty, we should not be insensible to the virtues exhibited by another class, belonging equally to the history of the period. These had their share of reverse and suffering. Many saw their children and relatives espousing opposite sides; and with ardent feelings of loyalty in their hearts, were forced to weep over the miseries of their families and neighbors. Many were driven from their homes, despoiled of property, and finally compelled to cast their lot in desolate wilds and an ungenial climate. And while their heroism, fortitude, and spirit of self-sacrifice were not less brightly displayed, their hard lot was unpitied, and they met with no reward. . . .

A British critic has charged me with having mentioned instances of cruelty among the royalists, without due notice of the forbearance and clemency frequently exercised. I am aware that it is difficult to avoid apparent partiality in narrating incidents received from descendants of the patriots, who, even if uninfluenced by any remains of political animosity, would naturally remember the noble acts and the sufferings of their ancestors, while forgetful of the provocations given, or the injuries inflicted by individuals of their party. It must be confessed, too, that the very boldness of many among the women who took an active part, and the impunity with which they indulged in severe speeches to the royal officers, form a strong argument to show the humanity and respect with which they were generally treated. So far am I from being unwilling to do full justice to the other side, that I only regret my inability, from want of details promised, but not yet received, to portray in this volume as in the preceding ones, the devotion, self-sacrificing zeal, and courageous enterprise in the cause of the destitute and suffering, by which loyalist women softened the grim features of war, and lighted a period of darkness and distress.

In widening the scope of history to include the whole complex of ideas and interests at work in the social process, Alice Baldwin has inquired into the generation and spread of revolutionary conceptions of liberty. Her NEW ENGLAND CLERGY IN THE AMERICAN REVOLUTION [2] deals with the part which the clergy played "in teaching political theory to the people," and throws light on the relation of economic interest to the nature of that theory. The importance of the meeting-house, suggested in Abigail Adams' letters, stands out clearly in Miss Baldwin's scholarly portrayal of clerical activities.

Something of the close connection between religion and political theory has been brought out in the preceding chapters. To

[2] Reprint obtained through the courtesy of the author and the Duke University Press.

realize it more fully and to gain a better understanding of the long background and the true meaning of many of the Revolutionary arguments, it is necessary to study in somewhat more detail the religious and ecclesiastical controversies of the period and especially the Great Awakening which so deeply affected men's emotions and thinking. Such a study will serve to make more clear the interest of the New Englander in fundamental law, his belief that any violation of it by those in authority was tyranny and that revolt against such tyranny was legal and not only legal but a religious duty. What civil and religious liberty, property and equality meant to both clergy and laity at the opening of the Revolution cannot be fully grasped without a study of the Great Awakening. But before attempting to show how the familiar terms were thus vitalized, it is necessary to review briefly their earlier meaning.

Before 1740, we have seen, the ministers had taught that civil liberty was a natural right. The natural man had been under no human authority of any sort. He was free to do what he liked for his own advantage. But under civil government which he set up for his own good, restraints were imposed by compact and by law that the freedom remaining might be better secured. Therefore, liberty did not mean license. On that point the ministers were unanimous. As to how much liberty remained to men, John Wise, alone, wrote that only so much was given up as was necessary for the public good. But though not distinctly stated by others before 1740, it was implied in the emphasis upon the end of government and the office of ruler. Liberty certainly meant that those in power, chosen by the people directly or by original compact, were also limited by law and could not exert any authority over them beyond those legal limits. Most of the clergy declared that the people were under obligation to obey authority only within these limits.

Property, another natural right, was as frequently asserted and was always linked with liberty, but was less clearly defined. It evidently meant freedom from burdensome taxation, the assurance that the fruit of a man's labor would not be taken from him by arbitrary means. At times the ministers named told those in authority that people who were put to unnecessary charge were oppressed and abused and their rulers were not permitted by God or Nature to lay such burdens upon them. Jared Eliot in 1738 gave some interesting details of the kind of taxes he considered just. A wise government, he said, may at times give bounties to this or that manufacture provided it be for the good of the whole, although the people might find fault thereat; it may lay import and excise duties upon such things as are superfluous or not necessary to life or upon such as may by their increase become hurtful to the commonwealth; such duties should be aimed at the common good, not private gain. Just and legal taxation was not an invasion of the natural right of property, so the ministers thought. No more complete account of its origin or nature was given before 1740, so far as has been learned.

Theories concerning the natural equality of men were rarely discussed by the clergy before 1740. As will be seen in later chapters, the term, as it was used later in the eighteenth century, was applied most frequently not to society as it actually existed but to the original state of nature before the organization of civil government and seems to have meant that men in this state had an equal right to the fruit of their labors and that no man had any authority over another. It was frequently defined as meaning equal in respect to authority. John Wise seems to have been the only minister before 1740 to write of the equality of the state of nature, and the right to retain that equality under civil government to the highest degree consistent "with all just distinctions." This implies that a part of the original equality is preserved after civil government is organized, and the problem then would be to determine just how much and what kind should be retained.

Many of the clergy of this period were deeply concerned over what seemed to them the dangerous tendency to ignore distinctions of rank in existing society. . . . The dislike of "levelism" is apparent throughout the first half of the eighteenth century and to some extent later. The election sermons, especially in

Connecticut, lament the tendency of the people to ignore distinctions of rank and dress, to criticize those in authority over them, and even to wish to reduce rulers and ruled to a level. One must of course discount these sermons to some extent. The ministers were chosen for the occasion by either the Assembly or Council and as a rule would naturally be those whose known opinions pleased the body which chose them, though it is obvious that some of them indulged in a free, bold tongue. They were usually the more prominent ministers of the colony, as were also those who published pamphlets other than sermons. There may have been less well-known men who disagreed but who did not publish their opinions.

Peace had its "victories no less than war." In the task of pacification many women stood out as gallantly against retaliation as they had upheld the prosecution of the struggle for independence. Among such was "Witty Kate of the Fort," a South Carolinian patriot of unquestioned loyalty and courage, who spent her post-war years, until her death in 1785, trying to heal the cruel feud between Tory and Whig. Her humor and kindness softened bitterness and promoted friendships essential to the continuance of independency.

How Eliza Lucas Pinckney met the issue of peace is discovered in a passage from one of her letters that should rank her among the immortals of the spirit.

When I take a retrospective view of our past sufferings, so recent too, and compare them with our present prospects, the change is so great and sudden it appears like a dream, and I can hardly believe the pleasing reality, that peace, with all its train of blessings is returned. . . . Blessed be God! the effusion of human blood is stopped. . . .

Were I to enumerate the distresses that have come to my own knowledge I should distress you and myself beyond measure. . . .

Both my Sons, their wives and Infants were exiled. Wounded, sick and emaciated with a very pittance to support them in a strange land [Philadelphia] they imbarked. Their estates had been long before sequestrated and mine was shattered and ruined, which left me little power to assist them; nor had I in Country or Town a place to lay my head, all was taken out of my possession; my house I lived in, that in Colleton Square, and at Belmont, all was taken from me, nor was I able to hire a lodging. But let me forget as soon as I can their cruelties, I wish to forgive and will say no more on this subject, and hope our joy and gratitude for our great deliverance may equal our former anguish, and our contentment in mediocrity, and moderation in prosperity, equal the fortitude with which the greatest number even of our sex sustained the great reverse of fortune they experienced. . . .

CHAPTER III

PIONEERING IN THE WEST

ALTHOUGH the American Republic, established by revolution, extended its dominion from the Alleghenies to the Pacific Ocean by arms and diplomacy, the leaders in that expansion regarded these instruments as means to a great end—the sweep of the Nation from sea to sea. Jefferson, under whom the Louisiana territory was acquired and under whose party the continental domain was rounded out, had a very definite idea of the kind of civilization that was to unfold within the borders of the two oceans. He was himself one of the most cultivated men of his age, with interests embracing law, education, economy, science, music and architecture. He believed that agriculture was the one secure foundation for republicanism and democracy. And his democracy was not to be that of peasant tillers of the soil bound to unhonored drudgery but a democracy of free homesteads, of enlightened communities with popular schools, universities, libraries, books, art, and a free press. If his dream was not fully realized, if many of his projects went awry, still in a large measure his hopes came true for a time and free homesteads had profound influence on the course of American civilization.

However, as in the case of the original settlements, the westward movement of the population has been, in general histories at least, treated principally in terms of politics, religion, and economics—election brawls, revivals, corn, bacon, and wheat, the "frontier" conceived in images of Daniel Boone and Davy Crockett—as the untrammeled habitation of rough, uncouth men, and often as if no women were there at all. According to this partial view of the movement westward, the people who com-

posed it took the wilderness as a harsh environment on its own
terms and were conquered rather than developed by virgin forests
and fertile fields. In his "Epic of America," for instance, James
Truslow Adams, speaking of the frontier conflict, says: "The
mark of that struggle remained on everyone." Then he proceeds
to describe the social process in the following language which
savors of the absolute, while ignoring sources of life: "Material
success became a good in itself that could not be questioned. The
only other success which the life offered was that of local leadership, becoming a known and followed man in one's community.
For that it was essential that one should be able, so to say, to
swing an axe, to get one's self on in the rough and hard life, to
mix with one's neighbors on a plane of equality, or, if a bit above
them, to be that bit only in the abilities they admired, the abilities
that enabled one to be a good frontiersman. On the one hand,
the man who was merely virile, strong, ambitious in a material
sense, was much more apt to make a success in that hard life
than the man who by training or environment possessed the
manners of good society, who was learned or cultivated and who
cared more about such things than about spending his life making a clearing and adding acre to acre. On the other hand, the
frontiersmen, possessing none of these things, but others of value,
naturally idealized themselves and their qualities, and came to
look down on those different from themselves, as the Puritan
had looked down upon those with whom he differed as being
morally inferior. Just as American Puritanism had become in-
tolerably narrow, so was life on the frontier; and thus two of the
strongest influences in our life, religion and the frontier, made
in our formative periods for a limited and intolerant spiritual
life."

To some extent this restricted view of the frontier as a place
where human life was harshly determined by harsh conditions of
forest and field derives support from the writings of Frederick
Turner; but while Turner dealt intensely with politics and economics, his wide knowledge of the West put him constantly on
his guard. Indeed, far from describing the West in terms of the

man with big biceps or of the bigot, Turner laid emphasis on its humanism, making cheap land and the accompanying culture the most distinctive feature of American history.

As old letters, diaries, newspapers, pamphlets and books are collected and sorted, the simple axe-swinging, camp-meeting, rowdyism thesis disappears as a complete covering for Western minds and manners. In the light of these materials, historians are directed to many things hitherto unknown or unheeded. Instead of the nameless uncouth, we meet personalities and families—men and women—from older states and from Europe bearing various cultures to the frontier. Sensitive to the evils of a slave economy, many Southerners early moved to the West for the sake of individual and community ideals. Northerners went to the West to secure the land for free labor when its future was in doubt. Such people did not go empty of mind and spirit to the wilderness, with no knowledge or aspirations save those derived immediately through the physical senses. In thousands of early Western settlements the handicrafts were nurtured, artistic work was done, learning was cherished and refinements were purchased at immense personal cost.

Through the eyes of women journalists and diarists something besides elections, camp-meetings, and bar-room quarrels can be seen by those who care to see. When these accounts are examined, the pertinent question arises: "Just where did narrowness and intolerance actually exercise undisputed dominion?" If hard-hitting and axe-swinging marked the leaders of "men," how did it happen that Lincoln, who was certainly more than an axe-swinger and hard-hitter, was contributed to the nation from a region encompassed by "a limited and intolerant spiritual life?" Who started and supported the schools and colleges that quickly appeared in forest clearings; who taught sons and daughters to read and write by the light of pine knots; who founded and read the newspapers; who bought the books offered in stores; who took part in the intellectual activities described by R. L. Lusk in his "Literature of the Middle Western Frontier"? Underneath the bucolic exterior the spirit of men and women was moving, preserving life, improving shelter, sustaining communities, and caring about the cultivation of the mind and the advancement of learning.

On Cutler's Ohio purchase, the family of "Grandmother Brown" settled in 1809 in a tiny place called "Athens," consisting of about one hundred fifty people, English and Irish, housed in log cabins. In the midst of the cabins stood five brick buildings—a schoolhouse, a tavern, two private homes, and the college established in 1804 by Act of Congress on land it had already set aside for such purpose in the Northwest Ordinance of 1787. By the time Maria Foster [Brown] was old enough to notice collegians, the college, named Ohio University, had two hundred students. Its president was the Reverend William H. McGuffey whose Readers were widely used in the schools of the country. Maria Foster's father set up a brick-making business and this helped to "boom" the town.

In GRANDMOTHER BROWN'S HUNDRED YEARS[1] the people who moved to the West take on real life.

The land on which our house stood sloped toward the east. From our front porch we could see Miles Mill on the Hocking River and the hills beyond, but not the river itself. Around our place ran a "post and rail" fence—that is, a fence that had slots cut in the posts with flat smooth rails fitted into the slots. Within our enclosure was everything to make a happy world for children. We had no need to go abroad for pleasure, although we often did run across the street and down the road to play at the homes of our numerous cousins.

Our house was of weatherboard inlaid with brick so that the

---

[1] Reprint obtained through the courtesy of Little, Brown, and Company.

walls were very thick and the window sills very deep. It was a two-story structure above the cellar kitchen. In the middle of the house, opening on to the porch that faced the street, was the main entrance. This porch had a railing around it and a seat against the railing, all the way around. It was a resort for old and young. There Ma sat with her sewing. There we all gathered on a summer afternoon. The front door opened directly into the big living room with its huge fireplace. Back of this were kitchen and summer kitchen, across the way the best room, —we never called it parlor,—upstairs the sleeping rooms. My mother used to say, after we had lived about in different places, that never was there any place where she could accomplish so much as in that house.

What kind of furniture did we have? Well, in the best room the chairs were of the kind called Windsor—the bottoms solid, the backs round. In that room was one large rocking-chair with the most beautiful cushion on it. I think the chairs must have been of cherry—perhaps mahogany; they were red. And in one corner stood a large bureau—the most work on it!—big claw feet, glass knobs. The walls of this room were painted white. The floor had a rag carpet. At that time, all window shades were made of paper, green paper. We had thin curtains over the shades. No pictures.

In our living room we had no carpet. The floor was of ash wood, very white, and kept white. Every morning, after sweeping it, we wiped it over with   clean, damp mop. It took but five minutes and kept the floor sweet and clean. That mop was rinsed then and hung in its place. We were always up at five o'clock in the morning, so that we had plenty of time for everything.

At the back of the house lay orchard and garden, the well and drying kiln, the milk house and smokehouse, with the stables at the farther end of the lot where my father drove his oxen in. I used to run, when I heard the oxen coming at night, to see them put their handsome heads into the stanchion. My father's oxen were famous for their beauty. Once, a little while after Dan'l and I were married and living in Amesville, we drove back to Athens. Stopping at a wayside place, Dan'l introduced me to the innkeeper, saying, "This is Eben Foster's daughter." And the man exclaimed, "Oh, those fine oxen that he had!" He was more interested in them than in the bride.

My father was always thoughtful of his oxen. Once he dismissed a hired man who swore at them. "They work hard for me six days in a week," he said, "and all they get is what they eat. They can't be sworn at or abused." Every Saturday in warm weather Pa turned the oxen out for a nice long Sabbath rest.

He used to send them to his farm. That was the first ground outside the corporation. The Baltimore and Ohio Railway station stands on that land to-day. There my father raised hay for his cattle and there our cows were pastured. We never kept less than two, for Pa always would have plenty of milk and butter. We children used to drive the cows back and forth to pasture. Other people kept theirs on the common. All the hills around Athens were covered with lovely grass where cows could walk knee-deep. But we knew where our cows were if we kept them on our own farm.

The oxen were used by my father for hauling the brick he manufactured. He always kept at least three teams. The brick he made was eight-sided, like a honeycomb design. Some of it I saw, a few years ago, in a pavement in Athens. The soil about there is full of iron, and the brick made from it was so hard that it wouldn't break when unloaded. They used to pull out the linchpin of the cart and just drive on.

Close to the house was the well. It was a natural spring. My father had walled it up. Our place used to be a tanyard. Think how much water is needed for a tannery! I've heard my mother say that in time of drought as many as fourteen families had been supplied from our well. The water from it flowed into the milk house through troughs of cut stone that came from my father's quarry. Everything was so sloped that whenever the least bit of water was spilt around the well it ran into the stone troughs and through the milk house and down to the street. Outside the fence was a great watering trough where Pa used to water his oxen.

The old milk house was a beauty, everything in it so spick and span and shiny, everything so conveniently arranged, smelling so fragrant too of sweet brier. Near by, in the smokehouse, we always had a good store of hams and bacon well smoked in corncob smoke.

Near the house too was the dry kiln where my mother dried fruit for the winter. The kiln consisted of a big oval flagstone, at least six feet long, which had been brought from my father's quarry. It was as smooth as if polished. It was set up on brick legs so as to be well off the ground, and a fire was built at one end with a flue running under the flag so as to warm the stone. The fire was made of chips and sticks and not allowed to get too hot, or it would bake the fruit. On this flagstone Ma spread out apples, peaches, pears, and quinces, cut in quarters. These she covered with a cloth which absorbed the moisture and kept off the flies and bees. From time to time she would turn the fruit over until it was thoroughly dried.

Fruit! We were rich in fruit those days, our trees and bushes burdened with it. Boys always know where apples grow. I've heard Judge Welch say, "We boys used to flock up to the Foster orchard. We never got yelled at or driven away from there." Well, we had all we needed. I never saw such prolific apple trees as we had, such wealth of early sweet apples and Vandevere pippins, such cherry trees. As for quinces and currants, there aren't such any more. Why, our quinces were great golden things like my two fists put together, yellow, the color of lemon, and no "furze" on them. Currants so abundant that we couldn't possibly use them all! Stems as long as my finger and tapering down just like it! My mother used to put them up with raspberries— how good they were!

My mother was a good housekeeper and used to try to save everything, but there was so much fruit that some of it had to go to waste. . . .

I have never seen any place kept so nice, inside and out, as ours was. In those days bedsteads had no springs, so we used to have straw beds to make them springy. Every spring the ticks were emptied and washed and filled with new straw. I remember hearing it said that my father wouldn't let the straw be carried through the grounds because some of it would be dropped on the grass and give the place an untidy look. No, everything about our place was neat and in order while my father lived. And there were roses, tidy rows of lovely roses to make things beautiful. I remember a row that ran the whole length of the house, a row of red roses big and round, as big as door knobs. We didn't have so many kinds of roses as nowadays, but we had them in abundance. When Ma would be sitting outdoors sewing, we'd stick roses in her hair. I can see her now with a big one flopping from her comb. . . .

The difference between those who were naturally clean and orderly and those who were not was perhaps more marked in those days than it is now. It was so easy, for instance, since we had no screens, to let the flies spoil everything. My mother just wouldn't have it so. We weren't allowed to bring apples into the house in summer, because apples attract flies. If any of us dropped a speck of butter or cream on the floor, she had to run at once for a cloth to wipe it up. . . . When Sister Libbie went to house-keeping, she had little round-topped screens for every dish on her table. That was considered quite stylish. . . .

Our forks were two-tined. They weren't much good for holding some things. But if we used our knives for conveying food to our mouths it had to be done with the back of the knife towards the face. We had no napkins. We used our handkerchiefs. Table-cloths were made of cotton diaper especially woven for the purpose. The first white bedspread I ever had was made of two widths of that same cotton whitened on the grass.

In warm weather we washed outdoors under the quince bushes. We used our well water. It was so soft, it was just beautiful. We'd draw a barrel of water, put one shovel of ashes into it, and it would just suds up like soft water, so white and clean. We used soft soap, of course. Our starch was of two kinds—either made from a dough of flour worked round and round until it was smooth and fine or made from grated potato cooked to the right consistency. . . .

It required more knowledge to do the things for everyday living than is the case nowadays. If one wants light now, all one has to do is pull a string or push a button. Then, we had to pick up a coal with tongs, hold it against a candle, and blow. And one had to make the candles, perhaps.

I remember the first matches that I ever saw. Someone handed me a little bunch of them, fastened together at the bottom in a solid block of wood about a half inch square. "Lucifer matches" they called them. I tore one off and set the whole thing afire.

Some people had tinder boxes. Some kept a kind of punk which would give off a spark when struck with steel or knife. Generally speaking, people kept the fire on their hearthstones going year in and year out.

We did not make our candles at home, but got them usually from Uncle Dean, who made candles for the town. I used to love to watch him and Aunt Maria at work dipping candles— she with the hot tallow in a big kettle on the hearth, he with stillyards beside him, weighing carefully. Occasionally we had some sperm candles made of fine white tallow. Besides candles, people sometimes burned sperm or whale oil in little lamps that looked like square-topped candlesticks. In the square top was a place for a bowl that would hold perhaps a half pint of oil. . . .

My mother used to spin. She made beautiful fine thread. She taught Sister Libbie how to spin, but decided, before my turn came, that spinning was doomed to become a lost art, and that I might be better employed in some other way. . . . Part of the thread was made with the open, part with the crossed, band. They colored it with butternut bark, but the two kinds would never color alike, so that part of it was a light and part a dark brown. They wove it into a plaid and had it pressed, and then they made fine dresses out of it to wear to church. I remember, too, that my mother raised flax, spun it into linen, wove it into cloth,—colored blue in the yarn,—made it up into a dress for me which she embroidered in white above the hem. I wish I had kept that dress to show my children the beautiful work of their grandmother. . . .

Women made their own designs for cloth as well as for dresses in those days. If a woman had taste, she had a chance to show it in her weaving. But, oh, it was hard work. You never saw warping bars, did you? Clumsy things, long as a bed. On them work was prepared for the loom. You had to draw each thread through a reed. I used to love to watch my mother weaving, her shuttle holding the spool with yarn shooting through the warp, then back the other way. When she had woven as far as she could reach, she would bend below the loom and wind the woven cloth into a roll beneath. Blankets made at home used to last a long, long time. Homespun things were good. . . .

The first lamp I ever saw Will brought home from Denmark when he was a young man. It was made of glass, and it exploded. . . . Just think what I have seen in my lifetime in the way of development in illumination! When I was a child, the only kind of lantern known was the tin can with holes punched in it to allow the checkered candlelight to shine through. Lanterns, candles, oil lamps, electric incandescents—I have seen them all.

We had all the things that were really necessary for our comfort in those days, and we had quite as much leisure as people have now. . . .

You see I had rather a severe course in Domestic Science, but the rest of my education didn't amount to much. . . .

We lived in Amesville eleven years. Then we sold out and joined the Western migration. We bought a farm in Iowa and moved there in the summer of 1856.

Dan'l had got the Western fever, and I was willing to go to any place where I thought we might better our fortunes. A cousin of Dan'l's who had been in California, going out by land and returning around the Horn, visited us in '55 and told interesting tales of his experience. Dan'l himself had made two trips to the West, looking for land. He thought of settling in Geneseo,

Illinois, where cousins had located. But he went on into Iowa, where another cousin, Oliver Brown, was living, and came back saying he had bought a farm across the road from Oliver's.

Brown and Dickey sold their business for $10,000, each getting $5000 in cash. The price of our Iowa farm was $3500 in gold. The rest of our money went to buy a fine team of mares, a new wagon, and a new carriage, which had taken prizes at the country fair. We sold the bulk of our household goods, but I managed to have the cherry dresser packed for transportation and also a big roll of Brussels carpet.

It was a considerable undertaking, in those days, to move one's family from Ohio to Iowa. There were no railroads to carry us across country and we had to go by steamboat down the Hocking River to the Ohio, down the Ohio to St. Louis, and then up the Mississippi River to Keokuk, and overland the rest of the way by carriage. We were twenty days on the journey. But compared with what our grandparents had had to overcome in moving from Massachusetts to New York and Vermont, and from those places on to Ohio, it was nothing. And then I never thought about its being hard. I was used to things being hard.

I was very busy, those last days in Amesville, getting myself and children ready for the journey. You may be sure that I fixed my children up so they looked nice. . . . Will and Charlie had such pretty little suits—long trousers with little roundabout coats and hats with visors. I made them ruffled linen collars that were very becoming with their suits, and I did those collars up on the boat, so that the boys looked fresh and clean all the way.

Whenever I stopped to think, my heart was heavy at the thought of leaving Ohio and going to such a far, strange country. But I didn't have much time for thinking. And one thing made it easier. My mother was going along. . . .

Finally we were off. The boats of those days were interesting places, carrying all kinds of human beings, black and white. The rough work was done by colored roustabouts. Some of the passengers were quite fashionable. There was dancing every night to music furnished by a band made up of colored waiters. There was card playing, too. Indeed, the boat was infested with black-leg gamblers. Every evening after dinner the card tables were set out. There was a bar, too, where you could get anything you'd a mind to pay for.

Our boat was a side-wheeler and was loaded to the guards with freight. It moved very slowly. I got *so* tired before the journey was ended. I had my children's clothes to wash and iron every day. . . .

When first I heard people talking about railroads I thought they meant roads made of fence rails laid across the mud to keep the wheels from sinking into the soft ground! Well, to continue: When we got to St. Louis there was a half mile of boats headed in at the wharf, and we had to wait a long time before we could land. We stopped in St. Louis long enough to buy some dishes and a cookstove. It was a good stove—there never was a better. Made by Bridge, Beech and Company, and called the "Golden Era." Those were the years of the California gold excitement, and every door of the stove had the picture of a gold piece on it.

Finally we reached Keokuk, "the head of navigation" in those days. We couldn't go above the rapids in the river, there being no canal as yet. So we landed at Keokuk, and Ma and I with baby and Lizzie were put into our fine new carriage with Grandpa Brown and Cousin Will Foster to drive us to our farm. That was eight miles from Fort Madison and twelve miles from Burlington, which were towns of considerable size. Dan'l stayed behind in Keokuk with the little boys to look after the landing of our goods.

After several hours' driving we arrived at Oliver Brown's house. We were welcomed with great excitement, for Oliver had begun to be awfully uneasy, fearing that Dan'l had been robbed and murdered for his money. The care of that money had been our main concern all through the trip. Dan'l had the paper money in a belt round his waist. . . . The gold for the farm was left with me. The gold pieces were wrapped separately in paper and put in a sack of linen bird's eye which had been woven by Dan'l's mother. This sack of gold I kept in a carpet bag where I had the children's soiled clothes. We did not, of course, want to give the impression that we had any quantity of money with us. I felt deeply the responsibility of looking after it.

As we were leaving Keokuk, Dan'l brought the carpet bag and, depositing it at my feet, said cheerfully: "There, Mother! There's your farm!" Then off we drove. . . .

We had a good farm of rich black soil. But it is people that really make a country, not soil. Those who had settled in that neighborhood were of American stock, but it was poor in quality. I like to be with people who know something, who want something. . . .

Probably it was I who made the first knit underwear for babies. At least I used to feel very proud of the beautiful gauze-like shirts I'd make for my babies out of the tops of my old white cotton stockings, and I never knew any other woman who thought of doing it.

I even made the men's clothes at times. . . . But I really had to draw the line at making clothes for the neighbors. . . .

I suppose that the most unusual piece of work I ever did while we were living on the farm was to make a casket for a little dead baby. . . .

Such a way of living is hard, *hard,* Hard. The only thing that can make it endurable for a woman is love and plenty of it. . . .

In the fifties there were no railroads in Iowa. It was some years after we came to Iowa before there was a bridge across the Mississippi or even a railway between Fort Madison and Burlington. In disposing of farm products we were not much beyond the period of barter and exchange that we had known at Amesville. Dan'l was more of a trader than he was a farmer. When our boys had raised things, he could drive a bargain with them. . . .

Schooling! That was the great mistake in our moving West. . . . The work of the farm always seemed to Dan'l more important than that of the schools. Nothing I said would change him. I never could understand why he was so blind on this one subject. Generally speaking, too, the Browns were a bookish lot and set great store by education. That was one thing I liked about Oliver Brown. He sent his children away to school. . . . But I must say this for Dan'l. He felt differently late in life—after his own children were grown up and gone. He was eager to do for Lizzie's children what he never thought necessary for his own. He saw, too, that his own boys were resentful of the way he had let them scramble for an education or go without, and it hurt him. He grieved over it a good bit at the last, especially over Herbert, who was having a hard struggle about the time Dan'l died. . . .

As time went on we became quite prosperous. The thing that set us on our feet was cheese making. Our neighbor, Mrs. Andrews, had a little vat big enough to make small cheeses in. I borrowed it once and made a few little cheeses. I pressed them under the fence rail with a weight on top. They were very nice. It put Dan'l in the mind of cheese making on a larger scale. The "Dan Brown Cheese" made quite a name for itself in southeastern Iowa. A good deal of it went to the Union Army. . . .

I took satisfaction in the improvements we had made, but it seemed to me that our life grew more burdensome each year. . . . And I couldn't see much opportunity in that part of the country for my children. . . .

Then Dan'l sold the farm—sold it for $10,000.

I've often thought that a considerable part of that $10,000 surely belonged to me. All our married life I was just saving, saving. We shouldn't have had anything if I hadn't been saving. The secret of the whole thing was just dimes, dimes. . . . Our neighbor, Mr. McChord, said to Brother John: "Some of the rest of us could own a farm and store and move into town if our wives knew how to save the dimes as your sister does."

We received $10,000 for a farm that had cost us only $3500. But it had cost us, in addition, fourteen years of our lives and most exhausting labor. It had been little better than a wilderness when we took it; we left it in a good state of cultivation. Those fourteen years seemed a long time to me, a big price to pay.

The same species of people could struggle with the aborigines and establish the arts of peace on the frontier. This fact is well illustrated in the "HISTORY OF WOMAN SUFFRAGE," where THE BATTLE OF ONE HUNDRED WOMEN *is quickly followed by the whir of spinning wheels, the ferment of social thought, and novel laws.*

The earliest settlement of Indiana was a missionary one, in 1777, though it was not admitted as a Territory until 1800, then including the present states of Michigan and Illinois. A number of Indian wars took place in this part of the country during the twenty-five years between 1780 and 1805. What was known as the Northwest Territory was organized in 1789, and General Arthur St. Clair appointed Governor, an office he held until 1802. In 1790 a war of unusually formidable character broke out among the Indian tribes of the Northwest, and in 1791 St. Clair was created General-in-Chief of the forces against them. Many of the settlers of this portion of the country joined his army, among whom were one hundred women, who accompanied their husbands in preference to being left at home subject to the surprises and tortures of the savages with whom the country was at war. In giving command of these forces to St. Clair, Washington warned him against unexpected assaults from the enemy; but this general who was of foreign birth, a Scotchman, was no match for the cunning of his wily foe, who suddenly fell upon him, November 4th, near the Miami villages (present site of Terre Haute), making great havoc among his forces.

When the terrible war-whoop was heard, the heroism of these hundred women rose equal to the emergency. They did not cling helplessly to their husbands—the women of those early days were made of sterner stuff—but with pale, set faces, they joined in the defense, and the records say most of them were killed fighting bravely. They died a soldier's death upon the field of battle in defense of home and country [like the natives]. They died that the prairies of the West and the wilderness of the North should at a later period become the peaceful homes of untold millions of

men and women. They were the true pioneers of the Northwest, the advance-guard of civilization, giving their lives in battle
against a terrible enemy, in order that safety should dwell at the
hearth-stones of those who should settle this garden of the continent at a future period. History is very silent upon their record;
not a name has been preserved; but we do know that they lived,
and how they died, and it is but fitting that a record of woman's
work for freedom should embalm their memory in its pages.
Many other women defended homes and children against the
savage foe, but their deeds of heroism have been forgotten.

There is scarcely a portion of the world so far from civilization
as Indiana was at that day. No railroads spanned the continent,
making neighbors of people a thousand miles apart; no steamboat sailed upon the Western lakes, nor indeed upon the broad
Atlantic; telegraphy, with its annihilation of space, was a marvel
as yet unborn; even the lucifer match, which should kindle fire
in the twinkling of an eye, lay buried in the dark future. Little
was known of these settlements; the Genesee Valley of New
York was considered the *far West,* to which people traveled (the
Erie Canal was not then in existence) in strong, springless
wagons, over which large hoops, covered with white cloth, were
securely fastened, thus sheltering the inmates from sun and storm.
These wagons, afterward known as "Prairie Schooners," were for
weeks and months the traveling homes of many a family of early
settlers.

But even in 1816 Indiana could boast her domestic manufactures, for within the State at this time were "two thousand five
hundred and twelve looms and two thousand seven hundred
spinning wheels," most of them in private cabins, whose mistresses, by their slow agencies, converted the wool which their
own hands had often sheared, and the flax which their own
fingers had pulled, into cloth for the family wardrobe.

Thus in 1816 the manufactures of Indiana were chiefly in the
hands of its women. It is upon the industries of the country that
a nation thrives. Its manufactures build up its commerce and
make its wealth. From this source the Government derives the

revenue which is the life-blood circulating in its veins. Its strength and its perpetuity alike depend upon its industries, and when we look upon the work of women through all the years of the Republic, and remember their patriotic self-devotion and self-sacrifice at every important crisis, we are no less amazed at the ingratitude of the country for their services in war than at its non-recognition of their existence as wealth-producers, the elements which build up and sustain every civilized people.

Viewing its early record, we are not surprised that Indiana claims to have organized the first State Woman's Rights Society, though we are somewhat astonished to know that at the time of the first Convention held in Indianapolis, a husband of position locked his wife within the house in order to prevent her presence thereat, although doubtless, as men have often done before and since, he deemed it not out of the way that he himself should be a listener at a meeting he considered it contrary to family discipline that his wife should attend.

December 11, 1816, Indiana was admitted into the Union. William Henry Harrison, who had been Governor of the Territory, and Brigadier-General in the army, with the command of the Northwest Territory, was afterward President of the United States. He encountered the Indians led by Tecumseh at Tippecanoe, on the Wabash, and after a terrible battle they fled. This was the origin of the song, "Tippecanoe and Tyler too," that was sung with immense effect by the Whigs all over the country in the presidential campaign of 1840, when Harrison and Tyler were the candidates; and when women, for the first time, attended political meetings.

Indiana, though one of the younger States, by her liberal and rational legislation on the questions of marriage and divorce, has always been the land of freedom for fugitives from the bondage and suffering of ill-assorted unions. Many an unhappy wife has found a safe asylum on the soil of that State. Her liberality on this question was no doubt partly due to the influence of Robert Owen, who early settled at New Harmony, and made the experiment of communal life; and later, to his son, the Hon. Robert

Dale Owen, who was in the Legislature several years, and in the Constitutional Convention of 1850. . . .

Before 1828, Frances Wright (a Scotchwoman) had visited Mr. Owen's colony, assisted him in the editorial department of the *New Harmony Gazette,* changed afterward to the *Free Enquirer,* published in New York. Such a circle of remarkably intelligent and liberal-minded people, all effective speakers and able writers, was not without influence in moulding the sentiment of that young community.

That "material success" was not always regarded as "a good in itself" and that rough physical environment did not necessarily transform pioneers into uncouth men and women are demonstrated in the life and work of Anna Howard Shaw. By common consent she is acknowledged a fine flower of American culture. Yet in THE STORY OF A PIONEER,[2] *she describes the hard and "brutalizing" conditions through which she passed in her youth—one of the most primitive experiences which any white woman encountered in the United States.*

Father preceded us to the Michigan woods, and there, with his oldest son, James, took up a claim. They cleared a space in the wilderness just large enough for a log cabin, and put up the bare walls of the cabin itself. Then father returned to Lawrence (Massachusetts) and his work, leaving James behind. A few months later (this was in 1859), my mother, my two sisters, Eleanor and Mary, my youngest brother, Henry, eight years of age, and I, then twelve, went to Michigan to work on and hold down the claim while father, for eighteen months longer, stayed on in Lawrence, sending us such remittances as he could. His second and third sons, John and Thomas, remained in the East with him. . . .

Like most men, my dear father should never have married.

---

[2] Reprint obtained through the courtesy of Harper & Brothers.

Though his nature was one of the sweetest I have ever known, and though he would at any call give his time to or risk his life for others, in practical matters he remained to the end of his days as irresponsible as a child. If his mind turned to practical details at all, it was solely in their bearing toward great developments of the future. To him an acorn was not an acorn, but a forest of young oaks.

Thus, when he took up his claim of three hundred and sixty acres of land in the wilderness of northern Michigan, and sent my mother and five young children to live there alone until he could join us eighteen months later, he gave no thought of the manner in which we were to make the struggle and survive the hardships before us. He had furnished us with land and the four walls of a cabin. Some day, he reasoned, the place would be a fine estate, which his sons would inherit and in the course of time pass on to their sons—always an Englishman's most irides-cent dream. That for the present we were one hundred miles from a railroad, forty miles from the nearest post-office, and half a dozen miles from any neighbors save Indians, wolves, and wild-cats; that we were wholly unlearned in the ways of the woods as well as in the most primitive methods of farming; that we lacked not only every comfort, but even the bare necessities of life; and that we must begin, single-handed and untaught, a struggle for existence in which some of the severest forces of nature would be arrayed against us—these facts had no weight in my father's mind. Even if he had witnessed my mother's despair on the night of our arrival in our new home, he would not have understood it. From his viewpoint, he was doing a man's duty. He was working steadily in Lawrence, and, inci-dentally, giving much time to the Abolition cause and to other big public movements of his day which had his interest and sympathy. He wrote to us regularly and sent us occasional re-mittances, as well as a generous supply of improving literature for our minds. It remained for us to strengthen our bodies, to meet the conditions in which he had placed us, and to survive if we could.

We faced our situation with clear and unalarmed eyes the morning after our arrival. The problem of food, we knew, was at least temporarily solved. We had brought with us enough coffee, pork, and flour to last for several weeks; and the one necessity father had put inside the cabin walls was a great fireplace, made of mud and stones, in which our food could be cooked. The problem of our water-supply was less simple, but my brother James solved it for the time by showing us a creek a long distance from the house; and for months we carried from this creek, in pails, every drop of water we used, save that which we caught in troughs when the rain fell.

We held a family council after breakfast, and in this, though I was only twelve, I took an eager and determined part. I loved work—it has always been my favorite form of recreation—and my spirit rose to the opportunities of it which smiled on us from every side. Obviously the first thing to do was to put doors and windows into the yawning holes father had left for them, and to lay a board flooring over the earth inside our cabin walls, and these duties we accomplished before we had occupied our new home a fortnight. There was a small saw-mill nine miles from our cabin, on the spot that is now Big Rapids, and there we bought our lumber. The labor we supplied ourselves, and though we put our hearts into it and the results seemed beautiful to our partial eyes, I am forced to admit, in looking back upon them, that they halted this side of perfection. We began by making three windows and two doors; then, inspired by these achievements, we ambitiously constructed an attic and divided the ground floor with partitions, which gave us four rooms.

The general effect was temperamental and sketchy. The boards which formed the floor were never even nailed down; they were fine, wide planks without a knot in them, and they looked so well that we merely fitted them together as closely as we could and light-heartedly let them go at that. Neither did we properly chink the house. Nothing is more comfortable than a log cabin which has been carefully built and finished; but for some reason—probably because there seemed always a more urgent duty calling to us around the corner—we never plastered our house at all. The result was that on many future winter mornings we awoke to find ourselves chastely blanketed by snow, while the only warm spot in our living-room was that directly in front of the fireplace, where great logs burned all day. Even there our faces scorched while our spines slowly congealed, until we learned to revolve before the fire like a bird upon a spit. No doubt we would have worked more thoroughly if my brother James, who was twenty years old and our tower of strength, had remained with us; but when we had been in our new home only a few months he fell ill and was forced to go East for an operation. He was never able to return to us, and thus my mother, we three young girls, and my youngest brother—Harry, who was only eight years old—made our fight alone until father came to us, more than a year later.

Mother was practically an invalid. She had a nervous affection which made it impossible for her to stand without the support of a chair. But she sewed with unusual skill, and it was due to her that our clothes, notwithstanding the strain to which we subjected them, were always in good condition. She sewed for hours every day, and she was able to move about the house, after a fashion, by pushing herself around on a stool which James made for her as soon as we arrived. He also built for her a more comfortable chair with a high back.

The division of labor planned at the first council was that mother should do our sewing, and my older sisters, Eleanor and Mary, the housework, which was far from taxing, for of course we lived in the simplest manner. My brothers and I were to do the work out of doors, an arrangement that suited me very well, though at first, owing to our lack of experience, our activities were somewhat curtailed. It was too late in the season for plowing or planting, even if we had possessed anything with which to plow, and, moreover, our so-called "cleared" land was thick with sturdy tree-stumps. Even during the second summer plowing was impossible; we could only plant potatoes and corn, and follow the most primitive method in doing even this. We took an ax, chopped up the sod, put the seed under it, and let the seed grow. The seed did grow, too—in the most gratifying and encouraging manner. Our green corn and potatoes were the best I have ever eaten. But for the present we lacked these luxuries.

We had, however, in their place, large quantities of wild fruit —gooseberries, raspberries, and plums—which Harry and I gathered on the banks of our creek. Harry also became an expert fisherman. We had no hooks or lines, but he took wires from our hoop skirts and made snares at the ends of poles. My part of this work was to stand on a log and frighten the fish out of their holes by making horrible sounds, which I did with impassioned earnestness. When the fish hurried to the surface of the water to investigate the appalling noises they had heard, they were easily snared by our small boy, who was very proud of his ability to contribute in this way to the family table.

During our first winter we lived largely on corn-meal, making a little journey of twenty miles to the nearest mill to buy it; but even at that we were better off than our neighbors, for I remember one family in our region who for an entire winter lived solely on coarse-grained yellow turnips, gratefully changing their diet to leeks when these came in the spring.

Such furniture as we had we made ourselves. In addition to my mother's two chairs and the bunks which took the place of beds, James made a settle for the living-room, as well as a table and several stools. At first we had our tree-cutting done for us, but we soon became expert in this gentle art, and I developed such skill that in later years, after father came, I used to stand with him and "heart" a log.

On every side, and at every hour of the day, we came up against the relentless limitations of pioneer life. There was not a team of horses in our entire region. The team with which my brother had driven us through the wilderness had been hired at Grand Rapids for that occasion, and, of course, immediately returned. Our lumber was delivered by ox-teams, and the absolutely essential purchases we made "outside" (at the nearest shops, forty miles away) were carried through the forest on the backs of men.

Our mail was delivered once a month by a carrier who made the journey in alternate stages of horseback riding and canoeing. But we had health, youth, enthusiasm, good appetites, and the wherewithal to satisfy them, and at night in our primitive bunks we sank into abysses of dreamless slumber such as I have never known since. Indeed, looking back upon them, those first months seem to have been a long-drawn-out and glorious picnic, interrupted only by occasional hours of pain or panic, when we were hurt or frightened.

Naturally, our two greatest menaces were wild animals and Indians, but as the days passed the first of these lost the early terrors with which we had associated them. We grew indifferent to the sounds that had made our first night a horror to us all— there was even a certain homeliness in them—while we regarded with accustomed, almost blasé eyes the various furred creatures of which we caught distant glimpses as they slunk through the forest. Their experience with other settlers had taught them caution; it soon became clear that they were as eager to avoid us as we were to shun them, and by common consent we gave each other ample elbow-room. But the Indians were all around us, and every settler had a collection of hair-raising tales to tell of them. It was generally agreed that they were dangerous only when they were drunk; but as they were drunk whenever they could get whisky, and as whisky was constantly given them in exchange for pelts and game, there was a harrowing doubt in our minds whenever they approached us.

In my first encounter with them I was alone in the woods at sunset with my small brother Harry. We were hunting a cow James had bought, and our young eyes were peering eagerly among the trees, on the alert for any moving object. Suddenly, at a little distance, and coming directly toward us, we saw a party of Indians. There were five of them, all men, walking in single file, as noiselessly as ghosts, their moccasined feet causing not even a rustle among the dry leaves that carpeted the woods. All the horrible stories we had heard of Indian cruelty flashed into our minds, and for a moment we were dumb with terror. Then

I remembered having been told that the one thing one must not do before them is to show fear. Harry was carrying a rope with which we had expected to lead home our reluctant cow, and I seized one end of it and whispered to him that we would "play horse," pretending he was driving me. We pranced toward the Indians on feet that felt like lead, and with eyes so glazed by terror that we could see nothing save a line of moving figures; but as we passed them they did not give to our little impersonation of care-free children even the tribute of a side-glance. They were, we realized, headed straight for our home; and after a few moments we doubled on our tracks and, keeping at a safe distance from them among the trees, ran back to warn our mother that they were coming.

As it happened James was away, and mother had to meet her unwelcome guests supported only by her young children. She at once prepared a meal, however, and when they arrived she welcomed them calmly and gave them the best she had. After they had eaten they began to point at and demand objects they fancied in the room—my brother's pipe, some tobacco, a bowl, and such trifles—and my mother, who was afraid to annoy them by refusal, gave them what they asked. They were quite sober, and though they left without expressing any appreciation of her hospitality, they made her a second visit a few months later, bringing a large quantity of venison and a bag of cranberries as a graceful return. These Indians were Ottawas; and later we became very friendly with them and their tribe, even to the degree of attending one of their dances, which I shall describe later.

Our second encounter with Indians was a less agreeable experience. There were seven "Marquette warriors" in the next group of callers, and they were all intoxicated. Moreover, they had brought with them several jugs of bad whisky—the raw and craze-provoking product supplied them by the fur-dealers—and it was clear that our cabin was to be the scene of an orgy. Fortunately my brother James was at home on this occasion, and as the evening grew old and the Indians, grouped together around the fire, became more and more irresponsible, he devised a plan for our safety. Our attic was finished, and its sole entrance was by a ladder through a trap-door. At James's whispered command my sister Eleanor slipped up into the attic, and from the back window let down a rope, to which he tied all the weapons he had—his gun and several axes. These Eleanor drew up and concealed in one of the bunks. My brother then directed that as quietly as possible, and at long intervals, one member of the family after another was to slip up the ladder and into the attic, going quite casually, that the Indians might not realize what we were doing. Once there, with the ladder drawn up after us and the trap-door closed, we would be reasonably safe, unless our guests decided to burn the cabin.

The evening seemed endless, and was certainly nerve-racking. The Indians ate everything in the house, and from my seat in a dim corner I watched them while my sisters waited on them. I can still see the tableau they made in the firelit room and hear the unfamiliar accents of their speech as they talked together. Occasionally one of them would pull a hair from his head, seize his scalping-knife, and cut the hair with it—a most unpleasant sight! When either of my sisters approached them some of the Indians would make gestures, as if capturing and scalping her. Through it all, however, the whisky held their close attention, and it was due to this that we succeeded in reaching the attic unobserved, James coming last of all and drawing the ladder after him. Mother and the children were then put to bed; but through that interminable night James and Eleanor lay flat upon the floor, watching through the cracks between the boards the revels of the drunken Indians, which grew wilder with every hour that crawled toward sunrise. There was no knowing when they would miss us or how soon their mood might change. At any moment they might make an attack upon us or set fire to the cabin.

By dawn, however, their whisky was all gone, and they were in so deep a stupor that one, after the other, the seven fell from their chairs to the floor, where they sprawled unconscious. When they awoke they left quietly and without trouble of any kind. They seemed a strangely subdued and chastened band; probably they were wretchedly ill after their debauch on the adulterated whisky the traders had given them. . . .

When I was fifteen years old I was offered a situation as school-teacher. By this time the community was growing around us with the rapidity characteristic of these Western settlements, and we had nearer neighbors whose children needed instruction. I passed an examination before a school-board consisting of three nervous and self-conscious men whose certificate I still hold, and at once began my professional career on the modest salary of two dollars a week and my board. The school was four miles from my home, so I "boarded round" with the families of my pupils, staying two weeks in each place, and often walking from three to six miles a day to and from my little log school-house in every kind of weather. During the first year I had about fourteen pupils, of varying ages, sizes, and temperaments, and there was hardly a book in the school-room except those I owned. One little girl, I remember, read from an almanac, while a second used a hymn-book. . . .

The problem of living grew harder with every day. [The Civil War came. Her father and brothers enlisted.] We eked out our little income in every way we could, taking as boarders the workers in the logging-camps, making quilts, which we sold, and losing no chance to earn a penny in any legitimate manner. Again my mother did such outside sewing as she could secure, yet with every month of our effort the gulf between our income and our expenses grew wider, and the price of the bare necessities of existence climbed up and up. The largest amount I could earn at teaching was six dollars a week, and our school year included only two terms of thirteen weeks each.

It was an incessant struggle to keep our land, to pay our taxes, and to live. Coffee was one dollar a pound. There were no men left to grind our corn, to get in our crops, or to care for our live stock; and all around us we saw our struggle reflected in the lives of our neighbors. . . . I was the principal support of our family.

When the various motives that carried men and women to the frontier are taken into account, the hard-and-fast conception of the Western community dissolves and the weakness of sweeping generalizations concerning "type" becomes evident. Even missionaries were not all of one stamp. There was Peter Cartwright. And there was Narcissa Whitman. Narcissa was the daughter of Judge Prentiss of Plattsburgh, New York. Reared in a comfortable home, she was early moved by reading about missionary effort in India to seek an adventure of the spirit for herself. When Marcus Whitman heard of her mood, he sought her in marriage in order to have a suitable companion on his mission to the Far Northwest in 1836.

Of their trip across the plains, Narcissa Whitman kept a daily record—a JOURNAL [3] *—that ends abruptly in 1847, when this advance-guard of an Oregon movement was slain by Indians among whom an epidemic of measles had spread which they attributed to the invasion of the white race.*

August 1. Dearest Mother: We commenced our journey to Walla Walla July 18, 1836, under the direction of Mr. McLeod. The Flathead and Nez Pierce Indians and some lodges of the Snake tribe accompany us to Fort Hall. Have travelled two months. Have lived on fresh meat for two months exclusively. Our ride today has been so fatiguing. Felt a calm and peaceful state of mind all day. In the morning had a season of prayer for my dear parents. We have plenty of dry buffalo meat. I can scarcely eat it, it appears so filthy, but it will keep us alive, and we ought to be thankful. Do not think I regret coming. No, far from it. I would not go back for the world; am contented and happy. Feel to pity the poor Indian women. Am making some progress in their language; long to be able to converse with them about the Saviour.

August 3. Came to Fort Hall this morning. Was much cheered with a view of the fort. Anything that looks like a house makes

[3] Printed in *The Souvenir of Western Women,* edited by Mary Osborn Douthit of Portland, Oregon.

us glad. Were hospitably entertained by Captain Wyeth from Boston, whom we saw at the Rendezvous, on his way to the East. Our dinner consisted of dry buffalo meat, turnips, and fried bread, which was a luxury. Mountain bread is simply coarse flour mixed with water and fried or roasted in buffalo grease. To one who has had nothing but meat for a long time, this relishes very well.

August 4. Enjoyed the cool retreat of an upper room this morning while writing. Was there ever a journey like this? Performed when the sustaining hand of God has been so manifest every moment. Surely the children of Israel could not have been more sensible of the "Pillar of cloud by day and the pillar of fire by night" than we have been of that hand that has led us safely on.

August 17. Came to salmon fishing; obtained some fish and boiled for breakfast; find it good eating. They are preparing to cross Snake river. I can cross the most difficult streams without the least fear. There is one manner of crossing husband has tried, but I have not. Take an elk skin and stretch it over you, spreading yourself out as much as possible, then let the Indian women carefully put you in the water and with a cord in the mouth they will swim and drag you over.

September 1. Arrived at Fort Walla Walla. . . . After breakfast was over we were shown the novelties. We were shown in the room Mr. Pambrun prepared for us, on hearing of our approach. It was the west bastion in the fort, full of portholes in the sides, but no windows, and was filled with firearms. A large cannon, always loaded, stood behind the door by one of the holes. These things did not move me.

At four we were called to dinner. It consisted of pork, potatoes, beets, cabbage, turnips, tea, bread and butter. I am this particular in my description of eatables, so that you may be assured we find something to eat beyond the Rocky mts. I have not introduced you to the lady of the house. She is a native born from a tribe east of the mts. She appears well, does not speak English, but her native tongue and French. Mr. Pambrun is from Canada; is very agreeable and much of a gentleman in appearance. About noon Mr. and Mrs. Spalding arrived with their company.

September 7. We set sail from Walla Walla to Vancouver yesterday. Our boat is an open one, manned with six oarsmen and the steersman. I enjoyed it much. The Columbia is beautiful.

September 12. We are now in Vancouver, the New York of the Pacific Coast. Before we reached the house of the chief factor, Dr. McLoughlin, were met by several gentlemen who came to give us welcome: Mr. Douglas, Dr. Tolmie, and Dr. McLoughlin of the Hudson's Bay Company, who invited us in and seated us on the sofa. Soon after we were introduced to Mrs. McLoughlin and Mrs. Douglas, both natives of the country (half-breeds). We were invited to walk in the garden. Here we found fruit of every description. I must mention the origin of the apples and grapes. A gentleman twelve years ago, while at a party in London, put the seeds of the apples and grapes he ate into his vest pocket, and soon after took a voyage to this country, and left them here. Now they are greatly multiplied. . . .

September 13. This morning visited the school to hear the children sing. It consists of about fifty scholars, children who have French fathers and Indian mothers, and many orphans. . . .

September 22. . . . We were invited to ride as often as once a week. Today Mrs. McLoughlin rode with us. She prefers the old habit of riding gentleman fashion. She is one of the kindest women in the world. Speaks a little French but mostly loves her native language. She wishes to go and live with me; her daughter and Mrs. Douglas also. . . . The doctor urges me to stay all winter. He is a very sympathetic man; is afraid we will suffer. I sing about an hour every evening with the children, teaching them new tunes at the request of Dr. McLoughlin. Mrs. McLoughlin has a fine ear for music and is greatly delighted. . . .

Nor in fact was there any typical frontier covering the wide region which included the forests of Wisconsin, the plains of Kansas, the ranges of Texas, and the mining districts of the Pacific slope. Even among gold seekers all sorts of men and women were represented. One hundred years after its first publication in 1833, Mary Austin Holley's book on Texas—a State she did so much to found—is republished. Our knowledge of frontier people is thus enlarged.

For the picture of a migration de luxe we are indebted to Margaret Alsip Frink, of Martinsville, Indiana, whose husband, Ledyard Frink, a prosperous merchant there, longed for new worlds to conquer as merchants have done since trade began, and, on a gold-rushing expedition to California in 1850, took her with him. There were mountain barriers to master and swollen streams to cross, deserts to endure and illness to overcome. But moonlight nights and music with song and violin, high adventure and buoyancy of spirit, made trials and tribulations more thrilling than grievous on the whole, if we may believe the account of this trip related in the JOURNAL[4] which Margaret kept of that eventful expedition.

The first thing on Mr. Frink's part was to have a suitable wagon made for the trip, while I hired a seamstress to make up a full supply of clothing. In addition to our finished articles of dress, I packed a trunk full of dress goods not yet made up. We proceeded in the spring (1850) to get our outfit completed. There was no one from our part of the country, so far as we knew, that intended to cross the plains that season, and we were obliged to make such preparations as our best judgment led us to do, without advice or assistance from others. We knew nothing of frontier life, nor how to prepare for it. And besides, we were met with all the discouragements and obstructions that our neighbors and the people of our country could invent or imagine, to induce us not to attempt such a perilous journey. But, nothing daunted, we kept at work in our preparations for the trip, think-

[4] Privately printed.

ing all the time that we should have to make the long journey
by ourselves, as no one in all that part of the country was offering
or expecting to go to California that season.

But it appeared as if there was a Providence planning for us.
First, we had a boy that we had taken into our family to live
with us when he was seven years of age, and now he was eleven.
He was much attached to us and could not be reconciled to be
left with his own friends and relatives. The child being so determined to cling to us, Mr. Frink consented to take him if his uncle
and guardian, Mr. W. Wilson, would give his consent. This he
very readily did, though with all his family opposed to the plan.
The consent was given about four days before we started.

The wagon was packed and we were all ready to start on the
twenty-seventh day of March. The wagon was designed expressly for the trip, it being built light, with everything planned
for convenience. It was so arranged that when closed up, it could
be used as our bedroom. The bottom was divided all into little
compartments or cupboards. After putting in our provisions, and
other baggage, a floor was constructed over all, on which our
mattress was laid. We had an India-rubber mattress that could
be filled with either air or water, making a very comfortable bed.
During the day we could empty the air out, so that it took up
but little room. We also had a feather bed and feather pillows.
However, until we had crossed the Missouri River we stopped
at hotels and farmhouses every night and did not use our bedding. After that, there being no more hotels nor houses, we used
it continually all the way to California.

The wagon was lined with green cloth, to make it pleasant and
soft for the eye, with three or four large pockets in each side to
hold many little conveniences—looking-glasses, combs, brushes,
and so on. Mr. Frink bought in Cincinnati a small sheet-iron
cooking-stove, which was lashed on behind the wagon. To prepare for crossing the desert, we also had two India-rubber bottles
holding five gallons each, for carrying water.

Our outfit for provisions was plenty of hams and bacons, covered with care from the dust, apples, peaches and preserved fruits

of different kinds, rice, coffee, tea, beans, flour, corn-meal, crackers, sea-biscuit, butter and lard. The canning of fruits had not been invented yet—at least in the west, as far as we knew.

Learning by letters published in the newspapers that lumber was worth $100.00 per thousand in California, while it was worth only $3.00 in Indiana, Mr. Frink concluded to send the material for a small cottage by the way of Cape Horn. The lumber was purchased and several carpenters were put to work. In six days the whole material was prepared, ready for putting it together. It was then placed on board a flatboat lying in White River, to be ready for the spring rise—as boats could not pass out except at high water. The route was down White River to the Wabash, to the Ohio, to the Mississippi, to New Orleans; thence by sail vessel around Cape Horn to Sacramento where it arrived the following March, having been just one year on the voyage.

Our team consisted of five horses and two mules. We had two saddles for the riding-horses, one for Mr. Frink and one for myself.

I believe we were all ready to start on the morning of the twenty-seventh of March. On the evening before, the whole family, including my mother, were gathered together in the parlor, looking as if we were all going to our graves the next morning, instead of our starting on a trip of pleasure, as we had drawn the picture in our imagination. . . .

We bade farewell. . . . Mr. Frink and myself, having each a horse to ride, rode out of town on horseback, and with the four-horse wagon [a well-to-do town boy almost twenty-one years of age joined in at the last and helped with the driving] went seven miles before stopping for lunch. It was a beautiful spring day. Our faces were now at last set westward. We arrived on the west bank of the Eel River about sundown. We were quite tired and there being a large brick house near by, we inquired there for quarters for the night. It appeared that the landlady was, for the moment, in the stable, and, hearing our inquiry, she thrust her head out of the stable window and answered rather impatiently that she had no time to give to strangers; that she had a cow in the stable that she was going to break if it took her all night to do it; that we had better go on about three miles, where we might be accommodated with lodgings. This looked like a poor chance for us; but Mr. Frink was not to be discouraged in this manner. He went to the stable and gave the milkman such instructions as enabled him in a short time to bring the unruly cow under subjection, so that the old lady came out highly pleased, and allowed us to stay in the house all night. . . .

Sunday, March 31. We continued our journey to-day and struck the national road at Manhattan, where we had dinner. We lost our road, however, and had to retrieve about three miles. We stopped at night about twenty miles east of Terre Haute; and were very pleasantly entertained. The landlord of the hotel had been a sea-captain, and volunteered some advice that afterwards proved very beneficial to us in regard to preparing to defend ourselves against scurvy, from which so many California emigrants had suffered in 1849.

Monday, April 1. We started again in good spirits, every one at the hotel, strangers and all, wishing us good luck on our long journey. On this great "national road" the towns are near together; and whenever we stopped, even to water the horses, there would be squads of people standing about, full of curiosity, and making comments upon ourselves and our outfit, thinking we were certainly emigrants bound for California. But some would remark, "There's a lady in the party, and surely there's no man going to take a woman on such a journey as that across the plains."

Wednesday, April 3. We started last night on Grand Prairie. Our hostess and her husband were German people, and made us very comfortable. We traveled all day on the prairie. The distance was seventeen miles between houses, and no timber in sight at many times, though occasionally we passed some beautifully timbered spots. . . .

April 4. We found good accommodations in a large backwoods cabin. There were two large rooms with great, wide fireplaces and huge, blazing logs piled on. That great, glowing fire [her feet had just been frozen] I shall never forget, nor the beautiful supper table, with its good warm coffee, and, best of all, the cheerful faces that welcomed us.

April 11. To-day we crossed the Missouri. . . . We got the privilege of stopping at a private farmhouse, it being then dark, where they consented to furnish us with supper and breakfast. . . . The gentleman and his wife . . . appeared to be considering the propriety of furnishing accommodations to people from a "free state"; for we were now in a "slave state" [Missouri].

April 22. Mr. Frink traveled sixteen miles through the farming country searching for pickled cucumbers [to ward off the scurvy. He found some still in salt, brought them back and Mrs. Frink pickled them in apple vinegar.]

May 20. . . . The country was so level that we could see the long trains of white-topped wagons for many miles. Finally, when the two roads came together and the army which had crossed the Missouri River at St. Joseph's joined our army which had crossed the river above Savannah, it appeared to me that none of the population had been left behind. It seemed to me that I had never seen so many human beings in all my life before. And, when we drew nearer to the vast multitudes, and saw them in all manners of vehicles and conveyances on horseback and on foot, all eagerly driving and hurrying forward, I thought, in my excitement, that if one-tenth of these teams and these people got ahead of us, there would be nothing left for us in California worth picking up. . . .

Mr. Frink was not with our wagons just at this moment. . . . So I took the responsibility, and gave orders to the drivers to whip up and drive fast and get ahead of that countless throng of wagons. But in a little while Mr. Frink appeared and wanted to know of the drivers what they had got in such a hurry about.

Already the horses were showing signs of being fretted, and Mr. Frink at once instructed the drivers that it would not do to attempt to travel at that rate of speed if we expected ever to reach California. But I was half frantic over the idea that every blade of grass for miles on each side of the road would be eaten off by the hundreds and thousands of horses, mules and oxen ahead of us. And, worse than all, there would only be a few barrels of gold left for us when we got to California.

With the freedom of movement across the continent went a spirit of liberty that found expression in the new Western constitutions.[5]

In the spring of 1852, when the great *furor* for going West was at its height, in the long trails of miners, merchants and farmers wending their way in ox-carts and canvas-covered wagons over the vast plains, mountains and rivers, two remarkable women, then in the flush of youth, might have been seen: one, Abigail Scott Duniway, destined to leave an indelible mark on the civilization of Oregon, and the other, Mary Olney Brown, on that of Washington territory. What ideas were revolving in these young minds in that long journey of 3,000 miles, six months in duration, it would be difficult to imagine, but the love of liberty had been infused in their dreams somewhere, either in their eastern homes from the tragic scenes of the anti-slavery conflict, or on that perilous march amidst those eternal solitudes by day and the solemn stillness of the far-off stars in the gathering darkness. That this long communion with great nature left its impress on their young hearts and sanctified their lives to the best interests of humanity at large, is clearly seen in the interesting accounts they give of their endeavors to mold the governments of their respective territories on republican principles. Writing of herself and her labors, Mrs. Duniway says:

[5] History of Woman Suffrage, Vol. III, p. 767 ff.

"I was born in Pleasant Grove, Tazewell County, Illinois, October 22, 1834, of the traditional 'poor but respectable parentage' which has honored the advent of many a more illustrious worker than myself. Brought up on a farm and familiar from my earliest years with the avocations of rural life, spending the early spring-times in the maple-sugar camp, the later weeks in gardening and gathering stove-wood, the summers in picking and spinning wool, and the autumns in drying apples, I found little opportunity, and that only in winter, for books or play. . . . Before I was seventeen I was employed as a district school teacher, received a first-class certificate and taught with success, though how I became possessed of the necessary qualifications I to this day do not know. . . .

"In the spring of 1852 my father decided to emigrate to Oregon. My invalid mother expostulated in vain; she and nine of us children were stowed away in ox-wagons, where for six months we made our home, cooking food and washing dishes around camp-fires, sleeping at night in the wagons, and crossing many streams upon wagon-beds, rigged as ferry-boats. When our weary line of march had reached the Black Hills of Wyoming my mother became a victim to the dreadful epidemic, cholera, that devastated the emigrant trains in that never-to-be-forgotten year, and after a few hours' illness her weary spirit was called to the skies. We made her a grave in the solitudes of the eternal hills, and again took up our line of march, 'too sad to talk, too dumb to pray.' But ten weeks after, our Willie, the baby, was buried in the sands of the Burnt River mountains. Reaching Oregon in the fall with our broken household, I engaged in school-teaching till the following August, when I allowed the name of 'Scott' to become 'Duniway.' Then for twenty years I devoted myself, soul and body, to the cares, toils, loves and hopes of a conscientious wife and mother. Five sons and one daughter have been born to us. . . .

"The first woman suffrage society ever formed in Oregon was organized in Salem, the capital of the State, in the autumn of 1870, and consisted of about a dozen members. Col. C. A. Reed was chosen president and G. W. Lawson, secretary. . . . In the winter of 1871 this society honored men with credentials to a seat in the woman suffrage convention which was to meet in San Francisco the following May. My business called me to the Golden City before the time for the convention, and a telegraphic summons compelled me to return to Oregon without meeting with the California Association in an official way, as I had hoped. But my credentials introduced me to the San Francisco leaders, among whom Emily Pitts Stevens occupied a prominent position as editor and publisher of *The Pioneer*, the first woman suffrage paper that appeared on the Pacific coast. Before returning to Oregon I resolved to purchase an outfit and begin the publication of a newspaper myself, as I felt that the time had come for vigorous work in my own State. . . .

"Soon after reaching my home in Albany I sold my millinery store and removed to Portland, where, on May 5, 1871, the *New Northwest* made its appearance, and a siege of the citadels of a one-sexed government began. . . .

"In June, 1878, a convention met in Walla Walla, Washington territory, for the purpose of forming a constitution for the proposed new State of Washington, and in compliance with the invitation of many prominent women of the territory, I visited the convention and was permitted to present a memorial in person, praying that the word 'male' be omitted from the fundamental law of the incubating State. But my plea failed of success, through a close vote however—it stood 8 to 7. . . .

"I went to Southern Oregon in 1879, and while sojourning in Jacksonville was assaulted with a shower of eggs (since known in that section as 'Jacksonville arguments') and was also burned in effigy on a principal street after the sun went down. Jacksonville is an old mining town, beautifully situated in the heart of the Southern Oregon mountains, and has no connection with the outside world except through the daily stage-coaches. Its would-be leading men are old miners or refugees from the bushwhacking district where they were driven by the civil war. The taint of slavery is yet upon them and the methods of border-ruffians are their hearts' delight. It is true that there are many good people among them, but they are often over-awed by the lawless crowd whose very instincts lead them to oppose a republican form of government. But that raid of the outlaws proved a good thing for the woman suffrage movement. It aroused the better classes, and finally shamed the border ruffians by its own reaction. . . .

"In addition to all that is being done in Oregon and Washington, we are actively engaged in pushing the work in Idaho and Montana territories, where the *New Northwest* has been thoroughly circulated in many localities and many spirited public meetings have been held. The Idaho legislature seriously considered and came near adopting a woman suffrage bill last winter. . . . Remembering Dakota's set-back through the governor's veto in 1885, they are carefully planning to avoid a like calamity in their own territory. In Montana the cause has made less apparent progress, but there is much quiet and constantly increasing agitation in its favor. Popular feeling is steadily ripening for this change, and let the rest of the world wag as it will, there cannot be much longer hindrance to the complete triumph of liberty in the Pacific Northwest."

CHAPTER IV

MACHINE INDUSTRY AND PLANTATION

As THE so-called "frontier" swept westward to the Pacific, the number of inventions, factories, railways and mines multiplied from decade to decade, finally outrunning in the value of the capital involved and the wealth produced all the free farms and plantations.

Here lay the basis of a movement and an antagonism of interests destined to eventuate in armed conflict. In this transformation of productive economy, women were actors, as inventors on a small scale and as industrial workers on a large scale. Throughout the industrial regions, the life and labor of women, their agelong habits, were revolutionized and the change was accompanied by revolutionary ideas—Fanny Wrightism, socialism, trade-unionism and all the other isms, which seemed so spectral to conservatives of the old culture. In the South, as the plantation system expanded, the menace of industrialism was early recognized and it was clear that the plantation, once regarded as a final economy, with fixed codes for women from the slave mistress to the field hand, was in mortal peril. So the wives and daughters of planters, accustomed to heavy managerial responsibilities but also to the fruits of the slave economy, saw their fate entangled in the swiftly growing conflict of cultures.

In all the activities of that conflict—economic, moral and intellectual—women participated on both sides of the geographical line. Great energies went into the discussion of slavery itself and as the attacks grew increasingly emotional, its defense became correspondingly vehement. To Northern criticism of plantation slavery, Southern leaders replied with attacks on the "wage slavery" of industry with its dangerous "socialistic" accompaniments. On both sides women waged the verbal battle with all the historical implements—argument and ridicule, essay and novel, economic rationalization and cultural defense mechanism. Not a phase of the struggle, with such deep implications for the Nation as well as for their individual fortunes, did they neglect and, were all the speeches of Congressmen lost, the intellectual imagery of the verbal battle could be entirely recovered from the writings of women, in the North and the South.

As in every great social movement in the United States, moreover, women of the Old World took a hand. English ladies now addressed open letters to American women calling upon them to abolish chattel slavery. After making a tour of the Southern states in person, Harriet Martineau created a commotion on both shores of the Atlantic by her reports on slavery—an experiment in "arousing the conscience of the world" long afterward repeated by Katherine Mayo, author of "Mother India," in another connection. In a second volume, Miss Martineau tried to modify her original account in the light of Southern criticism but apparently nothing could stay the sharpening clash of cultures, for such it was at bottom. While each side of the alignment was accusing the other of cruelty to labor, each was also erecting a philosophy of "perfect good" in its own defense.

Just what was happening to the life and labor of women in the early days of the factory system of the North is described in great detail by Edith Abbott in her volume on WOMEN IN INDUSTRY, from which these pages are taken.[1]

The relation of women and children to the early factory system can be understood only in connection with the whole labor situation as it existed at the close of the eighteenth and the beginning

[1] Reprint obtained through the courtesy of D. Appleton & Company.

of the nineteenth century. The labor problem of that period was fundamentally different from ours to-day. The ease with which any man could become a freeholder and the superior chances of success in agriculture made it difficult to find men who were willing to work in manufacturing establishments and it was questionable whether sufficient labor could be found to run the new mills when they were constructed. Moreover, as a question of national economy, fear was expressed regarding the possible injury to our agricultural interests if much labor were diverted from the land. Manufactures, if they were to be established, must not, it was emphatically said, be built up at the expense of agriculture.

It has already been pointed out that, in many respects, the situation in England was quite different from our own. There the manufacture of cloth had become an industry of large proportions before the industrial revolution; and the establishment of the factory system created a disaffected class of unemployed workmen who were jealous of the new machinery which could be easily managed by women and children and which was taking the work away from them. In this country, however, a comparatively small number of persons were employed, and because of the absorption of our male laborers in agriculture, in so far as there was such an industry, it was for the most part in the hands of women and girls.

The establishment of the factory system, therefore, substantially meant, with us, the creation of new work, and made imperative a large increase in our wage-earning population. Moreover, this new work was identical with the work which women had long been doing in their own homes, and it was inevitable that the difficulties caused by the scarcity and high cost of male labor should be met by the employment of women. So long as land remained cheap and agriculture profitable, it was taken for granted that men could not be induced to work in the new mills and factories; and just as confidently it was expected that women could be counted on to continue, in the mills, the work they had formerly done at home.

The economic ideals of our early statesmen must also be taken into account as a factor of importance. Hamilton and his followers had visions of the complete development of the virgin resources of the new republic; and they hoped to formulate a policy for obtaining the maximum utility, not only from our territory, but from our population. It was logical, therefore, that Hamilton, in his famous "Report on Manufactures," should argue that one great advantage of the establishment of manufactures was "the employment of persons who would otherwise be idle. . . . In general," he said, "women and children are rendered more useful by manufacturing establishments than they otherwise would be." He also pointed out that "the husbandman himself [would experience] a new source of profit and support from the increased industry of his wife and daughters, invited and stimulated by the demands of the neighboring manufactories."

In 1794, when Trench Coxe found it necessary to reply to the argument that labor was so dear as to make it impossible for us to succeed as a manufacturing nation and that the pursuit of agriculture should occupy all our citizens, he at once called attention to the fact that the importance of woman's labor must not be overlooked, since manufactures furnished the most profitable field for its employment. And in the early part of the last century, a new factory was called a "blessing to the community," among other reasons, because it would furnish employment for the women of the neighborhood. Later it was said that women were "kept out of vice simply by being employed and instead of being destitute provided with an abundance for a comfortable subsistence."

The availability of women's labor to meet the demand for hands to police the new machines was one of the arguments with which the early protectionists most frequently met their opponents. The objection that American labor was more profitably employed in agriculture than in manufactures and that to "abstract" this labor from the soil would be unwise and unprofitable, was answered by pointing to the women and children. In the

. pages of *Niles's Register* this is done again and again. The work of manufactures does not demand able-bodied men, it is claimed, but "is now better done by little girls from six to twelve years old." To the "Friends of Industry," as the early protectionists loved to call themselves, it was, therefore, a useful argument to be able to say that of all the employees in our manufacturing establishments not one fourth were able-bodied men fit for farming; and the question was raised, Would agriculture be benefited if "on the stopping of the cotton and woolen manufactures, these women returned to idleness?"

During the period following the close of the War of 1812, when the tariff was, for a time, the most important subject of public discussion, the fact that women formed so large a proportion of the employees in the "infant industries" proved a valuable protectionist argument. Niles and Matthew Carey frequently made use of it, and memorials to Congress during the period called attention to the additions to the national wealth and prosperity made possible by the utilization in factories of women's labor which had hitherto been less advantageously employed. In 1815, a group of manufacturers, in a petition to Congress urging the prohibition of the importation of coarse cottons, pointed out that their establishments had afforded "the means of employment to thousands of poor women and children for whom the ordinary business of agriculture [supplied] no opportunities for earning a livelihood," and that any loss to manufacturing interests would mean that hundreds of poor women would be "thrown back on the community for support." Thus the charge that manufactures would produce pauperism had already been met and it was only necessary to repeat that the number of those unable to earn their own subsistence was decreased when new or more remunerative occupations for women were provided.

During the tariff controversy of the early thirties, free-traders and protectionists alike agreed in commending the manufacturing industries which had furnished employment for women. It was no new thing for the "Friends of Industry" to argue that the decline of our manufacturing interests would mean that the women employees would become "the tenants of charitable institutions or be consigned to prisons and penitentiaries by the vices contracted during idleness." But to have their arguments obliged to yield this point, was, in its way, a considerable victory.

Precisely this happened, however, in 1831, when in the "Memorial for the Free-Trade Convention" of that year, Gallatin frankly admitted that although labor generally was less productive in manufactures than if applied to other pursuits, there was one exception which seemed "to alleviate the evil." Women's work in the cotton and woolen industries was, as he said, "much more productive than if applied to the ordinary occupations of women." And, he added, that with the fund out of which they had been previously supported thus set free, large accumulations might be annually added to the wealth and capital of the country. Gallatin even proceeded to make a precise computation as to the additional quantity of productive labor put in motion, and concluded that the surplus product obtained by the employment of women in a single cotton mill of two hundred employees was $14,000 annually.

That the convention, in its official memorial, should be obliged to make an exception which included so large a proportion of the total number of employees, was a distinct concession to the protectionists.

The committee on cotton of the "Convention of the Friends of Industry," which was held in New York in 1931, reported similarly that "thirty-nine thousand females" were employed in the various cotton factories of the United States, their aggregate wages amounting to "upwards of four million dollars annually." In the words of the committee: "This immense sum paid for the wages of females may be considered so much clear gain to the country. Before the establishment of these and other domestic manufactures, this labor was almost without employment. Daughters are now emphatically a blessing to the farmer. Many instances have occurred within the personal knowledge of individuals of this committee in which the earnings of daughters have been scrupulously hoarded to enable them to pay off mortgages on the parental farm."

It was in short easy to point out that there was a clear economic gain to the community in the establishment of factories in which women's labor, which was very unproductive in agriculture, could be advantageously employed. Thus a writer in the *Boston Centinel* attempted to summarize the situation: "In Europe as in America," he said, "machinery not only facilitates labor in a tenfold ratio, but enables women and children who are unable to cultivate the earth to make us independent of foreign supplies." Matthew Carey argued similarly: "The services of females of the specified ages (10–16–25) employed in agriculture, for which above one half of them are too young or too delicate, are very unproductive. At manufactures they are far more valuable and command higher wages."

In brief, it was claimed that "thousands of persons were turned from the consuming to the productive class"; that a maximum return was more nearly obtained from the country's labor force; that the national prosperity was increased by making women "a source of wealth, rather than an incumbrance"; and that their work represented so much clear gain to society, an argument to which, as we have seen, even so able a free-trader as Gallatin could not reply.

Another point of interest in connection with the employment of women in the early mills and factories is that their work in these establishments was approved on social as well as on economic grounds. It has already been pointed out that in the colonial period great apprehension existed lest women and children, particularly those who were poor and in danger of becoming a public charge, should fall into the sin of idleness. This old Puritan fetich of the virtue of industry survived long into the nineteenth century and in some quarters the introduction of cotton machinery was regarded with disfavor "from the fear that the female part of the population by the disuse of the distaff should become idle."

Public attention was, therefore, frequently called to the fact that women found increased rather than diminished opportunities for employment as a result of the introduction of machinery and the establishment of factories. The new system, it was thought, not only gave women a chance of earning their livelihood, but educated them in habits of honest industry. The rise of manufactures was said to have "elevated the females belonging to the families of the cultivators of the soil in their vicinity from a state of penury and idleness to competence and industry." It was pointed out that young women who, before the introduction of the factory system, were "with their parents in a state of poverty and idleness, bare-footed and living in wretched hovels," had "since that period been comfortably fed and clothed, their habits and manners and dwellings greatly improved"; and they had in general become "useful members of society."

In the same spirit of unreasoning exaggeration the women in villages remote from manufacturing centers were described as "doomed to idleness and its inseparable attendants, vice and guilt." A picture of a village where "free, independent and happy workmen with their wives and children were employed," was a sign of prosperity that seemed to arouse no misgivings in the first quarter of the last century.

Matthew Carey, one of the well-known philanthropists of his day, declared in a public address, in 1824, before the Philadelphia "Society for Promoting Agriculture" that one half of the "young females" in the cotton mills, "would be absolutely or wholly idle but for this branch of business," and although his account of the beneficial effects of their work there was absurdly extravagant, it is an interesting illustration of the point of view of the times. "They contract," he said, "habits of order, regularity and industry, which lay a broad and deep foundation of public and private usefulness. They become eligible partners for life for young men, to whom they will be able to afford substantial aid in the support of families." Thus, his crowning argument was, "the inducement to early marriages . . . is greatly increased . . . and immensely important effects produced on the welfare of society."

The employment of children in the early factories was regarded from much the same point of view as the employment of women. Philanthropists, who still cherished colonial traditions of the value of an industrious childhood, supported statesmen and economists in warmly praising the establishment of manufactures because of the new opportunities of employment for children. They pointed out the additional value that could be got from the six hundred thousand girls in the country, between the ages of ten and sixteen, most of whom were "too young or too delicate for agriculture," and in contrast called attention to the "vice and immorality" to which children were "exposed by a career of idleness."

The approval of child labor was, in short, met with on all sides. Early inventors worked to discover possible means of using the labor of children as well as women. Commendation was solicited for Baxter's machines on the ground that they could be turned, one sort by children from five to ten years and the other by girls from ten to twenty years.

Governer Davis of Massachusetts called attention, in a message in 1835, to the fact that not only machines in the textile manufactures but "thousands of others equally important, were managed and worked easily by females and children." Mr. E. B. Bigelow of Boston, in 1842, patented a series of devices "for making the carpet loom automatic, so that the costly labor of man might be dispensed with, and the whole process of weaving be conducted by women and boys."

Tariff arguments, too, made use of the fact that children as well as women were employed in large numbers in the new mills. One protectionist carefully worked out in the pages of *Niles's Register* the exact gain that came to a typical village from the fact that its children could find work in neighboring textile factories. He came to the conclusion that "if we suppose that before the establishment of these factories, there were two hundred children between seven and sixteen years of age, that contributed nothing toward their maintenance and that they are now employed, it makes an immediate difference of $13,500 a year to the value produced in the town!"

Now and then an interesting document is found which throws light on conditions which prevailed at this time. The memorandum from the "Poignaud and Plant Papers" showing the wages paid to Dennis Rier for himself and his family of children and to Abigail Smith and "her daughter Sally, 8 years of age, and son Samuel, 13 years of age," which is quoted in a later chapter dealing with wages, is of interest from this point of view. Of similar interest is a wages book for the year 1821, still in the possession of the agent of the Waltham cotton mills, which shows that one Gideon Haynes in that year, came regularly to collect the wages of his children: for Cynthia Haynes, who worked in the cloth room, two dollars and a quarter a week; for the three children who were employed in the card room, Ann, one dollar and a half a week, Sabre, two dollars, and Sophia, two dollars and eight cents. Samuel Longley also came to collect the three dollars and a half, which represented the joint weekly earnings of his daughters, Sarah and Rebecca.

In general, however, it should be said that a relatively larger number of women and fewer children were employed in the mills of eastern Massachusetts and in New Hampshire than in Rhode Island and Connecticut, where the so-called "family system" prevailed. This point, however, will be dealt with in some detail in a later chapter dealing with the early mill towns.

A brief summary of the industrial situation during the first part of the last century so far as it concerned the employment of women may be useful, even at the risk of repetition. The introduction of machinery had created new and great industrial possibilities, but we were confronted with the problem of establishing manufactures in a country where labor was scarce and dear and where there was a strong national prejudice against "diverting labor from the land." This problem was solved by the employment of women and children to police the new machines, a natural solution since the machines were doing work which women had been doing in their own homes. Moreover, to have the women of the country fully employed meant the more complete utilization of the country's labor force, which was a clear economic gain to the nation and in line with the policy of achieving the maximum utility not only from our boundless and unexplored territory, but from our population. It should be noted, too, that in addition to the fact that an economic justification was found for the employment of women in the new mills and factories, there was no social prejudice against it. Following in the wake of Puritan tradition which loathed idleness as a vice and cherished ideals of industry and thrift, anything which offered new opportunities of employment for either women or children was eagerly welcomed.

On January 24, 1853, from her home, "Sherwood Forest," in Virginia, Julia Gardiner Tyler, Northern by birth, the wife of ex-President John Tyler, dispatched the following stern REPLY TO THE DUCHESS OF SUTHERLAND AND OTHER LADIES OF ENGLAND *who had just sent an "Address" to the women of America calling for their nation-wide action to end slavery. Mrs. Tyler's reply was first printed in the "RICHMOND ENQUIRER" and then other Southern papers carried it. The "Southern Literary Messenger" in February of that year declared that it deserved the widest possible circulation.*

Your address to your sisters, the women of the United States, on the subject of domestic slavery, as it exists among us, which has appeared in our public journals, should be acknowledged by some one of the vast number of those to whom it is addressed, without awaiting the publication of the more formal communication. There are some of the concerns of life in which conventionalities are properly to be disregarded, and this is one of them. A reply to your address must necessarily be the work of some one individual among us, or must go altogether unperformed. Woman, in the United States, with but few exceptions, confines herself within that sphere for which the God who created her seems to have designed her. Her circle is, literally and emphatically, that of her family; and such she is content that it shall be. Within that circle her influence is felt over the relations of life, as wife, mother, mistress—and as she discharges the duty of one or all of these relations, so is she respected or otherwise. To cast a doubt upon her fidelity in any one of them, is to excite against her the odium of the community, and, in a great measure, to dethrone her from her high position. She knows nothing of political conventions, or conventions of any other sort than such as are held under suitable pastors of the Church, and are wholly directed to the advancement of the Christian religion. Such is emphatically the case with the women of the Southern States. Do you wish to see them, you must visit their homes. Do you desire to ascertain the nature of their employments, you must enter their family circle, and, believe me, good sisters of England, you would find in their Christian deportment, and perfect amiability of manners, enough, at once, to inspire you with the most exalted respect and esteem. You might find no splendid vestments of dress, no glittering diamonds, no aristocratic displays. No, the vestments they wear are those of meekness and charity, their diamonds are gems of the heart, and their splendor the neatness and order and contentment which everywhere greets the eye; and that neatness, that order, and that contentment is in nothing more observable than in the well-clothed and happy domestics who welcome your arrival, and heap upon you every comfort during your sojourn under the roofs of their masters. You will see then how utterly impossible it would be to expect the women of the United States to assemble in convention, either in person or by proxy, in order to frame an answer to your address. Nay, I must, moreover, in all frankness, declare to you, that the women of the South, especially, have not received your address in the kindest spirit. They regard it as entirely incompatible with all confidence in, or consideration for them, to invoke the imposition of the women of what are called the free States, in a matter with which they have no more to do than have yourselves, and whose interference in the question can produce no other effect than to excite disturbance and agitation and ill-will, and, possibly in the end, a total annihilation of kind feeling between geographical sections. It is the province of the women of the Southern States to preside over the domestic economy of the estates and plantations of their husbands—it is emphatically their province to visit the sick, and attend to the comfort of all the laborers upon such estates; and it is felt to be but a poor compliment to the women of the South, to suppose it necessary to introduce other superintendence than their own over the condition of their dependents and servants. They see, too, or fancy they see, in the fact that the address which you have made them, was handed to you already prepared for signature, by the editors of the newspaper press of England, and that, according to the admission of the Duchess of Sutherland in her opening address to your Convention, your Convention itself is but the offspring of the same political newspaper press—I say, they see enough in all this to excite not their sympathies, but their apprehensions. They also see, or fancy that they see, in your movement, the fingers of your greatest statesmen. The *Countess of Derby, the Viscountess Palmerston, the Countess of Carlisle, Lady John Russell,* not to mention others of distinction and notoriety, would scarcely be complimented by a supposition that they had signed or openly approved such an address without the concurrence of their husbands. The women of the Southern States are, for the most part, well educated; indeed they yield not in this respect to any females on earth, and they have peculiar opportunities of acquiring knowledge in regard to the public concerns of the world. Politics is almost universally the theme of conversation among the men, in all their coteries and social gatherings, and the women would be stupid indeed, if they did not gather much information from this abundant source. Hence they are not ignorant of the rapid growth of their beloved country, or of the promises of its early future. . . .

The women of the United States comprehend the fact that all confederacies have heretofore, in the history of the world, been broken up and destroyed by the machinations of foreign governments; and if such has been the fate of other confederacies, how much more vigilant ought we to be to guard against the fatal results which have attended others, and to look with suspicion, come from what quarter it may, on all interference in our domestic concerns! . . .

Nor is this suspicion in any degree removed by the fact on which you predicate your address, viz: the fact that your country inflicted on her then colonies the "curse" of slavery in opposition to their frequent and solemn protests. The colony of Virginia, and, I believe, most of the other colonies, were constant and earnest in their remonstrances; and one of the causes set forth in the Declaration of Independence, as prepared and written by a son of Virginia, was a continuance of the slave trade by the mother country, in despite of all remonstrances on the part of the colonies. Thus, then, England not only permitted but encouraged the slave trade, for a period of a century and a half, as a means of swelling her coffers; and the infamous traffic could only be expelled from this country by the force and power of the sword. Your Kings and Queens, sustained by your Parliament and people, entered into treaties, and formed contracts, for the purpose of reaping a rich harvest of profit from the trade—and the voice of the slave-dealer on the shores of Africa was perfect music in their ears, because it was the music of gold told into the treasury, and all merry England danced with joy at the pleasant sound. You have been well informed, doubtless, of the treaties made by your Queen Anne, of "blessed memory," and the crown of Spain, which stipulated a monopoly of the trade in close partnership between those royal personages, to the exclusion of all the world beside. . . .

Would England, with a continuance of a monopoly of the trade over our broad acres up to the present day, have clothed herself in sackcloth and ashes, as she now has done? . . . Will it be an easy task to convince us, that the people of the present generation are better, more moral and more Christian than all who have gone before them—that your right reverend Bishops and Prelates are more pure and orthodox than all their predecessors—that your Kings and Queens, your nobles and gentry, are influenced by a higher spirit of Christianity than all who have preceded them—that your statesmen of the present day are superior, in moral excellence, to those illustrious men who shaped the destinies of England in past times, and left to history undying names? . . . Such interference implies either a want of proper and becoming conduct on our part, in the management of our negroes, or it seeks to enlist the sympathies of the world against us. Your own address represents the Southern States as denying to their slaves all religious instruction—a calumny more false was never uttered. So far from it, no Sabbath goes by that the places of worship are not numerously attended by the black population —edifying discourses are delivered to them, and often by colored pastors, and large numbers of them are in communion with the churches. . . .

If you wish a suggestion as to the suitable occupation of your idle hours, I will point you to the true field for your philanthropy; the unsupplied wants of your own people of England. . . . I remember to have seen lately, that there were in the city of London alone, 100,000 persons who rose in the morning without knowing where or how they were to obtain their "daily bread"; and I remember, also, somewhere to have seen that the Eleemosynary establishment of England costs annually £10,000,000 sterling— a sum greater than that expended by this frugal and economical government of ours, with its army and navy, and civil and diplomatic list. Surely, surely, here is a field large enough for the exercise of the most generous sympathy, the most unbounded charity. Go, my good Duchess of Sutherland, on an embassy of mercy to the poor, the stricken, the hungry and the naked of your own land—cast in their laps the superflux of your enormous wealth; a single jewel from your hair, a single gem from your dress, would relieve many a poor female of England who is now cold, and shivering, and destitute. . . . The negro of the South lives sumptuously in comparison with the 100,000 of the white population of London. . . .

The poor serf may toil and labor, and stretch his heart strings until they crack in agony, and yet the noble ladies of England will express no sympathy for him, and present no address to their sisters of Russia upon the subject of serfdom. . . . The newspaper press would admonish you of the danger of interference in that quarter, and the Emperor Nicholas will go unquestioned as to the manner and extent of his royal sway. . . .

Even if you are horror-stricken at the highly colored picture of human distress, incident to the separation of husband and wife. and parents and children under our system of negro slavery—a thing, by the way, of rare occurrence among us, and then attended by peculiar circumstances—you have no occasion to leave your own land for a similar, and still harsher, and more unjust exercise of authority. Go, and arrest the proceedings of your admiralty! Throw your charities between poor Jack and the press-gang! He has fought the battles of England all over the seas. He was at the Nile. He bled and conquered at Trafalgar. He caught your gallant Nelson in his arms as he was falling on the bloody deck; received his last breath, and consigned his remains to the bosom of St. Paul's Cathedral. He has made England what she is, great and powerful. . . . He has perilled his life for England—he has returned from a five years' absence in distant seas—his wife and children look with rapture upon his weather-beaten countenance—he holds the loved ones in his embrace; but the press-gang comes, and his fitful dream of happiness is over. If he resists, there are fetters for his limbs! If he talks of England's proudly boasted common law, there is no law for him. Magna Charta is a farce, and the Petition of Right a mockery, as far as he is concerned. Go, sisters of England, to your Queen, your Prime Minister, your Parliament and your Courts, and ask their interference to arrest this moral and political iniquity, and you will be told, "Woman should have no concern with politics—back to your drawing-rooms and nurseries."

For another subject, quite as fruitful of sympathy, I need only refer you to the condition of Ireland. . . .

I pray you to bear in mind, that the golden rule of life is for each to attend to his own business, and let his neighbor's alone! . . .

*The Address from the Ladies of England encountered other
protests, such as the reply in De Bow's "Review" in March,
1853, under the caption, BRITISH PHILANTHROPY AND
AMERICAN SLAVERY. It was signed "A Southern Lady."*

Ladies of Stafford-house, believe us, you have not the monopoly
of woman-feelings, and were the evil of our institutions so
"enormous," and prevailing with *"such frightful results"* as you
suppose, long ere this would we women of the Southern United
States, *"as sisters, as wives, and as mothers,"* have raised *"our
voices to our fellow-citizens and our prayers to God for the removal of this affliction from the Christian world."* Believe us,
ladies, we have not waited for your appeal *"to ask council of God
how far such a state of things is in accordance with His holy
Word, the inalienable rights of immortal souls, and the pure and
merciful spirit of the Christian religion?"* We can think as
women, and feel as women, and act as women, without waiting
for the promptings of your appeals, or of Mrs. Stowe's imaginative horrors. It seems to us, that you should receive it as a strong
proof of how much you have mistaken our system, that so many
millions of women—mothers, sisters, and daughters, loving and
beloved, civilized women, Christian women, have contentedly
lived in the midst of it, and yet the common woman-heart among
us has not risen up to call it *cursed*. . . .

Can the ladies of Stafford-house coolly contemplate the feasi-
bility of such an unraveling of this Gordian knot? Will their
admiration for Mrs. Stowe not stop short of amalgamation? We
answer for them boldly. We do them more justice than they
have done to us. As Christian and as civilized women, they
shrink with horror from the idea. What then, we repeat, can be
done with the negro? Amalgamation cannot be thought of.
Barbarism then—cannibal barbarism—slavery or extinction is his
fate. Will our self-constituted teachers in the A, B, C, of humanity, have the goodness to inform us which of these alternatives they would advise as a first experiment? . . .

The *North British* expatiates upon the power of pathos and

other admirable qualities of this authoress, and cheers her on to
work, recalling the fact that it was "a woman, Elizabeth Heyrick,
who wrote the pamphlet that moved the heart of Wilberforce
to pity and to pray over the wrongs of the oppressed sons of
Africa." We can only say that if so, Elizabeth Heyrick was almost as mischievous a woman in her day, as Mrs. Stowe now
threatens to be; for those tears of Wilberforce have caused more
shedding of blood, more anguish of soul, more agony of body
and mind, than it often falls to the lot of one man to give scope
to. He attacked crime, not with the philosophic coolness which
examines, compares, probes causes and effects, and thus has at
least the fairest chance for cure;—but with a species of feminine
pathetics and wailings, caught perhaps from Mrs. Heyrick, he set
the example, and opened that sluice of sickly sentimentality
which too often, taking the place of sound sense and argument,
now inundates the world, causing agonies of body and soul, to
which the worst scenes of the slave trade, heinous as they were,
stand but as dust in the balance. . . .

Our system, abhorrent as it seems to your ladyships, has the
sanction of our hearts and heads, and in the conscientious exercise of it, we find enough to occupy both without the necessity
of joining any of the world-improving and God-improving societies which at present are so much in vogue, and each one of
which threatens the world with some new *fiat lux.* . . .

Our poor, we have already told you, cannot be shoved into gar-
rets and cellars. They are with us at bed and at board; and when
there is woe with them, the wailing of it is in our ears. . . . We
can weep with them, nurse them, comfort them. . . .

A SOUTHERN CHURCHWOMAN'S VIEW OF SLAV-
ERY *was published in the "CHURCH INTELLIGENCER" of
November 22, 1860, anonymously.*

I have thought it might be interesting to some of your readers,
especially the Northern portion, to hear something of what the

Germans call "Our inner life." In a word, it may be interesting to them to hear, honestly, a Southern woman's opinion on slavery. I know, in spite of the great effort made to enlighten the world in general, and the Northern portion of these United States in particular, by Emerson, Greeley, Mrs. Stowe, Henry Ward Beecher, and others, there is a very great amount of ignorance as to the position and feelings of the white population of the South on this subject. I promise you to express frankly and truly, in the presence of God and the world, as an honest "Daughter of the Church," my belief on these matters. . . .

In very early times, perhaps, there may have been some excesses committed by slave-owners. There may be, even yet, exceptions; I have heard of such; thank God, I never knew them. But I will say, "setting down naught in malice," that, in every instance, these lawless acts were committed, not by Southern men and women, born and bred, but by men who came from other portions of the world, who bought negroes and land to make money as fast as possible, then to sell out and go back from whence they came to spend it, and to become very loud-mouthed Abolitionists. They demanded of the negro more than he is physically capable of performing, broke his spirit by overwork and want of sympathy, and then deserted him in helplessness and inefficiency. We do not act so. Our interest forbids it, if no other feelings actuate us. Our homes are here; our lives, our fortunes, our associations, past, present, and future, are here. . . .

As for Southern mistresses—noble, Southern women, whose peers I have never met, in any class of women, in any portion of the civilized world!—I throw the gauntlet down and defy any man to point out such a class of women in the world as they are. Moral, chaste, devoted wives; tender and self-denying mothers; active, industrious housekeepers—not disdaining the most menial occupations, if it but add to the comfort and welfare of their dear ones; faithful mistresses—providing with their own hands, often, the clothing of their negroes, visiting and nursing the sick day by day, and by night; caring for the little children; teaching, to the best of their knowledge, these poor ones; refined, accom-

plished, intellectual, as many Southern mistresses are, thinking it
no more than their duty to exhaust their time, their sympathies,
their affections, their lives, for these objects of their love; where
can their equals be found? I do not know of such women, except in the days when Penelope spun, and Lucretia and Cornelia
sat with their maidens. . . .

What can you know, our Northern sisters, of the life and work
of a planter's wife—you who are so comfortably fixed; your
houses so conveniently arranged; your markets near and well
furnished? If your servants do not suit you, they are discharged.
Water, gas, coal, social advantages, books, lectures, music—how
can you understand the position of a Southern mistress—her
many cares and anxieties, her responsibilities, her frequent isolation, her daily self-sacrifice? Would you like to stand all day
long, with a pair of heavy shears in your hand, and cut out coarse
negro clothing, till your hand ached with weariness? I know
many hands, small and delicate as yours, that do this! Would
you like to go into the negro houses and stand hour after hour by
the bed of the sick and dying, cheering and comforting the poor
creature? I know many, as refined as you, who do this, and
think nothing of it. Would you like to struggle and wrestle with
ignorance, stupidity and the fearful tendency to immorality—
alas! almost inherent in the negro? All around me, throughout
the length and breadth of the land, are women who do this. And
these are the women who, I have been told, were helpless, indolent, weak, tyrannical creatures, who scarcely spoke "good English," but drawled out their apathetic sentences, in a mixed jargon
of Africanisms and English! I have been all over England, and
my conclusion is that we speak better English than the English
themselves; and many of us speak French, and Italian, and Spanish, and German, as well as English; and almost every Southern
woman has knowledge of music. . . . I recommend to my coun-
trywomen to use the Choral Service for their negroes, because,
as a usual thing, they all have some knowledge of music.

I could go on and tell you of the experiments made, and still
making, by Southern people, to improve and Christianize their

servants—tell you of a neighbor of ours, who has even tried to introduce trial by jury among them, making them judge, among themselves, their misdemeanors; but I should be also obliged to inform you that the experiment failed—he finding, as Dr. Krapf and all other African missionaries have, "that Africans live better under a monarchy than under republics"; that under the latter form of government, "the Africans are profitable *in nothing, either to God or man.*" Dr. Livingstone says, "running away is a disease among these people"; and so, I suppose, we will have to endure that idiosyncrasy as well as we can. I am happy to say it is of much rarer occurrence among us now than formerly.

Southern outcries against "Uncle Tom's Cabin," Harriet Beecher Stowe's novel of slavery, led her to follow it with the "Key," in which she undertook to meet objections by supplying the proofs of her right to present slavery in that manner. Reviews of the "Key" accordingly flooded Southern papers. One was written by a "Lady of Georgia" and captioned SOUTHERN SLAVERY AND ITS ASSAILANTS. It appeared in De Bow's "Review" in 1853.

Out of source material, hitherto inaccessible to the students of American history, material now being assembled at the University of North Carolina, the anti-bellum woman of the South is destined to emerge as a personality too long incognito.

In writing her Key, Mrs. Stowe seems to have been aware that the public would expect from her not only a verification of incidents which she says were essentially true, but also, in so great, so vehement an accusation against a people, some proof that she was not unfairly arguing from the abuse to the use, from the exception to the rule. The Key is divided into four parts. Part First contains simply a sort of verification of her characters, and beyond certain incidental statements and arguments discloses nothing particularly to be discussed. Parts Third and Fourth contain her examination of the slave code, with certain trials

under it, and embody the chief force of her argument. We also
find in it her attack on the arguments for slavery usually drawn
from the Old Testament. Part Fourth contains a view of the
action of the Church on the subject of slavery, with an attempt to
prove the Epistle to Philemon an abolition document, and winds
up by an effort to prove that the spirit of the Gospel commands
us instantly to free our slaves.

In reviewing a book, it is best to have distinctly before the mind
the full bearing and force of it; so we will endeavor to state
succinctly what we conceive to be the general plan of Mrs. Stowe's
reasoning.

Her general argument places the matter upon a wrong issue,
and in reality makes two counts on one indictment. While she
does not directly say that we are responsible for the act of the
British government in bringing slaves into this country, she
implies that we originated it, and makes us responsible for its
continuance, by making it appear that in giving up property so
unjustly acquired, we should make no sacrifice, and incur no in-
convenience beyond the loss of the slaves' pecuniary value. These
views, so easily controverted if directly put, she has so artfully
involved in the book, that any one whose ideas were derived
solely from it, would imagine they were so plain that all parties
had agreed to take them for granted, while he would be apt to
think the suggestion that there could be any disadvantage to the
negroes in emancipation could only come from a Bedlamite.
By thus artfully shifting the ground of our defence from slavery
made necessary by the force of circumstance to slavery in the
abstract, she takes from us the legitimate defence of many apparent violations of right as necessitated by that force of circumstance, and she makes slavery really the creature of our own
convenience and pleasure, pursued with total disregard to the
good or rights of the negro. And though, when thus placed before us, the sophistry is so evident, the true state of the case so
plain, that it seems quite unnecessary directly to confute it, still,
by skilfully evading the direct enunciation of these false premises,
she has contrived to render quite plausible a great many wrong
conclusions.

Besides this general argument or one count of the indictment, she has made another by examining the subject in detail. In reviewing the slave code, she pronounces it both incomplete and inefficient, and so, quite in consonance with her theory that it is the creature of our own selfishness, and though it contains a great many protective enactments totally at war with that action, she attempts to destroy the force of this evidence of our desire to be humane, by making it appear that, by the protective enactments, we simply intended to deceive the world as to our total inhumanity and selfishness, and that we have so artfully contrived the matter, that by a perfectly legitimate construction of these protective laws, they mean absolutely nothing. That of the humane class of Southerners, those who are not blinded by prejudice see this, and are abolitionists at heart. The rest of the humane class, feeling their own comfort and happiness involved in the well-being of their slaves, are too weak to see the drift of the vast mass, who, whether their eyes are open or closed to the total inhumanity and selfishness of the system, are themselves so selfish they do not care for it.

Mrs. Stowe says directly she does not confound slaveholders with the system in her hatred of it; but so long as she thus misrepresents them, they may be permitted to entertain some doubts as to whether she really knows her own feelings. It is a melancholy exemplification of the facility with which a philanthropist, who devotes herself exclusively to the eradication of one form of evil, can deceive herself, and come to regard any means justifiable, in the pursuance of a supposed good end. That subtle analyst of character, Nathaniel Hawthorne, has ably dissected this species of delusion in the "Blithedale Romance," whose hero, Hollingsworth, we commend to Mrs. Stowe's study. It is easy to see how she misleads herself, by first assuming a position, and then trying to collect facts to support it, a course which will lead the best-intentioned person into twisting facts to suit his purpose. It is evident that Mrs. Stowe's mind is in that excited state which fitted her rather to defend a pre-adopted conclusion, than to investigate facts to arrive at conclusions. . . .

But the Southern women did not all take the defensive position. The attitude of the Grimké sisters, who freed their slaves and moved to the North, where they joined in the abolition movement, is fairly well known in America. Less a matter of common knowledge is the criticism of other Southern women, such as Maria J. McIntosh, member of an illustrious county family of Georgia descended from the famous Scottish clan, who "viewed with alarm" the trend of pro-slavery opinion in the South. From WOMAN IN AMERICA: HER WORK AND HER REWARD, published in 1850, the following passage is taken.

The South! the sunny South! The land where the snow-spirit never comes, where the forest-trees are never stripped of their green coronal, where Spring flings her flowers into the very lap of Winter! Let us stand beneath her soft skies, inhale the perfume of her myrtle-bowers and orange-groves, press her violet-covered turf, and weave fragrant wreaths of the jessamine which flings its yellow clusters so gracefully from tree to tree. Or, if you would look on nature in a soberer dress, we will walk through her forests of pine, and listen to the whispering of the winds as they pass over them; or we will stand beneath the giant oaks, from whose branches a gray, mossy drapery hangs waving in the summer breeze, while the ocean wave breaks with a lulling murmur at our feet. To eyes accustomed to bolder views—to precipitous rocks and lofty mountains, and all the pleasing variety of hill and dale—these beauties may seem tame, yet no true lover of nature can look long without some melting of the heart, upon that rich and varied foliage, that flowery earth, and those ever sparkling, ever dancing waters. Theirs is not the beauty which strikes with sudden, overpowering admiration, but they steal not less surely to the heart; and when, bruised and worn with the conflicts of life, we shrink from great emotions and long only for repose, the memory of their peaceful loveliness comes back on our spirits, with an influence soothing as that of the mother's smile which lulled our infancy to rest.

It will be evident to those acquainted with the physical features

of our country that we have been describing only the Atlantic
coast of the Southern States; for as we advance into the interior,
the face of the country becomes more broken, and rises to greater
elevation, until, at the distance of less than one hundred miles
from the sea, the Allegheny rears its lofty summits. A noble
country is this interior—its aspect wild and picturesque, its soil
fertile, and its mineral wealth unbounded; but it is yet, like the
West, in that state of transition, which offers few distinctive
features to the observers of moral and social life. New settlers
are still migrating thither from the North and East, bearing with
them the impressions and habits of their former homes; and it
will probably be long before they are welded together in one
homogeneous mass. But on the Southern seacoast, we have a
social life which has existed nearly as long as any in our land, and
which is marked by peculiar characteristics, the result of peculiar
institutions.

In sketching the circumstances under which the earliest settlements in these United States were made, we did not allude to one
element introduced into Southern life, and Southern life alone.
It is one, in truth, which we would fain have avoided altogether,
for its very name has been of late years a signal for strife. But
to write of the South and say nothing of slave-labor, were indeed
—to borrow the words of John Randolph, on another subject—
"to give the tragedy of Hamlet, with the part of Hamlet omitted";
for from this domestic institution does the South derive many
of those traits which have given her a distinctive character, and
assigned to her a distinctive part in the great drama acting in this
land. We have seen that in every part of our country the prosperity of the colonists began only when they threw off their dependence on their foreign patrons; but ere this had been done,
those patrons had, in some instances, accomplished plans whose
influence, for good or for evil, is still felt by us. Such was the act
introducing African laborers, as slaves, into the Southern colonies.
Vainly did the colonists protest against this act—vainly seek its
annulment by the Board of Directors in England. Wise men
were those who formed that board! Did the future unroll itself

before their wondering eyes? Did they see, far down the tide of time, those feeble colonies become a great nation, no longer bringing tribute to England, or accepting laws from her; and did a mocking laugh rise to their lips as they heard their own sons—the sons of those by whose command, if not by whose very hands, the African was brought to America, and condemned to his life-bondage—the sons of those either in England or in New England who received all the gain of this infamous traffic, branding as men-stealers the children of the very men now petitioning to be delivered from the incubus of slavery? Strange things must the angels see in this our world! But we are nearing the abyss of strife (1850)—we feel its hot fires burning on our brow and kindling a flame in our heart, and we gladly turn from the acts of men, inconsistent, vacillating, and unjust, to those of the all-perfect One, "with whom is no variableness nor shadow of turning"; and we think it will not be difficult to prove from the annals of African slavery in this land, that He has made the wrath of man to praise Him—transmuting, with heavenly alchemy, the loathsome selfishness and heartlessness of the slave-trader into the partial civilization and Christianization of the race enslaved, and into the means of promoting the intellectual culture and social refinement of those who were forced into the position of their masters.

The improvement of the African race among us is sufficiently attested by the contrast which even the slaves in our Southern States present, to the specimens of the same race occasionally re-captured from some slave-ship and brought to our shores, some forty or fifty years ago. And now, yearly, many of this oppressed and much-wronged people are returning to their own land, bearing with them the seeds of all that has made us what we are. They went forth weeping, and they return bearing precious sheaves. The foul spirits which haunted the shores of Africa have been exorcised; Christian temples are rising there, and around these temples are clustered the habitations of civilized men, from which the voice of prayer and praise ascends to Heaven like the evening and the morning incense.

In proof of our second proposition, that the introduction of slavery into the United States had been made to subserve the promotion of intellectual culture and social refinement among ourselves, we will refer the reader to a work by one who cannot be suspected of favoring slavery—Dr. Bushnell, of Hartford. The argument to which we allude is contained in a sermon, published by him some months since, entitled, "Barbarism our first danger." He there asserts that, in colonization, the colony must always retrograde from the civilization of the parent-land, since little time can be spared for the refinements of life, by those who are engaged in a hand-to-hand contest with nature for the indispensable requisites of existence. From the action of this law, however, he confesses that those colonies in our land into which slavery was introduced, were comparatively free. There, the owner of property, having his land tilled by other hands, had leisure for the cultivation of his mind, and the practice of all the gentle courtesies of life. His gains, too, were immediate, and he was thus able to command the means of sending his sons to England for their education, while the youth of other portions of our land were educated at native schools and by native teachers. Was not the great prominence of our Southern statesmen, in the earlier years of our republic, the result of the superiority in the education which they thus received? This, her glorious crown, has fallen from the head of the South, and the sceptre is fast falling from her hands. Since they could not send their sons abroad for education, the Northern colonists struggled nobly and successfully to establish within their own borders the institutions necessary to mental culture. The result was another proof that in self-dependence lies self-reliance, self-help; for it has been hither, to this rude, laborious North, that Southern youth have come to receive an education, for the last fifty years.

We have presented these results of African slavery in our land, not to excuse the wrong-doing of men, by whom they could not have been foreseen, and of whose motives they could therefore have formed no part, but as evidence of the infinite wisdom and goodness of the world's Ruler. May we not be encouraged by such evidence to believe that He will yet bring *all good* out of this evil? With hearts strengthened by such a faith, we may return to that fair Southern land, whose physical features we attempted to portray at the commencement of this chapter;--we will enter her habitations, and hold converse with her children—we will mark her social life, and see what woman has done there, and what yet remains for her to do. In fulfilling this design, it is not necessary that we should enter into the moral question involved in the existence of slavery; for we write not for men, who make and may therefore unmake the laws, but for women, whose benevolence and charity should be a law unto themselves, softening the pressure of the fetters which they cannot break, and lightening the darkness which they may not wholly dispel.

At the first glance which we give to Southern life, we perceive one point of striking contrast to life in the Northern and Middle States. The latter are chiefly commercial, and in them wealth, talent, and energy, are concentrated in cities. The former is agricultural, and there towns are few and small. The largest towns increase slowly, and some that were built a century ago have been deserted, their inhabitants having retired to their plantations. Nor could this well be avoided, for he who continues in the relation of a master cannot absolve himself from its obligations, and those obligations cannot be fulfilled in continual absence from the dependents for whose interests, temporal and eternal, he is bound "to watch as one that must give account." Especially should the gentle care of woman not be withdrawn from the home of the slave. She should be there to interpose the shield of her charity between the weak and the strong, to watch beside the sick, to soothe the sorrowing, to teach the ignorant, to soften by her influence the haughty master, and to elevate the debased slave. We know that there are women—women in the often misrepresented South—who have lived and do live for such objects. They will have their reward; their names may be cast out as evil in the world, but "they shall be found within the Lamb's book of life." Such should be the life of every Southern woman. She is a missionary to whose own door God has brought the

Pagans to be instructed. Ah! could she but understand all her mission, could she possess her soul in patience in the midst of the warring elements which surround her—could she pour the oil of her own loving and gentle thoughts upon the raging waters of strife, winning the fiery natures around her to see the good even in their enemies, to adopt wise counsel even though it come mingled with bitter taunt, to foster the rare magnanimity which will not be withheld from a right action by the apprehension that a foe may regard it as a concession—could she induce, or even strive to induce them to do all this—exercising her influence, not by public associations, and debates, and petitions, but in the manifestations of all feminine grace, and all womanly delicacy— she would prove herself indeed, what one of old named her, the connecting link between man and the angelic world.

On Southern plantations the houses are generally of wood, large and commodious, but built with little regard to elegance, and furnished with a simplicity which would shock the eye of a third-rate votary of fashion in a Northern city. In these simple homes, however, you may enter without fear; "stranger" is there a sacred name; and you will find yourself entertained with an open-hearted hospitality which may well reconcile you to the absence of some accustomed luxuries. In the dwellers in these homes, you will find generally the easy, courteous bearing which distinguishes the best society everywhere. In them, too, you will find the highest intelligence in the land; and it will be readily perceived, that the result of this attainment of high cultivation in the inartificial life of the country, must be the formation of a character uniting, in a rare degree, refinement and simplicity. To this union, we think, Southern women are indebted for the charm so generally attributed to their manner—a charm which is never felt so fully as in their own homes, where all around them wears the impress of their own spirits. In the life they lead, there is little of moment but personal qualities. The fact that the changes of property are less frequent and violent in an agricultural than in a commercial country—that families remain longer in their relative positions in the first than in the last—has given, it is true, a higher value to blood,—to family distinction,—at the South than at the North, yet scarcely sufficient to affect the reception of an individual in society. The true gold of character will there pass current, even though it may lack "the guinea stamp."

Yet, even in this life, simple, unostentatious as it is, we find some vestiges of the old feudalism. One of these vestiges we recognize in the universal contempt for labor—not perhaps in itself considered, but as pursued for gain. A *gentleman* may labor, he may be his own blacksmith or carpenter, if such be his taste, but he must make it evident that it is his taste—that he has no ulterior design to profit by his labors—if he would not lose caste. Were this prejudice entertained only against such rude employments as we have named, however, we would scarcely represent it as characteristic of the South. The hard-handed mechanic, however intelligent and even polite, is as completely shut out from the pale of good society everywhere; but at the South, even the merchant finds himself somewhat slightly regarded, because engaged in a money-getting occupation. This has doubtless been the result of that severance of the natural connection between property and labor which has obtained at the South, and in which lies the very essence of feudalism. Through this, the association of *otium cum dignitate* was established and has been perpetuated at the South. Through this, the military profession has been honored there, even as in European countries in old feudal times. Next in dignity stands the legal profession, the great nursery of statesmen in our land; then the clerical and medical professions; while the life of elegant leisure, which the resources of a few enable them to lead, is regarded as equal or superior to any of these in the social position it confers.

In the Northern and Middle States, an idle man seems in an awkward position, as the world of his acquaintance is hurrying by him; he must assume a bustling manner, that he may, at least, *seem* to be employed. At the South, he stands in an attitude of graceful repose, and looks with conscious superiority upon the workers around him. But this state of things cannot endure. Every day, and in every place, the conviction is becoming more decided, that this is a working world. There is work here for each and all, and he who does not his own share makes his brother's burden by so much the heavier. Work! though it be only to improve your own land; and if you work successfully, the world has become so much richer by your labors. Especially in a country professedly republican, can no wise or conscientious man remain an idler. Do you really value your country, her freedom, her intelligence? Awake, sluggard! lift up your eyes, and see how the darkness from other lands is overshadowing her intelligence—how the oppressed multitudes of other nations, escaping from their galling bonds, threaten, in their wild transports, to trample freedom under foot, and to introduce in her place the anarchy which has ever ended, and must ever end, in despotism. Here are the ignorant to be taught, the weak to be guided, the vicious to be reclaimed. Up, then, and be doing!—while a school or a church is needed in the remotest district, you have something for which to labor. We feel persuaded that even in the South, the listless repose of the idle will not long continue undisturbed. Changes have already taken place there which betoken the infusion of new elements into the indolent *poco-curante* life. These elements are, we believe, the overflowing of the ever-boiling and bubbling caldron of life in the New England and Middle States. A happy admixture will this be, if the South will receive strength and activity, and give refinement, without suffering simplicity to be lost in the exchange.

Changes, we repeat, have already taken place at the South. Manufactories have been erected there, mines have been worked, and railroads opened, in almost every available direction. Should the prejudice against labor continue in its full force at the South, these newly-opened sources of wealth must fall into the hands of the strangers who first found the key to them, and the old proprietors be overshadowed till they die out of the soil which gave them birth. But of this we have little fear. We do not think that any part of our country can much longer remain unenlightened on the beneficence, the true nobleness of labor, nay, of labor for money, since in money lies the germ of all the good we may do, as well as of that we may enjoy. We will suppose all error on this subject to have been rectified, and Southern society to have become an industrious, active, energetic, money-getting society. Then arises another, and, to us, not less interesting question. Will it, in acquiring the virtues of the North, retain its own? Will its members, while adding to their homes the mechanical improvements which minister to comfort, and the treasures of art which at once form and gratify the taste—while thus gaining all that is truly valuable in the most advanced civilization, still wisely refuse to exchange their simple, social habits for the ostentatious display and vulgar pretension which too often mark a sudden increase of wealth? If they do, if maintaining their simplicity of life, they awake to a sense of their responsibility to God and to the world for the improvement and proper use of every talent entrusted to them, if they become *"workers* with God," seeking wealth,

> Not to hide it in a hedge,
> Nor for a train attendant—
> But for the glorious privilege

of opening to others a nobler life, of elevating to the dignity of man their own dependents, of sending the purifying streams of Christian education through the land—that, each man learning he is the brother of all, the bitter prejudices of sect and party may be discarded, and our country, our whole country, become what God intended it to be, united in one spirit, as well as in one body; if they do all this, then will they have attained to our conception of a true American life.

And has woman at the South nothing to do in promoting this "consummation most devoutly to be wished"? It must be mainly her work. Let her place it before her as an object of her life. Let her improve every gift and cultivate every grace, that the increased influence thus obtained may aid in its accomplishment. Let her light so shine that it may enlighten all who come within her sphere. Let her be a teacher of the ignorant, a guide to the straying of her own household. Let her make it a law of the social life in which she rules, that nothing so surely degrades a man as idleness, and the vices to which it almost inevitably leads. Thus she will proclaim the dignity and worth of labor, and she will find her reward in the new impress made on the yet ductile minds of her children. She has seen them hitherto too often go forth, like bright but wandering stars, into a life containing for them no definite object. In this vast void, she has seen them too often driven hither and thither by their own reckless impulses; and her heart has been wrung, and her imploring cry has arisen to Heaven for God's restraining grace, as they have seemed about to rush into the unfathomable realm of night. With almost Spartan heroism she has offered her "Te Deums," as again and again the sound has come up to her from the battlefield of life— "Mother! all is lost, but honor!" But labor will tame these wild impulses—will give to life a decided aim; and, as the strong hand, loosed from the bonds of prejudice, obeys the command of the stout heart, her "pæans" will be sounded, not for defeat nobly sustained, but for victory won. We have placed before her, her work and her reward.

While the popular discussion of slavery was filled with moral fervor, Lydia Maria Child, a Northerner, as early as 1833, saw clearly that underlying this dispute was a fundamental economic clash. In her APPEAL IN FAVOR OF THAT CLASS OF AMERICANS CALLED AFRICANS, she set forth this thesis in straightforward terms.

Machiavel says that "the whole politics of rival states consist in checking the growth of one another." It is sufficiently obvious, that the slave and free States are, and must be, rivals, owing to the inevitable contradiction of their interests. It needed no Machiavel to predict the result. A continual strife has been going on, more or less earnest, according to the nature of the interests involved, and the South has always had strength and skill to carry her point. Of all our Presidents, Washington alone had power to keep the jealousies of his countrymen in check; and he used his influence nobly.—Some of his successors have cherished those jealousies, and made effective use of them.

The people of the North have to manage a rocky and reluctant soil; hence commerce and fisheries early attracted their attention. The products of these employments were, as they should be, proportioned to the dexterity and hard labor required in their pursuit. The North grew opulent; and her politicians, who came in contact with those of the South with anything like rival pretensions, represented the commercial class, which was the nucleus of the old Federal party.

The Southerners have a genial climate and a fertile soil; but in consequence of the cumbrous machinery of slave labor, which is slow for everything (except exhausting the soil), they have always been less prosperous than the free States. It is said, I know not with how much truth, but it is certainly very credible, that a great proportion of their plantations are deeply mortgaged in New York and Philadelphia. . . .

A striking difference of manners, also caused by slavery, serves to aggravate other differences. . . .

It has been already said, that most of the wealth in New England was made by commerce; consequently the South became unfriendly to commerce. There was a class in New England, jealous, and not without reason, of their own commercial aristocracy. It was the policy of the South to foment these passions, and increase these prejudices. Thus was the old Democratic party formed; and while that party honestly supposed they were merely resisting the encroachments of a nobility at home, they were actually playing a game for one of the most aristocratic classes in the world—*viz.,* the Southern planters. A famous slave-owner and politician openly boasted that the South could always put down the aristocracy of the North, by means of her own democracy. In this point of view, democracy becomes a machine used by one aristocratic class against another, that has less power and is therefore less dangerous. . . .

The statesmen of the South have generally been planters. Their agricultural products must pay the merchants—foreign and domestic—the ship owner, the manufacturer—and all others concerned in the exchange or manipulation of them. It is universally agreed that the production of the raw materials is the least profitable employment of capital. The planters have always entertained a jealous dislike of those engaged in the more profitable business of the manufacture and exchange of products; particularly as the existence of slavery among them destroys ingenuity and enterprise, and compels them to employ the merchants, manufacturers, and sailors of the free States. Hence there has ever been a tendency to check New England, whenever she appears to shoot up with vigorous rapidity. Whether she tries to live by *hook* or by *crook,* there is always an effort to restrain her within certain limited bounds. The embargo, passed without limitation of time (a thing unprecedented), was fastened upon the bosom of her commerce, until life was extinguished. . . .

It is true, agriculture suffered as well as commerce; but agricultural products could be converted into food and clothing; they would not decay like ships, nor would the producers be deprived of employment and sustenance, like those connected with navigation.

Whether this step was intended to paralyze the North or not, it most suddenly and decidedly produced that effect. We were told that it was done to save our commerce from falling into the hands of the English and French. But our merchants earnestly entreated not to be thus saved. At the very moment of the embargo, underwriters were ready to *insure* at the *usual* rates.

The non-intercourse was of the same general character as the embargo, but less offensive and injurious. The war [1812] crowned this course of policy; and like the other measures, was carried by slave votes. It was emphatically a Southern, not a national, war. . . .

If the protection of commerce had been the real object of the war, would not some preparations have been made for a navy? It was ever the policy of the slave States to destroy the navy.

Vast conquests by *land* were contemplated, for the protection of Northern commerce. Whatever was intended, the work of destruction was done. The policy of the South stood for a while like a giant among ruins. New England received a blow, which crushed her energies, but could not annihilate them. Where the system of free labor prevails, and there is work of any kind to be done, there is a safety valve provided for *any* pressure. In such a community there is a vital and active principle, which cannot be long repressed. You may dam up the busy waters, but they will sweep away obstructions, or force a new channel.

Immediately after the peace, when commerce again began to try her broken wings, the South took care to keep her down, by multiplying permanent embarrassments, in the shape of duties. The *direct* tax (which would have borne equally upon them, and which in the original compact was the equivalent for slave representation) was forthwith repealed, and commerce was burdened with the payment of the national debt. The encouragement of *manufactures,* the consumption of domestic products, or *living within ourselves,* was then urged upon us. This was an ancient doctrine of the democratic party. Mr. Jefferson was its strongest advocate. Did he think it likely to bear unfavorably upon the "nation of shopkeepers and peddlers"? The Northerners adopted it with sincere views to economy, and more perfect independence. The duties were so adjusted as to embarrass commerce, and to guard the interests of a few in the North, who, from patriotism, party spirit, or private interest, had established manufactures on a considerable scale. The system of protection, opposed by the North, was begun in 1816 by Southern politicians, and enlarged and confirmed by them in 1824. It was carried nearly as much by Southern influence, as was the war itself; and if the votes were placed side by side, there could not be a doubt of the identity of the interests and passions which lay concealed under both. But enterprise, that moral perpetual-motion, overcomes all obstacles. Neat and flourishing villages rose in every valley of New England. The busy hum of machinery made music with her neglected waterfalls. All her streams, like the famous Pactolus, flowed with gold. From her discouraged and embarrassed commerce arose a greater blessing, apparently indestructible. Walls of brick and granite could not easily be overturned by the Southern *lever,* and left to decay, as the ship timber had done. Thus Mordecai was again seated in the king's gate, by means of the very system intended for his ruin. As soon as this state of things became perceptible, the South commenced active hostility with manufactures. Doleful pictures of Southern desolation and decay were given, and all attributed to manufactures. The North was said to be plundering the South, while she, poor dame, was enriching her neighbors, and growing poor upon her extensive labors. . . .

The bitter discussions in Congress have grown out of this strong dislike to the free States; and the crown of the whole policy is nullification. The single state of South Carolina has undertaken to abolish the revenues of the whole nation; and threatened the Federal Government with secession from the Union, in case the laws were enforced by any other means than through the judicial tribunals. . . .

What would the South have? They took the management at the very threshold of our government, and, excepting the rigidly just administration of Washington, they have kept it ever since. They claimed slave representation, and obtained it. For their convenience the revenues were raised by imposts instead of direct taxes, and thus they gave little or nothing in exchange for their excessive representation. They have increased the slave States, till they have twenty-five votes in Congress—They have laid the embargo, and declared war—They have controlled the expenditures of the nation—They have acquired Louisiana and Florida for an eternal slave market, and perchance for the manufactory of more slave States—They have given five presidents out of seven to the United States—And in their attack upon manufactures, they have gained Mr. Clay's *concession* bill. . . . The free States must be kept down. But change their policy as they will, free States *cannot* be kept down. There is but one way to ruin them; and that is to make them slave States. If the South with all her

power and skill cannot manage herself into prosperity, it is because the difficulty lies at her own doors, and she will not remove
it. At one time her deserted villages were attributed to the undue
patronage bestowed upon settlers on the public lands; at another, the tariff is the cause of her desolation. Slavery, the real
root of the evil, is carefully kept out of sight, as a "delicate subject" which must not be alluded to. It is a singular fact in the
present age of the world that delicate and indelicate subjects
mean precisely the same thing. . . .

We next come [after the history of slavery] to the influence of
this diabolical system on the *slave-owner;* and here I shall be
cautioned that I am treading on delicate ground, because our own
countrymen are slave-holders. But I am yet to learn that wicked-
ness is any the better for being our own.—Let the truth be spoken
—and let those abide its presence who can.

The following is the testimony of Jefferson, who had good opportunities for observation, and who certainly had no New England prejudices: "There must, doubtless, be an unhappy influence on the manners of the people, produced by the existence of
slavery among us. The whole commerce between master and
slave is a perpetual exercise of the most boisterous passions: the
most unremitting despotism on the one part, and degrading submission on the other. Our children see this, and learn to imitate
it; for man is an imitative animal. The parent storms; the child
looks on, catches the lineaments of wrath, puts on the same airs
in a circle of small slaves, gives loose rein to the worst of passions;
and thus nursed, educated, and daily exercised in tyranny, cannot
but be stamped by it with odious peculiarities. The man must be
a prodigy, who can retain his morals and manners undepraved in
such circumstances."

In a community where all the labor is done by one class, there
must of course be another class, who live in indolence; and we all
know how much people that have nothing to do are tempted by
what the world calls pleasures; the result is, that slave-holding
states and colonies are proverbial for dissipation. Hence too the
contempt for industry, which prevails in such a state of society.

Where none work but slaves, usefulness becomes degradation. The wife of a respectable mechanic, who accompanied her husband from Massachusetts to the South, gave great offence to her new neighbors by performing her small household avocations; they begged her to desist from it (offering the services of their own blacks), because the sight of a white person engaged in any labor was extremely injurious to the slaves; they deemed it very important that the negroes should be taught, both by precept and example, that they alone were made to work!

Whether the undue importance attached to merely external gentility, and the increasing tendency to indolence and extravagance throughout this country, ought to be attributed, in any degree, to the same source, I am unable to say; if *any* influence comes to us from the example and ridicule of the slave-holding States, it certainly must be of this nature.

There is another view of this system, which I cannot unveil so completely as it ought to be. I shall be called bold for saying so much; but the facts are so important, that it is a matter of conscience not to be fastidious.

The negro woman is unprotected either by law or public opinion. She is the property of her master, and her daughters are his property. They are allowed to have no conscientious scruples, no sense of shame, no regard for the feelings of husband, or parent; they must be entirely subservient to the will of their owner, on pain of being whipped as near unto death as will comport with his interest, or quite to death, if it suit his pleasure.

Those who know human nature would be able to conjecture the unavoidable result, even if it were not betrayed by the amount of mixed population. Think for a moment, what a degrading effect must be produced on the morals of both blacks and whites by customs like these!

Considering we live in the nineteenth century, it is indeed a strange state of society where the father sells his child, and the brother puts his sister up at auction! Yet these things are often practiced in our republic. . . .

I have more than once heard people, who had just returned from the South, speak of seeing a number of mulattoes in attendance where they visited, whose resemblance to the head of the family was too striking not to be immediately observed. What sort of feeling must be excited in the minds of those slaves by being constantly exposed to the tyranny or caprice of their own brothers and sisters, and by the knowledge that those near relations will, on a division of the estate, have power to sell them off with the cattle!

But the vices of white men eventually provide a scourge for themselves. They increase the negro race, but the negro can never increase theirs; and this is one great reason why the proportion of colored population is always so large in slave-holding countries. As the ratio increases more and more every year, the colored people must eventually be the stronger party; and when this result happens, slavery must either be abolished, or government must furnish troops, of whose wages the free States must pay their proportion. . . .

It is said that when the first pack of blood-hounds arrived in St. Domingo, the white planters delivered to them the first negro they found, merely by way of experiment; and when they saw him immediately torn to pieces, they were highly delighted to find the dogs so well trained to their business.

Some authentic records of female cruelty would seem perfectly incredible, were it not an established law of our nature that tyranny becomes a habit, and scenes of suffering, often repeated, render the heart callous. . . .

The ladies who remove from the free States into the slave-holding ones almost invariably write that the sight of slavery was at first exceedingly painful; but that they soon became habituated to it; and after a while, they are very apt to vindicate the system, upon the ground that it is extremely convenient to have such submissive servants. This reason was actually given by a lady of my acquaintance, who is considered an unusually fervent Christian. Yet Christianity expressly teaches us to love our neighbor as ourselves. This shows how dangerous it is, for even the best of us, to become *accustomed* to what is wrong. [She cites instances of cruelty.]

I shall be told that such examples as these are of rare occurrence; and I have no doubt that instances of excessive severity are far from being common. I believe that a large proportion of masters are as kind to their slaves as they can be, consistently with keeping them in bondage; but it must be allowed that this, to make the best of it, is very stinted kindness. And let it never be forgotten that the negro's fate depends entirely on the character of his master; and it is a mere matter of chance whether he fall into merciful or unmerciful hands; his happiness, nay, his very life, depends on chance.

The slave-owners are always telling us, that the accounts of slave misery are abominably exaggerated; and their plea is supported by many individuals, who seem to think that charity was made to *cover* sins, not to *cure* them. But without listening to the zealous opposers of slavery, we shall find in the judicial reports of the Southern States, and in the ordinary details of their newspapers, more than enough to startle us; besides, we must not forget that where one instance of cruelty comes to our knowledge, hundreds are kept secret; and the more public attention is awakened to the subject, the more caution will be used in this respect. . . .

But it is urged that it is the interest of planters to treat their slaves well. This argument no doubt has some force; and it is the poor negro's only security. But it is likewise the interest of men to treat their cattle kindly; yet we see that passion and shortsighted avarice do overcome the strongest motives of interest. Cattle are beaten unmercifully, sometimes unto death; they are ruined by being over-worked; weakened by want of sufficient food; and so forth. Besides, it is sometimes directly *for* the interest of the planter to work his slaves beyond their strength. When there is a sudden rise in the prices of sugar, a certain amount of labor in a given time is of more consequence to the owner of a plantation, than the price of several slaves; he can well *afford* to waste a few lives. This is no idle hypothesis—such calculations are gravely and openly made by planters. Hence, it is the slave's prayer that sugar may be cheap. When the negro is old, or feeble from incurable disease, is it his master's *interest* to feed him well, and clothe him comfortably? Certainly not: it then becomes desirable to get rid of the human brute as soon as convenient. It is a common remark, that it is not quite safe, in most cases, for even parents to be entirely dependent on the generosity of their children; and if human nature be such, what has the slave to expect, when he becomes a mere bill of expense? . . .

If we were educated at the South, we should no doubt vindicate slavery, and inherit as a birthright all the evils it engrafts upon the character. If they lived on our rocky soil, and under our inclement skies, their shrewdness would sometimes border upon knavery, and their frugality sometimes degenerate into parsimony. We both have our virtues, and our faults, induced by the influences under which we live, and, of course, totally different in their character. *Our* defects are bad enough; but they cannot, like slavery, affect the destiny and rights of millions.

All this mutual recrimination about horse-jockeys, gamblers, tin-peddlers, and venders of wooden nutmegs, is quite unworthy of a great nation. Instead of calmly examining this important subject on the plain grounds of justice and humanity, we allow it to degenerate into a mere question of *sectional* pride and vanity. (Pardon the Americanism, would we had less use for the word!) It is the *system*, not the *men*, on which we ought to bestow the full measure of abhorrence. If we were willing to forget ourselves, and could, like true republicans, prefer the common good to all other considerations, there would not be a slave in the United States, at the end of half a century.

The arguments in support of slavery are all hollow and deceptive, though frequently very specious. No one thinks of finding a foundation for the system in the principles of truth and justice; and the unavoidable result is, that even in *policy* it is unsound. The monstrous fabric rests on the mere *appearance* of present expediency; while, in fact, all its tendencies, individual and national, present and remote, are highly injurious to the true interests of the country. The slave-owner will not believe this. The stronger the evidence against his favorite theories, the more strenuously he defends them . . . all who ground their arguments in policy, and not in duty and plain truth, are really blind to the highest and best interests of man. . . .

The difficulty of subduing slavery, on account of the great number of interests which become united in it and the prodigious strength of the selfish passions enlisted in its support, is by no means its least alarming feature. This Hydra has ten thousand heads, every one of which will bite or growl, when the broad daylight of truth lays open the secrets of its hideous den.

I shall perhaps be asked why I have said so much about the slave *trade,* since it was long ago abolished in this country? There are several good reasons for it. In the first place, it is a part of the system; for if there were no slaves, there could be no slave trade; and while there are slaves, the slave trade *will* continue. . . . The breeding of negro cattle for the foreign markets (of Louisiana, Georgia, Alabama, Arkansas, and Missouri) is a very lucrative branch of business. Whole coffles of them, chained and manacled, are driven through our Capital on their way to auction. Foreigners, particularly those who come here with enthusiastic ideas of American freedom, are amazed and disgusted at the sight. A troop of slaves once passed through Washington on the fourth of July, while drums were beating, and standards flying. One of the captive negroes raised his hand, loaded with irons, and waving it toward the starry flag, sang with a smile of bitter irony, "Hail Columbia! *happy* land!". . . .

Washington is the great emporium of the internal slave trade! The United States jail is a perfect store-house for slave merchants; and some of the taverns may be seen so crowded with negro captives that they have scarcely room to stretch themselves on the floor to sleep. Judge Morrel, in his charge to the grand jury at Washington, in 1816, earnestly called their attention to this subject. He said the frequency with which the streets of the city had been crowded with manacled captives, sometimes even on the Sabbath, could not fail to shock the feelings of all humane persons; that it was repugnant to the spirit of our political institutions, and the rights of man; and he believed it was calculated to impair the public morals, by familiarizing scenes of cruelty in the minds of youth.

A free man of color is in constant danger of being seized and carried off by these slave-dealers. Mr. Cooper, a Representative in Congress from Delaware, told Dr. Torrey of Philadelphia that he was often afraid to send his servants out in the evening, lest they should be encountered by kidnappers. Wherever these notorious slave jockeys appear in our Southern States, the free people of color hide themselves, as they are obliged to do on the coast of Africa. . . .

It may indeed be said, in palliation of the internal slave trade, that the horrors of the *middle passage* are avoided. But still the amount of misery is very great. Husbands and wives, parents and children, are rudely torn from each other;—there can be no doubt of this fact: advertisements are very common, in which a mother and her children are offered either in a lot, or separately, as may suit the purchaser. In one of these advertisements, I observed it stated that the youngest child was about a year old.

The captives are driven by the whip, through toilsome journeys, under a burning sun; their limbs fettered; with nothing before them but the prospect of toil more severe than that to which they have been accustomed. . . .

Finally, I have described some of the horrors of the slave trade, because when our constitution was formed, the government pledged itself not to abolish this traffic until 1808. We began our career of freedom by granting a twenty years' lease of iniquity—twenty years of allowed invasion of other men's rights—twenty years of bloodshed, violence and fraud! And this will be told in our annals—this will be heard of to the end of time!

Every man who buys a slave promotes this traffic, by raising the value of the article; every man who owns a slave, indirectly countenances it; every man who allows that slavery is a lamentable *necessity,* contributes his share to support it; and he, who votes for admitting a slave-holding State into the Union, fearfully augments the amount of this crime.

Between ancient and modern slavery there is this remarkable distinction—the former originated in motives of humanity; the latter is dictated solely by avarice. The ancients made slaves of captives taken in war, as an amelioration of the original custom of indiscriminate slaughter; the moderns attack defenceless people, without any provocation, and steal them, for the express purpose of making them slaves.

Modern slavery, indeed, in all its particulars, is more odious than the ancient; and it is worthy of remark that the condition of slaves had always been worse just in proportion to the freedom enjoyed by their masters. . . .

Poetry was Julia Ward Howe's favorite medium of expression. Her "Battle Hymn of the Republic," as every American knows, whipped up the martial fury for marching men when that which was irrepressible finally broke its leash. We learn from her REMINISCENCES [2] what was going on in her mind before she composed so robust a pæan for soldiers.

Returning to Boston in 1851, I found the division of public sentiment more strongly marked than ever. The Fugitive Slave Law was much in the public mind. The anti-slavery people attacked it with might and main, while the class of wealthy conservatives and their followers strongly deprecated all opposition to its enactments. During my absence Charles Sumner had been elected to the Senate of the United States, in place of Daniel Webster, who had hitherto been the political idol of the Massachusetts aristocracy. Mr. Sumner's course had warmly commended him to a large and ever increasing constituency, but had brought down upon him the anger of Mr. Webster's political supporters. My husband's sympathies were entirely with the class

[2] Reprint obtained through the courtesy of Houghton Mifflin Company.

then derided as "a band of disturbers of the public peace, enemies of law and order." I deeply regretted the discords of the
time, and would have had all people good friends, however diverse in political persuasion. As this could not be, I felt constrained to cast in my lot with those who protested against the
new assumptions of the slave power. . . .

I did not then, or at any time, make any willful breach with
the society to which I was related. It did, however, much annoy
me to hear those spoken of with contempt and invective, who, I
was persuaded, were in advance of the conscience of the time. . . .

It was in the early years of this decade (1850–1860) that I
definitively came before the world as an author. My first volume
of poems, entitled "Passion Flowers," was published by Ticknor
and Fields without my name. . . .

The work, such as it was, dealt partly with the stirring questions of the time, partly with things near and familiar. The
events of 1848 were still in fresh remembrance; the heroic efforts
of Italian patriots to deliver their country from foreign oppression, the struggle of Hungary to maintain her ancient immuni-
ties. The most important among my "Passion Flowers" were
devoted to these themes. . . .

The publication of my Cuban notes brought me an invitation
to chronicle the events of the season at Newport for the *New
York Tribune*. This was the beginning of a correspondence
with that paper which lasted well into the time of the civil war.
My letters dealt somewhat with social doings in Newport and in
Boston, but more with the great events of the time. To me the
experience was valuable in that I found myself brought nearer in
sympathy to the general public, and helped to a better understanding of its needs and demands. . . .

The years between 1850 and 1857, eventful as they were, appear to me almost a period of play when compared with the time
of trial which was to follow. It might have been likened to the
tuning of instruments before some great musical solemnity. The
theme was already suggested, but of its wild and terrible development who could have had any foreknowledge?

CHAPTER V

DISSOLVING THE CULTURAL HERITAGE

THE extent of the slavery literature of the middle nineteenth century, if segregated from other writing, gives an exaggerated notion of the area of interest which it occupied. The abolitionists, it is true, were energetic in heaping fuel upon the fire of anti-slavery agitation, but in numbers they represented an inconsequential proportion of citizens and even they usually had other interests as well. Radical experiments were made by idealists along the lines of coöperative living, such as Brook Farm in Massachusetts and New Harmony in Indiana, inspired by Plato or Saint-Simon, by Fourier or Owen—undertakings in economic utopianism. On the utmost frontiers discussion took place over such issues as temperance, popular and equal education and the currents of criticism and philosophy borne to the American shores from the European upheavals in the forties. Throughout the debates on all these matters ran the speeches and writings of women. Nor was the ferment of opinion, as provincialism often assumes, confined to any section.

Northern writers had entry to Southern papers and magazines when they were not arguing the slavery question; for example, Mrs. Elizabeth Ellet, with a series of articles on European literature and thought. The very title of a book by a planter's daughter, Mary E. Bryan of Florida, "Hunger is Power," revealed vigor of mind. Lizzie Petit, of Virginia, when but nineteen years of age, so effectively depicted the follies and foibles of her environment that her first book, "Light and Darkness," was republished in London and translated into French. Southern women were also raising the issue of better institutional education for their sex.

Given the cultural heritage with which the American colonies began their careers and the rôle of the clergy as the élite in early American society, it was inevitable that religion should be the first focus of intellectual energies, apart from politics, until displaced by competing interests. Therefore endless discussions by laymen, the custom in Protestant circles, turned upon the ancient issues of theology—creation, sin, salvation, and the nature of the cosmos as conceived in religion. In the middle period, although the debate had widened, theological concepts still colored most notions of the social proprieties. But a swift dissolution had set in; and women, bending their minds to the sifting process, aided in the break-up of theological authority and the secularization of thought through skepticism and the diversion of attention to mundane interests.

North and South, East and West, the religious criticism was at work. New England was rapidly producing Unitarians. Philadelphia Quakers were considering the "superstitions" within their Quietest circles. On lonely plantations in the South, ladies were pondering on the heights and depths of spiritual meanings. From Fundamentalism of the purest dye to the pale hues of Transcendentalism ranged the concern with matters divine, as the conflict divided thinkers into religious sects and sent a few into the realm of free thought. At opposite poles in this division, for instance, stood Mary Lyon, missionary-minded and zealous in founding a school for the training of young envoys to the heathen, and Sarah Ripley, skeptical in faith and universalist in cultural interest.

At a time when "men of letters" were still rare in this country, a "woman of letters" undertook a task of large proportions— nothing short of a history of religions, highly appropriate as a theme when Church and State were being divorced.

Hannah Adams, the author, was born in 1755 at Medfield, Massachusetts, a small town about eighteen miles from Boston. Her father owned a little country store and among his merchandise offered books for sale. His private library was exceptionally large and his daughter browsed among the poetry and fiction on the shelves, with his encouragement, as she grew to maturity. The family was exceedingly poor and the father had not had the advantage of a collegiate education; but he respected learning and Hannah was permitted to study Latin, Greek, Geography and Logic with scholars who boarded in the house. Lacking institutional education and with every handicap to overcome, including Puritan religious dogmas, she steadily worked toward her literary goal and more than made up by conversations with intellectuals what she missed in classes at school. In 1831, at the age of seventy-six, she published a remarkably impartial history of religions and explains in her MEMOIR how she accomplished this feat.

Until I had attained the twentieth year of my age, my reading had chiefly consisted of works of imagination and feeling; such as novels and poetry. Even the religious works I perused were chiefly devotional poetry, and such works as Mrs. Rowe's Devout Exercises, and the lives of persons who were eminently distinguished for their piety. I was almost a stranger to controversial works, and had never examined the points in dispute between different denominations of Christians. But at length an incident in my life gave a different turn to my literary pursuits.

While I was engaged in learning Latin and Greek, one of the gentlemen who taught me had by him a small manuscript from Broughton's Dictionary, giving an account of Arminians, Calvinists, and several other denominations which were most common. This awakened my curiosity, and I assiduously engaged myself in perusing all the books which I could obtain, which gave an account of the various sentiments described. I soon became disgusted with the want of candor in the authors I consulted, in giving the most unfavorable descriptions of the denominations they disliked, and applying to them the names of heretics, fanatics, enthusiasts, &c. I therefore formed a plan for myself, made a blank book, and wrote rules for transcribing, and adding to, my compilation. But as I was stimulated to proceed only by curiosity, and never had an idea of deriving any profit from it, the compilation went on but slowly, though I was pressed by necessity to make every exertion in my power for my immediate support. During the American revolutionary war, I learned to weave bobbin lace, which was then salable, and much more profitable to me than spinning, sewing or knitting, which had previously been my employment. At this period I found but little time for literary pursuits. But at the termination of the American war, this resource failed, and I was again left in a destitute situation. My health did not admit of my teaching a school, and I was glad to avail myself of every opportunity of taking any kind of work which I could do, though the profit was very small, and inadequate to my support. One pleasing event occurred in this gloomy period. I had the satisfaction of teaching the rudiments of Latin and Greek to three young gentlemen, who resided in the vicinity. This was some advantage to me. Besides, it was a pleasant amusement. One of these young gentlemen was the Rev. Mr. Clark, of Norton, who pursued his studies with me till he entered Cambridge University. . . .

The difficulty of taking in such kinds of work as I could do, for I was not, like my sister, ingenious in all kinds of needle work, induced me, as the last resort, to attend to my manuscript, with the faint hope that it might be printed, and afford me some little advantage. . . .

I was sensible, that, in printing my manuscript, I had various obstacles to encounter. It was difficult to procure proper materials for the work in my sequestered abode. I felt that my ignorance of the world, and little acquaintance with business, would put me in the power of every printer to whom I might apply. I, however, resumed my compilation on an enlarged scale, which included a few of the reasons which the various denominations give in defence of their different religious systems. Stimulated by

an ardent curiosity, I entered into the vast field of religious controversy, for which my early reading had ill prepared me. I
perused all the controversial works I could possibly obtain with
the utmost attention, in order to abridge what appeared to me
the most plausible arguments for every denomination. As I read
controversy with a mind naturally wanting in firmness and decision, and without that pertinacity which blunts the force of
arguments which are opposed to the tenets we have once imbibed,
I suffered extremely from mental indecision, while perusing the
various and contradictory arguments, adduced by men of piety
and learning in defence of their respective religious systems.
Sometimes my mind was so strongly excited, that extreme feeling obliged me for a time to lay aside my employment. Notwithstanding it required much reading to perform my task, the
painful feelings I suffered while preparing my work for the
press far outweighed all the other labor. Reading much religious
controversy must be extremely trying to a female, whose mind,
instead of being strengthened by those studies which exercise
the judgment, and give stability to the character, is debilitated
by reading romances and novels, which are addressed to the
fancy and imagination, and are calculated to heighten the feelings.

After my View of Religions was prepared for the press, the
difficulty still remained of finding any printer willing and able
to print it without money immediately paid. But at length, after
various perplexities, this compilation was put to the press in
1784. The profit to myself was very small; for, as it might well
have been expected from my father's inexperience in the business of book making, he was completely duped by the printer,
in making the bargain. After being at the trouble of procuring
upwards of four hundred subscribers, all the compensation I
was able to obtain was only fifty books; and I was obliged to
find a sale for them, after the printer, (whose name, out of respect to his descendants, I omit to mention), had received all
the subscription money. As my books sold very well, the printer
must have made something handsome by the publication.

The effect of reading so much religious controversy, which had been very trying to my mind, was extremely prejudicial to my health, and introduced a train of the most painful nervous complaints. I was at length brought so low, that the physician who attended me supposed I was in a decline. But after a tedious interval of extreme suffering, I began gradually to recover; and afterwards found my complaints were increased, by following the injudicious advice of the physician who attended me. To the skill and attention of my friend Dr. Mann, formerly of Wrentham, I owe, under Heaven, the preservation of my life at this period.

Soon after I began to recover, I received a letter from the printer of my View of Religions, informing me that he had sold the greatest part of the edition, and was about to reprint it; and requesting me to inform him if I wished to make any additions to my work. As I had the precaution to secure the copy-right, agreeably to the law passed in Massachusetts, 1783, I returned a laconic answer, forbidding him to reprint it; and he finally relinquished the design.

The information, that the first edition of my View of Religions was sold, gave me the idea of reprinting it for my own benefit. But as I was entirely destitute of pecuniary resources, ignorant of the world, incapable of conducting business, and precluded from almost all intercourse with persons of literature and information, and consequently destitute of friends who were able and willing to assist me, the execution of the plan was extremely difficult. Even the few friends I had gained at that time supposed the disadvantages in my situation too great to encourage my undertaking. Instead of assisting me, they considered my plan as chimerical, and depressed my hopes and discouraged my exertions. . . .

But notwithstanding all the difficulties in my situation, I determined to use every possible exertion to help myself; considering that, if I was unsuccessful in attempting to extricate myself from poverty, my efforts would awaken the activity of my mind, and preserve me from sinking under the weight of affliction I sustained in losing the best of sisters. It was, perhaps, a happy circumstance, that necessity stimulated me to exertion in this most gloomy period of my existence.

After I began to prepare the additions to my View of Religions, I found it required a great effort to detach my mind from the recollection of past sufferings, and force myself to that mental exertion which is naturally so congenial to my mind. At length, however, I completed the task of preparing my work for the press. I had previously, in 1790, sent a petition to Congress, which was presented by the late Fisher Ames, Esq., for a general law to be passed, to secure to authors the copy-right of their publications. I now applied to a large number of printers to know on what terms they would publish my work. . . .

I at length concluded to accept the terms of one of the printers to whom I applied, who offered me one hundred dollars in books, for an edition of one thousand copies. When I went to Boston for this purpose, a friend of mine introduced me to the Rev. Mr. Freeman, whom I had only once before seen· but I was well apprised of his benevolent character, which I found more than realized the ideas which I had formed of it from report. I shall ever recollect the generous interest he took in my affairs, with the most lively gratitude. He removed my perplexity, by transacting the business with the printer. By his advice, a subscription paper was published; and I soon found the benefit of his patronage, in procuring a large number of subscribers, and concluding an advantageous bargain for me with Mr. Folsom, the printer. The second edition was published in 1791; and the emolument I derived from it not only placed me in a comfortable situation, but enabled me to pay the debts I had contracted during mine and my sister's illness, and to put out a small sum upon interest. . . .

Encouraged and animated by this success, I soon formed the design of engaging in another publication, and set myself to choose a subject. It was poverty, not ambition, or vanity, that first induced me to become an author, or rather a compiler. But I now formed the flattering idea, that I might not only help myself, but benefit the public. With this view, I engaged in writing a Summary History of New England. . . .

When I compiled this work, there was not any history of New England extant, except Mather's Magnalia, and Neale's History; and these extended only to an early period in the annals of our country. If there had been only one work, which reached to the acceptance of the Federal constitution, my task had been far less laborious. There was no authentic account of Rhode Island, except that of Callender's. This induced me to spend some time in Providence, in order to examine the Records in the Secretary's office. The perusal of old manuscripts, which were damaged by time, was painful to my eyes. . . .

When I first consulted the doctor, he had not any expectation that my eyes would recover so as to enable me to make the use of them I have since done. But by applying laudanum and sea water several times in the course of the day, for two years, I recovered so far as to resume my studies and by employing an amanuensis to assist me in transcribing my manuscript, I was enabled to print the work in 1799. . . . As my eyes were still weak, I could not bestow the same attention in condensing the last part of my History, as the first; and consequently the History of the American Revolution was much more prolix than I originally intended. In giving an account of the war, my ignorance of military terms rendered it necessary to transcribe more from Dr. Ramsay's History, than I had done in any other part of the work. I therefore wrote an apology to the doctor. . . . I was obliged to publish the work almost entirely at my own expense. The printers were in low circumstances, and required payment before I could dispose of the books. I was therefore obliged to borrow a sum of money to defray the expenses of the work, which, as it was printed on very good paper, were large, and I derived but little profit from my labor.

My next publication was the third edition of my View of Religions, to which I made the addition of a hundred pages. The Rev. Mr. Freeman, who continued his kind attentions, made the bargain for me with the printer, by which I was entitled to receive five hundred dollars in yearly payments, for an edition of two thousand copies. This relieved me from the embarrassments in which I was involved by printing my History of New England at my own expense. As my eyes still continued too weak to engage in any new laborious work, I determined to wait till a large part of my History of New England was sold; and then, if my life continued, to abridge it for the use of schools.

In the meantime, however, I set about writing a concise View of the Christian Religion, selected from the writings of eminent laymen. . . . I found it difficult to procure proper materials for the work, as I was utterly unable to purchase books. A considerable part of this compilation, as well as the additions to the third edition of my View of Religions, was written in booksellers' shops. . . . At length, in 1804, I agreed with a printer to execute the work, upon the small consideration of receiving only one hundred dollars in books. . . .

I formed the design of writing the History of the Jews, though I was sensible it would require much reading, and that I must wander through a dreary wilderness, unenlivened by one spot of verdure. My curiosity was strongly excited, and I determined to persevere in my attempt to investigate the fate of this wonderful people. I began the introduction with their state under the Persian monarchy, after their restoration from the Babylonian captivity. The standard works for this History were Josephus, and Basnage, the latter of whom brings his narrative down only to the 19th century. After this period, I was obliged to compile from desultory publications and manuscripts. I had at this time the privilege of corresponding with the celebrated Gregoire, who had attained great celebrity for the conspicuous part he acted during the French Revolution, and exerted all his energy in the first constitutional assembly to procure the rights of citizens for the Jews. He had the goodness to send me some writings in their favor. . . .

Mr. Buckminster was so kind as to give me the use of his large and valuable library, which was of great advantage to me in compiling my History of the Jews. . . .

In the decline of life, I was so far debilitated by repeated fevers . . . that I was unable to write for the press. At length, I so far recovered, as to resume a work which I had formerly begun, upon the New Testament, which I designed to be much larger than it is; but my advanced age induced me only to publish a little book, entitled "Letters on the Gospels," which has passed through two editions.

I have already mentioned the perplexity and embarrassment of my mind, while writing my View of Religions. After removing to Boston, and residing in that city while the disputes upon Unitarian sentiments were warmly agitated, I read all that came in my way upon both sides of the question; and carefully examined the New Testament, with, I think, a sincere and ardent desire to know the truth. I deeply felt the difficulties upon both sides of the question; yet prevailingly give the preference to that class of Unitarians, who adopt the highest idea of the greatness and dignity of the Son of God. I never arrived to that degree of decision that some have attained on that subject. In this, and every other disputable subject, I would adopt the following:

> If I am right, thy grace impart
> Still in the right to stay;
> If I am wrong, O teach my heart,
> To find the better way.

An unquestioned leader in the dissolving process was Lucretia Mott, a Philadelphia Quaker, who helped to establish the right to free expression of opinion even while she enlarged her mind. Her work was done from the public platform, in the meeting-house and by correspondence rather than in the form of books, and hence her power is apt to be forgotten by those who think only of immortal treatises. But Elizabeth Cady Stanton, herself a forceful critic of Church and State, acknowledged Lucretia Mott as her Master, as the following eulogy[1] shows—words spoken at a memorial service in 1881.

[1] History of Woman Suffrage, Vol. I, p. 407 ff.

Mrs. Mott was to me an entirely new revelation of womanhood. I sought every opportunity to be at her side, and continually plied her with questions, and I shall never cease to be grateful for the patience and seeming pleasure, with which she fed my hungering soul. On one occasion, with a large party, we visited the British Museum, where it is supposed all people go to see the wonders of the world. On entering, Mrs. Mott and myself sat down near the door to rest for a few moments, telling the party to go on, that we would follow. They accordingly explored all the departments of curiosities, supposing we were slowly following at a distance; but when they returned, there we sat in the same spot, having seen nothing but each other, wholly absorbed in questions of theology and social life. She had told me of the doctrines and divisions among "Friends"; of the inward light; of Mary Wollstonecraft, her social theories, and her demands of equality for women. I had been reading Combe's "Constitution of Man," and "Moral Philosophy," Channing's works, and Mary Wollstonecraft, though all tabooed by orthodox teachers; but I had never heard a woman talk what, as a Scotch Presbyterian, I had scarcely dared to think.

On the following Sunday I went to hear Mrs. Mott preach in a Unitarian church. Though I had never heard a woman speak, yet I had long believed she had the right to do so, and had often expressed the idea in private circles; but when at last I saw a woman rise up in the pulpit and preach earnestly and impressively, as Mrs. Mott always did, it seemed to me like the realization of an oft-repeated, happy dream. The day we visited the Zoölogical Gardens, as we were admiring the gorgeous plumage of some beautiful birds, one of our gentlemen opponents remarked, "You see, Mrs. Mott, our Heavenly Father believes in bright colors. How much it would take from our pleasure, if all the birds were dressed in drab." "Yes," said she, "but immortal beings do not depend on their feathers for their attraction. With the infinite variety of the human face and form, of thought, feeling, and affection, we do not need gorgeous apparel to distinguish us. Moreover, if it is fitting that woman should dress in every color of the rainbow, why not man also? Clergymen, with their black clothes and white cravats, are quite as monotonous as Quakers.". . .

I found in this new friend a woman emancipated from all faith in man-made creeds, from all fear of his denunciations. Nothing was too sacred for her to question, as to its rightfulness in principle and practice. "Truth for authority, not authority for truth," was not only the motto of her life, but it was the fixed mental habit in which she most rigidly held herself. . . . When I confessed to her my great enjoyment in works of fiction, dramatic performances, and dancing, and feared that from underneath that Quaker bonnet would come some platitudes on the demoralizing influence of such frivolities, she smiled, and said, "I regard dancing a very harmless amusement"; and added, "The Evangelical Alliance, that so readily passed a resolution declaring dancing a sin for a church member, tabled a resolution declaring slavery a sin for a bishop."

Sitting alone one day, as we were about to separate in London, I expressed to her my great satisfaction in our acquaintance, and thanked her for the many religious doubts and fears she had banished from my mind. She said, "There is a broad distinction between religion and theology. The one is a natural, human experience, common to all well-organized minds. The other is a system of speculations about the unseen, and unknowable, which the human mind has no power to grasp, or explain; and these speculations vary with every sect, age, and type of civilization. No one knows any more of what lies beyond our sphere of action, than you and I; and we know nothing."

In her own correspondence, printed in the LIFE AND LETTERS OF JAMES AND LUCRETIA MOTT, the spirit of Mrs. Mott's thought and the conclusions to which she was led by inquiry and meditation are simply stated.

We are now engaged in reading Southey's "Life of Wesley, with the Rise and Progress of Methodism." An interesting work, though some parts we thought might have been omitted, such as the supernatural appearances. The author appears as much attached to the doctrines of the Episcopal Church, as some of us Quakers are to ours. I was pleased with the rule laid down for Wesley, by his mother, to enable him to judge of the lawfulness or unlawfulness of pleasure, which is as follows: "Whatever weakens your reason, impairs the tenderness of your conscience, obscures your sense of God, or takes off the relish of spiritual things; in short, whatever increases the strength and authority of your body over your mind, that thing is sin to you, however innocent it may be in itself." . . .

Cannot you enlightened ones set us a good example by making some improvement in the Discipline relative to out-goings in marriage? . . .

It is with heartfelt regret that we learn the state of things at Jericho M^g, as well as in many others. If we c^d only do as our beloved grand^{fr} advised, "leave the present unprofitable discussion, and endeavor to go on unto perfection," how much better w^d it be for us all. The apostle has truly forewarned us, "But if ye bite and devour one another, take heed that ye be not consumed one of another": for have we not found this to be the case, that the stronger are consuming the weaker, in the several M^{gs} where these party feelings exist. I know it is a serious thing to set up individual judgment against that of a Mo. M^g; but when we see those of unblemished lives repeatedly arraigned before their tribunal, and remember the test which the Blessed Master laid down, "By their fruits shall ye know them," it is difficult always to refrain, though we still endeavor to do so. . . .

I regret that we cannot procure for thee all that Stuart has written opposed to Channing, because justice requires that we should acquaint ourselves with both sides, before we judge. What is furnished may satisfy thy mind, as far as controversial writings can do this: but permit me to question whether thy

present wants will be met by the perusal of works of this character. Rather consult the volume of thy own experience, and as
thou acknowledges thy views slowly brightening, be patient, and
rest in full faith for the rising of the sun, when, as thou art able
to bear it, all mists and clouds will be dispelled. In the meantime,
while reading and studying the Scriptures, let the *general tenor*
of these invaluable writings govern thy conclusions, making
all due allowance for the time and circumstances in which they
were written; but do not puzzle and perplex thy mind with in-
ferences from isolated passages here and there, which are contrary to the spirit of the whole, and do violence to the noble gift
of reason, divinely bestowed upon us . . . while thou holds fast
to that excellent sentiment that no text of Scripture however
plain can shake thy belief in a truth which thou perceives by
intuition, or make thee believe a thing which is contrary to thy
innate sense of right and wrong, it will lead thee to frequent
introversion, and thou wilt know "of whom thou learnest these
things," and wilt not have need that any man should teach
thee. . . .

Worcester's "Causes of Contentions among Christians" I have
in vain looked for, to send thee. Mine was returned a few days
since. I enclose it for thy perusal; to be returned when thou hast
done with it. John Woolman's "Journal," will, as we told thee,
bear an attentive perusal; and although thou may see some
parts strongly marked with Quaker superstitions and technicalities, yet lay it not aside on that account. Thou art capable
of judging of the spirit of the writer; let that, with his sound
reasoning, commend it to thy notice. I defend not the visionary
part. . . .

I do not wonder at thy doubts of the propriety of occupying
thy "station as minister" in preaching any system of Faith, and
care not how soon thy Orthodox brethren detect thy heresies;
although I shall be careful how I expose thee, well as I know
that thy religious or *theological* opinions have been for some years
past undergoing a change. I want thee to have done with calling
Unitarian rationalities, "icy philosophizing." The step thou art

taking is a serious one, and thy conclusions are of great importance. . . .

About the year 1825, feeling called to the gospel of Christ, and
submitting to this call, and feeling all the peace attendant on
submission, I strove to live in obedience to manifest duty. Going one day to our meeting, in a disposition to do that to which
I might feel myself called, most unexpectedly to myself the duty
was impressed upon my mind to abstain from the products of
slave labor, knowing that Elias Hicks long, long before had done
this. I knew that in the boarding-school, where I had received
such education as was then customary, we had had the middle
passage of the slave-ship represented to us, and the appeals from
Clarkson's works for the abolition of the slave trade were familiar
to all the children in the school. I knew that some of our committee were not free to partake of the sweets obtained from this
unrighteous channel, so I was somewhat prepared for this duty,
and yet it was unexpected. It was like parting with the right
hand, or the right eye, but when I left the meeting I yielded to
the obligation, and then, for nearly forty years, whatever I did
was under the conviction, that it was wrong to partake of the
products of slave labor. . . .

Although we [four women at a church conclave] were not recognized as a part of the convention by signing the document, yet
every courtesy was shown to us, every encouragement given to
speak, or to make suggestions of alteration. I do not think it occurred to any one of us at that time, that there would be a
propriety in our signing the document. It was with difficulty,
I acknowledge, that I ventured to express what had been near to
my heart for many years, for I knew we were there by suf-
ferance; but when I rose, such was the readiness with which the
freedom to speak was granted, that it inspired me with a little
more boldness to speak on other subjects. When the declaration
was under consideration, and we were considering our principles
and our intended measures of action, when our friends felt that
they were planting themselves on the truths of Divine Revelation, and on the Declaration of Independence, as an Everlasting

Rock, it seemed to me, as I heard it read, that the climax would be better to transpose the sentence and place the Declaration of Independence first, and the truths of Divine Revelation last, as the Everlasting Rock; and I proposed it. I remember one of the younger members turning to see what woman there was who knew what the word "transpose" meant. . . .

Among the path-breakers of the new way was Lucy Stone, who declared that "if women could secure education and the right to speak, they could win everything else for themselves." Amid trials and tribulations she won that coveted instrument and then proceeded to use it for the extension of privileges to her sex. From Oberlin College she wrote letters to her mother which indicate the passion that drove her forward. Her daughter, Alice Stone Blackwell, in LUCY STONE, PIONEER OF WOMAN'S RIGHTS [2] gives the setting for the movement, led by this young person and a few friends, which finally broke down the legal barriers to privilege.

"I know, Mother, you feel badly about the plan I have proposed to myself, and that you would prefer to have me take some other course, if I could in conscience. Yet, Mother, I know you too well to suppose that you would wish me to turn away from what I think is my duty, and go all my days in opposition to my convictions of right, lashed by a reproaching conscience.

"I surely would not be a public speaker if I sought a life of ease, for it will be a most laborious one; nor would I do it for the sake of honor, for I know that I shall be disesteemed, nay, even hated, by some who are now my friends, or who profess to be. Neither would I do it if I sought wealth, because I could secure it with far more ease and worldly honor by being a teacher. But, Mother, the gold that perishes in the using, the honor that comes from men, the ease or indolence which eats out the energy of the

[2] Reprint obtained through the courtesy of Little, Brown, and Company.

soul, are not the objects at which I aim. If I would be true to myself, true to my Heavenly Father, I must be actuated by high and holy principles, and pursue that course of conduct which, to me, appears best calculated to promote the highest good of the world. Because I know that I shall suffer, shall I, for this, like Lot's wife, turn back? . . . If, while I hear the wild shriek of the slave mother robbed of her little ones, or the muffled groan of the daughter spoiled of her virtue, I do not open my mouth for the dumb, am I not guilty? Or should I go, as you said, from house to house to do it, when I could tell so many more in less time, if they should be gathered in one place? You would not object, or think it wrong, for a man to plead the cause of the suffering and the outcast; and surely the moral character of the act is not changed because it is done by a woman. . . .

"I expect to plead not for the slave only, but for suffering humanity everywhere. *Especially do I mean to labor for the elevation of my sex.* . . . I will not speak further upon this subject at this time, only to ask that you will not withhold your consent from my doing anything that I think is my duty to do. You will not, will you, Mother? . . .

"We are trying to get the faculty to let the ladies of our class read their own pieces when they graduate. They have never been allowed to do it, but we expect to read for ourselves, or not to write. . . .

"I must write you about my affairs here, and then I want you to tell me honestly just whether you think I have done right. This coming Commencement, you know, I graduate, and several members of the class are appointed to speak and write for that occasion. The class appoints its own speakers and writers, after the faculty have decided how many shall be appointed. This year they decided that half the class, that is, half the ladies and half the gentlemen, should take part in the Commencement exercises.

"It has been the custom for the ladies who were appointed to write for the Commencement to have their essays read by Professor Thome. Some of them thought ladies ought to have the

privilege of reading for themselves. Accordingly, I prepared a
petition to the faculty, and to the Ladies' Board, asking that we
might do so; but the petition was rejected, on the ground that
it was improper for women to participate in public exercises with
men. I came at once to the conclusion that I would not write.

"The day for the appointment came. President Mahan and Mr.
Whipple, principal of the Preparatory Department, met with the
class to count votes. I received an appointment by a very large
vote. I said to President Mahan that I could not accept without
a violation of principle that I had no right to make, and I wished
to be excused. Several members of the class spoke at once; said
they hoped I would not then resign, but would take time to consider. I told them that I had already considered, and that it was
not at all probable that an after consideration would change my
mind. President Mahan said he thought that we ought to have
the privilege of reading for ourselves; that he did all he could
to get the consent of the faculty, but they were all against him.
He thought I had better wait a little before I refused the appointment. . . . He said it must be referred to the faculty whether
I should be excused. Mr. Whipple came home with me, and
urged all the reasons he could think of to persuade me to write
and let Professor Thome read for me. I told him that by so doing I would make a public acknowledgement of the rectitude
of the principle which takes away from women their equal
rights, and denies to them the privilege of being co-laborers with
men in any sphere to which their ability makes them adequate;
and that no word or deed of mine should ever look toward the
support of such a principle, or even to its toleration. Miss Adams
and some members of the class, who were particularly anxious
that I should read, called on President Mahan and asked him to
request the faculty that it might be granted to me as a special
privilege, in view of my conscientious scruples. He said that he
had just been speaking of the same thing to Mrs. Mahan; that
he was very, very desirous that Miss Stone should read; that he
thought she ought to; that she understood herself, and would
represent the class well; that there had never been a student here

who had gone through a course of study with whom he was better satisfied, etc., etc., etc. . . . .

"The matter has been before the faculty and the Ladies' Board more than two weeks. I don't know what they will decide, but I certainly shall not write if I cannot read for myself. . . . I never was in a place where women are so rigidly taught that they must not speak in public. . . .

"I have been accustomed for the last year to meet with four other ladies, sometimes at the house of an old colored woman, and sometimes in the woods, and practice declamation and discussion; but I need more general practice before I can do justice to myself or the cause as a public speaker. . . .

"I am glad that you all approved of the course I took relative to writing for Commencement. I felt that I had done right, but it gave a kind of wholeness to the feeling to know that you agreed with me. . . ."

[Referring to this incident, Miss Blackwell writes:] Many of the students evidently sympathized with Lucy's point of view, for "all the ladies (quoting Lucy), except one, who were appointed to write essays resigned, as did two of the gentlemen. Others were appointed to fill their places, and these too refused to accept the conditions."

It illustrates the curious vagaries of anti-woman prejudice that Antoinette [Brown, the first woman minister in the United States], who had also been chosen to write an essay for Commencement, was allowed to read it, without the least objection. The reason was that she had been taking the "Ladies' Literary Course," instead of the regular classical course. The students of the two courses recited together in many subjects, and had their graduating exercises on successive days, in the same auditorium, and before practically the same audience. But when the graduates of the Ladies' Literary Course took their diplomas, the persons on the platform were all women, except the president; and when the students of the regular classical course received their degrees, the persons on the platform were almost all men. . . .

When Oberlin celebrated its semicentennial, thirty-six years later, Lucy was invited to be one of the speakers at that great gathering—the only woman on the program. . . .

The Whole World's Temperance Convention (1853) passed off peacefully and triumphantly. At the Half World's Convention, Antoinette L. Brown unexpectedly became a storm center.

Her troubles at Oberlin had begun when Lucy's ended, with their graduation from the collegiate department. There was consternation among the authorities when it was learned that she meant to enter the theological school. Faculty meeting after faculty meeting was held on the subject; but the founders of Oberlin had put it into the charter that all its opportunities were to be open to women. Finally Professor Morgan said, "Antoinette, I think you are all wrong. If I could keep you out, I would; but, since I cannot, I will do my very best to teach you." Her father and brother ceased to send the money they had been contributing toward her expenses, not wishing to aid what they considered so wild a project as her plan to enter the ministry. She had been teaching drawing in the preparatory department and had expected to continue to do so; but the Ladies' Board made a special rule to bar her out. Then Miss Atkins, the Assistant Lady Principal, got up a drawing class for her, of which Professor (afterwards President) Fairchild and several of the theological students were members, besides many younger pupils; and she thus paid her expenses with ease.

She had one colleague, Lettice Smith, who wished to study theology, but was not intending to preach. They were allowed to study with the rest, but had no part in the Commencement exercises, except as listeners, and for many years their names did not appear in the Alumni Catalogue as graduates of the theological class of 1850. Long afterwards, Oberlin became very proud of them, restored their names to the list of graduates, and gave Antoinette the degree of D.D.

She could have been ordained at Oberlin when she left the theological school. Father Shepherd and several other ministers were willing to take part in the ceremony. But it would have embarrassed the university authorities, most of whom were opposed to women's preaching. Also, she preferred to wait till she could be ordained in her own denomination. For several years she lectured with success, and preached as she had opportunity. Horace Greeley and Charles A. Dana of the *New York Sun* were so impressed by her ability that they invited her to preach regularly in New York City, promising to provide a hall and pay her board, and to give her one thousand dollars a year—in those days a large salary for a woman. But she thought herself too inexperienced for a metropolitan pulpit, and accepted instead a call to the struggling little Congregational Church of South Butler, New York, at a salary of three hundred dollars a year. She was about to be ordained at the time when the Whole World's and Half World's Temperance Conventions were held. . . .

She had credentials to the Half World's Temperance Convention, both from the church at South Butler and from a temperance society.

Leaders of the anti-woman party, wishing to discourage the holding of the Whole World's Convention, had declared that it was needless, as they were going to allow women to take part. At the suggestion of Wendell Phillips, Antoinette decided to test this. . . .

Antoinette Brown was ordained a few days later. The affair made a great commotion. Press and pulpit thundered denunciations. Doctor Cheever declared that any woman who would seek ordination was an infidel, and any church that would ordain her was an infidel church. But Harriet Beecher Stowe wrote: "If it is right for Jenny Lind to sing to two thousand people, 'I know that my Redeemer liveth,' why is it wrong for Antoinette L. Brown to say the same thing?"

She wanted Lucy to come and address her congregation. Lucy refused, for fear her heterodoxy and her Bloomers (the women's "freedom dress") might make trouble for her friend. Antoinette replied:

"You are the greatest little goose and granny-fuss that I ever did see! What nonsense to think of your injuring in any way

my success as a minister by lecturing to them! They are all expecting you, and they know besides that you wear Bloomers and
are an 'infidel.' Any congregation I may preach to will not be
scared overmuch by anything you will say. They believe in
free speech. Everybody knows you and your reputation as well,
almost, now as they will after seeing you, for your fame is abroad
in the land. They think you, of course, worse than you are."

Later Antoinette passed through a period of religious doubt
which led her to resign her pastorate. For a time she did social
work with Mrs. Abby Hopper Gibbons in the prisons and slums
of New York. . . . She emerged from her period of religious
doubt a Unitarian, and continued to preach as often as opportunity offered and many family cares permitted. She had six
children, wrote nine books, and lived to be ninety-six years old.
When she died, the census showed that there were more than
three thousand women ministers and preachers in the United
States. . . .

Long before Lucy's time, an occasional voice had been lifted
in America in behalf of larger rights for women—by Margaret
Brent of Maryland in 1647, by Abigail Adams of Massachusetts
in 1776, and by the sister of Richard Henry Lee of Virginia in
1778. Frances Wright of Scotland, who lectured in this country,
the Grimké sisters, Mrs. Ernestine L. Rose, a beautiful Polish
Jewish who settled in the United States, and Margaret Fuller,
had all spoken for woman's rights. But they had pleaded this
cause only incidentally to other subjects, which were their chief
themes. Lucy Stone was the first and for years the only woman
who made it her main topic, and went up and down the country lecturing upon it. It is for this that she has been called "the
morning star of the woman's rights movement." In those early
years, it was she who stood to the public as the representative of
that cause, and bore the chief brunt of the obloquy connected
with it. Elizabeth Cady Stanton said, "Lucy Stone was the first
person by whom the heart of the American public was deeply
stirred on the woman question."

CHAPTER VI

THE GREAT SOCIAL WAR

IT has sometimes been lightly assumed that the conflicts leading to war and war itself are the products of purely masculine will and purpose. Herbert Spencer, among others, has given currency to this opinion. But when the acts of war are placed in their environment and movement, the validity of the theory vanishes. At all events, modern wars—civil and international— are not just marauding expeditions of militant males. They spring from deep-rooted social and economic antagonisms, from clashes of cultures shaped in large measure by the habits and desires of women. As we have already seen, American women, Northern and Southern, took part in the formulation of attack and defense mechanisms which sharpened the antithesis that culminated in one of the world's harshest social wars. Their philosophy of family life, of proper social arrangements, of the instant need of things, and their activities, both economic and intellectual, entered into the concentration of energies preparing the way for the ultimate arbitration by arms.

For the sustenance upon which the fighting depended, for the martial spirit which inflamed the soldiers, women considered themselves responsible in high degree at the time. And after the close of the armed struggle, they meditated upon its nature and significance. Thus they were involved in overt acts and crusading, in the actualities of war, in the determination of objectives to be gained, in the reconstruction which followed, in the consideration of policy, in the new labor economy, in the rise of former slaves to position in the new order, and in the adjustment of interracial relations.

In her "Diary from Dixie," Mary B. Chesnut, whose husband had just left the Senate to cast in his lot with secession, set down at Charleston, South Carolina, on December 10, 1860, this honest entry: "As a woman, of course, it is easy for me to be brave under the skins of other people; so I said, 'Fight it out. Bluffton has brought on a fever that only bloodletting will cure.'" In her journal, "The Last Ninety Days of the War," published in 1866, Mrs. Cornelia P. Spencer, who felt from the beginning that North Carolina had been betrayed into secession, recounted her participation in the fierce struggle for Southern independence when it reached the point of arms. In numerous war journals, other Southern women described their action in the midst of realities. And at the close of the conflict, explanations and justifications came from the pens of women: for example, Varina Howell Davis' memoir of her husband, Jefferson Davis, President of the Confederacy.

"God's Angry Man" committed an act which helped to plunge the Nation into war. Julia Ward Howe, who composed its greatest Battle Hymn, recorded in her REMINISCENCES [1] the attitude of New England toward that deed and her own judgment in the case at the time.

It may have been a year or more later that Dr. Howe said to me: "So you remember that man of whom I spoke to you—the one who wished to be a savior for the negro race?" I replied in the affirmative. "That man," said the doctor, "will call here this afternoon. You will receive him. His name is John Brown." Thus admonished, I watched for the visitor, and prepared to admit him myself when he should ring at the door.

This took place at our house in South Boston, where it was

[1] Reprint obtained through the courtesy of Houghton Mifflin Company.

not at all infra dig, for me to open my own door. At the expected
time I heard the bell ring, and, on answering it, beheld a middle-
aged, middle-sized man, with hair and beard of amber color,
streaked with gray. He looked a Puritan of the Puritans, forceful,
concentrated, and self-contained. We had a brief interview, of
which I only remember my great gratification at meeting one of
whom I had heard so good an account. I saw him once again at
Dr. Howe's office, and then heard no more of him for some time.

I cannot tell how long after this it was that I took up the
Transcript one evening, and read of an attack made by a small
body of men on the arsenal at Harper's Ferry. Dr. Howe presently came in, and I told him what I had just heard. "Brown has
got to work," he said. I had already arrived at the same conclusion. The rest of the story is a matter of history: the failure of the
slaves to support the movement initiated for their emancipation,
the brief contest, the inevitable defeat and surrender, the death
of the rash, brave men upon the scaffold. All this is known, and
need not be repeated here. In speaking of it, my husband assured
me that John Brown's plan had not been so impossible of realization as it appeared to have been after its failure. Brown had been
led to hope that, upon a certain signal, the slaves from many
plantations would come to him in such numbers that he and
they would become masters of the situation with little or no
bloodshed. Neither he nor those who were concerned with him
had it at all in mind to stir up the slaves to acts of cruelty and
revenge. The plan was simply to combine them in large numbers, and in a position so strong that the question of their freedom
would be decided then and there, possibly without even a battle.

I confess that the whole scheme appeared to me wild and
chimerical. . . . None of us could exactly approve an act so
revolutionary in its character, yet the great-hearted attempt
enlisted our sympathies very strongly. The weeks of John
Brown's imprisonment were very sad ones, and the day of
his death was one of general mourning in New England. Even
there, however, people were not all of the same mind. I heard
a friend say that John Brown was a pig-headed old fool. In the

Church of the Disciples, on the other hand, a special service was held on the day of the execution, and the pastor took for his text the saying of Christ, "It is enough for the disciple that he be as his master." Victor Hugo had already said that the death of John Brown would thenceforth hallow the scaffold, even as the death of Christ had hallowed the cross.

The record of John Brown's life has been fully written, and by a friendly hand. I will only mention here that he had much to do with the successful contest which kept slavery out of the territory of Kansas. He was a leading chief in the border warfare which swept back the pro-slavery immigration attempted by some of the wild spirits of Missouri. In this struggle, he one day saw two of his own sons shot by the Border Ruffians (as the Missourians of the border were then called), without trial or mercy. Some people thought that this dreadful sight had maddened his brain, as well it might.

The nation had not only an angry man but also an extremely angry young woman, Anna Dickinson by name and called the "American Joan of Arc" by her satellites. She was not clad in armor and she wore no sword. Yet she felt a similar call from God to serve as avenging angel, having the emancipation of slaves in view; and if the spirit of Northern soldiers seemed at any time to flag, she was soon in their camps pleading for action with the assurance of one who had taken upon herself the burden of her Nation. She did not hesitate to criticize the strategy of Generals in Blue and her political leadership was as vigorous as her military fervor. She was only a girl in her twenties when she was invited to address the Congress of the United States on the subject of slavery. Her story appears in the HISTORY OF WOMAN SUFFRAGE—the cause she espoused at the end of the war.

Foremost among the women who understood the political significance of the great conflict, was Miss Dickinson, a young girl of Quaker ancestry, who possessed remarkable oratorical power, a keen sense of justice, and an intense earnestness of purpose. In the heated discussions of the Anti-Slavery Conventions, she had acquired a clear comprehension of the province of laws and constitutions; of the fundamental principles of governments, and the rights of man. Like a meteor, she appeared suddenly in the political horizon, as if born for the eventful times in which she lived, and inspired by the dangers that threatened the life of the republic.

At the very beginning of the war her radical utterances were heard at different points in her native State. Her admirable speech on the higher law, first made at Kennett Square, and the discussion that followed, in which Miss Dickinson maintained her position with remarkable clearness and coolness for one of her years, were a surprise to all who listened. The flattering reports of this meeting in several of the Philadelphia journals introduced her at once to the public. . . .

Forney's *Press* said: "Miss Anna E. Dickinson, of Philadelphia, aged seventeen years, handsome, of an expressive countenance, plainly dressed, and eloquent beyond her years, made the speech of the occasion. After the listless, monotonous harangues of the day, the distinct, earnest tones of this juvenile Joan of Arc were very sweet and charming. . . ." "We are told," said she, "to maintain constitutions because they are constitutions, and compromises because they are compromises. But what are compromises, and what is laid down in those constitutions? Eminent lawyers have said that certain great fundamental ideas of right are common to the world, and that all laws of man's making, which trample on these ideas, are null and void—wrong to obey—right to disobey. The Constitution of the United States recognizes human slavery, and makes the souls of men articles of purchase and of sale." . . .

Soon after, she entered the United States Mint, to labor from seven o'clock in the morning to six at night. Although she was ever faithful to her duties and skillful in everything she undertook, soon becoming the most rapid adjuster in the Mint, her

radical criticisms of the war and its leaders cost her the loss of
the place. At a meeting just after the battle of Ball's Bluff, in
summing up the record, after exonerating Stone and Baker, she
said, "Future history will show that this battle was not lost
through ignorance and incompetence, but through the treason
of the commanding general, George B. McClellan, and time
will vindicate the truth of my assertion." She was hissed all over
the house, though some cried, "Go on!" "Go on!"

When Gen. McClellan was running against Lincoln in 1864,
after she had achieved a world-wide reputation, she was sent
by the Republican Committee of Pennsylvania to this same town,
to speak to the same people, in the same hall. In again summing up the incidents of the war, when she came to Ball's Bluff,
she said, "I say now, as I said three years ago, history will record
that this battle was lost, not through ignorance or incompetence,
but through the treason of the commanding general, George B.
McClellan." "And time has vindicated your assertion," was
shouted all over the house. . . .

With remarkable prescience all through the war and the period
of reconstruction, Miss Dickinson took the advance position.
Wendell Phillips used to say that "she was the young elephant
sent forward to try the bridges to see if they were safe for
older ones to cross." When wily politicians found that her
criticisms were applauded by immense audiences, they gained
courage to follow her lead. As popular thought was centering
everywhere on national questions, Miss Dickinson thought less
of the special wrongs of women and negroes and more of the
causes of revolutions and the true basis of government; hence she
spoke chiefly on the political aspects of the war, and thus made
herself available in party politics at once. . . .

In the intervals of public speaking, she made frequent visits to
the Government hospitals, and became a most welcome guest
among our soldiers. In long conversations with them, she learned
their individual histories, experiences, hardships, and sufferings;
the motives that prompted them to go into the army; what they
saw there; what they thought of war in their hours of solitude,

away from the camp and the battle-field. Thus she acquired an insight into the soldier's life and feelings, and from these narratives drew her material for that deeply interesting lecture on hospital life, which she delivered in many parts of the country.

This lecture given in Concord, New Hampshire, in the autumn of 1862, was the turning-point of her fortunes. In this speech she proved slavery to be the cause of the war, that its continuance would result in prolonged suffering to our soldiers, defeat to our armies, and the downfall of the Republic.

Her march through the State [of New Hampshire] was a succession of triumphs, and ended in a Republican victory. . . . The Governor-elect made personal acknowledgment that her eloquent speeches had secured his election. She was serenaded, feasted and fêted, the recipient of many valuable presents, and eulogized by the press and the people. . . .

New Hampshire safe, all eyes were turned to Connecticut. The contest there was between Seymour and Buckingham. It was generally conceded that, if Seymour was elected, Connecticut would give no more money or troops for the war. . . . No resistance was made to this impending calamity until Anna Dickinson went into the State, and galvanized the desponding Loyalists to life. . . . The halls where she spoke were so densely packed that Republicans stayed away to make room for Democrats, and the women were shut out to give place to those who could vote. There never was such enthusiasm over an orator in this country. . . . Ministers preached about her, prayed for her, as a second Joan of Arc, raised up by God to save that State to the loyal party, and through it the nation to freedom and humanity. . . .

Fresh from the victories in New Hampshire and Connecticut, she was announced to speak in Cooper Institute, New York. . . . There never was such excitement over any meeting in New York. . . . There were clergymen, generals, admirals, judges, lawyers, editors, the literati, and leaders of fashion, and all alike ready to do homage to this simple girl, who moved them alternately to laughter and tears, to bursts of applause and the most profound silence. . . .

After her remarkable success in New York, the Philadelphia Union League invited her to speak in that city. The invitation, signed by leading Republicans, she readily accepted. . . .

In July, 1862, the first move was made to enlist colored troops in Pennsylvania. A meeting was called for that purpose in Philadelphia. Judge Kelley, Frederick Douglass, and Anna Dickinson were there, and made strong appeals to the people of that State to grant to the colored man the honor of bearing arms in defense of the country. The effort was successful. . . . In September a field-day was announced at Camp William Penn. General Pleasonton reviewed the troops. . . . At the close of the day when the people began to disperse it was noised round that Miss Dickinson was there; a cry was heard at once on all sides, "A speech! a speech!" The moon was just rising, mingling its pale rays with those of the setting sun, and throwing a soft, mysterious light over the whole scene. The troops gathered round with bristling bayonets and flags flying, the band was hushed to silence, and when all was still, mounted on a gun-wagon, with General Pleasonton and his staff on one side, General Wagner and his staff on the other, this brave girl addressed "our boys in blue." She urged that justice and equality might be secured to every citizen in the republic; that slavery and war might end forever and peace be restored; that our country might indeed be the land of the free and the home of the brave.

As she stood there uttering words of warning and prophecy, it seemed as if her lips had been touched with a live coal from the altar of heaven. Her inspired words moved the hearts of our young soldiers to deeds of daring, and gave fresh courage to those about her to bid their loved ones go and die if need be for freedom and their country. The hour, the mysterious light, the stillness, the novel surroundings, the youth of the speaker, all gave a peculiar power to her words, and made the scene one of the most thrilling and beautiful on the page of history.

In January, 1864, she made her first address in Washington. . . . To speak before the President, Chief-Justice, Judges, Senators, Congressmen, Foreign Diplomats, all the dignitaries and honorables of the Government was one of the most trying ordeals in her experience. She had one of the largest and most brilliant audiences ever assembled in the Capitol, and was fully equal to the occasion. . . . At the close of her address she was presented to many of the distinguished ladies and gentlemen, and chief among them the President. . . . She was honored as no man ever had been before. . . .

One of the most powerful and impressive appeals she ever made was in the Convention of Southern Loyalists held in Philadelphia in September, 1866. In this Convention there was a division of opinion between the Border and the Gulf States. The latter wanted to incorporate negro suffrage in their platform, as that was the only means of success for the Liberal party at the South. The former, manipulated by Northern politicians, opposed that measure, lest it should defeat the Republican party in the pending elections at the North. This stultification of principle, of radical public sentiment, stirred the soul of Miss Dickinson, and she desired to speak. . . .

She went on in spite of interruptions, reviewing the conduct of the Border States with scorn, and an eloquence never equalled in any of her previous efforts, in favor of an open, manly declaration of the real opinion of the Convention for justice to the colored Loyalist, not in the courts only, but at the ballot-box. The speech was in Miss Dickinson's noblest style throughout— bold, but tender, and often so pathetic that she brought tears to every eye. . . . Kentucky and Maryland now listened as eagerly as Georgia and Alabama; Brownlow's iron features and Botts' rigid face soon relaxed, and tears stood in the old Virginian's eyes; while the noble Tennesseean moved his place, and gazed at the inspired girl with an interest and wonderment which no other orator had moved before. She had the audience in hand, as easily as a mother holds her child, and like the child, this audience heard her heart beat. It was a marvelous speech. Its greatness lay in its manner and effect, as well as its argument. When she finished, one after another of the Southern delegates came forward and pinned on her dress the badges of their States until she wore the gifts of Alabama, Missouri, Tennessee, Texas, Florida, Louisiana, and Maryland.

And thus it was from time to time that this remarkable girl uttered the highest thought in American politics in that crisis of our nation's history. While in camp and hospital she spoke words of tenderness and love to the sick and dying, she did not hesitate to rebuke the incapacity and iniquity of those in high places. She was among the first to distrust McClellan and Lincoln, and in a lecture, entitled "My Policy," to unveil his successor, Andrew Johnson, to the people. She saw the scepter of power grasped by the party of freedom, and the first gun fired at Sumter in defence of slavery. She saw our armies go forth to battle, the youth, the promise, the hope of the nation—two million strong—and saw them return with their ranks thinned and broken, their flags tattered and stained, the maimed, the halt and the blind, the weary and worn; and this, she said, is the price of liberty. She saw the dawn of the glorious day of emancipation when four million African slaves were set free, and that night of gloom when the darkest page in American history was written in the blood of its chief. Through the nation's agony was this young girl born into a knowledge of her power; and she drew her inspiration from the great events of her day.

How the Southern women she saw and knew responded to the war is described by Mrs. Roger A. Pryor in REMINISCENCES OF PEACE AND WAR.[2] *She engaged in every sort of work herself in its behalf.*

It is well known that General Lee did not approve the hasty, ill-considered action of the early seceders from the Union. He foresaw the perils and doubtful results of such action. He knew that war—as my own husband had so earnestly said in Congress —"meant widows and orphans, the punishment of the innocent,

[2] Reprint obtained through the courtesy of The Macmillan Company.

the ruin of the fortunes of all." Still, the "Old Mother" had been forced to accept it at the hands of others. The simple question was: "With or against blood and kin? For or against the Old Mother?" And the question answered itself in the asking.

I am sure that no soldier enlisted under Virginia's banner could possibly be more determined than the young women of the state. They were uncompromising.

"You promised me my answer to-night," said a fine young fellow, who had not yet enlisted, to his sweetheart.

"Well, you can't have it, Ben, until you have fought the Yankees," said pretty Helen.

"What heart will I have for fighting if you give me no promise?"

"I'll not be engaged to any man until he has fought the Yankees," said Helen, firmly. "You distinguish yourself in the war, and then see what I'll have to say to you."

This was the stand they took in Richmond and Petersburg. Engagements were postponed until they could find of what mettle a lover was.

"But suppose I don't come back at all!" suggested Ben.

"Oh, then I'll acknowledge an engagement and be good to your mother—and wear mourning all the same—*provided*— your wounds are all in front." . . .

To be idle was torture. We women resolved ourselves into a sewing society—resting not on Sundays. Sewing-machines were put into the churches, which became depots for flannel, muslin, strong linen, and even uniform cloth. When the hour for meeting arrived, the sewing class would be summoned by the ringing of the church bell. . . . We instituted a monster sewing class, which we hugely enjoyed, to meet daily at my home on Market Street. My Colonel was to be fitted out as never was colonel before. He was ordered to Norfolk with his regiment to protect the seaboard. I was proud of his colonelship, and much exercised because he had no shoulder-straps. I undertook to embroider them myself. We had not then decided upon the star for our colonel's insignia, and I supposed he would wear the eagle like all the colonels I had ever known. No embroidery bullion was to be had, but I bought heavy bullion fringe, cut it in lengths, and made eagles, probably of some extinct species, for the like were unknown in Audubon's time, and have not since been discovered. However, they were accepted, admired, and, what is worse, worn.

The Confederate soldier was furnished at the beginning of the war with a gun, pistol, canteen, tin cup, haversack, and knapsack —no inconsiderable weight to be borne in a march. The knapsack contained a fatigue jacket, one or two blankets, an oilcloth, several suits of underclothing, several pairs of white gloves, collars, neckties, and handkerchiefs. Each mess provided a mess-chest containing dishes, bowls, plates, knives, forks, spoons, cruets, spice-boxes, glasses, etc. Each mess also owned a frying-pan, oven, coffee-pot, and camp-kettle. The uniforms were of the finest cadet cloth and gold lace.

This outfit—although not comparable to that of the Federal soldiers, many of whom had "Saratoga" trunks in the baggage train, was considered sumptuous by the Confederate volunteer.

As if these were not enough, we taxed our ingenuity to add sundry comforts, weighing little, by which we might give a touch of refinement to the soldier's knapsack.

There was absolutely nothing which a man might possibly use that we did not make for them. We embroidered cases for razors, for soap and sponge, and cute morocco affairs for needles, thread, and court-plaster, with a little pocket lined with a bank-note. "How perfectly ridiculous!" do you say? Nothing is ridiculous that helps anxious women to bear their lot—cheats them with the hope that they are doing good. . . .

My resolution was taken. My children were safe with their grandmother. I would write. I would ask that every particle of my household linen, except a change, should be rolled into bandages, all my fine linen be sent to me for compresses, and all forwarded as soon as possible.

I would enter the new hospital which had been improvised in Kent & Paine's warehouse, and would remain there as a nurse as long as the armies were fighting around Richmond. . . .

Kent & Paine's warehouse was a large, airy building, which had, I understood, been offered by the proprietors for a hospital immediately after the battle of Seven Pines. McClellan's advance upon Richmond had heavily taxed the capacity of the hospitals already established.

When I reached the warehouse, early on the morning after the fight at Mechanicsville, I found cots on the lower floor already occupied, and other cots in process of preparation. An aisle between the rows of narrow beds stretched to the rear of the building. Broad stairs led to a story above, where other cots were being laid.

The volunteer matron was a beautiful Baltimore woman, Mrs. Wilson. When I was presented to her as a candidate for admission, her serene eyes rested doubtfully upon me for a moment. She hesitated. Finally she said: "The work is very exacting. There are so few of us that our nurses must do anything and everything—make beds, wait upon anybody, and often a half a dozen at a time."

"I will engage to do all that," I declared, and she permitted me to go to a desk at the farther end of the room and enter my name.

As I passed by the rows of occupied cots, I saw a nurse kneeling beside one of them, holding a pan for a surgeon. The red stump of an amputated arm was held over it. The next thing I knew I was myself lying on a cot, and a spray of cold water was falling over my face. I had fainted. Opening my eyes, I found the matron standing beside me.

"You see it is as I thought. You are unfit for this work. One of the nurses will conduct you home."

The nurse's assistance was declined, however. I had given trouble enough for one day, and had only interrupted those who were really worth something.

I resolved I would conquer my culpable weakness. It was all very well,—these heroics in which I indulged, these paroxysms of patriotism, this adoration of the defenders of my fireside. The defender in the field had naught to hope from me in case he should be wounded in my defence.

I took myself well in hand. Why had I fainted? I thought it was because of the sickening, dead odor in the hospital, mingled with that of acids and disinfectants. Of course this would always be there—and worse, as wounded men filled the rooms. I provided myself with sal volatile and spirits of camphor—we wore pockets in our gowns in those days—and thus armed I presented myself again to Mrs. Wilson. . . .

But I found myself reinstated—with surgeons, matron and Miss Deborah who meant business—when I appeared a few days later, accompanied by a man bearing a basket of clean, well-rolled bandages, with promise of more to come. The Petersburg women had gone to work with a will upon my table-cloths, sheets, and dimity counterpanes—and even the chintz furniture covers. My springlike green and white chintz bandages appeared on many a manly leg and arm. My fine linen underwear and napkins were cut, by the sewing circle at the Spotswood, according to the surgeon's directions, into lengths two inches wide, then folded two inches, doubling back and forth in a smaller fold each time, until they formed pointed wedges for compresses.

Such was the sudden and overwhelming demand for such things, that but for my own and similar donations of household linen, the wounded men would have suffered. The war had come upon us suddenly. Many of our ports were already closed, and we had no stores laid up for such an emergency. . . .

The women who worked in Kent & Paine's hospital never seemed to weary. After a while the wise matron assigned us hours, and we went on duty with the regularity of trained nurses. . . . Efficient, kindly colored women assisted us. Their motherly manner soothed the prostrate soldier, whom they always addressed as "son."

Many fine young fellows lost their lives for want of prompt attention. They never murmured. They would give way to those who seemed to be more seriously wounded than themselves, and the latter would recover, while from the slighter wounds gangrene would supervene from delay. Very few men ever walked away from that hospital. They died, or friends found quarters for them in the homes in Richmond. None complained! Unless a poor man grew delirious, he never groaned. There was an atmosphere of gentle kindness, a suppression of emotion for the sake of others. . . .

Each of the battles of those seven days brought a harvest of wounded to our hospital. I used to veil myself closely as I walked to and from my hotel, that I might shut out the dreadful sights on the street,—the squads of prisoners, and, worst of all, the open wagons in which the dead were piled. Once I *did* see one of these dreadful wagons! In it a stiff arm was raised, and shook as it was driven down the street, as though the dead owner appealed to Heaven for vengeance; a horrible sight never to be forgotten. . . .

The Emancipation Proclamation did not create a ripple of excitement among the colored members of our households in Virginia. Of its effect elsewhere I could not judge. As to fighting, our own negroes never dreamed of such a thing. The colored troops of the North were not inferior, we were told, in discipline and courage to other soldiers; but the martial spirit among them had its exceptions.

My Petersburg beauties were all wearing hats of their own manufacture, the favorite style being the Alpine with a pointed crown. For trimming, very soft and lovely flowers were made of feathers, the delicate white feather with a tuft of fleecy marabout at its stem. The marabout tuft would be carefully drawn off, to be made into swan's-down trimming. A wire was prepared and covered with green paper for a stem, a little ball of wax fastened on the end, and covered with a tiny tuft of the down for a centre, and around this the feathers were stuck—with incurving petals for apple blossoms and half-open roses, and reversed for camellias. Neatly trimmed and suitably tinted, these flowers were handsome enough for anybody, and were in great demand. Cocks' plumes were also used on hats, iridescent, and needing no coloring. With the downy breast of a goose which came from my possession I essayed the making of a powder-puff for my baby, but alas! the oil in the cuticle proved a perennial spring which could not be dried up by soda or sunning, and finally I saw my powder-puff disappearing in a hole, drawn downward by a vigorous and hungry rat.

The young girls who visited me never complained of their privations in the matter of food, but they sorely grieved over their shabby wardrobes.

"I really think," said one, "if we can only get along until we can wear white waists, we shall do very well. Every time a white waist is washed it's made new—but these old flannel sacks—ugh!"

One day Mary Meade made me a visit. Always beautiful, her face wore on this afternoon a seraphic, beatific expression.

"Tell me, dear," I said, "all about it." I supposed she had heard her lover had been promoted or was coming home on a furlough.

She held up her two hands. *"It's just these gloves!"* said Mary. "I can't help it. They make me perfectly happy! They have just come through the blockade."

The butcher shops were closed, and many of the dry-goods stores; but somebody had ordered a quantity of narrow crimson woollen braid, and had failed to accept it. We seized upon it. Every one of us had garments embroidered with it—in scrolls, Maltese crosses, undulating lines, leaves; all of which goes to prove that the desire for ornament is an instinct of our nature, outliving the grosser affection for the good things of the table. The consciousness of being well dressed, we have been told, will afford a peace of mind far exceeding anything to be derived from the comforts of religion.

It had not been many years since every Virginia farm owned a house for a great cumbrous loom, with beams supported against the ceiling. The door of the loom-house was again opened, and the weaver installed upon her high bench. Cotton cloth was woven and dyed yellow with butternut, black with walnut-bark, gray with willow. A mordant to "set the dye" was unattainable —but at last rusty iron nails, old horseshoes, old clamps and hinges, were found to be effective. Every atom of black silk was a treasure. It was shredded to mix with the cotton before carding. Even now the cells of my brain waken at the sight of a bundle of old black silk, and my fingers would fain respond.

Pins became scarce. People walked about with downcast eyes; they were looking for pins! Thorns were gathered and dried to use as pins. Dentists' gold soon disappeared. The generation succeeding the war period had not good teeth. Anæsthetics—morphine, chloroform, opium—were contraband of war. This was our great grief. Our soldier boys, who had done nothing to bring the war upon the country, must suffer every pang that followed the disasters of battle. The United States gave artificial limbs to its maimed soldiers. Ours had only their crutches, and these of rude home manufacture. The blockade-running, for which our women were so much blamed, was often undertaken to bring morphine and medicine to our hospitals. The fashions of the day included a small round cushion worn at the back of a lady's belt, to lift the heavy hoop and many petticoats then in vogue. It was called "a bishop," and was made of silk. These were brought home from "a visit to friends at the North" filled with quinine and morphine. They were examined at the frontier by a long pin stuck through them. If the pin met no resistance, they were allowed to pass.

The famine moved on apace, but its twin sister, fever, never visited us. Never had Petersburg been so healthy. No garbage was decaying in the streets. Every particle of animal or vegetable food was consumed, and the streets were clean. Flocks of pigeons would follow the children who were eating bread or crackers. Finally the pigeons vanished, having been themselves eaten. Rats and mice disappeared. The poor cats staggered about the streets, and began to die of hunger.

At times meal was the only article attainable except by the rich. An ounce of meat daily was considered an abundant ration for each member of the family. To keep food of any kind was impossible—cows, pigs, bacon, flour, everything, was stolen, and even sitting hens were taken from the nest.

In the presence of such facts as these General Lee was able to report that nearly every regiment in his army had reënlisted—

and for the war! And very soon he also reported that the army was out of meat and had but one day's rations of bread. . . .

With all our starvation we never ate rats, mice, or mule-meat. We managed to exist on peas, bread, and sorghum. We could buy a little milk, and we mixed it with a drink made from roasted and ground corn. The latter, in the grain, was scarce. Mr. Campbell's chickens picked up the grains wherever the army horses were fed.

My little boys never complained, but Theo, who had insisted upon returning to me from his uncle's safe home in the country, said one day: "Mamma, I have a queer feeling in my stomach! Oh, no! it doesn't ache the least bit, but it feels like a nutmeg grater." . . .

Our friends in town sent many invitations to us dwellers in tents. Of course, I accepted none of them. I had no heart for gayety, and not one moment's time to spare from my sewing. It is passing strange—this disposition to revel in times of danger and suffering. Florence was never so gay as during the Plague! The men of our army who had been absent three years were now near their homes, and they abandoned themselves to the opportunities of the hour. Some of them were engaged to the beautiful young women of Petersburg.

"This is no time for marriage," said General Lee, "no time while the country is in such peril"; and yet he granted a furlough now and then to some soldier who was unwilling to wait.

There were parties, "starvation parties," as they were called on account of the absence of refreshments impossible to be obtained. Not even the lump of sugar allowed by Lady Morgan at her *conversazione* was possible here; but nothwithstanding this serious disadvantage, ball followed ball in quick succession. "The soldier danced with the lady of his love at night, and on the morrow danced the dance of death in the deadly trench on the line." There the ranks closed up; and in the ball room they closed up also. There was always a comrade left for the partner of the belle; and not one whit less valiant was the soldier for his brief respite. He could go from the dance to his place in the trenches with a light jest, however heavy his heart might be.

To Clara Barton belongs the star rôle as war-worker at this time. Her biographer says: "She could never be kept from the firing line. All of the appointments to all of the offices in the world could not hold her back from personally going to the front." And after the war she spent four years searching for missing men. Then her work widened to a world range. She served as nurse in the Franco-Prussian War, at the Siege of Paris and the Commune, in the Spanish-American War. Next the Galveston flood claimed her energy and she became a peace-time servant in another species of disaster.

In her writings, to be found in the LIFE OF CLARA BAR-TON [3] by Percy H. Epler, her opinions about war as a method of settling disputes are not minced.

I was strong and thought I might go to the rescue of the men who fell. The first regiment of troops, the old 6th Mass. that fought its way through Baltimore, brought my playmates and neighbors, the partakers of my childhood; the brigades of New Jersey brought scores of my brave boys, the same solid phalanx; and the strongest legions from old Herkimer brought the associates of my seminary days. They formed and crowded around me. What could I do but go with them, or work for them and my country? The patriot blood of my father was warm in my veins. The country which he had fought for, I might at least work for, and I had offered my service to the government in the capacity of a double clerkship at twice $1400 a year, upon discharge of two disloyal clerks from its employ—the salary never to be given to me, but to be turned back into the U. S. Treasury then poor to beggary, with no currency, no credit. But there was no law for this, and it could not be done and I would not draw

[3] Reprint obtained through the courtesy of The Macmillan Company.

salary from our government in such peril, so I resigned and went into direct service of the sick and wounded troops wherever found.

But I struggled long and hard with my sense of propriety—with the appalling fact that I was only a woman whispering in one ear, and thundering in the other the groans of suffering men dying like dogs—unfed and unsheltered, for the life of every institution which had protected and educated me!

I said that I struggled with my sense of propriety and I say it with humiliation and shame. I am ashamed that I thought of such a thing. . . .

When our armies fought on Cedar Mountain, I broke the shackles and went to the field. . . . And if you chance to feel, that the positions I occupied were rough and unseemly for a *woman*—I can only reply that they were rough and unseemly for *men*. But under all, lay the life of the nation. I had inherited the rich blessing of health and strength of constitution and I felt that some return was due from me and that I ought to be there. . . .

Our coaches were not elegant or commodious; they had no windows, no seats, no platforms, no steps, a slide door on the side was the only entrance, and this higher than my head. For my manner of attaining my elevated position, I must beg of you to draw on your own imaginations and spare me the labor of reproducing the boxes, barrels, boards, and rails, which in those days, seemed to help me up and on in the world. We did not criticize the unsightly helpers and were only too thankful that the stiff springs did not quite jostle us out. This description need not be limited to this particular trip or train, but will suffice for all that I have known in Army life. This is the kind of conveyance by which your tons of generous gifts have reached the field with the precious freights. These trains through day and night, sunshine and rain, heat and cold, have thundered over heights, across plains, through ravines, and over hastily built army bridges 90 feet across the rocky stream beneath.

At 10 o'clock Sunday (August 31, 1862) our train drew up at

Fairfax Station. The ground, for acres, was a thinly wooded slope—and among the trees, on the leaves and grass, were laid the wounded who were pouring in by scores of wagon loads, as picked up on the field under the flag of truce. All day they came and the whole hillside was covered. Bales of hay were broken open and scattered over the ground like littering for cattle, and the sore, famishing men were laid upon it.

And when the night shut in, in the mist and darkness about us, we knew that standing apart from the world of anxious hearts, throbbing over the whole country, we were a little band of almost empty-handed workers literally by ourselves in the wild woods of Virginia, with 3000 suffering men crowded upon the few acres within our reach.

After gathering up every available implement or convenience for our work, our domestic inventory stood 2 water buckets, 5 tin cups, 1 camp kettle, a stewpan, 2 lanterns, 4 bread knives, 3 plates, and a 2-quart tin dish, and 3000 guests to serve.

You will perceive by this, that I had not yet learned to equip myself, for I was no Pallas, ready armed, but grew into my work by hard thinking and sad experience. It may serve to relieve your apprehension for the future of my labors if I assure you that I was never caught so again.

You have read of adverse winds. To realize this in its full sense you have only to build a camp fire and attempt to cook something on it.

There is not a soldier within the sound of my voice, but will sustain me in the assertion that go whichsoever side of it you will, wind will blow the smoke and flame directly in your face. Notwithstanding these difficulties, within fifteen minutes from the time of our arrival we were preparing food, and dressing wounds. You wonder what, and how prepared, and how administered without dishes.

You generous, thoughtful mothers and wives have not forgotten the tons of preserves and fruits with which you filled our hands. Huge boxes of these stood beside that railway track. Every can, jar, bucket, bowl, cup or tumbler, when emptied, that instant became a vehicle of mercy to convey some preparation of mingled bread and wine or soup or coffee to some helpless, famishing sufferer who partook of it with the tears rolling down his bronzed cheeks and divided his blessings between the hands that fed him and his God. I never realized until that day how little a human being could be grateful for and that day's experience also taught me the utter worthlessness of that which could not be made to contribute directly to our necessities. The bit of bread which would rest on the surface of a gold eagle was worth more than the coin itself.

But the most fearful scene was reserved for the night. I have said that the ground was littered with dry hay and that we had only two lanterns, but there were plenty of candles. The wounded were laid so close that it was impossible to move about in the dark. The slightest misstep brought a torrent of groans from some poor mangled fellow in your path.

Consequently here were seen persons of all grades from the careful man of God who walked with a prayer upon his lips to the careless driver hunting for his lost whip—each wandering about among this hay with an open flaming candle in his hand.

The slightest accident, the mere dropping of a light, could have enveloped in flames this whole mass of helpless men.

How we watched and pleaded and cautioned as we worked and wept that night! How we put socks and slippers upon their cold, damp feet, wrapped your blankets and quilts about them, and when we had no longer these to give, how we covered them in the hay and left them to their rest! . . .

[On the field of second Bull Run and Chantilly] The slight, naked chest of a fair-haired lad caught my eye, and dropping down beside him, I bent low to draw the remnant of his torn blouse about him, when with a quick cry he threw his left arm across my neck, and, burying his face in the folds of my dress, wept like a child at his mother's knee. I took his head in my hands and held it until his great burst of grief passed away. "And do you know me?" he asked at length. "I am Charley Hamilton, who used to carry your satchel home from school!"

My faithful pupil, poor Charley. That mangled right arm would never carry a satchel again.

About three o'clock in the morning I observed a surgeon with his little flickering candle in hand approaching me with cautious step far up in the wood. "Lady," he said as he drew near, "will you go with me? Out on the hills is a poor distressed lad, mortally wounded and dying. His piteous cries for his sister have touched all our hearts and none of us can relieve him but rather seem to distress him by our presence."

By this time I was following him back over the bloody track, with great beseeching eyes of anguish on every side looking up into our faces, saying so plainly, "Don't step on us."

"He can't last half an hour longer," said the surgeon as we toiled on. "He is already quite cold, shot through the abdomen, a terrible wound." By this time the cries became plainly audible to me.

"Mary, Mary, sister Mary, come—Oh come, I am wounded, Mary! I am shot. I am dying—Oh come to me—I have called you so long and my strength is almost gone—Don't let me die here alone. O Mary, Mary, come!"

Of all the tones of entreaty to which I have listened, and certainly I have had some experience of sorrow, I think these, sounding through that dismal night, the most heart-rending. As we drew near some twenty persons attracted by his cries had gathered around and stood with moistened eyes and helpless hands waiting the change which would relieve them all. And in the midst, stretched upon the ground, lay, scarcely full grown, a young man with a graceful head of hair, tangled and matted, thrown back from a forehead and a face of livid whiteness. His throat was bare. His hands, bloody, clasped his breast, his large, bewildered eyes turning anxiously in every direction. And ever from between his ashen lips pealed that piteous cry of "Mary! Mary! Come."

I approached him unobserved, and motioning the lights away, I knelt by him alone in the darkness. . . . I listened till his blessings grew fainter and in ten minutes with them on his lips he fell asleep. So the gray morning found us. My precious charge had grown warm, and was comfortable. . . . When finally he woke, he seemed puzzled for a moment but then he smiled and said:—"I knew before I opened my eyes that this couldn't be Mary. I know now that she couldn't get here but it is almost as good. You've made me so happy. Who is it?" . . .

"Will they take away the wounded?" he asked. "Yes," I replied, "the first train for Washington is nearly ready now." "I must go," he said quickly. "Are you able?" I asked. "I must go if I die on the way. I'll tell you why. I am poor mother's only son, and when she consented that I go to the war, I promised her faithfully that if I were not killed outright, but wounded, I would try by every means in my power to be taken home to her dead or alive. If I die on the train, they will not throw me off, and if I were buried in Washington, she can get me. But out here in the Virginia woods in the hands of the enemy, never. I *must* go!"

I sent for the surgeon in charge of the train and requested that my boy be taken.

"Oh, impossible! Madam, he is mortally wounded and will never reach the hospital. We must take those who have a hope of life." "But you must take him." "I cannot."—"Can you, Doctor, guarantee the lives of all you have on that train?" "I wish I could," said he sadly. "They are the worst cases, nearly fifty per cent must die eventually of their wounds and hardships."

"Then give this lad a chance with them.". . . Whether yielding to argument or entreaty, I neither knew nor cared so long as he did yield nobly and kindly. And they gathered up the fragments of the poor, torn boy and laid him carefully on a blanket on the crowded train and with stimulants and food and a kind-hearted attendant, pledged to take him alive or dead to Armory Square Hospital and tell them he was Hugh Johnson of New York, and to mark his grave.

Although three hours of my time had been devoted to one sufferer among thousands, it must not be inferred that our general work had been suspended or that my assistants had been equally inefficient. They had seen how I was engaged and nobly redoubled their exertions to make amends for my deficiencies.

Probably not a man was laid upon those cars who did not receive some personal attention at their hands, some little kindness, if it were only to help lift him more tenderly.

This finds us shortly after daylight Monday morning. Train after train of cars were rushing on for the wounded and hundreds of wagons were bringing them in from the field still held by the enemy, where some poor sufferers had lain three days with no visible means of sustenance. If immediately placed upon the trains and not detained, at least twenty-four hours must elapse before they could be in the hospital and properly nourished. They were already famishing, weak and sinking from loss of blood and they could ill afford a further fast of twenty-four hours. I felt confident that unless nourished at once, all the weaker portion must be past recovery before reaching the hospitals at Washington. If once taken from the wagons and laid with those already cared for, they would be overlooked and perish on the way. Something must be done to meet this fearful emergency. I sought the various officers on the grounds, explained the case to them and asked permission to feed all the men as they arrived before they should be taken from the wagons. It was well for the poor sufferers of that field that it was controlled by noble-hearted, generous officers, quick to feel and prompt to act.

They at once saw the propriety of my request and gave orders that all wagons would be stayed at a certain point and only moved on when every one had been seen and fed. This point secured, I commenced my day's work of climbing from the wheel to the brake of every wagon and speaking to and feeding with my own hands each soldier until he expressed himself satisfied.

Still there were bright spots along the darkened lines. Early in the morning the Provost Marshal came to ask me if I could use fifty men. He had that number, who for some slight breach of military discipline were under guard and useless, unless I could use them. I only regretted there were not five hundred. They came—strong, willing men—and these, added to our original force and what we had gained incidentally, made our number something over eighty, and believe me, eighty men and three women, acting with well directed purpose will accomplish a good deal in a day. Our fifty prisoners dug graves and gathered and buried the dead, bore mangled men over the rough ground in their arms, loaded cars, built fires, made soup, and administered it. And I failed to discern that their services were less valuable than those of the other men. I had long suspected, and have since been convinced, that a private soldier may be placed under guard, court-martialed, and even be imprisoned without forfeiting his honor or manliness, that the real dishonor is often upon the gold lace rather than the army blue. . . .

The departure of this train cleared the grounds of the wounded for the night, and as the line of fire from its ploughing engines died out in the darkness, a strange sensation of weakness and weariness fell upon me, almost defying my utmost exertion to move one foot before the other.

A little Sibley tent had been hastily pitched for me in a slight hollow upon the hillside. Your imagination will not fail to picture its condition. Rivulets of water had rushed through it during the last three hours. Still I attempted to reach it, as its white surface, in the darkness, was a protection from the wheels of wagons and trampling of beasts.

Perhaps I shall never forget the painful effort which the making of those few rods, and the gaining of the tent, cost me. How many times I fell from sheer exhaustion, in the darkness and mud of that slippery hillside, I have no knowledge, but at last I grasped the welcome canvas, and a well established brook, which washed in on the upper side at the opening that served as door, met me on my entrance. My entire floor was covered with water, not an inch of dry, solid ground.

One of my lady assistants had previously taken train for Washington and the other, worn out by faithful labors, was crouched upon the top of some boxes in one corner fast asleep. No such convenience remained for me, and I had no strength to arrange one. I sought the highest side of my tent, which I remembered was grass grown, and ascertaining that the water was not very deep, I sank down. It was no laughing matter then. But the recollection of my position has since afforded me amusement.

I remember myself sitting on the ground, upheld by my left arm, my head resting on my hand, impelled by an almost uncontrollable desire to lie completely down, and prevented by the certain conviction that, if I did, water would flow into my ears.

How long I balanced between my desires and cautions, I have no positive knowledge, but it is very certain that the former carried the point by the position from which I was aroused at twelve o'clock by the rumbling of more wagons of wounded men. I slept two hours, and oh, what strength I had gained! I may never know two other hours of equal worth. I sprang to my feet dripping wet, covered with ridges of dead grass and leaves, wrung the water from my hair and skirts, and went forth again to my work. . . .

Darkness brought silence and peace, and respite and rest to our gallant men. As they had risen, regiment by regiment, from their grassy beds in the morning, so at night the fainting remnant again sank down on the trampled blood-stained earth, the weary to sleep, and the wounded to die.

Through the long starlit night, we wrought and hoped and prayed. But it was only when, in the hush of the following day, as we glanced over that vast Aceldama, that we learned at what a fearful cost the gallant Union army had won the battle of Antietam.

Antietam! With its eight miles of camping armies, face to face; 160,000 men to spring up at dawn like the old Scot from the heather! Its miles of artillery shaking the earth like a chain of Etnas! Its ten hours of uninterrupted battle! Its thunder and its fire! The sharp unflinching order—"Hold the Bridge, boys—always the Bridge." At length, the quiet! The pale moonlight on its cooling guns! The weary men—the dying and the dead!

The flag of truce that buried our enemy's slain, and Antietam was fought, and won, and the foe turned back! . . .

No one has forgotten the heart sickness which spread over the entire country as the busy wires flashed the dire tidings of the terrible destitution and suffering of the wounded of the Wilderness whom I attended as they lay in Fredericksburg. But you may never have known how many hundredfold of these ills were augmented by the conduct of improper, heartless, unfaithful officers in the immediate command of the city and upon whose actions and indecisions depended entirely the care, food, shelter, comfort, and lives of that whole city of wounded men. One of the highest officers there has since been convicted a traitor. And another, a little dapper Captain quartered with the owners of one of the finest mansions in the town, boasted that he had changed his opinion since entering the city the day before—that it was in fact a pretty hard thing for refined people like the people of Fredericksburg to be compelled to open their homes and admit "these dirty, lousy, common soldiers," and that he was not going to compel it.

This I heard him say and waited, until I saw him make his words good—till I saw, crowded into one old sunken hotel, lying helpless upon its bare, wet, bloody floors, 500 fainting men hold up their cold, bloodless, dingy hands, as I passed, and beg me in Heaven's name for a cracker to keep them from starving (and I had none); or to give them a cup that they might have something to drink water from, if they could get it (and I had no cup, and could get none), till I saw 200 six-mule army wagons in a line, ranged down the street to headquarters, and reaching so far out on the Wilderness road that I never found the end of it; every wagon crowded with wounded men, stopped, standing in the rain and mud, wrenched back and forth by the restless hungry animals all night from four o'clock in the afternoon till eight next morning and how much longer I know not.—The dark spot in the mud under many a wagon told only too plainly where some poor fellow's life had dripped out in those dreadful hours. . . .

I remembered one man who would set it right, if he knew it, who possessed the power and who would believe me if I told him. I commanded immediate conveyance back to Belle Plain. With difficulty I obtained it, and four stout horses with a light army wagon took me ten miles at an unbroken gallop, through field and swamp, and stumps and mud to Belle Plain, and a steam tug at once to Washington. Landing at dusk I sent for Henry Wilson, Chairman of the Military Committee of the Senate. A messenger brought him at eight, saddened and appalled like every patriot in that fearful hour, at the weight of woe under which the nation staggered, groaned, and wept.

He listened to the story of suffering and faithlessness, and hurried from my presence, with lips compressed and face like ashes. At ten he stood in the War Department. They could not credit his report. He must have been deceived by some frightened villain. No official report of unusual suffering had reached them. Nothing had been called for by the military authorities commanding Fredericksburg.

Mr. Wilson assured them that the officers in trust there were not to be relied upon. They were faithless, overcome by the blandishments of the wily inhabitants. Still the department doubted. It was then that he proved that my confidence in his firmness was not misplaced, as facing his doubters he replied: "One of two things will have to be done—either you will send some one to-night with the power to investigate and correct the abuses of our wounded men at Fredericksburg—or the Senate will send some one to-morrow."

This threat recalled their scattered senses.

At two o'clock in the morning the Quartermaster-General and staff galloped to the 6th Street wharf under orders; at ten they were in Fredericksburg. At noon the wounded men were fed from the food of the city and the houses were opened to the *"dirty, lousy* soldiers" of the Union Army.

Both railroad and canal were opened. In three days I returned with carloads of supplies.

No more jolting in army wagons! And every man who left

Fredericksburg by boat or by car owes it to the firm decision of one man that his grating bones were not dragged 10 miles across the country or left to bleach in the sands of that city. . . .

I had been making the rounds of the hospital tents [at Petersburg, Virginia] and for a moment stepped into the commission quarters when this tall, sun-burned, honest-faced soldier stepped in after me and approaching the agent said he should like to get a pair of stockings.

The agent replied with great kindness that he was very sorry he could not oblige him, but they were out of stockings, except some very fine ones they had saved for *dead men!*

If you could have seen the look of puzzled astonishment which spread over the veteran's face, as he strove to comprehend the meaning of the reply! He looked at me, at his own turtle-backed feet, innocent of stockings for months, until finally giving it up, he broke out with, "Stockings for dead men!" And turning on his heel he stalked out of the tent, no richer and apparently no wiser than when he entered. Doubtless he went back to the camp and trenches in disgust. And the young agent who had been from home only a fortnight, and had never learned by observation that men could lie quietly in their graves without stockings and shirts was just as deeply puzzled to comprehend the astonishment of the soldier and stood gazing after him in silent wonder as he walked away. From their different standpoints neither could get a glimpse of the other's thoughts any more than the good lady could understand how war should increase the price of candles. "Candles higher!" she exclaimed. "Why, bless me, do they fight by candle light?" . . .

Narratives of battles, as they are found in histories and official reports, are all wonderfully alike. There is the same intricate and incomprehensible machinery of divisions—brigades—regiments—battalions and squadrons of right centers and left wings. There are some attempts to flank; some other incomprehensible mechanism to prevent being flanked. The same advancing and falling back, extending and contracting—whirling—charging— deploying and enfilading. A perfect chaos—intelligible to few, and interesting to still fewer—where the natural eye can discern no human being—or scarce a sign of human presence. . . .

I shall not essay to enlighten you upon the subject of war. Were I to attempt it, I should doubtless miserably fail, for it has so long been said, as to amount to an adage, that "women don't know anything about war."

I wish men didn't either. They have always known a great deal too much about it for the good of their kind. They have worshiped at Valkyrie's shrine, and followed her siren lead, till it has cost a million times more than the whole world is worth, poured out the best blood and crushed the fairest forms the good God has ever created.

General Sherman was right when addressing an assemblage of cadets he told them war was Hell! Deck it as you will, it is this, and whoever has looked active war full in the face has caught some glimpses of regions as infernal, as he may ever fear to see. If any listener of mine on this subject expects ever to hear me converse on the war side of it, he had best prepare early for a disappointment, because that was not my side. The war side of the war could never have called me to the field—*Through and through—thought and act—body and soul—I hate it!*

The side of the picture which history never shows [belongs] to those who must follow the track of conquering armies, faces bathed in tears and hands in blood—the lees in the wine, the dregs in the cups of military glory. It would be out of such as this that I must sketch the battle glimpses I could bring you, were I to attempt it, for there was my lowly place in all wars I have known. . . .

[From Europe in 1872] If there be any power on earth which can right the wrongs for which the nations go to war, I pray that it may be made manifest, but when I think, I fear—How supreme an International court must it have been to be able to induce the Southerners to liberate their slaves or to convince them the "mudsills," and "greasy mechanics" and "horned Yankees" are a people entitled to sufficient respect to be treated on fair International ground? And how much legislation would it have taken to convince the world what a worthless bubble of assumption was France, so utterly unworthy the leadership she assumed and to have laid her in all respects so open before the world that it should with one voice repudiate her leadership, and refuse to follow her as heretofore in frivolity, immorality, folly, fashion, vice, and crime. It seems to me to have been only one great balloon and now that bayonets and bombs have pierced it full of holes, it sends out tens of thousands of little balloons in its collapse. It is bad for France, but I am not certain but the lesson will be beneficial to the rest of the world. I don't know if we may always trust councils. We had one at Rome not half a year ago that voted a dogma which turned backward the progress of enlightened thought two centuries; and how great a power of legislation would have been required to overthrow that decision? But I suspect the fear of Victor Emmanuel's bayonets has seriously interfered with it. Ah, I don't know; it is such a mystery, and mankind the greatest mystery of all. I shall never get it right in this world, whatever may happen in the one "that sets this right." . . .

Our position [with respect to the Red Cross] was incomprehensible to them (the president and members of the International Committee for the Relief of the Wounded in War). If the treaty had originated with a monarchical government they could see some ground for hesitancy. But it originated in a Republic older than our own. To what did America object, and how could these objections be overcome? They had twice formally presented it to the government at Washington, once in 1864, through our Minister Plenipotentiary at Berne, who was present at the convention; again in 1868, through Rev. Henry W. Bellows, the great head of war relief in America. They had failed in both instances. No satisfactory or adequate reason had ever been given by the nation for the course pursued. They had thought the people of America, with their grand sanitary record, would be the first to appreciate and accept it. I listened in silent wonder to all this recital, and when I did reply it was to say that I had never heard of the Convention of Geneva or knew of the treaty, and was sure that as a country America did not know that she had declined; that she would be the last to withhold recognition of a humane movement; that it had doubtless been referred to and declined by some one department of the government, or some one official, and had never been submitted to the people; and as its literature was in languages foreign to our English-speaking population, it had no way of reaching us.

You will naturally infer that I examined it. I became all the more deeply impressed with the wisdom of its principles, the good practical sense of its details, and its extreme usefulness in practice. Humane intelligence had devised its provisions and peculiarly adapted it to win popular favor. The absurdity of our own position in relation to it was simply marvelous. As I counted up its roll of twenty-two nations, not a civilized people in the world but ourselves missing, and saw Greece, Spain, and Turkey there, I began to fear that in the eyes of the rest of mankind we could not be far from barbarians. This reflection did not furnish a stimulating food for national pride. I grew more and more ashamed.

Although the gradual growth of the idea of something like humanity in war, stimulated by the ignorant and insane horrors of India and the Crimea, and soothed and instructed by the sensible and practical work of Florence Nightingale, had slowly but surely led up to the conditions which made such a movement possible, it was not until the remarkable campaign of Napoleon III in Northern Italy again woke the slumbering sympathies of the world that any definite steps revealed themselves. . . .

The War had its politics as well as battles, as Susan B. Anthony understood. In her public speeches and in her office as Secretary of the Women's Loyal League, she insisted again and again that the war must have freedom for slaves as its goal no less than the preservation of the Union. One of the earliest demands for a Federal amendment to that end was expressed in a Resolution of May, 1863, passed at a meeting of her organization, which read as follows:

We talk about returning to the "Union as it was" and the "Constitution as it is"—about "restoring our country to peace and prosperity—to the blessed conditions which existed before the war." I ask you what sort of peace, what sort of prosperity, have we had? Since the first slave ship sailed up the James River with its human cargo and there, on the soil of the Old Dominion, it was sold to the highest bidder, we have had nothing but war. When that pirate captain landed on the shores of Africa and there kidnapped the first negro and fastened the first manacle, the struggle between that captain and that negro was the commencement of the terrible war in the midst of which we are today. Between the slave and the master there has been war, and war only. This is but a new form of it. No, no; we ask for no return of the old conditions. We ask for something better. . . . By the Constitution as it is, the North has stood pledged to protect slavery in the States where it existed. We have been bound, in case of insurrections, to go to the aid, not of those struggling for liberty, but of the oppressors. It was politicians who made this pledge at the beginning, and who have renewed it from year to year. These same men have had control of the churches, the Sabbath-schools and all religious institutions, and the women have been a party in complicity with slavery. They have made the large majority in all the churches throughout the country, and have, without protest . . . accepted pro-slavery preaching from their pulpits; suffered the words "slavery a crime" to be expurgated from all the lessons taught their children. . . . Woman must now assume her God-given responsibilities and make herself what she was clearly designed to be, the educator of the race. Let her no longer be the mere reflector, the echo of the worldly pride and the ambition of man. Had the women of the North studied to know and to teach their sons the law of justice to the black man, they would not now be called upon to offer the loved of their households to the bloody Moloch of war.

As a sample of the response which Miss Anthony and her liberty party received from other Northern women, we quote a letter from Clarissa G. Olds of Hampton, New Hampshire, dated May 4, 1863.[4] Behind the Emancipation Proclamation was an unremitting moral pressure reinforcing military tactics.

Miss Anthony—Dear Madam:—I cheerfully respond to the call, published in *The Liberator,* to the loyal women of the North, to meet on the 14th inst. I am sensible that you will have responses from many whose words will be more potent, and who can do braver deeds than I can do. But I want to add my feeble testimony, notwithstanding, to encourage this first effort of American women in a national capacity, to sustain the Government, and help guide it through the perils which threaten its existence, thus demonstrating not only their loyalty, but their ability to understand its genius; the quickness of their perception of the cause and also of the remedies of the dangers which imperil the nation; and also their fitness to be admitted to take part in its deliberations. Not long since, men here at the North— loyal men—men who were not in favor of slavery, denied that they had any responsibility in regard to its existence. Marvelous, that they could not see that slavery is a moral pestilence, poisoning all the fountains of society, spreading infections over all the nation. Now the war teaches them that they have a responsibility, and that it would have been better had they seen it earlier. The right to take any responsibility in regard to it was denied to woman; it was out of her sphere; it ran into politics, which were unfit for woman, and into government affairs, which she was supposed incompetent to comprehend. But this painful hour of warfare crowds home upon us the conviction that woman's interests equally with man's are imperilled—private as well as public, individual as well as social. . . .

Wishing that the women of every State may be largely represented by earnest and faithful representatives, able to give counsel and efficient action, I am very cordially with you in spirit.

[4] History of Woman Suffrage, Vol. II, p. 875.

The ensuing year, 1864, Miss Anthony was continuing to unburden her soul on this matter.[5] She was deeply concerned over the character of the Nation that was to be preserved.

Miss Susan B. Anthony made a speech arguing that the decision of the anti-slavery question should not be left to the "stern logic of events" which is wrought by the bullet and the bayonet. More knowledge is needed. The eyes and the ears of the whole public are now open. It should be the earnest work of every lover of freedom to give those eyes the right thing to see and those ears the right thing to hear. It pains her to receive, in answer to a call for assistance and funds, letters saying that the day for discussion and petition is past. It looks as if we had returned to the old condition of barbarism, where no way is known of settling questions except by fighting. Women, who are noted for having control of the moral department of society and for lifting the other half of the race into a high moral condition, should not relapse into the idea that the status of any human being is to be settled merely by the sword. Miss Anthony then spoke of the constitutional right of Congress to pass an emancipation law. She read a letter from a lady who, on receiving documents from the League, first doubted the power of Congress to pass such a law; then she thought perhaps it had; then she compared the petition and the Constitution; then she thought it had no such power, and finally she concluded to circulate the petition anyhow. Miss Anthony proceeded at some length to expound the Constitution, showing that it does not say that slaves shall not be emancipated, and therefore concluding that they may. But if Congress cannot emancipate slaves constitutionally, it should do so unconstitutionally. She does not believe in this red-tapism that cannot find a law to suppress the wrong, but always finds one to oppress the innocent. If she was a mayor, or a governor, or a legislator, and there was no law to punish mobocrats, she thought she would go to work to make one pretty quick. She requested the opinion of some gentleman.

[5] History of Woman Suffrage, Vol. II, p. 898.

Petitions for EMANCIPATION, *accompanied by a letter from Elizabeth Cady Stanton, started rolling toward the capital of the nation. The instigation of this movement was discussed in the New York "Evening Post" of May 15, 1863.*

It has sometimes been made a reproach to the women of the Northern States, that while their sisters of the South are the very life of the rebellion, exceeding the men in zeal and devotion and self-sacrifice, they, with a noble cause against a base one, show less zeal, less earnestness, do less to animate and inspire the combatants; in short, are less active in maintaining the Union than the ladies of the Slave States in working to destroy it.

If, however, the members of the "Women's Loyal National League," an association recently commenced in this city, succeed in what they have just undertaken, it will go far to show that there is neither lukewarmness nor lack of energy in the women of the North; and that, in practical industry exerted in aid of the war and the Government, they are not to be outmatched by the zeal of the fair mischief-makers who oppose both.

We learn that the League has already obtained several thousand names and addresses of persons and societies throughout the Northern and Border States who are favorable to emancipation, to whom they propose to address their circulars; and that they are organizing, after a business fashion, the machinery necessary to effect their object in the six months still intervening before the meeting of Congress. It is a great undertaking, this obtaining of one million signatures, such an undertaking as has seldom if ever been carried out before. If it succeeds it will obtain record in the history of the time as an enterprise most honorable to the sex which conceived and completed it.

The following January, 1864, Mrs. Stanton sent out another appeal.

The Women's Loyal National League, to the Women of the Republic:—We ask you to sign and circulate this petition for the entire abolition of slavery. We have now one hundred thousand signatures, but we want a million before Congress adjourns. Remember the President's Proclamation reaches only the slaves of rebels. The jails of loyal Kentucky are to-day "crammed" with Georgia, Mississippi, and Alabama slaves, advertised to be sold for their jail fees "according to law," precisely as before the war! While slavery exists anywhere, there can be freedom nowhere. There must be a law abolishing slavery. We have undertaken to canvass the nation for freedom. Women, you cannot vote or fight for your country [some did fight]. Your only way to be a power in the Government is through the exercise of this, our sacred, constitutional "right of petition"; and we ask you to use it now to the utmost. Go to the rich, the poor, the high, the low, the soldier, the civilian, the white, the black—gather up the names of all who hate slavery—all who love liberty, and would have it the law of the land—and lay them at the feet of Congress, your silent but potent vote for human freedom guarded by law.

You have shown courage and self-sacrifice from the beginning of the war. You have been angels of mercy to our sick and dying soldiers in camp and. hospital, and on the battlefield. But let it not be said that the women of the republic, absorbed in ministering to the outward alone, saw not the philosophy of the revolution through which they passed; understood not the moral struggle that convulsed the nation—the irrepressible conflict between slavery and liberty. Remember the angels of mercy and justice are twin-sisters, and ever walk hand in hand. While you give yourselves so generously to the Sanitary and Freedmen's Commissions, forget not to hold up the eternal principles on which our republic rests. . . .

An aged Negro, Sojourner Truth, frequently a speaker at suffrage meetings,[6] thus delivered her mind in 1867 in New York City.

There is a great stir about colored men getting their rights, but not a word about the colored women; and if colored men get

---

[6] History of Woman Suffrage, Vol. II, p. 193 ff.

their rights, and not colored women theirs, you see the colored men will be masters over the women, and it will be just as bad as it was before. So I am for keeping the thing going while things are stirring; because if we wait till it is still, it will take a great while to get it going again. White women are a great deal smarter, and know more than colored women, while colored women do not know scarcely anything. They go out washing, which is about as high as a colored woman gets, and their men go about idle, strutting up and down; and when the women come home, they ask for their money and take it all, and then scold because there is no food. I want you to consider on that, chil'n. I call you chil'n; you are somebody's chil'n, and I am old enough to be mother of all that is here. I want women to have their rights. In the courts women have no right, no voice; nobody speaks for them. I wish woman to have her voice there among the pettifoggers. If it is not a fit place for women, it is unfit for men to be there.

I am above eighty years old; it is about time for me to be going. I have been forty years a slave and forty years free, and would be here forty years more to have equal rights for all. . . . I have done a great deal of work; as much as a man, but did not get so much pay. I used to work in the field and bind grain, keeping up with the cradler; but men doing no more, got twice as much pay. . . . We do as much, we eat as much, we want as much. . . . I suppose I am about the only colored woman that goes about to speak for the rights of the colored women.

The mere tool of the ballot was not enough in the view of Mrs. Josephine Griffing, whose home in Ohio had been one of the secret stations for refugee slaves. She believed that the government would have to take care of the freed people until they could manage for themselves. A plan for such care which she laid before President Lincoln was approved and would probably have been put into effect if the assassination of the President, sympathetic with such ideals, had not placed post-war policies in other hands. On September 12, 1870, Mrs. Griffing addressed the following letter [7] to Horace Greeley who was one of the leading critics of her relief proposals.

Dear sir:—Much as I respect your judgment, and admire your candor, I must express entire dissent with your views in reference to those who are laboring to befriend the Freedmen, and also with your estimate of the character of the black race.

When you condemn my work for the old slaves, who can not labor, and are "crowded into Washington" by force of events uncontrollable, as a "great injury," I am at a loss to perceive your estimate of any and all benevolent action. If, to provide houses, food, clothing, and other physical comforts, to those broken-down aged slaves whom we have liberated in their declining years, when all their strength is gone, and for whom no home, family friendship, or subsistence is furnished; if this is a "great injury," in my judgment there is no call for alms-house, hospital, home, or asylum in human society, and all appropriations of sympathy and material aid are worse than useless, and demand your earnest rebuke and discountenance, and to the unfortunates crowded into these institutions, you should say, "You must find work, go out and seek it." So far as an humble individual can, I am substituting to these a Freedman's (relief) bureau; sanitary commission; church sewing society, to aid the poor; orphan asylum; old people's home; hospital and alms-house for the sick and the blind; minister-at-large, to visit the sick, console the dying, and bury the dead; and wherein I fail, and perhaps you discriminate, is the want of wealthy, popular, and what is called honorable associations. Were these at my command, with the field before me, it would be easy to illustrate the practical use as well as the divine origin of the Golden Rule.

If, in your criticism, you refer to my secondary department in which I have labored to furnish employment to the Freedmen both in the District and out, is it not a direct reflection upon all efforts made for the distribution of labor? Is my course more

[7] History of Woman Suffrage, Vol. II, p. 36.

aggravating to the weakness of destitute unemployed freed people, than emigrant societies, intelligence offices, benevolent ladies' societies, and young men's Christian associations, who give work to the poor of all nations; and lastly the Government Indian department, that has wisely called to its aid the American missionary, and the Quaker societies, to farm out the poor Indians? Or, if the measures put forth by these admissible agents can raise the ambition and stimulate to self-reliance their beneficiaries, will you be good enough to show wherein the same means, which I claim to employ, must have the opposite effect upon the Freedmen crowded into Washington?

Is it possible that the swarming of the Irish, Swiss, and German poor, to the city of New York, is attributable to the intelligence offices and immigration societies of your city, and not, as we have supposed, to the want of work and bread at home, and is there really a danger, that in providing and calculating for them, we shall strengthen the argument of race, while our institutions of charity are filled with descendants of the Saxon, the Norman, the Goth, and the Vandal? I think not.

The tasks of reconstruction in the South, as Southern women undertook them, were very different in kind from those rendered famous in the annals of carpetbaggers and scalawags. Contrary to customary opinion, the Negro laborers did not all remain as of old the loyal servitors of masters and mistresses who survived the war. Released from the ownership of those who had made their work compulsory, it was easier for them to idle and be satisfied with the minimum of needs. Hence those Southern women who had to employ Negroes on a new basis found their problems increased not only by devastated fields and ruined homes but by the changed attitude of servants.

In PATIENCE PENNINGTON, A WOMAN RICE PLANTER,[8] *Elizabeth Pringle genially pictures Southern economy under the new régime.*

[8] Reprint obtained through the courtesy of The Macmillan Company.

When we got back to Cherokee, Chloe had a cup of tea ready and the party returned to Gregory. I felt anxious, it being late and cold. They left a large basket of things for me to keep for further distribution (among the poor). I wish so I could get at the poor Lewis family with some of them.

Miss Chevy answered when I asked about the Lewises in a high and righteous voice:—

"Yes, Miss Pashuns, they've gone away bag and baggage an' I tell you truly it's a good riddance, Mis' Lewis she acted that ridiklous with them children.

"A man come there one day in a wagon from de up country lookin' for han's to pick cotton, an' he asked me if them Lewises could pick cotton, an' I spoke up an' said, 'Yes, sir, they kin pick cotton every one o' them,' 'en he jes' drove right to the house an' asked them to go with him en he carried them all off, father and mother and three children, en I'll tell you, Miss Pashuns, it's me that's thankful.

"You see I didn't tell no lie; he didn't ask me if they would pick cotton, but he ask me if they cud, an' I up an' says they cud, but I didn't say they's that shiftless that they won't do it." . . .

The purchase of Cherokee does more credit to my heart than to my head, and it is very doubtful if I shall ever pay off the mortgage. I have lost two entire crops by freshet, and the land is now under water for the third time this winter, and, though I have rented 125 acres, it is very uncertain if I can get the half of that in. March is the month when all the rice-field ploughing should be done. The earliest rice is planted generally at the end of March, then through April, and one week in May. Last season I only got in fifty acres of rent rice and ten of wages; for in the same way the freshet was over the rice land all winter, and when it went off, there was only time to prepare that much. The renters made very fine crops—30, 40, and 45 bushels to the acre, while the wages fields only made 17! This is a complete reversal of the ordinary results, for I have very rarely, in all these years, made less than 30 bushels to the acre on my fields, and I was greatly discouraged and anxious to understand the reason of this sudden failure in the wages rice at both plantations.

By the merest chance I found out the cause. Early in December I was planting oats in a six-acre field. We broadcast winter oats in this section and then plough it in on fields which have been planted in peas before. I was anxious to get the field finished before a freeze, and had six of the best ploughmen in it. Grip had prevented my going out until they had nearly finished, but Bonaparte had assured me it was being well done. When I went into the field, it looked strange to me—the rich brown earth did not lie in billowy ridges as a ploughed field generally does. Here and there a weed skeleton stood erect. I tried to pull up one or two of these and found they were firmly rooted in the soil and had never been turned. I walked over that field with my alpenstock for hours, and found that systematically the ploughmen had left from eight to ten inches of hard land between each furrow, covering it skilfully with fresh earth, so that each hand who had been paid for an acre's ploughing had in reality ploughed only one-third of an acre. And then I understood the failure of all the wage rice! . . .

I have just come in from the corn-field, where two women have been paid for cutting down the corn-stalks, so that there will be nothing to interfere with the plough. They have only broken off the tops of the stalks, leaving about eighteen inches of stout corn-stalks all through the field. I shall have to send some one else to do the work and pay once more. . . .

8 P.M.—Spent the day at Cherokee fighting with incompetency and unwillingness.

The loose, irregular stacks of hay were, of course, wet to the heart, and I had them taken down entirely, much to Green's dismay. He thought it pure folly and fussiness, and I had to stand by and see it done, lending a helping hand now and then, to get it done at all.

He was loud in his abuse of Gibbie, his brother, for his incompetency and determination not to work, saying, "He's too strifflin' to libe," but that he himself was capable of everything;

not only stacking hay but everything else he did in the most perfect way. I let him talk on, for his manner was respectful, and I was really interested and amused to see unveiled his opinion of himself.

It would be very comfortable to see one's self in that perfect light, instead of being always so fiercely conscious of one's own shortcomings. I almost envied Green his fool's paradise.

I went to a stack which he assured he had " 'zamined, an' it was puffectly dry, 'cause, I put dat stack up myself." With ease I ran my hand in up to the elbow and brought out a handful of soaking wet hay. But that had no effect; he said that was some he had just thrown back, fearing to have it exposed, as it might rain, looking wisely at the clear sky.

One has to pray inwardly all the time to keep from a mighty outburst. He is better than any one else I could get just now. . . .

Job knew what he was talking about when he said: "Man is born to trouble as the sparks fly upward." I went to Cherokee in quite an excitement this morning because the cotton-field was snowy yesterday and I expected to make a big picking, but last night, on a plantation three miles away, an old woman died and not a creature has come out to work.

Eva is the "Presidence of the Dessiety," her son tells me, to which Lizette belonged, and so, of course, she could not be expected to work to-day, but the other women have no such eminence nor can they claim kin nor even friendship; meanwhile should the weather change and a rain come down, my precious cotton will be ruined.

Another brilliant morning, but no hands in the cotton-field but Eva. She, having accomplished the duties falling on her as "presidence" of the burial society and pinked out yards and yards of frilling for the dressing of the coffin and shroud and sat up all last night, did not feel bound to remain to the funeral, as they had not been friends; indeed the departed Lizette had been the cause of great domestic infelicity to Eva, so she came and picked her usual thirty-five pounds alone. . . .

The harvest of my June field (wages) began today. Though

very weak and miserable from grip, I drove the twelve miles to Casa Bianca, and in a lovely white piqué suit went down on the bank. I timed myself to get there about 12 o'clock, and as I expected I met a procession of dusky young men and maidens coming out of the field. I greeted them with pleasant words and compliments on their nice appearance, as they all reserve their gayest, prettiest clothes for harvest, and I delight to see them in gay colors, and am careful to pay them the compliment of putting on something pretty myself, which they greatly appreciate. After "passing the time of day," as they call the ordinary polite greetings, I asked each: "How much have you cut?" "A quarter, Miss." "Well, turn right back and cut another quarter—why, surely, Tom, you are not content to leave the field with only a quarter cut! It is but a weakling who would do that!" And so on till I have turned them all back and so saved the day.

A field of twenty-six acres is hard to manage, and unless you can stir their pride and enthusiasm they may take a week over it. One tall, slender girl, a rich, dark brown, and graceful as a deer, whose name is Pallas, when I ask, "How much?" answers, "Three quarters, Ma'am, an' I'm just goin' to get my break'us an' come back an' cut another quarter." That gives me something to praise, which is always such a pleasure. Then two more young girls have each cut a half acre, so I shame the men and urge them not to let themselves be outdone; and in a little while things are swimming. I break down some of the tops of the canes and make a seat on the bank, and as from time to time they come down to dip their tin buckets in the river to drink, I offer them a piece of candy and one or two biscuits, which I always carry in the very stout leather satchel in which I carry my time-books, etc. . . .

The women are very graceful as they sow the rice with a waving movement of the hands, at the same time bending low so that the wind may not scatter the grain; and a good sower gets it all straight in the furrow. Their skirts are tied up around their hips in a very picturesque style, and as they walk they swing in a wonderful way. This peculiar arrangement allows room for one or two narrow sacks (under the skirt), which can hold a peck of rice, and some of the sowers, if weighed on the homeward trip, would be found to have gained many pounds. They are all very gentle and considerate in their manner to-day, for a great sorrow has fallen on the family. Their tender, sympathetic manner is more to me than many bushels of rice, and I turn my back when they are dipping it out. . . .

I paid off this afternoon, as the Fourth of July is the day of all days the negroes celebrate. It was always so before the war. Every creature has to be finely dressed.

Chloe came in yesterday in great excitement to say Miss Penelope had opened a big box of the most beautiful hats and she wanted the money to buy one, "Quarter of a dollar and 10 cents." I exclaimed at the cheapness, but when she returned and showed me a very large black straw trimmed with a wealth of black and white veiling and a huge purple orchid on top I was still more filled with wonder how it is possible.

Chloe is perfectly happy. The cloud which has hung over her for the last week is dispelled by the consciousness that she is suitably provided to celebrate the country's birthday. . . .

The new beater for the threshing mill engine has arrived and is being put up. Last year I lost my engineer, he having been absorbed by a neighboring mill-owner, and I felt much at a loss, but I turned at once to an old "befo' de wah" darkey, who had learned his trade under my father. Every one said old Tinny could not possibly run the mill: he was too old and stupid; but I sent for him and he came promptly, and when I asked if he could run the engine and thresh the crop for me he answered, with great spirit, "Suttinly I kin," as though I had insulted him by the question. He has showed himself a competent engineer, careful and vigilant, though he looks as if he had not intelligence or capacity enough to kindle the fire. His first action was to tell me after examining the machinery, that I must get a new beater, as he did not consider the one in use safe. When I demurred he said, "Miss, lemme mek you sensible. I kin patch um up en run de ingin ef yo' kyan't possible buy a new one; but it's a resk, en my old marsta 'ood never expose none o' him peeple to run a ingin wid sech a beater, yo' onderstan', ma'am?" I needed nothing more than that, and wrote at once to beg Capt. L. to come and examine it, and, if necessary, to order a new one for me. He took a long time to come, being a very busy man, but when he did come he said Tinny was quite right and a new one was necessary, and now Tinny is engaged in putting in the new beater. It seems almost a miracle to me that he should be able to do it; but it just shows what it is to have been thoroughly trained to a thing in youth. This pygmy of 75, who has not looked at an engine for thirty years, and has just lived under his own vine and fig tree and worked his own little farm, the moment he is called upon, is perfectly at home in the engine room and really more competent than the very intelligent, smart young man I had before, who reads, writes, and speaks correctly and has learned his trade since the war. . . .

Just at the end of the war, when things were being adjusted after the upheaval of the Emancipation Proclamation, my mother was trying to arrange a contract which would be just to all parties, so that the lands might be worked and the starvation and want which was threatening this region prevented. The intelligent negroes saw the necessity and gave what help they could, acquiescing in the terms of the contract. The inferior element among the negroes was very turbulent and rebellious and it was a very exciting scene.

At my mother's request a United States soldier had been detailed by the commandant in Gregory to be present, witness the contract, and keep order. During the turmoil and uproar the soldier said:—

"I should think you'd rather get white help."

From time to time it has recurred to me with renewed humor, and now I think the time has come when I really must try and "get white help.". . .

To-day I went down to Casa Bianca to receive Marcus' resignation of his place as foreman. He is going to move "to town"; to enjoy the money he has made in my service and planting rice. He has bought land there and built four houses, which he rents out. He is a preacher, or, as he says, "an ordain minister." I have wondered he stayed these last few years, but he has made so good an income that his wife was willing to forego the joys of the town; he owns a horse and buggy, three very fine cows and calves, and three splendid oxen.

I feel very sad at parting with him; he has been here so long, and as foreman he has been most satisfactory in every way. When he turned over the keys of the barn to me I almost broke down, for I hate change anyway, and I really do not know to whom I can give the keys. . . .

They think that to scratch over many acres of land, guiltless of manure or help of any kind, with a yoke of oxen and then to have all the family from the oldest to the youngest turn out and plant the corn by hand, disturbing it as little as possible by work until it is ready to harvest, is to be a farmer, and they are satisfied. In the spring R.L.A. was trying to persuade one of these very satisfied old men to plant a few acres under the direction of the Department. He turned on him.

"Look a' yere, young man," he said, "I bin fa'ming long before y'u ever wuz thought of, en I want y'u to onderstan' I don't believe in deep ploughin', I don't."

R.L.A. used all his blandishments until the old man promised to plant two acres by his directions, beginning with deep ploughing. He told me that when he went back some months later the man said:

"Youngster, I don't know what's the reason, but I kyan't get any of my corn to grow but them two akers o' yourn—the dry drought is just a-burning up the rest o' my corn."

And still later when the steady rains set in and he went that way the old man clapped him on the back and said with much embellishment of action:

"Well, you've got me; the rain's done finished the rest of the corn, but them akers of yourn jest keep on a-growin' en a-growin', en I jest tell you now next year I plants jest about half o' what

I bin a-plantin' en I ploughs it all deep en does jest es you tells me to do.". . .

Yesterday I gave Gibbie a severe talk because of his total neglect of his work—the stables not cleaned, no pine straw hauled for bedding, the calves starved, yet the cows only half milked. I would not mind losing the milk so much if only the calves got it, but they look miserable, especially Heart, the little Guernsey I so wish to raise.

He is intoxicated with the rice bird and coot fever and spends every night out hunting, and of course in the day he is too sleepy to do anything. He answered almost insolently for the first time, for usually he has the grace of civility. . . .

Now I know why I have had so much trouble in getting my wood cut and sold. I had put Billy in charge and he has been steadily stealing my wood, he and his brother together, shipping it in a flat owned by their father, who is a gentleman of leisure living on his own land on a pension which he receives from the great Government of these United States. . . .

Elihu is of a peculiarly rich shade of black, almost blue black. His own mother when he was a boy always spoke of him as "dat black nigger." Through all the trials and tribulations of his fifty years of life he has never been in danger of the chain gang before, for he has kept a good character for one of his hue, and now the certain prospect of the gang unless some miracle happened had crushed the spirit out of him. I scarcely would have known him. I walked out of the gate and said:

"Why, Mr. Stout, what does this mean?"

"It means, Miss Patience, that I'm a-taking Elihu to the chain gang. I've got the warrant in my pocket."

"And on what ground?"

"For cursing, Miss Patience, and making a disturbance on the public highway."

"Was he not in his son's house?"

"Yes, Miss Patience, but the Judge says that is within fifty yards of the public road."

"Has it been measured, Mr. Stout?"

"No, ma'am, Miss Patience, 'tain't been measured, but the woman said it was only forty yards from the road, en the Judge said he knowed the place and that was right."

"What is the sentence?"

"Thirty days on the gang, Miss Patience, or a fine of $50."

"Mr. Stout," I said, "you turn right round with me and drive back to Mr. Haman with Elihu. That house is more than fifty yards from the highway."

This he said he dared not do.

By this time Jim had brought Ruth in the buckboard, and I got in and drove out of the gate. . . .

"Mr. Haman, you must sign that release until the distance is measured. I know that it is more than fifty yards from the road to Bill's house, and until that distance is measured his committal to the gang is illegal. Elihu is a hard-working, docile, respectable negro. If I wanted anything hard done to-night such as to send by land or water ten miles Elihu is the man I could call upon, knowing he would not refuse. If I had occasion to drive forty miles this night through the darkness, Elihu is a man I could trust to take me safely through the darkness and do it cheerfully. And you think I will see him put on the chain gang illegally? You don't know me, Mr. Haman.". . .

In the morning I found Eva had not come out to do the work I had pointed out to her, and I went out to the street, meaning to go to her house and see what was the matter. I found no gate to her large enclosure and could not get in, so went to Gibbie's house to ask the way. It was about 11 o'clock and Gibbie was supposed to be at work. Saw the children and asked for their mother, but they did not seem to understand, but when I repeated my question the little one answered:

"Pa dey een 'e baid."

I looked through the door and there was Gibbie fast asleep across the bed. I went in and poked him with my parasol, but he did not wake, so I left the house feeling hopeless—how can any work be done with this going on?

As I went through his yard I met his wife carrying a burning coal between two sticks. She had been over to a neighbor's, as she said, "to ketch fish fo' cook Gibbie little." She directed me to her mother-in law's house through a labyrinth of fences and gates.

I was much interested for it is just what Stanley describes in "Darkest Africa," a system of passages of stockades, making hasty entrance impossible and so guarding against surprise. . . .

This corn had been stolen in a very clever way. About a month ago I went through the field to mark what I wished kept for seed from the stalks that had more than one fine ear. I found that about every eighth stalk had two ears and some few had three ears; to-day, when gathered, not a single stalk had more than one ear. In spite of this and the damage from the storm, these two acres made seventy-two bushels of shelled corn, which is a comfort. . . .

Every year more hands leave the plantations and flock to the town, and every year more funerals wend their slow way from the town to the country; for though they all want to live in town, none is so poor but his ashes must be taken "home"; that is, to the old plantation where his parents and grandparents lived and died and lie waiting the final summons. . . . The expense of a railroad journey does not deter them from bringing their dead "home." The whole family unites and "trow een" to make up the sum necessary to bring the wanderer home, and even the most careless and indifferent of the former owners respect the feeling and consent to have those who have been working elsewhere for years, and who perhaps left them in the lurch on some trying occasion, laid to rest in the vine-covered graveyard on the old plantation.

Troublesome labor, however, if endlessly talked about and worried over, must not obscure the force and intelligence of those Negro leaders who rose out of bondage to assume burdens connected with the education of their race. Lucy Laney, whose story is told by Mary White Ovington in PORTRAITS IN COLOR,[9] *is one of the competent and courageous descendants of slaves who became leaders of their people.*

Everybody knows of Booker Washington and of how he went out from Hampton Institute in 1883 and founded a school for Negroes at Tuskegee. But only a few know that three years later Lucy Laney, graduate of Atlanta University, started in Augusta, Georgia, what was to be known as Haines Institute, a secondary school for Negro boys and girls. Washington was fired by the spirit of Hampton and General Armstrong. Lucy Laney was fired by the spirit of Atlanta University and the Wares. Tuskegee became the most famous school for industrial training in America. Miss Laney's accomplishment was less spectacular, but Haines Institute was long known as the best school of its kind for Negroes in Georgia. Its students, as they went out to teach, or as they continued their education at college or professional school, compared favorably with white students in training and capability. Haines Institute maintained a high standard of scholarship and rectitude.

The raising of money to support Tuskegee Institute was a tremendous task. Booker T. Washington died in 1915, worn out with the strain of it. But I doubt if it was as difficult to secure the money to run Tuskegee as it was to get support for Lucy Laney's school, though one had a budget very many times that of the other. Those who gave to Tuskegee saw the Negro becoming a good laborer, of service to the whites. They were doing well for him and also for themselves. But to give money to teach Negroes algebra and the classics was of no help to the whites, and was considered ridiculous and perhaps dangerous for a newly emancipated race.

So, when Lucy Laney, dark-skinned, stocky, with cropped hair and plain dress, taught her class to decline Latin nouns and conjugate Latin verbs, she was regarded as foolish and obstinate. But this did not alter her purpose. She knew the value of the

---

[9] Reprint obtained through the courtesy of the Viking Press.

education she had had at Atlanta, and she knew also how extremely difficult it was for colored boys and girls in the South to prepare for college. The public grammar schools were few and inadequate and high schools for Negroes, until quite recently, were unknown. Of good colored teachers there was the greatest need. She meant to send out from her school graduates who would have had as good a training as white graduates, and if her students wished to go to college they should enter thoroughly prepared. This she accomplished. Her school maintained a high standard, though the cold lean years were many and disaster lurked around the corner.

Haines Institute took some time to reach the place where it was pointed to as one of the best schools of its kind for Negroes in the South. Lucy Laney, on graduating from Atlanta, taught for ten years in the public schools of Augusta, Milledgeville, and Savannah. She learned a great deal in those years, and found that, despite her youth, she could handle the worst hoodlum, keeping him at work and interested. But public-school teaching had its drawbacks; it did not give full swing to her virile personality, and she gladly accepted an invitation from the Board of Missions for Freedmen to go to Augusta and start a private school.

The Board of Missions for Freedmen was doing educational as well as religious work in the South. It did not see its way, however, to maintaining the school, the opening of which it had sanctioned, and Lucy Laney had to raise the money alone. The school soon outgrew the church lecture room in which it started, and the principal moved it to a two-story house in Calhoun Street. She had day scholars and boarding scholars. She had boys and girls. At first she had meant to take girls only, but when some boy, poor, ragged, looking at her out of pathetic brown eyes, arrived on her doorstep, she took him in. In two years her school numbered three hundred pupils. There were children in plenty, but no funds. She had counted on tuitions, but the child who appealed to her most was the child whose parents could do least, or who had no parents at all. With her vivid imagination, she had only to look at a ragged, dirty boy to see a well set-up, cleanly, clear-eyed figure in his place. Her imagination saw this; it was for her practical self to bring about the metamorphosis. Sometimes she did refuse destitute boys or girls of Augusta; but the boarding pupil, ambitious, needing her help, she could not turn away. She put all her savings into the school; she begged and borrowed and paid back when she could. She went hungry and she slept cold. She prayed in her chill room at night, trusting that somehow the way would be made for her to pull through.

Her life before this had not been an easy one, but it had not known real privation. Her parents were Savannah people, and she had grown up in that pleasant, kindly city. Her father was a preacher, an exhorter, as such folks were called in slavery days, who later became an ordained Presbyterian minister. Her mother belonged to the Campbell family and was personal maid to Miss Campbell, a kindly mistress, who, seeing her slave's ability, taught her to read and write. On their marriage her father and mother were allowed to live together in a home of their own, to which they returned after their day's work. Here Lucy Laney grew up amid many children, for, besides their own large family, the Laneys took in cousins and orphaned children of friends. There was romping and fighting in which this stocky girl held her own. But there was something else. Another world was opened to her in the big house where her mother served.

When Lucy was four years old, she was taught to read and write. Then, sometimes, her mother would take her to the Campbells'; and while the mother was dusting the library, the little girl would snuggle in a deep chair to wander through fairyland with Dick Whittington or Jack-and-the-Beanstalk. Miss Campbell chose books for her and was interested in her education. It was a fine background for this teacher, who later was to gather children about her. She knew the rough-and-tumble side of life, but she knew also the quiet library and the friendliness of great books. Not until she tried to bring this friendliness to others, however, did she experience grinding worry and real privation.

It was extraordinary, but under all this strain, Lucy Laney built up a high-standard graded school. She has always had excellent co-workers. . . . New ideas in education appealed to her. She had a kindergarten when they were scarcely known in the South. She had manual training, laying great stress on household knowledge—cooking, sewing, laundering, carpentry. She got an elderly German to organize a school orchestra that held concerts in the city and outlying places. She kept up the regular curriculum. Little by little her graduates became known throughout the country. Then, as today, if you came from Lucy Laney's school, you must have character, discipline, and a great, unfailing belief in your race. If you went on to college or professional school, you must make a record as a conscientious worker. These things were naturally expected, because they were so often found. . . .

The city of Augusta owes much to Lucy Laney. It was she who introduced the trained nurse to Augusta. The city authorities let her have an old pest-house as a hospital. She brought a white graduate nurse from Canada, put her in charge, and then sent ten girls to her as students. Today, the city has a hospital with two hundred beds, over which the Canadian nurse first presided, but which has now a colored nurse as superintendent. Miss Laney heads the colored section of the Interracial Committee, and has worked with the white to secure drainage in the Negro section, and, unsuccessfully as yet, to obtain adequate schools for the colored children. It is a great grief to this woman who has given forty years to educating the children of Augusta to see the niggardliness with which the city matches her efforts.

Lucy Laney is a pioneer woman. She belongs with Lucretia Mott, Frances Willard, Lillian Devereaux Blake. She was ahead of her time, and men, especially those in her profession, looked askance at her. What business had a woman at the head of a school? As Haines Institute grew, as one dignified building after another was erected on its campus, it was unseemly that she should be principal. . . . This woman, too, had such an undignified way of sweeping up the leaves in the yard, or making biscuits in the kitchen, when she should have been sitting at her desk receiving visitors in her office. No one looking at her would imagine that she held a prominent position in the educational world. She never spent anything on clothes or considered any work beneath her dignity. . . .

Since the colored race is put in a position of inferiority, life cannot be easy for a woman of masterful ability and temper. Lucy Laney never toadies. She may have to hold her tongue, but she does not pretend an acquiescence in what she believes to be wrong. During the war, when the exodus from the South was under way, and Southern employers urged the Negro to stay at home, she would not acquiesce in this doctrine. . . .

The Negro audience is blamed for remaining unresponsive when the white man weeps over the loss of his colored mammy. But the reason is obvious. The Negro knows that its womanhood was drawn away from the service that it owed its own, that it was confined, contorted. Now the dam is broken and the maternal spirit released. What that stream can accomplish when it is allowed to rush unobstructed is shown by this colored woman's life.

By 1930 Southern women, through organizations in every Southern State, were seeking to abolish lynching—the remaining blot on their sectional escutcheon. Feminine leaders, distinguished in the religious, educational and social life of the South, were declaring that the defense of womanhood must be left to more civilized procedure. The care-of-life sentiment had broadened to include all races.

Interracial committees were working, experimentally, to bring about a better adjustment by the people involved, after the hardships suffered by Northern control. From their publications a few extracts are taken to convey something of the spirit animating this enterprise.

In the South's entire history there has probably been no sociological development more unique and important than the recent movement for interracial coöperation, which took organic form in Atlanta in 1919, with the creation of the Commission on Interracial Coöperation.

The purpose of this organization and its affiliated state and local committees is to bring about *better understanding, justice and fair dealing* between the white and colored races. The Commission believes that the white race, as the more fortunate group and the one responsible for the Negro's presence in America, is under obligation to be both just and generous toward the latter. It believes further that the welfare and even the racial integrity of the two groups can be effectively preserved in no other way.

The results of this policy, as worked out by hundreds of interracial committees, have attracted nationwide and even international attention. Though the Commission has made no effort to organize outside the South, similar committees have recently been set up in many northern states and cities where there are considerable Negro populations. The plan is even being put into effect in South Africa.

In this movement *southern women* have been a most important factor. At the call of the Commission on Interracial Coöperation, a hundred women, leaders in their respective circles, met in Memphis in October, 1920, for the purpose of considering the situation. Four representative Negro women were invited to interpret to the meeting the viewpoint and the needs of colored women and children.

A profound impression was made upon the group and out of the meeting came a remarkable statement, expressing *"a deep sense of responsibility* to the womanhood and childhood of the Negro race and a great desire for a Christian settlement of the problems that overshadow the homes of both races." The statement recommended the conservation of the life and health of Negro children through day nurseries, kindergartens, clinics and playgrounds; the study of Negro housing and sanitary conditions with a view to their improvement; equitable provision of educational opportunities; improved conditions of travel; justice in the courts; and with especial emphasis, the suppression of lynching. A Continuation Committee of seven was created, representing respectively the Methodist, Baptist, Presbyterian, Episcopal and Disciples Churches, the Y.W.C.A., and the Women's Clubs.

CHAPTER VII

THE ADORNMENTS OF CAPITALISM

AFTER industrialism triumphed in the social war and spread across the continent, exploiting natural resources, through the connivance of the government, with little let or hindrance, the civilization of urbanism steadily supplanted the simpler culture of the old rural and village life. Thus the artificialities of a money economy exfoliated and extended, as wealth concentrated in the hands of a few and the values of wealth rose supreme over the values of culture. Things which the early Romans had feared, as tending to the effeminacy of spirit, once again multiplied and became in fact the almost universal objects of desire—profoundly affecting ideas, interests, moralities and manners from the top to the bottom of the social ladder.

American women now had a new scene to survey. Some looked on it with amusement and laughed out loud. Others were solemnly reminded of decaying empires. An "unregenerate Southerner," admitted to its very center of ceremonies, regarded it with quiet geniality. An artist, profiting from its patronage, viewed it with her art in mind. The great novelist of the era, Edith Wharton, habituated to the ways of an order marked by more restraint, named it "The Age of Innocence." From such as these we may learn of the classes that set the fashions for the masses and began to build up the civilization of the North.

To Marietta Holley the new freedom was mostly ludicrous. Under the pseudonym of "Samantha Allen" or "Josiah Allen's

Wife," she gave rein to her feeling for the absurd which never reached the point of bitterness. Her wit was too sure for that. With SAMANTHA AT SARATOGA we meet the new-rich creating for themselves a "spa."

We arrived at Saratoga jest as sunset with a middlin' gorgeous dress on wuz a walkin' down the west and a biddin' us and the earth goodbye. There wuz every color you could think on almost, in her gown, and some stars a shinin' through the floatin' drapery and a half moon restin' up on her cloudy foretop like a beautiful ornament.

(I s'pose mebby it is proper to describe sunset in this way on goin' to such a dressy place, though it haint my style to do so. I don't love to describe sunset as a female and don't, much of the time, but I love to see things correspond.) . . .

Wall, after supper (a good supper and enough on't), Josiah proposed that we should take a short walk, we two alone. . . . I wuz tired enough myself to lay down my head and repose in the arms of sleep, and told my companion so, but he said:

"Oh shaw! Let old Morpheus wait for us till we get back, there'll be time enough to rest then."

Josiah felt so neat, that he wuz fairly beginnin' to talk high learnt, and classical. But I didn't say nothin' to break it up, and tied on my bonnet with calmness (and a double bow knot) and we sallied out.

Soon, or mebby a little after, for we didn't walk fast on account of my deep tucker, we stood in front of what seemed to be one hull side of a long street, all full of orniments and openwork, and pillows, and flowers, and carvin's, and scollops, and down between every scollop a big basket full of posys, of every beautiful color under the heavens. And over all, and way back as far as we could see, wuz innumerable lights of every color gorgeousness a shinin' down on gorgeousness, glory above, a shinin' down on glory below. And sweet strains of music wuz a floatin' out from somewhere, a shinin' somewhere, renderin' the seen fur more beautiful to all 4 of our enraptured ears.

And Josiah sez, as we stood there nearly rooted to the place by our emotions, and a picket fence, sez he dreamily:

"I almost feel as if we had made a mistake, and that this is the land of Beuler." And he murmured to himself some words of the old him:

"'Oh Beuler land! Sweet Beuler land!'"

And I whispered back to him and sez—"Hush! they don't have brass bands in Beulah land."

And he sez, "How do you know what they have in Beuler?"

"Wall," sez I, "'tain't likely they do."

But I don't know as I felt like blamin' him, for it did seem to me to be the most beautiful place that I ever sot my eyes on. And it did seem fairly as if them long glitterin' chains and links of colored lights, a stretchin' fur back into the distance sort a begoned for us to enter a land of perfect beauty and Pure Delight.

And then them glitterin' chains of light would jine onto other golden, and crimson, and orange, and pink, and blue, and amber links of glory and hang there all drippin' with radiance, and way back as fur as we could see. And away down the shinin' lanes the white statues stood, beautiful snow-white females, a lookin' as if they enjoyed it all. And the lake mirrored back all of the beauty.

Right out onto the lake stood a fairy-like structure all glowin' with big drops of light and every glitterin' drop reflected down in the water and the fountain a sprayin' up on each side. Why, it sprayed up floods of diamonds, and rubys, and sapphires, and topazes, and turkeys, and pearls, and opals, and sparklin' 'em right back into the water agin.

And right while we stood there, neerly rooted to the spot and gazin' through extacy and 2 pickets, the band gin a loud burst of melody and then stopped, and after a minute of silence, we hearn a voice angel-sweet a risin' up, up, like a lark, a tender-hearted, golden-throated lark.

High, high above all the throngs of human folks who wuz cheerin' her down below—up above the sea of glitterin' light—up above the bendin' trees that clasped their hands together in silent applaudin' above her, up, up into the clear heavens, rose that glorious voice a singin' some song about love, love that wuz deathless, eternal. . . .

And Josiah stood stun still till she had got done, and then he sithed out: "Oh, it seems as if it must be Beuler land! Do you s'pose, Samantha, Beuler land is any more beautiful?"

And I sez, "I haint a thinkin' about Beulah." I sez it pretty middlin' tart, partly to hide my own feelin's, which wuz perfectly rousted up, and partly from principle, and sez I, "Don't for mercy's sake call it Beuler."

Josiah always will call it so. . . . Truly in some things a pardner's influence and encouragement fails to accomplish the ends aimed at.

Wall, it wuz after some words that I drew Josiah away from that seen of enchantment—or he me, I don't exactly know which way it wuz—and we wended onwards in our walk.

The hull broad street wuz full of folks, full as they could be, all on 'em perfect strangers to us and who knew what motives or weapons they wuz a carryin' with 'em; but we knew we wuz safe, Josiah and me did, for way up over all our heads, stood a big straight soldier, a volunteer, volunteerin' to see to the hull crew on 'em below, a seein' that they behaved themselves. His age wuz seventy-seven as near as I could make out, but he didn't look more'n half that. He had kep' his age remarkable.

Wall, it wuz, if I remember right, jest about now that we see a glitterin' high up over our heads some writin' in flame. I never see such brilliant writin' before nor don't know as I ever shall ag'in.

And Josiah stopped stun still, and stood a lookin' perfectly dumbfoundered at it. And finally he sez, "I'd give a dollar bill if I could write like that."

I see he wuz deeply rousted up for 2 cents is as high as he usually goes in bettin'. I see he felt deep and I didn't blame him. "Why," sez he, "jest imagine, Samantha, a hull letter wrote like that! how I'd love to send one back to Uncle Nate Gowdey. How Uncle Nate's eyes would open, and he wouldn't want no

spectacles nor nothin' to read it with, would he? I wonder if I
could do it," sez he, a beginnin' to be all rousted up.

But I sez, "Be calm"; for so deep is my mind that I grasped
the difficulties of the undertakin' at once. "How could you send
it, Josiah Allen? Where would you get a envelop? How could
you get it into the mail box?" Sez I, "When any body would
send a letter wrote like that, they would want to write it on
sheets of lightnin', and fold it up in the envelopin' clouds of the
skies, and it should be received by a kneelin' and reverent
soul. . . ."

And so we meandered along, keepin' our 2 heads as nigh as we
could under that long glitterin' chain of golden drops that wuz
high overhead. And on, and on, we followed it diligently; till
for the land's sake! if it didn't lead us to another one of them
openwork buildin's, fixed off beautiful, and we could see inside
2 big wells like, with acres of floor seemin'ly on each side on 'em,
and crowds of folks a walkin' about and settin' at little tables
and most all of 'em a drinkin'. . . .

And ag'in Josiah asked me if I thought Beuler land could
compare with it? . . .

Wall, the next mornin' Josiah and me sallied out middlin'
early to explore still further the beauties and grandness of Saratoga. I had on a black straw bonnet, a green vail, and a umberell.
I also had my black alpacky, that good moral dress.

My dress bein' such a high mission one choked me. It wuz
so high in the neck it held my chin up in a most uncomfortable
position, but sort a grand and lofty lookin'. My sleeves wuz so
long that more'n half the time my hand wuz covered up by 'em
and I wuz too honerable to wear 'em for mits; no, in the name
of principle I wore 'em for sleeves, good long sleeves, a pattern
to other grandmas that I might meet.

I felt that when they see me and see what I wuz doin' and
endurin' for the cause of female dressin' they would pause in
their wild career, and cover up their necks and pull their sleeves
down. . . .

I can truly say that I thought I knew sunthin' about parasols, havin' owned 3 different ones in the course of my life, and havin' one covered over. I thought I knew sunthin' of their nater and habits, which is a good deal, so I had always s'posed, like a umberell's. But good land! I gin up that I knew them not, nor never had.

Why, anybody could learn more on 'em through one jerney down that street, than from a hull life time in Jonesville. Truly travel is very upliftin' and openin' and spreadin' out to the mind, both in parasols and human nater. . . .

And it wuz anon that we see in the distance a fair white female a standin' kinder still in the edge of the woods, and Josiah spoke in a seemin'ly careless way, and sez he, "She don't seem to have many clothes on, Samantha."

Sez I, "Hush, Josiah! she has probable overslept herself, and come out in a hurry, mebby to look for some herbs or sunthin'. I persoom one of her children are sick, and she sprung right up out of bed, and come out to get some weather-wort, or catnip, or sunthin'."

And as I spoke I drawed Josiah down a side path away from her. But he stopped stun still and sez he, "Mebby I ought to go and help her, Samantha."

Sez I, "Josiah Allen, sense I lived with you, I don't think I have been shameder of you"; sez I, "it would mortify her to death if she should *mistrust* you had seen her in that condition."

"Wall," sez he, still a hangin' back, "if the child is very sick, and I can be of any help to her, it is my duty to go."

His eyes had been on her nearly every moment of the time, in spite of my almost voyalent protests, and sez he, kinder excited like, "She is standin' stun still, as if she is skairt; mebby there is a snake in front of her or sunthin', or mebby she is took paralysed, I'd better go and see."

Sez I, in low deep axents, "You stay where you be, Josiah Allen, and I will go forward, bein' 2 females together, it is what is right to do and if we need your help I will holler."

And finally he consented after parlay.

Wall, as I got up to her I see she wuzn't a live, meat woman, but a statute and so I hastened back to my Josiah and told him "there wuzn't no need of his help and he wuz in the right on't —she was stun still."

More formidably Sarah Orne Jewett reported on her day. At another watering-place, Poland Spring House, which she visited in 1902, positively ominous thoughts took form.

The line between being innocently amused and wickedly bored is very narrow. It is a little like what crossing the continent with a big train party must be,—not the people you or I run across very often, but all sorts of terrible, rich and splendid westerners and southerners of a sort who must have had German grand-mas and have prospered in the immediate past. Their jewels and their gowns are a wonder, and the satisfaction in life must be very great, though the best of them look as if keeping things just right and *according to* at this high rate were almost too much effort. It is the kind of rich creatures who are more at home in big hotels than in fine houses. They are apt to speak of last winter at "Pa'm Beach", and altogether they made me understand what my old grand-father, who had travelled wide, meant when he said, "Oh, they're not people, they're nothing but a pack of images!" This is in the mass; one individual opposite me at the table has been quite entertaining; such a diamond cross she wears upon her; but I must hold back from relating such parts of her history as have been ascertained,—automobile and private car. A great many puzzling facts were brought together into simple certainty yesterday when I heard somebody say she was a prosperous retired hotel-keeper. It made you see her fine and masterful about quailing maids. These dazzle one's eyes; but now and then, when you see the backs of two dear heads of ladies a table or two away, you feel as if you must stop and speak! I feel sure out of two or three hundred fellow pilgrims I must find as many of my betters, but I have been so long away that my country seems strange in its great crowd of citizens. One thing certain is, it is a rich country,—it is like Rome before it fell!

The upper crust of the planting South, ruined by the social war, made such adjustments as it could to a changed America. Many old families settled back in secluded mansions and lived in their memories if they could. Others sent sons and daughters to Northern schools with the thought that they might learn to make their way in the new order. In some cases Northern men married Southern women, and brought their brides to the center of the industrial system, the great metropolis of New York, where a "Society" assuming regal rights of selection was taking form.

Thus Constance Cary, a distant relative of Thomas Jefferson, became a member of ruling circles as the wife of Burton Harrison. In RECOLLECTIONS GRAVE AND GAY,[1] she limned New York of the gilded period—at a little distance but with sympathy.

What an odd, provincial pleasant little old New York was that of the seventies, just when the waves of the after-the-war prosperity had begun to strike its sides and make it feel the impulse toward a progress never afterward to cease!

Broadway, a long unlovely thoroughfare, was filled with huddled buildings, monotonous in line and tint. Union and Madison Squares were still inclosed in high railings (removed after 1871 and sold at auction), their grasses and trees, as now, a great relief to the eye in passing. Fifth Avenue, fringed on either side with telegraph poles, was abominably paved with irregular blocks of stone, so that a drive to the park, or "away up-town to Fiftieth Street," was accompanied by much wear and tear to the physical and nervous system. The celebrated and delightful Dr. Fordyce Barker used to say he actually could not recommend a convalescent patient to take the air, because of the necessary jolting in a carriage in any direction away from the residential quarter.

[1] Reprint obtained through the courtesy of Charles Scribner's Sons.

Apart from this discomfort, the noise of continuous passage of vehicles, knowing not rubber tires, made open windows in one's home a purgatorial trial. Certainly we modern grumblers in asphalted streets heave no sigh of regret for that feature of the dear old by-gone days!

Plodding up and down town jogged the lamentable old omnibuses, filled, as Mr. J. W. Cross once said of them, "exactly the way we stuff the carts with calves in London." A sorry spectacle, indeed, was that of well-dressed, well-bred New Yorkers clinging to straps, jaded, jammed, jostled, panting in the aisle of these hearse-like equipages, to reach their goal. An astute traveller from France, Monsieur Simonet, in an article published at that time in the *Revue des Deux Mondes,* guilelessly records that he was "told in New York" it was the custom of "the ladies," on getting into a full omnibus in Fifth Avenue, to seat themselves on the knees of "gentlemen" already placed! The conditions of horse-cars in the neighboring avenues showed for many years no improvement upon this discomfort, and the prices of "hacks" and "coaches," procured after much preamble at the livery stables, were prohibitive save for the solvent citizen. On New-Year's Day, when calls were made by men upon the families of their friends, it was common for four of the intending visitors to unite in paying forty dollars for the hire of a ponderous old hack, of the Irish-funeral variety, and go their rounds clad in evening dress, rumbling over the stony streets from mid-day till dinner-time at six o'clock.

In the absence of cabs, hansoms and the sportive "taxis"— then as unimaginable as the air-ship in common use appears to-day—walking was very much in vogue. It was a general practice of professional men, possessing offices down town, to go afoot in all weathers from their dwellings to their business haunts and back again. A lawyer, prominent in that day, lately said to me: "And weren't we the better for it, I'd like to know?" Who doesn't remember Clarkson Potter's handsome, erect figure, and springing step, like a boy's in middle age; and David Dudley Field, who always took his exercise in that way (as well as on horseback, with a rest before dinner)? Wasn't he a picture of vigor in later life? No dieting and health foods about those men, I'll promise you. . . . And what a cheery meeting-place Broadway was for friends!

Central Park was already beginning to be beautiful in verdant slopes and flowering shrubs and trees, although still surrounded, and the way to it disfigured, by hill-sides from which segments were cut away like slices from a cheese, upon the summit of which perched the cabins of Irish squatters left high and dry by the march of municipal progress. The territory around these dwellings was populous with curs, urchins, goats, pigs, and mounds of débris revealing old tin cans and discarded hoop-skirts. . . .

What would have been thought in that epoch of New York of a table stretched to the limit of the dining-room with chairs so pushed together as to prevent free movement with spoon and fork; where forty or more guests, corralled to eat insidious messes served by caterers and shepherded by strange waiters on tiptoe thrusting between them fish, flesh, and fowl, with their attendant condiments, at quarters so close the alarmed diner must shrink back in order to avoid contact with the offered dish!

No, that was hardly the way they served dinners in the seventies! Rather were friends convened to the number of ten or twelve around mahoganies of generous size and space (small enough for talk to fly easily across them), the host and hostess near enough to their guests to mark their own individuality upon the feast. Upon the authority of the late Mr. Ward McAllister we are told that "Blue Seal Johannisberg flowed like water; incomparable '48, superb Burgundies and amber-colored Madeira were there to add to the intoxicating delight" of the best New York dinner and supper tables. But, as the present chronicler has never been able to distinguish old wine from new, she fears in this matter she is in the category of a certain well-known literary lady of New York of whom Mr. Ward McAllister once remarked to me with scathing emphasis: "She write stories of New York Society! Why, I have seen her, myself, buying her Madeira at Park & Tilford's in a demijohn!"

It is not in me to offer regretful comparison of the New York of my first acquaintance, its people, content to dwell in barns of brick with brown-stone fronts, its chief avenues as yet untouched by the finger of art in beautiful buildings, some of its streets yet encumbered with rows of trucks and wagons kept there by their owners for want of a place of shelter, ash and refuse barrels in all their hideous offensiveness standing by the basement doors of refined citizens, with our later city of wondrous progress, a gathering place of art of the whole world, as well as a sovereign of finance.

But putting aside the physical aspect of the place, forgetting certain inherited crudities of custom, its vulgar or lifeless architecture, I have never seen reason to renounce my belief that the period I write of was illustrated by the best society New York has known since colonial days. It is generally admitted by commentators of our social life to-day that the rock we split upon is the lack of leadership. As to who are the present real great ladies of New York there is in the public mind a nebulous uncertainty only occasionally dispelled by the dictum of some writer for the newspapers.

In the earlier period, New York possessed what none could question: a sovereignty over its body corporate divided between five or six gentlewomen of such birth, breeding, and tact that people were always satisfied to be led by them. Mrs. Hamilton Fish, Mrs. Lewis Morris Rutherfurd, Mrs. Belmont, Mrs. Theodore Roosevelt, and the two Mrs. Astors were the ladies whose entertainments claimed most comment, whose fiat none was found to dispute.

Of these, Mrs. Theodore Roosevelt seemed to me easily the most beautiful; and in the graciousness of her manner and that inherent talent for winning and holding the sympathetic interest of those around her, I have seen none to surpass her. . . . This lady was of Southern birth, and many stories were whispered of her unhappiness during the war because of the fulminations of the Northern family into which she had married against her Confederate kin and sympathies. I remember her, first, in a small, inconspicuous house, one of a brown-stone row in a street between Broadway and Fourth Avenue where her afternoon at home seemed to convey a waft of violets. . . . In the course of time, the Roosevelts moved uptown into a handsome modern house in West Fifty-seventh Street. There a great ball was given, to which we went. I believe it was to celebrate the entrance into society of the eldest daughter, and the story was circulated that eleven hundred invitations had been sent forth. I find this mentioned in a letter written to my mother in Baltimore, by whom I was besought to keep her *au courant* of everything, big or little, in my new experience. I have no souvenirs to contribute concerning the early youth of the future President but I fancy he was enjoying the glorious indifference of sturdy boyhood to the social happenings of the hour.

Mrs. Belmont was a woman of charm and distinction, to whom fortune had allotted means and opportunity to take the lead in entertainment of the grandiose foreign order, in a great house, with an illumined picture-gallery and everything on a corresponding scale. . . .

Mrs. John Jacob Astor was at the time I first came to New York a noble-looking woman, full of gracious sweetness and wide humanity. Her parties were a happy union of the best elements procurable in New York, surrounded by all that wealth and taste could add to originality of conception. Her Southern blood revealed itself in the cordiality and simplicity with which this lady bore her honors of leadership.

Mrs. Hamilton Fish, a matron of exemplary dignity, who transferred her regnant attitude toward Society from New York to Washington, where her husband was Secretary of State in Grant's administration, belonged to the Faubourg St. Germain side of New York, the Second Avenue "set," embracing a number of old-school families of colonial ancestry who had not thought it worth their while to remove from their broad and spacious residences on the East Side to emulate the mere fashion of living in Fifth Avenue.

In this quarter also abode Mrs. Rutherfurd, wife of the gentle

and learned astronomer. Their oldest son, Stuyvesant Rutherfurd, had reversed his name on inheriting the Stuyvesant fortune.
. . . Mrs. Rutherfurd was a law-giver in her circle, and no weak
one; she invited whom she pleased, as she pleased; and an of-
fender against her exactions came never any more. But she had
the prettiest way in the world of putting people in appropriate
place.

It was on the East Side of town that we, "reconstructed" rebels,
first pitched our tent in New York. . . . I am sure no perfectly
equipped Fifth Avenue establishment, fitted up beforehand by
the fairies who obey the wands of millionaires ever gave to a
young couple the delight we took in our simple quarters. The
contrast with surroundings in the war-worn South made the
simple necessaries of life, disposed with taste and harmony, seem
a fairy tale. I had brought from Paris some understanding of
the decorative value of crétonne in small rooms, and the French
gray of my little salon, with its draperies and furniture of gray
crétonne relieved by medallions of pale blue enshrining shepherds
and shepherdesses, hearts and darts, pipes and tabors tangled
with knots of ribbon, filled the measure of my ambition as a
housekeeper. . . .

We now found ourselves in a circle of acquaintances, alien in
political creed, with a few exceptions among the Southerners
already established in New York, but most kind and considerate
always, and every year the number grew and firmer friendships
were cemented. . . .

We went out a great deal. . . . There is the record of a ball
at the Academy of Music of which Lord Dufferin was the bright
particular star among the guests, with Sir Tatton and Lady
Sykes and some other smart English folk in the party. . . .

To the Academy of Music we repaired for public balls and
operas. Till late at night on these occasions, quiet, sleepy Irving
Place would resound with the roll of fashionable carriages and
the hoarse call by the doormen of fashionable names or their
equivalent numbers. And oh! the song-birds caged for our delec-
tation in that dear old Temple of Music! There Patti, Nilsson,

Gerster, Pauline Lucca, Annie Louise Cary, Kellogg, Minnie Hauk, Parepa-Rosa, Brignoli, Capoul, Campanini, Del Puente, and a host of others, sang our hearts out of our bodies many a time. . . .

It was not only the "Four Hundred" who experimented socially in the early years of prosperity. New York was also the abode of THE TERRIBLE SIREN, Victoria Woodhull,[2] whose career is sketched by Emanie Sachs. She who had been a child of the "submerged tenth," as the phrase ran current to identify the poor, rose through newspaper editing, political campaigning, Wall Street speculating, and friendships to a post of considerable power until she departed for England and by a marriage into the nobility settled down to a ripe old age as a country gentle-woman. Victoria Woodhull illustrated the mobility of classes at home and abroad, in the days of laissez faire.

Victoria Woodhull was the firebrand of her time, and her story is as strange as her personality.

It is a story of violent action and romantic contrasts, dominated by the courage and vitality of a woman who was brilliant and ignorant and beautiful; who emerged from a background which explains much that seems inexplicable, since few have ever emerged into public notice from such a sordid beginning. Deeds that bewildered those with any standards of behavior were only natural to a hungry creature with none. She did anything she wanted to do, and then denied that she had done so, and died at eighty-nine in the odor of sanctity.

Throughout, like a tiger, she had purred when she was stroked, and torn when she was lashed. And like a tiger, she could see in the dark; she was a spiritualist. But she had an itch for greatness and an urge for reform, which brought her out of the jungle.

[2] Reprint obtained through the courtesy of the author and Harper & Brothers.

She was the first suffragist to have an official hearing in Washington. She memorialized Congress to claim votes for women under the Fourteenth Amendment. But she fought the folkways that oppressed her sex more than she fought for the franchise. She defied prudery in her life and in the press and on the platform. She was a great orator, and people flocked to hear her lecture on constitutional equality, and spiritualism, the social revolution, and the principles of finance, as well as free love. She was a priestess of publicity. And she figured in every history of Socialism in America, as well as in every history of Wall Street.

In 1870, she and her sister, Tennessee Claflin, were the famous Lady Brokers of Wall Street, or the Bewitching Brokers, according to some. They made a fortune, and lost most of it, through publishing *Woodhull & Claflin's Weekly,* which had *"Progress! Free thought! Untrammeled lives!* Breaking the Way for Future Generations," on the cover. Anthony Comstock suppressed it for printing a scandal about the Rev. Henry Ward Beecher, and sent Victoria and Tennessee to Ludlow Street jail, though Victoria was a candidate for the Presidency of the United States. She was nominated by the Equal Rights party, and her running mate for Vice-President was Frederick Douglass, the negro reformer.

Born in Homer, Ohio, in 1838, she was bred in poverty and chicanery. She died in 1927, the widow of a wealthy English banker, a lady-bountiful in an English village, esteemed by the estimable. She had a varied life.

In the 'seventies, her heyday, newspapers called her "The Queen of the Prostitutes," but some said in representing suffrage, an unpopular cause, she paid the pioneer's penalty of misrepresentation, though none of the other suffragists paid it. One man called her a dual personality, half saint, half sinner, but altogether fascinating.

She fascinated me. My purpose, however, is neither to vindicate her nor to attack her, but to tell the story I found, after nearly two years' research. I went to Homer, Ohio, her birthplace, and saw old settlers there who remembered her and her family. I followed her trail to Mt. Gilead, Ohio, and to Columbus. It led to court records in Ottawa, Illinois, in Chicago, New York, and Brooklyn, to folk-lore in Pennsylvania, and old letters from everywhere. Newspaper files have been searched from Maine to California, and Mr. Daniel R. Maué of Columbia University went to England for material. The story of Mr. Benjamin R. Tucker's experience with Victoria Woodhull is printed from his own handwriting. Several published memoirs of her contemporaries mentioned her, and she was the subject of many biographical pamphlets, which are colorful, dramatic, and contradictory. Moreover, she had an engaging habit of public confessional in print and on the platform.

Hundreds who knew her, or whose parents knew her, have told me her legends. They are hearsay evidence, but inasmuch as they came from disconnected sources, without any reason for animus, they are consistent enough to be believable. And surely, when anyone has been interesting enough to inspire legends, they are valuable as an index of human behavior. Both the false and the true are significant, because both show what people thought and felt about Victoria Woodhull, what she meant in their minds and their emotions. Maybe she was merely a symbol of feminine activity in an age of male bluster when feminine activity was dreaded and feared. Maybe she personified men's erotic dreams, too, and women's audacious impulses, and like Johnny Appleseed and Paul Bunyan and other Gargantuan American figures, she and her remarkable family were only half real.

But it is undeniable that in Victoria Woodhull's heyday she wanted to live in the white glare of publicity. She sought it. Because she went into public life, she belongs to history, and because she was vivid and conspicuous there, her story cannot fade into the mists of oblivion with which decency covers the dead who had wanted privacy.

I shall try to tell what seems true to me, to revive the personality of Victoria Woodhull, a woman who dared to do anything she wanted to do. Those who lack her strength or her ruthlessness; those whose training or circumstances, or deepest desires, prevent them from obeying piratical impulses, may release them vicariously in her adventures without doing harm to anyone. And those who haven't any piratical impulses will find Americana.

In the eighties attendance upon the Opera was made the sine qua non *of social perfection and New York thus felt itself properly Parisian in its taste. At the zenith of capitalism, feminine beneficiaries of the system listened to the arias from a circle known as the "Diamond Horseshoe" on account of the gems which flashed there. The coming of the Opera into high favor is told by Mrs. Harrison from the standpoint of the audience. But Clara Louise Kellogg, in the MEMOIR OF AN AMERICAN PRIMA DONNA,[3] takes us behind the scenes where the artist who served that audience lived and worked. She began her musical career in 1861 in "Rigoletto," at the old Academy of Music in New York, at a time when Americans were still looking to Europe for voices. But in 1883 her fame and popularity as a native lyric artist were fully established.*

Everybody [in war time] went about singing Mrs. Howe's *Battle Hymn of the Republic* and it was then that I first learned that the air—the simple but rousing little melody of *John Brown's Body*—was in reality a melody by Felix Mendelssohn. Martial songs of all kinds were the order of the day and all more classic music was relegated to the background for the time being. It was not until the following winter [after the draft riots] that public sentiment subsided sufficiently for us really to consider another musical season. . . .

We had all gone to Chicago for our spring opera season and were ready to open, when the tragic tidings came [of the assassination of Lincoln] and shut down summarily upon every

---

[3] Reprint obtained through the courtesy of G. P. Putnam's Sons.

preparation for amusement of any kind. Every city in the Union went into mourning for the man whom the country idolized. . . . However, nations go on even after the beloved rulers of them are laid in the ground. Our Chicago season opened soon—I in Lucia—and everything went along as though nothing had happened. . . .

My mother hated the atmosphere of the theatre even though she had wished me to become a singer and always gloried in my successes. To her rigid and delicate instinct there was something dreadful in the free and easy artistic attitude, and she always stood between me and any possible intimacy with my fellow-singers. I believe this to have been a mistake. Many traditions of the stage come to one naturally and easily through others; but I had to wait to learn them all by experience. I was always working as an outsider, and, naturally, this attitude of ours antagonized singers with whom we appeared.

Not only that. My brain would have developed much more rapidly if I had been allowed—no, if I had been *obliged* to be more self-reliant. To profit by one's own mistakes;—all the world's history goes to show that is the only way to learn. By protecting me, my mother really robbed me of much precious experience. For how many years after I had made my *début* would she wait for me in the *coulisses,* ready to whisk me off to my dressing-room before any horrible opera singer had a chance to talk with me!

Yet she grieved for my forfeited youth—did my dear mother. She always felt that I was being sacrificed to my work, and just at the time when I would have most delighted in my girlhood. Of course, I was obliged to live a life of labour and self-denial, but it was not quite so difficult for me as she felt it to be, or as other people sometimes thought it was. Not only did I adore my music, and look forward to my work as an artist, but I literally never had any other life. I knew nothing of what I had given up; and so was happy in what I had undertaken, as no girl could have been happy who had lived in a less restricted, hard-working and yet dream-filled existence.

My mother was very strait-laced and puritanical, as I have said, and, naturally, by reflection and association, I was the same. I lay stress on this because I want one little act of mine to be appreciated as a sign of my ineradicable girlishness and love of beauty. When I earned my first money, I went to Mme. Percival's, the smart lingerie shop of New York, and bought the three most exquisite chemises I could find, imported and trimmed with real lace.

I dare say this harmless ebullition of youthful daintiness would have proved the last straw to some of my Psalm-singing New England relatives. There was one uncle of mine who vastly disapproved of my going on the stage at all, saying that it would have been much better if I had been a good, honest milliner. He used to sing: "Broad is the road that leads to Hell!" in a minor key, with the true God-fearing, nasal twang in it.

How I detested that old man! And I had to bury him, too, at the last. I wonder whether I should have been able to do so if I had gone into the millinery business! . . .

The week after my *début* we went to Boston to sing. Boston would not have *Rigoletto*. It was considered objectionable, particularly the ending. For some inexplicable reason *Linda di Chamounix* was expected to be more acceptable to the Bostonian public, and so I was to sing the part of Linda instead of that of Gilda. . . . It is a dear little story; but I never could comprehend how Boston was induced to accept the second act since they drew the line at *Rigoletto!*

I liked Linda and wanted to give a truthful and appealing impersonation of her. But the handicaps of those crude and primitive theatre conditions were really almost insurmountable. Now, with every assistance of wonderful staging, exquisite costuming, and magical lighting, the artist may rest upon his or her surroundings and accessories and know that everything possible to art has been brought together to enhance the convincing effect. In the old days at the Academy, however, we had no system of lighting except glaring footlights and perhaps a single, unimaginative calcium. We had no scenery worthy the name; and as for costumes, there were just three sets, called by the theatre *costumier* "Paysannes" (peasant dress); "Norma" (they did not know enough even to call it "classic"); and "Rich!" The last were more or less of the Louis XIV period and could be lightly modified for various operas. These three sets were combined and altered as required. Yet, of course, the audiences were correspondingly unexacting. . . . Once during a performance of *Il Barbiere* the man who was playing the part of Don Basilio sent his hat out of doors to be snowed on. . . . It was also the time when hoops were universally fashionable, so we all wore hoops, no matter what the period we were supposed to be representing. . . . Indeed there was no illusion nor enchantment to help one in those elementary days. One had to conquer one's public alone and unaided. . . .

It was not generally conceded that Americans could appreciate, much less interpret opera; and I, as the first American *prima donna,* was in the position of a foreigner in my own country. The chorus was made up of Italians. . . . The Italians were always bitter against me for, up to that time, Italians had had the monopoly of music. The chorus, indeed, could sometimes hardly contain themselves. "Who is she," they would demand indignantly, "to come and take the bread out of our mouths?" . . .

It was after the first performance of *Linda,* some time about midnight . . . when a knock came at the door. . . . My mother opened the door; and there stood two ladies who overwhelmed us with gracious speeches. . . . "Now, *would* we both come the following evening to a little *musicale;* and they would ask that delightful Signor Brignoli too. It would be *such* a pleasure! etc." . . .

This was by no means the first time that I had contended with a lack of consideration in the American hostess, especially toward artists. Her sisters across the Atlantic have better taste and breeding, never subjecting an artist who is their guest to the annoyance and indignity of having to "sing for her supper." But whenever I was invited anywhere by an American woman, I always knew that I would be expected to bring my music and to contribute toward the entertainment of the other guests. . . .

Literary Boston of that day revolved around Mr. and Mrs. James T. Fields, at whose house often assembled such distinguished men and women as Emerson, Longfellow, Oliver Wendell Holmes, Lowell, Anthony Trollope, Harriet Beecher Stowe, and Julia Ward Howe. Mr. Fields was the editor of *The Atlantic Monthly,* and his sense of humor was always a delight.

"A lady came in from the suburbs to see me this morning," he once remarked to me. "Well, Mr. Fields," she said, with great impressiveness, "what have you new in literature today? I'm just *thusty* for knowledge!"

Your true New Englander always says "thust" and "fust" and "wust," and Mr. Fields had just the intonation—which reminds me somehow—in a roundabout fashion—of a strange woman who battered on my door once after I had appeared in *Faust,* in Boston, to tell me that "that man Mephisto-fleas was just great!"

It was a wonderful privilege to meet Longfellow. He was never gay, never effusive, leaving these attributes to his talkative brother-in-law, Tom Appleton, who was a wit and a humorist. Indeed, Longfellow was rather noted for his cold exterior, and it took a little time and trouble to break the ice, but, though so unexpressive outwardly, his nature was most winning when one was once in touch with it. His first wife was burned to death and the tragedy affected him permanently, although he made a second and a very successful marriage with Tom Appleton's sister. . . .

Longfellow and I became good friends. I saw him many times and often went to his house to sing to him. He greatly enjoyed my singing of his own *Beware.* It was always one of my successful *encore* songs, although it certainly is not Longfellow at his best. But he liked me to sit at the piano and wander from one song to another. The older the melodies, the sweeter he found them. Longfellow's verses have much in common with simple, old-fashioned songs. They always touched the common people, particularly the common people of England. They were so

simple and so true that those folk who lived and laboured close
to the earth found much that moved them in the American
writer's unaffected and elemental poetry. Yet it seems a bit
strange that his poems are more loved and appreciated in England than in America, much as Tennyson's are more familiar to
us than to his own people. Some years later, when I was singing
in London, I heard that Longfellow was in town and sent him a
box. He and Tom Appleton, who was with him, came behind
the scenes between the acts to see me and, my mother being with
me, both were invited into my dressing-room. In the London
theatres there are women, generally advanced in years, who
assist the *prima donna* or actress to dress. . . . I had a maid, of
course, but there was this woman of the theatre, also, a particularly ordinary creature who contributed nothing to the gaiety of
nations and who, indeed, rarely showed feeling of any sort. I
happened to say to her: "Perkins, I am going to see Mr. Longfellow."

Her face became absolutely transfigured.

"Oh, Miss," she cried in a tone of awe and curtseying to his
name, "you don't mean 'im that wrote *Tell me not in mournful
numbers?* Oh, Miss! 'im!" . . .

The evening that stands out most clearly in my memory was
one, in the 'seventies, that I spent at the house of dear Charlotte
Cushman. . . . Sidney Lanier was there with his flute, which he
played charmingly. Indeed he was as much musician as poet,
as anyone who knows his verse must realize. He was poor then,
and Miss Cushman was interested in him and anxious to help
him in every way she could. There were two dried-up, little,
Boston old maids there too—queer creatures—who were much
impressed with High Art without knowing anything about it.
One composition that Lanier played somewhat puzzled me—my
impertinent absolute pitch was, as usual, hard at work—and at
the end I exclaimed:

"That piece doesn't end in the same key in which it begins!"

Lanier looked surprised and said:

"No, it doesn't. It is one of my own compositions."

He thought it remarkable that I should catch the change of key in such a long and intricately modulated piece of music. The little old maids of Boston were somewhat scandalized by my effrontery; but there was even more to come. After another lovely thing which he played for us, I was so impressed by the rare tone of his instrument that I asked:

"Is that a Bôhm flute?"

He, being a musician, was delighted with the implied compliment; but the old ladies saw in my question only a shocking slight upon his execution. Turning to one another they ejaculated with one voice, and that one filled with scorn and pity:

"She thinks it's the *flute!*" . . .

In that age, characterized by the uproars of the new civilization, which Edith Wharton, its greatest novelist, named "The Age of Innocence," the seasoned aristocracy did not completely succumb to the wiles of the plutocracy. Its resistance and the basis of resentments are the substance of Mrs. Wharton's thought and emotion. However, she tried to analyze herself, while she looked out upon the new society taking form, and examine her art as an intellectual operation keyed into the thought of Western culture—a feat marvelous and rarely performed, according to Matthew Arnold. In this effort she was guided by the best thought of literary critics from the seventeenth century to her own. In a recent essay on THE WRITING OF FICTION,[4] she summarizes the recognition by critics that social taste and theories rest on assumptions and, after dealing with the technique of writing, closes with the following comment on the subject matter, so pertinent to her own interests and ideas.

It has been often said that subject in itself is all-important, and at least as often that it is of no importance whatever. Definition is again necessary before the truth can be extracted from

[4] Reprint obtained through the courtesy of Charles Scribner's Sons.

these contradictions. Subject, obviously, is *what the story is about;* but whatever the central episode or situation chosen by the novelist, his tale will be about only just so much of it as he reacts to. A gold mine is worth nothing unless the owner has the machinery for extracting the ore, and each subject must be considered first in itself, and next in relation to the novelist's power of extracting from it what it contains. There are subjects trivial in appearance, and subjects trivial to the core; and the novelist ought to be able to discern at a glance between the two, and know in which case it is worth while to set about sinking his shaft. But the novelist may make mistakes. He is exposed to the temptation of the false good-subject, and learns only by prolonged experience to resist surface-attractions, and probe his story to the depths before he begins to tell it.

There is still another way in which subject must be tested. Any subject considered in itself must first of all respond in some way to that mysterious need of a judgment on life of which the most detached human intellect, provided it be a normal one, cannot, apparently, rid itself. Whether the "moral" be present in the guise of the hero rescuing the heroine from the villain at the point of the revolver, or whether it lurk in the quiet irony of such a scene as Pendennis' visit to the Grey Friars' Chapel, and his hearing the choir singing, "I have been young, and now am old, yet have I not seen the righteous forsaken, nor his seed begging bread," at the very moment when he discovers the bent head of Colonel Newcome among the pauper gentlemen—in one form or another there must be some sort of rational response to the reader's unconscious but insistent inner question: "What am I being told this story for? What judgment on life does it contain for me?"

There seems to be no escape from this obligation except into a pathological world where the action, taking place between people of abnormal psychology, and not keeping time with our normal human rhythms, becomes an idiot's tale, signifying nothing. In vain has it been attempted to set up a water-tight compartment between "art" and "morality." All the great novelists whose books have been used to point the argument have invariably declared themselves on the other side, not only by the inner significance of their work, but also, in some cases, by the most explicit statements. Flaubert, for instance, so often cited as the example of the writer viewing his themes in a purely "scientific" or amoral light, has disproved the claim by providing the other camp with that perfect formula: *"Plus la pensée est belle, plus la phrase est sonore"*—not the metaphor, not the picture, but the *thought*.

A good subject, then, must contain in itself something that sheds a light on our moral experience. If it is incapable of this expansion, this vital radiation, it remains, however showy a surface it presents, a mere irrelevant happening, a meaningless scrap of fact torn out of its context. Nor is it more than a half-truth to say that the imagination which probes deep enough can find this germ in any happening, however insignificant. The converse is true enough; the limited imagination reduces a great theme to its own measure. But the wide creative vision, though no fragment of human experience can appear wholly empty to it, yet seeks by instinct those subjects in which some phase of our common plight stands forth dramatically and typically, subjects which, in themselves, are a kind of summary or foreshortening of life's dispersed and inconclusive occurrences.

CHAPTER VIII

THE IMPERIALIST FANTASY

WHILE great industrialism was still scattering its golden profits from Knob Hill in San Francisco to Fifth Avenue in New York, raising up the new rich amid the old but proud poor, even before the domestic market was saturated leaders in business and politics began to look abroad for trade and investment opportunities for the purpose of keeping the huge economic mill running at increasing tempo. History seemed to point the way— the British Empire had torn her peasants from the soil to become proletarians working and living within the confines of manufacturing cities where they produced the goods which were forced upon distant peoples by means of the sea power. Referring to Pitt, London merchants had said that commerce had been made to flourish by war and empire. Hence the aggressive Americans thought that Jefferson's republic of farmers must likewise be transformed into an expanding and conquering empire, although John Ruskin, with the insight of a prophet and the passion of an artist, had been trying to drive home to all the Western world the truth that "there is no wealth but life." Into this game of invading, exploiting and draining gold from provinces, Germany too was feverishly trying to break, rattling her sword and disturbing the dividers of spoils by her claims to a larger share. To activists this performance, "worthy of real men," was the best adventure of all.

In the United States three young citizens, Theodore Roosevelt, Henry Cabot Lodge, and Alfred Thayer Mahan, as if unaware that the world was very old and had seen and endured many things, resolved to arouse America and set her in the new path to "glory." Dragging hesitant elders—William McKinley, John

D. Long, and John Hay—in their train, they inflamed the country with their "vision." America was now to have a big Navy, was to "come of age," was to be a "world power" of the highest magnitude. In distant places naval bases were to be seized and islands acquired, "little brown brothers" were to be subdued, "civilized," and "Christianized." Trade was to be won, by force if necessary, and was to be "protected" by force. The "big stick" was to be shaken in the faces of the "world powers" and they were to be compelled to open doors and give American capitalists "their share" of the spoils of empire. Meanwhile millions of immigrants from Europe were to supply the "hands" to keep American mills and mines running.

In due course, to be sure, the American Nation was to sicken of the clamor and fruits of empire, of the World War to which imperial rivalry brought "the great powers," of the "rattling saber;" empire did not in fact supply the eternally expanding market; the flood of "brown brothers," which immigrated into the United States, created alarms; the competition of raw materials from the provinces brought protests from impoverished American farmers; and the arrangement for the ultimate independence of the Philippines, won by blood and treasure, was being made. But in the closing years of the nineteenth century, this outcome, though it could have been foretold—had in truth often been foretold—was hidden to the men who were bent on making America "grow up and become great." They thundered with assurance, they carried on propaganda in behalf of "manifest destiny," they moved the multitudes to cheers, and they ridiculed the "mollycoddles," going so far as to accuse the doubters of treason.

Even the mild-mannered and soft-spoken Sarah Orne Jewett was stirred to the deeps by the eloquent plea of Captain Mahan for the sea power which was to demonstrate the "new American virtue and resolve" in the four corners of the earth.

"What do you think I am reading with deepest interest?" Miss Jewett asked a friend in 1898. And replied: " 'Mahan's Influence of the Sea Power in History,' " which is perfectly delightful! I don't know whether you would care much about it, though it is not too technical and nautical, but rather historical. One thing is so nice, about the fleets that are attacked having the best chance (according to the French). They stay in their places while the enemy comes at them, but wastes power in coming, and then, the principle holding good from the days of galleys until now, the attacked fleet has kept its power in reserve and its men fresh to resist. You get so interested before you know it. . . . The use of English words is so fresh and good and the whole tone so manly and sailor-like."

However, when the first demonstration of the new American sea power was made in the Spanish-American War and distant dominions were brought under the hegemony of the United States, citizens divided in their opinions of imperialism. At one pole were the ideologists of the Kipling school who saw in such expansion an excursion in higher morality through the assumption of responsibility for improving the manners and minds of "backward people." At the other pole were critics who saw in the adventure a manifestation of crass capitalism seeking new places for exploitation.

Between these extremes stood, citizens expressing various nuances of opinion. Many Americans accepted the decision of sea power as a *fait accompli* and laid their emphasis upon immediate and unremitting attention to the extension of the "benefits of civilization" as rapidly as possible to the people of the dependencies.

And what were women thinking about this business?

Dr. Anna Garlin Spencer, of Chicago University, ever concerned with the cultural aspects of action, in a speech delivered in 1898, presented the case of the WOMEN OF OUR NEW POSSESSIONS.[1]

[1] History of Woman Suffrage, Vol. III, p. 329.

Bebel says, "Woman was the first human being to taste of bondage." True, and her bondage has been long and bitter; but the subjection of woman to man in the family bond was a vast step upward from the preceding condition. It gave woman release from the terrible labor-burdens of savage life; it gave her time and strength to develop beauty of person and refinement of taste and manners. It gave her the teaching capacity, for it put all the younger child-life into her exclusive care, with some leisure at command to devote to its mental and moral, as well as physical, well-being. It led to a closer relationship between man and woman than the world had known before, and thus gave each the advantage of the other's qualities. And always and everywhere the subjection of woman to man has had a mitigation and softening of hardships unknown to other forms of slavery, by reason of the power of human affection as it has worked through sex-attraction. As soon, however, as the slavery of woman to man was outgrown and obsolete it became (as was African slavery in a professedly democratic country like our own) "the sum of all villainies." And to-day there is no inconsistency so great, and therefore no condition so hurtful and outrageous, as the subjection of women to men in a civilization which like ours assumes to rest upon foundations of justice and equality of human rights. . . .

To-day these considerations (especially the failure fully to apply the doctrine of equality of human rights to women, even in the most advanced centers of modern civilization) have an especial and most fateful significance in relation to the women of the more backward races as they are brought into contact with our modern civilization. I said the peoples with whom we are now being brought as a nation into vital relationship may be still in the matriarchate. If they are not, most of them are certainly in some transition stage from that to the father-rule. Not all peoples have had to pass through the entire subjection of women to men which marked our ancestral advance. The more persistent tribal relationship and collective family life have sometimes softened the process of social growth which was so harsh for women under the old Roman law and the later English common law. It may be that the dusky races of Africa and of the islands of the sea, as well as our Aryan cousins of India, may pass more easily through the stages of attainment of man's responsibility to the family life than we, with our tough fibre of character, were able to do. If so, in the name of justice they should have the chance!

But if we, who have not yet "writ large" in law and political rights that respect for woman which all our education, industry, religion, art, home life and social culture express; if we, who are still inconsistent and not yet out of the transition stage from the father-rule to the equal reign of both sexes; if we lay violent hands upon these backward people and give them only our law and our political rights as they relate to women, we shall do horrible injustice to the savage women, and through them to the whole process of social growth for their people. When we tried to divide "in severalty" the lands of the American Indian, we did violence to all his own sense of justice and coöperative feeling when we failed to recognize the women of the tribes in the distribution. We then and there gave the Indian the worst of the white man's relationship to his wife, and failed utterly, as in the nature of the case we must have done, to give him the best of the white man's relation to his wife. . . .

If to-day, in the Hawaiian Islands or in Cuba we fail to recognize the native women, who still hold something of the primitive prestige of womanhood, fail to recognize them as entitled to a translation, under new laws and conditions, of the old dignity of position, we shall not only do them an injustice, but we shall forcibly give the Hawaiian and Cuban men lessons in the wrong side and not the right side of our domestic relations. Above all, if in the Philippines we abruptly and with force of arms establish the authority of the husband over the wife, by recognizing men only as property-owners, as signers of treaties, as industrial rulers and as domestic law-givers, we shall introduce every outrage and injustice of women's subjection to men, without giving these people one iota of the sense of family responsibility, of protection of and respect for women, and of deep and self-sacrificing devotion to childhood's needs, which mark the Anglo-Saxon man.

In a word, if we introduce one particle of our belated and illogical political and legal subjection of women to men into any savage or half-civilized community, we shall spoil the domestic virtues that community already possesses, and we shall not (because we can not so abruptly and violently) inoculate them with the virtues of civilized domestic life. Nature will not be cheated. We can not escape, nor can we roughly and swiftly help others to escape, the discipline of ages of natural growth.

This all means that we need another Commission to go to all the lands in which our flag now claims a new power of oversight and control—a Commission other than that so recently sent to the Philippines—to see what can be done to bring order to that distracted group of islands. We need a Commission which shall study domestic rather than political conditions, and which shall look for the undercurrents of social growth rather than the more showy political movements. We should have on that Commission two archæologists, a man and a woman, and I can name them— Otis T. Mason and Alice C. Fletcher.

While the official view of early imperial transactions in the Philippines is to be found in the formal documents and reports sent to the State Department by William Howard Taft, the first civil governor, a more human and intimate account is given in RECOLLECTIONS OF FULL YEARS,[2] written by Mrs. Taft on the basis of her observation of the actors in the play and of conditions which impressed her as she travelled about the Islands.

There had never been any unusual interest in our family as to the results of the Spanish-American War. Like most patriotic Americans we had been greatly excited while the war was in

[2] Reprint obtained through the courtesy of the author and Dodd, Mead and Company.

progress and had discussed its every phase and event with a warmth of approval, or disapproval, as the case might be, but it did not touch us directly, except as citizens, any more than it touched the vast majority of the people of the United States. And yet, it came to mean more to us personally, than any other event in our times. The whole course of my husband's career was destined to be changed and influenced by its results.

Mr. Taft was strongly opposed to taking the Philippines. He was not an anti-imperialist in the sense that he believed the Constitution required us to keep the boundaries of the United States within their continental limits, but he thought the Antipodes rather a far stretch for the controlling hand, and he thought the taking of the Philippines would only add to our problems and responsibilities without increasing, in any way, the effectiveness and usefulness of our government.

Oddly enough, he had expressed himself to that effect when he happened, during the Spanish War, to be dining with a number of judges, including Justice Harlan, who, although later an anti-imperialist, was at that time strongly upholding the policy of taking over Spanish territory in both oceans.

Mr. Taft knew just about as much about the Filipino people as the average American knew in those days. What he definitely knew was that they had been for more than three centuries under Spanish dominion and that they now wanted political independence. He was heartily in favor of giving it to them. . . .

"The President and Mr. Root want to establish a civil government in the Philippines," said Mr. Taft, "and they want me to go out at the head of a commission to do it." It was only after I had accepted the invitation to go ten thousand miles away that I asked for an explanation.

In answer to the President's proposal, Mr. Taft said that he didn't approve of the acquisition of the Philippines in the first place, and that in the second place he knew nothing about colonial government and had had really no experience in executive work of any kind. But Mr. McKinley did not accept these objections as final. . . . Neither Mr. McKinley nor Mr. Root had rejoiced in the taking over of the Philippines for that matter, but that was beside the question; the Philippines were taken, and it behooved the United States to govern them until such time as their people had learned the difficult art of governing themselves.

My husband promised to consult with me and with his brother Charles and give his answer in a few days. He didn't know whether or not I would be willing to go, but that was a question soon settled.

His resignation of his judgeship was the greatest difficulty. The President told him that he did not think it would be at all necessary for him to resign since the work in the Philippines would take only about six months—nine months at the longest —and that he could absent himself from his duties for that length of time, and for such a purpose, without fear of any kind of unfortunate consequences. Mr. Taft's investigation and study of the situation immediately convinced him that Mr. McKinley was wrong in his expectation that the work could be done so quickly. Nor did Mr. Root have any such idea. Even with the meagre information which was then available, my husband at once saw that it would be years before the Philippine problem would begin to solve itself. So he resigned from the Bench; the hardest thing he ever did. . . .

We found intense interest in our mission, in California and San Francisco. If there were any anti-imperialists there, they successfully concealed themselves. The East was uncomfortably crowded with them in those days, but the evident interest and profit that the West coast would derive from a large Philippine trade may have been responsible for the favorable attitude of the Californians. However, we must not impeach their patriotism, and we ought to attribute some of their enthusiasm in reference to the Philippines, and our assuming control over them, to the natural enterprise of a people who had themselves gone so far in a land of development and hope.

Everything that could be done to make smooth the path of the

new Commission was done. At their own request the powers of
the Commissioners were carefully defined so that complications
with the military government, then in force in the Islands, might
be avoided. They were given equal rank with ministers plenipotentiary in the matter of naval courtesies and precedence; and
Mr. Root drafted a letter of instructions, which the President
signed, outlining their duties in such precise and correct detail
that it was afterward adopted and ratified in its entirety in the
act of Congress by which the Philippine government was established.

So—I believed we were going to have "smooth sailing" in
every sense, when we started on the long voyage. . . .

The men of the Commission, coming, as they did, from different parts of the United States, were widely contrasted, no less in
associations than in their varied accents and family traditions.

General Wright was, and is, one of the ablest lawyers in
Tennessee, and enjoyed, at the time of his appointment on the
Commission, the finest practice in Memphis. He is a Democrat;
and old enough to have been a lieutenant in the Civil War on
the Confederate side. But perhaps his finest laurels for bravery
and devotion to duty were won at the time when he exerted himself to save Memphis in the days when she was in the grip of
a terrible epidemic of yellow fever. I don't know the exact year,
but the epidemic was so out of control that all, who could, left the
city, while General Wright remained to organise such resistance
as could be made to the spread of the dreaded disease.

Mrs. Wright was a daughter of the famous Admiral Semmes
of the Confederate Navy and for some time after the war she
travelled with her father in Mexico and abroad, thereby acquiring at an early age a very cosmopolitan outlook. Admiral
Semmes was a great linguist and Mrs. Wright inherited his gift.
She learned to speak Spanish in her girlhood, so when she arrived in Manila she had only to renew her knowledge of the
language. . . .

Judge Ide was born and bred a Vermonter and had many of
the rugged characteristics of the Green Mountain State, not the

least among which is a certain indefinable, but peculiarly New England, caution. In addition to a large and active law practice in both New Hampshire and Vermont, he had banking connections through which he had gained a better knowledge of business and finance than is possessed by the average lawyer. Moreover, a long term as Chief Justice of Samoa had given him diplomatic experience and a knowledge of the Polynesian races which were to serve him well in his work in the Philippines. As Chief Justice he exercised diplomatic and consular as well as judicial functions, and his position brought him in close relations with the English and German officials of the joint protectorate of the Samoan islands and in constant social contact with the naval officers of many countries whose ships very frequently called at Apia. He was a widower with two young daughters. . . . A large part of their girlhood had been spent in Samoa; they were the product of an intermittent, but very picturesque, education, and there was ingrained in them some of that happy-go-lucky attitude toward life, and that freedom from useless convention which the Ocidental is not unlikely to acquire in the Orient. These girls had, in Samoa, been great friends of Robert Louis Stevenson. . . .

General Wright, Judge Ide and Mr. Taft were the lawyers on the Commission and it was felt that their familiarity with law and governmental matters greatly enhanced the strength and preparedness of the Commission for the work they had to do.

Mr. Worcester was an assistant professor at the University of Michigan. He too was a Vermonter, with quite as much *fortiter in re,* but with somewhat less of the *suaviter in modo* than Judge Ide inherently had, or had acquired in his Samoan experience.

Mr. Worcester was the only member of the party who had ever been to the Philippines before. I think he had been there twice with scientific expeditions before the Battle of Manila Bay had thrust the guardianship of the Filipinos upon our country, and in the course of his trips, with his fluency in Spanish as it is spoken in the Philippines, he had acquired a very intimate knowledge of the people and their customs, as well as of the flora and fauna of the islands. He had written a book on the Philippines which came out at a most fortunate time, just when Dewey's victory had turned the eyes of the country upon that never-before-thought-of corner of the world. This book led to his appointment on the first Commission and his useful, loyal, courageous and effective labours with that body led Mr. McKinley to appoint him on the second.

He is a large, forceful man with rather abrupt manners and very decided opinions and perhaps no greater contrast could be imagined than exists between him and Mrs. Worcester, who, in outward seeming, is the frailest kind of little woman, with a sweet face and engagingly gentle manners which suggest timidity. Mrs. Worcester has proved herself to possess the frailty of flexible steel. At that time we were quite concerned about her, I remember, thinking she would not be able to endure the Philippine climate even for a short period. But she has lived there from that day to this [1914]. She has been with her husband through many experiences from which the strongest woman would shrink, toiling with him over hundreds of miles of mountain and jungle trail on his frequent expeditions into the countries of the wild tribes and meeting every difficulty without comment. She is in excellent health and is a living refutation of the familiar exaggerations as to the effect of climate. They had with them two little white-haired children, one of them quite delicate, who have grown up in the Philippines strong and healthy and have received most of their education in the schools established there under American government.

The last member of the Commission was Professor Bernard Moses of the political and historical department of the University of California. He was a man of profound learning, a Connecticut Yankee, combining a very excellent knowledge of business with his unusual qualifications as an historian, economist and student of politics. He was especially familiar with all Spanish-American countries, had travelled extensively in the South American republics and had written a learned book on the constitution of

Colombia. My husband always says that he thinks Mr. McKinley exercised the widest discretion in the selection of all the members of this Commission since they possessed, among them, qualifications for every line of work in practical government and original research.

Mrs. Moses, a graduate from the University of California, was a very attractive woman. She had a gift for vivid description and for seeing the funny side of every situation. Her book, "Unofficial Letters of an Official's Wife," gives an interesting and accurate picture of social life in the early days of military rule, which are known in Manila history as "the days of the Empire" and of that period when American civil government was in the process of organisation. . . .

The principal impression I received was that between the Commission and the military government, in the person of General Arthur MacArthur, there did not exist that harmony and agreement which was considered to be essential to the amicable adjustment of Philippine affairs. In other words, General MacArthur seemed to resent the advent of the Commission and to be determined to place himself in opposition to every step which was taken by them or contemplated. It was not very easy for the Commissioners, but as far as I can see now, after a careful reading of all the records, they exercised the most rigid diplomacy at times when it would have been only human to have risen up and exercised whatever may be diplomacy's antithesis. . . .

Their reception was so cool that Mr. Taft said he almost stopped perspiring. There were few Filipinos to be seen, and as General MacArthur's reception to the Commission was anything but cordial or enthusiastic they began to feel a disconcerting sense of being decidedly not wanted.

If they had any doubts on this point General MacArthur soon cleared them up. He frankly assured them that he regarded nothing that had ever happened in his whole career as casting so much reflection on his position and his ability as their appointment under the direction of the President. They suggested that he could still rejoice in considerable honour and prestige as

a man at the head of a division of more troops than any general
had commanded since the Civil War and that he was, moreover,
still enjoying the great power of Chief Executive of the Islands.

"Yes," said he, "that would be all right if I hadn't been exercising so much more power than that before you came. . . ."

General MacArthur succeeded General Otis in command of
the United States Army in the Philippines and he had fallen
heir to a policy with which he was entirely out of sympathy.
General Otis had scattered the troops in small divisions and de-
tachments all over the Islands, and General MacArthur found
himself in command of about seventy thousand men, but with
only a few regiments where he could lay his hands on them for
action in his own immediate vicinity. He believed that the only
way to get rid of the predatory bands and bring order out of
a chaotic state was to concentrate the army on the island of
Luzon where most of the active *insurrectos* operated. And he
thought it would be many years before the Filipinos would be
ready for anything but the strictest military government. But
the trouble was that thousands of Filipinos all over the Islands
had already sworn fealty to the United States, or had gone
quietly back to work, and it was known that the lives of many
of these would not be worth a moment's purchase if the protection of the American troops was withdrawn from them. That
was the situation.

The last engagement between real insurgents and American
troops had taken place in February before the Commission arrived. There had been men of some ability and real patriotism
in Aguinaldo's cabinet and among his followers at Malalos, but
by this time the best of them had come in and taken the oath of
allegiance to the United States, others were in prison slowly making up their minds as to whether they would or would not follow
this course, while still others had gone over to Hongkong to join
in the activities of the "junta." Aguinaldo was still roaming
around the mountain fastnesses of Luzon, posing as a dictator and
issuing regular instructions to his lieutenants for the annihilation
of American regiments; but the insurrection had degenerated . . .

Most of the remaining "patriots" had become *ladrones* and were harrying their own people much more than they were opposing the American forces.

These conditions led the Commission to think the time had come to organise a native constabulary, under American officers, with which thoroughly to police the Islands. But General MacArthur did not agree with them; thought it would be folly to trust any Filipino with arms and cited instances of where those who had been armed as scouts had proved entirely un-trustworthy. But the suggestion was received by many of his own officers with the utmost approval and one man, in the Ilocos country in northern Luzon, said he had only to issue a call and he could have five thousand as loyal men as ever wore uni-form enlisted in twenty-four hours. I may say here that the Filipino people are divided into a number of distinct tribes and that some of them never did take much, if any, part in the in-surrection. The insurrection is to-day referred to as the Tagalog rebellion, the Tagalogs being one of the principal tribes, though not the largest. . . .

General MacArthur merely reiterated his belief that the only way to meet the situation was with additional American troops. . . .

All that was needed to discourage the last of the *insurrectos* was Mr. McKinley's election, and the Presidential campaign of 1900 was probably not watched anywhere with more breathless interest than it was in the Philippine Islands. . . .

The Commission had been for three months busily engaged in investigating conditions, as directed by the President, before they assumed any authority, and then they acted with no haste. We were impatiently awaiting news from America with regard to the Presidential election. It was thought to be futile to take any definite steps toward the establishment of local governments and the inauguration of far-reaching reforms until the status of American control should be settled. Mr. Bryan had promised political independence, and if Mr. Bryan were elected all the Commission's plans would go for naught.

The provincial and municipal codes were completed; certain important questions between the Church and the people were being considered, and many open sessions were held for discussion, with the purpose of advising the people that they would be listened to by a civil government. In the meantime the *insurrectos* were keeping things lively in a guerilla warfare with small squads of greatly harassed and very much disgusted American soldiers. There were occasional rumors about uprisings in Manila—when the guard at our gate would be doubled—but Mr. Taft assured us that Manila was as safe as New York or Chicago and we really had few fears. . . .

General MacArthur saw military dangers in all manner of things without being able to state just what they were, and he was always calling for more troops, while the Commission was entertaining hopes that it would not be a great length of time before a large part of the troops already there could be recalled. . . .

The Commissioners were engaged upon legislative matters of the gravest import, which would be rendered entirely superfluous should Mr. Bryan be elected and his announced policies be carried into effect. In that event they proposed immediately to turn matters back to the military government and withdraw, leaving Mr. Bryan to face the problems which they knew he would soon discover had to be dealt with from the standpoint of constructive statesmanship. . . .

The popularity of the Commission, as offering a change from the strictness of military rule, was becoming every day more marked. . . .

We insisted upon complete racial equality for the Filipinos, and from the beginning there were a great many of them among our callers and guests. Their manners are models of real courtesy, and, while their customs are not always like ours, wherever they are able they manifest a great willingness to be *conforme,*—to adapt themselves,—and their hospitality is unbounded. . . .

So many were the problems to be met and dealt with that in

the beginning the Commissioners were each given a set of subjects for investigation and study, their findings being submitted for debate and consideration in the general meetings.

Taxation, civil service, provincial and municipal organisation, currency and finance, police, harbour improvements, roads and railways, customs, postal service, education, health, public lands, an honest judiciary and the revision of the code of laws; these were some of the vital problems, but underlying them all was the immediate necessity for the establishment of tranquillity and confidence throughout the archipelago.

In order to make clear, in any degree, the Philippine situation as we found it, it is essential that, briefly, the position of the Catholic Church and its representatives, the Friars, be explained. For the first time in its history the American government found itself compelled to adjust a seemingly insurmountable difficulty between a Church and its people.

With us the Church is so completely separate from the State that it is difficult to imagine cases in which the policy of a Church in the selection of its ministers, and the assignment of them to duty, could be regarded as of political moment, or as a proper subject of comment in the report of a public officer, but in the first reports of the Philippine Commission to Washington this subject had to be introduced with emphasis.

The Spanish government of the Philippine Islands was a government by the Church through its monastic orders, nothing less. In the words of the Provincial of the Augustinians, the Friars were the "pedestal or foundation of the sovereignty of Spain," which being removed "the whole structure would topple over." The Philippine people, with the exception of the Mohammedan Moros and the non-Christian tribes, belonged, during the Spanish dominion, to the Roman Catholic Church, and the Church registry of 1898 showed a total membership of 6,559,998. The parishes and missions, with few exceptions, were administered by Spanish Friars of the Dominican, Augustinian and Franciscan orders, and it was to the nature of this administration that Spain owed the insurrections of 1896 and 1898, the latter of which terminated only upon our assuming control of the Islands.

In 1896 there were in the Philippines 1,124 monks of the Augustinian, Dominican and Franciscan orders, which body included a company of Recolletos, who are merely an offshot of the order of St. Augustine and differ from the Augustinians only in that they are unshod. In addition to these there were a few Jesuits, Capuchins, Benedictines and Paulists, but they engaged in mission and educational work only and did not share with the other orders the resentment and hatred of the people. Filipinos were not admitted to any of the orders, but they were made Friar curates and served as parish priests in some of the smaller places.

When a Spanish Friar curate was once settled in a parish he remained there for life, or until he was too old for service, and because of this fact he was able to establish and maintain an absolutism which is difficult to explain in a few words. He was simply everything in his parish. As a rule he was the only man of education who knew both Spanish and the native dialect of his district, and in many parishes he was the only Spanish representative of the government. In the beginning, through his position as spiritual guide, he acted as intermediary in secular matters between his people and the rest of the world, and eventually, by law, he came to discharge many civil functions and to supervise, correct or veto everything which was done, or was sought to be done in his pueblo.

He was Inspector of Primary Schools, President of the Board of Health and the Board of Charities, President of the Board of Urban Taxation, Inspector of Taxation, President of the Board of Public Works, Member of the Provincial Council, Member of the Board for Partitioning Crown Lands, Censor of Municipal Budgets, and Censor of plays, comedies or dramas in the dialect of his parish, deciding whether or not these were against the public peace or morals. In a word, he was the government of his parish; and in addition to all things else, it was he who, once a year, went to the parish register, wrote on slips of paper the names of all boys who had reached the age of twenty, and putting these into a receptacle, drew them out one by one and called every fifth man for military service. So hateful was this forced duty to the Filipino youths that many of them would run away into the mountains and hide, become outlaws in order to escape it. But the civil guard would go after them and when they were captured they would be put in jail and watched until they could be sent to their capital.

The monastic orders had behind them a powerful church organisation the heads of which took an active and official part in the administration of government. The Archbishop and the Bishops formed part of what was known in Manila as the Board of Authorities; and they, with the Provincials of the orders, belonged to the Council of Administration, a body analogous to the Council of State in Spain or France, charged with advising the Governor General on matters of urgent moment, or in times of crises. The Friars, Priests and Bishops constituted a solid, permanent and well-organized political force which dominated all insular politics, and the stay in the Islands of the civil or military officer who attempted to pursue a course at variance with that deemed wise by the orders, was invariably shortened by monastic influence. Each order had in Madrid a representative through whom the Court of Spain easily could be reached without the intervention of any authority. . . .

The three great orders of St. Francis, St. Augustine and St. Dominic owned, in different parts of the Islands, more than 400,000 acres of the best agricultural land, and this they rented out in small parcels to the people. Their income from their immense holdings was not what a prudent and energetic landlord would have realized, but they paid no taxes, while the Filipino was taxed in every possible way.

In the province of Cavite alone, the Friar estates amounted to 131,747 acres, and it was in the province of Cavite, which is just across the bay from Manila, that the two insurrections against Spain, or rather against Friar domination, began.

When we arrived in Manila all but 472 of the 1,124 Friars

had either been killed or had fled the country. In each of the uprisings many of them lost their lives, and many more were taken
prisoners. Indeed, the last of them were not released until the
rapid advance of the American troops in our own encounter with
the *insurrectos* made it necessary for the insurgent army to
abandon all unnecessary impedimenta. All the Friars remaining
in the Islands had taken refuge in Manila.

Strange to say, this resentment against the Friars interfered in
no way with the Filipino's love for the Church. With a strong
and real emotion he loves the religion which has been given him;
and the elaborate and beautiful forms of the Roman Catholic
Church are calculated, especially, to make a powerful appeal to
his mind. It is really an astonishing commentary on the character
of these people that they should be able to rise against the men
who administered the sacraments which they so deeply loved
and revered. Or, is it more of a commentary on the conditions
which caused the uprisings?

Without exception the Spanish Friars had been driven from
their parishes, and the most burning of all the burning political
questions, which the Commission met and had to settle, was
whether or not they should be permitted to return. It was impossible to make the people understand that the government of
the United States and the government of Spain were two different matters, and that if the Friars were returned to their
parishes they would exercise no secular functions of any kind.
The people had the proverbial dread of the "burnt child" and
no amount or kind of reasoning could move them from the
position they had taken, nor could any of them, from the highest
to the lowest, talk calmly and rationally about the subject. The
one point upon which the Filipinos were united was that the
Friars should not be reinstated.

Universal agitation, uneasiness, fear, hatred, a memory of
wrongs too recently resented and resented at too great a cost;
these were the factors which made necessary the stand which the
Commission finally adopted. The question with the Friars became one, largely, of getting value for their property, their title

to which was never seriously disputed, and it was decided that on condition of their leaving the Islands, the insular government would undertake the purchase of their vast estates. The intention was then to make some arrangement whereby the lands might be sold back to the people in homestead tracts, and on terms which the poorest man might be able, in time, to meet.

It was to negotiate this transaction, involving the expenditure of $7,000,000, that my husband was sent to Rome the following year as an emissary of the United States government to the Vatican. This was in the time of Pope Leo, and it made a most interesting experience which I shall detail in another chapter.

The first thing, really, that the Commission undertook when they arrived in Manila, was the settlement of a definite dispute between the Church and the People as to which had the right to administer the affairs of the Medical College of San José. Their manner of procedure in this case instituted in the Islands a new and never-before-thought-of system of evenly balanced justice, and made a tremendous sensation. . . .

The method adopted by the Commission for organising provincial government was extremely simple. The people were instructed to send delegates from all the towns in a province to meet the Commission on a given date at the provincial capital. Having gathered this popular assembly in the largest available hall Mr. Taft, or some other member of the Commission, would proceed to read and explain the new Provincial Code which covered every governmental function and which provided for the appointment by the Commission of a provincial governor, a treasurer and a secretary. It was the intention of the Commission to name a Filipino for governor in each province, thereby giving them an immediate opportunity for the exercise of self-government, but in several instances they were almost unanimously petitioned by the people to appoint to this office the American Army officer who had been in command in the district. Considering the attitude of the Filipinos toward military rule and their eagerness to substitute a purely civil form of government, it was really astonishing that they should have wished to retain any representative of the hated régime, but personality counts for a great deal with the Filipinos, and the Army officer who displayed tact and kindly justice in his dealings with them was sure to win for himself a peculiar popularity.

For treasurer an American was almost invariably chosen. During Spanish times the Filipinos had not learned much about the proper use of public funds and they have had to be very painstakingly taught that government money is for government purposes only. To our poignant and everlasting shame, object lessons had to be given them by the drastic punishment meted out to certain American treasurers who were unable to resist temptation. . . .

The Filipinos were greatly pleased at having the Commission bring their wives and daughters along. It was new to them and they were not slow to grasp its significance. Much to the disgust of the military authorities present, we all shook hands with everybody and assumed the friendliest kind of attitude. That the Army officers did not approve of our cordiality toward the Filipinos can hardly be wondered at. They had been subjected to the risks of a campaign of ambush and assassination for many months, and even then they were trying to bring in a band of about one hundred and fifty *insurrectos,* with as many rifles, who were hiding in the Meriveles Mountains and preying upon the people; so, it was natural for them to think that a policy of disdain and severity was the only one suited to the apparent unreliability and deceitfulness of the native. However, these same officers very shortly admitted to us, though rather unwillingly, that our mode of dealing with the people had had an extraordinary effect on the general tone in Bataan.

It was about this time that President McKinley communicated through Secretary Root the intention of the Administration to abolish the military governorship and to install a civil Governor under the power of the President as Commander-in-Chief, and to create civil departments also. When Mr. Taft received a cable from Secretary Root advising him of this fact, he went to see General MacArthur for the purpose of discussing with him the mode of procedure and to get his ideas as to how and when the transfer of power should be made.

The General had begun to look upon the work of the Commission from a somewhat less prejudiced angle and was by this time freely admitting that the establishment of provincial and municipal governments was having a good effect. He, of course, did not wish to surrender his power as military governor and remain in the Islands in a less important position, but he thought somebody would soon be named to succeed him and that the proper time for the transfer was after his successor arrived. Mr. Taft was going, with [Mrs. Taft and] the other members of the Commission, on a long organizing trip through the southern islands, and he thought he could not be ready for the adjustment of affairs before the end of June, so it was decided that the civil Governor should be inaugurated on the 4th of July, and my husband soon received assurances that he would be asked to serve in that capacity. . . .

General Chaffee and General MacArthur were two quite different types of men. General Chaffee was less precise, less analytical. General MacArthur had always been given to regarding everything in its "psychological" aspect and, indeed, "psychological" was the word so frequently on his lips that it became widely popular. General Chaffee was impetuous; he was much less formal than his predecessor both in thought and manner, and Mr. Taft found coöperation with him much less difficult. He made no secret of his conviction, which was shared by most of the Army, that civil government was being established prematurely, but he was not unreasonable. . . .

A great many Filipinos, clever politicians as they are, thought that after Mr. McKinley's death Mr. Bryan would become President, and that, after all, they would get independence.

Then came the awful tragedy of Balangiga. It happened only a few days after the President died, while our nerves were still taut, and filled us all with unspeakable horror intensified by the first actual fear we had felt since we had been in the Philippine Islands. Company "C" of the 9th Infantry, stationed at the town of Balangiga on the island of Samar, was surprised at breakfast, without arms and at a considerable distance from their quarters, and fifty of them were massacred. About thirty fought their way bare-handed through the mob, each man of which had a boloy or gun, and lived to tell the tale. It was a disaster so ghastly in its details, so undreamed of under the conditions of almost universal peace which had been established, that it created absolute panic. . . . Of course this made the Army officers more certain than ever that the Islands should have remained under military control indefinitely, and I cannot deny that, at the time, their arguments seemed to have some foundation. It was a frightful nervous strain and it took several months of tranquillity to restore confidence.

CHAPTER IX

BENEATH ADORNMENT AND POWER

THROUGHOUT the turmoil of reconstruction accompanying the great social war, amid the rush for riches and the beginnings of prosperity, during the belligerent adventures of empire, the care of life remained imperative if society was to endure. Its problems, rendered increasingly complicated, called for reflection and action correspondingly wise.

Awakened to the inadequacies and horrors of warfare which she had helped to encourage with her martial pæan, Julia Ward Howe revolted against the whole procedure of settling disputes by arms and, when the Franco-Prussian battle lines were drawn up in 1870, she appealed to the mothers of the world to end the barbarism of wholesale slaughter in the fields. She took the platform in her own country in an effort to arouse the will-to-peace and went to England to work in its interest. Her appeal to mothers was translated into French, Spanish, Italian, German and Swedish. New peace societies sprang into life everywhere.

Other American women gathered up other threads of humanitarian interest which had been snapped by the peril to the Nation, in the middle of the century, and tried to fit them together again. For example, the cause of temperance, long an ideal inspiring organisation among them, now became a veritable mania as the traffic in alcoholic liquors planted saloons to the right and the left and sodden drunkenness was thus stimulated by lust for profits; but in the first flush of the women's crusade against this evil, their attack was made directly on the saloon rather than on the commercial and political aspects of the business. Gradually temperance leaders placed their emphasis on the political aspects of their cause.

As for the great issue of poverty, raised in the very noon of new riches by a frightful panic and attending violence, if it was approached more gingerly, its menace to the classes was appreciated and studies were undertaken in its "scientific," political, economic and social relations.

In her Introduction to the HISTORY OF THE WOMAN'S TEMPERANCE CRUSADE, Annie Wittenmyer paints the background of the prohibition movement, eventuating in a government experiment with enforcement.

What did the Crusade do? . . . In front of a saloon that had refused them entrance, knelt a crusading group. Their leader was also the most prominent Methodist lady of the community. Her head was crowned with the glory of gray hairs; her hands were clasped; her sweet and gentle voice was lifted up in prayer. Around her knelt the flower of all the churches of that city— Congregationalists, Baptists, Presbyterians—many of whom had never worked outside their own denominations until now. At the close, an Episcopal lady offered the Lord's prayer, in which joined Unitarians, Swedenborgians, and Universalists; and when they had finished, a dear old lady in the dove-colored garb of the Friends' Society was moved to pray, while all the time below them on the curbstone's edge knelt Bridget with her beads and her *Ave Maria.*

"Going out on the street" signified a good deal when one comes to think about it. First of all, it meant stepping outside the denominational fence, which, properly enough, surrounds one's home. The Crusaders felt that "unity of the Spirit" was the one essential nor feared to join hands with any who had the Bible and the temperance pledge of the two articles in their "Confession of Faith"—who rallied to the tune of "Rock of Ages, cleft for me" or had for their watchword: "Not willing that any should perish."

Best of all, "going out on the street" brought women face to face with the world's misery and sin. And here I may be pardoned a bit of personal reminiscence. Never can I forget the day I met the great unwashed, untaught, ungospelled multitude for the first time. Need I say it was the Crusade that opened before me, as before ten thousand other women, this wide, "effectual door?" It was in Pittsburgh, the summer after the Crusade. Greatly had I wished to have a part in it, but this one experience was my first and last of "going out with a band." A young teacher from the public schools, whose custom it was to give an hour twice each week to crusading, walked arm-in-arm with me. Two school-ma'ams together, we fell into the procession behind the experienced campaigners. On Market street we entered a saloon, the proprietor of which, pointing to several men who were fighting in the next room, begged us to leave, and we did so at once, amid the curses of the bacchanalian group. Forming in line on the curbstone's edge in front of the saloon, we knelt, while an old lady, to whose son that place had proved the gate of death, offered a prayer full of tenderness and faith, asking God to open the eyes of those who, just behind that screen, were selling liquid fire and breathing curses on his name. We rose, and what a scene was there! The sidewalk was lined by men with faces written all over and interlined with the record of their sin and shame. Soiled with "the slime from the muddy banks of time," tattered, dishevelled, there was not a sneering look or a rude word or action from any of them. Most of them had their hats off; many looked sorrowful; some were in tears; and standing there in the roar and tumult of that dingy street, with that strange crowd looking into our faces—with a heart stirred as never until now by human sin and shame, I joined in the sweet gospel song:

> Jesus the water of life will give
> Freely, freely, freely!

Just such an epoch as that was in my life has the Crusade

proved to a mighty army of women all over this land. Does anybody think that, having learned the blessedness of carrying
Christ's gospel to those who never come to church to hear the
messages we are all commanded to "Go, tell," we shall ever lay
down the work? Not until the genie of the Arabian Nights
crowds himself back into the fabulous kettle whence he escaped
by expanding his pinions in nebulous bars—not until then! To-
day and every day they go forth on their beautiful errands—the
"Protestant nuns" who a few years ago were among the "anxious
and aimless" of our crowded population, or who belonged to
trades and professions overfull—and with them go the women
fresh from the sacred home-hearth and cradle-side. . . . If you
would find them, go not alone to the costly churches which now
welcome their voices, while to those who are "at ease in Zion"
they gently speak of the great, whitened harvest. But go to the
blacksmith shop and billiard-hall, the public reading-room and
depot waiting-room, to the North End in Boston, Water Street,
New York, the Bailey coffee-houses of Philadelphia, the Friendly
Inns of Cleveland, the Woman's Temperance Room of Cincinnati, and Lower Farwell Hall, Chicago, and you will find
the glad tidings declared by the new "apostolic succession"
dating from the Pentecost of the Crusade. . . .

What is the Crusade doing now? . . . It has come and gone
—that whirlwind of the Lord—but it has set forces in motion
which each day become more potent, and will sweep on until
the rum power in America is overthrown. . . .

It came about that, though they had gone forth only as skir-
mishers, they soon fell into line of battle. . . . The Women's
Praying Bands, earnest, impetuous, inspired, became the Women's
Temperance Unions, firm, patient, persevering. . . .

It is safe to say that never did any form of philanthropic work
afford scope for so great diversity of talent and of method as this
branch of the temperance reform "of the women, by the women."
In the days of the Crusade a dear old grandmother said: "I'm of
no use except to go along and cry" and in the same spirit a negro
servant said to the lady for whom she worked: "I be'ant good

for much, but I kin hold the ole ombereller over you"; and even the family dog sometimes walked with stately step beside his mistress as she led her "Band."

The bête noire of the "Wets" from 1874 until her death in 1898 was Frances Willard, head of the Women's Christian Temperance Union, capable organizer of prohibition sentiment and "wearer of the white ribbon"—symbol of purity. She was a person of broader outlook than the hatchet-swinger, Carrie Nation. Her recognition of the right to birth control and the need of woman suffrage swelled the ranks of her followers.

How Frances Willard's Methodist ardor was inflamed by thinking about the sacrifices of St. Francis is explained in her own words in the HISTORY OF THE WOMAN'S TEMPER-ANCE CRUSADE, edited by Annie Wittenmyer.

From my earliest recollection there hung on the dining-room wall at our house, a pretty steel engraving. It was my father's certificate of membership in the Washingtonian Society, and was dated about 1835. He had never been a drinking man, was a reputable young husband, father, business man and church member, but when the movement reached Churchville, near Rochester, N. Y., he joined it. The little picture represented a bright, happy temperance home with a sweet woman at the center, and over against it a dismal, squalid house with a drunken man staggering in, bottle in hand. Unconsciously and ineffaceably I learned from that one object-lesson what the precepts and practice of my parents steadily enforced, that we were to let strong drink alone.

In 1855 I cut from my favorite *Youth's Cabinet,* the chief juvenile paper of that day, the following pledge, and pasting it in our family Bible, insisted on its being signed by every member of the family—parents, brother, sister and self.

> A pledge we make no wine to take,
> Nor brandy that turns the head,

Nor fiery rum that ruins home,
Nor brewers' beer, for that we fear,
And cider, too, will never do.
To quench our thirst, we'll always bring
Cold water from the well or spring;
So here we pledge perpetual hate
To all that can intoxicate.

. . . Nobody asked me to sign it, nor was there a demand because of exterior temptation, for we were living in such isolation
on a farm three miles from Janesville, Wis. . . .

Coming to Evanston, Ill., in 1858, we found a prohibition village, the charter of the University forbidding the sale of any
intoxicating liquor as a beverage.

Temperance was a matter of course in this "Methodist heaven"
where we have lived from that day to this, from the time it had
but a few hundred, until now when it claims seven thousand
inhabitants.

About 1863–'65 a "Temperance Alliance" was organized here
by L. L. Greenleaf, then our leading citizen, the Chicago representative of the Fairbanks' firm, who have made St. Johns-
bury, Vt., a model temperance town. Before that Alliance I read
one temperance essay when I was a quiet school teacher amid
these shady groves, and one evening at the "Alliance sociable"
I offered the pledge for the first time and was rebuffed by a now
distinguished literary man, then a pastor and editor in our village.
This was my first attempt and his brusque and almost angry
negative hurt me to the heart. . . .

In all my teaching, in Sunday-school, public school and seminary, I never mentioned total abstinence until the winter of the
Crusade, taking it always as a matter of course that my pupils
didn't drink, nor did they as a rule.

I never in my life saw wine offered in my own country but
once, when Mrs. Will Knox, of Pittsburgh, a former Sunday-
school scholar of my sister Mary, brought cake and wine to a
young lady of high family in our church, and to me, when we
went to call on her after her wedding. "Not to be singular" we

touched it to our lips—but that was twenty-five years ago, before
the great examples burnt into the Nation's memory and conscience by Lucy Webb Hayes, Rose Cleveland and Frances
Folsom Cleveland.

That was truly a prophetic innovation at the White House
when our gracious Mrs. Hayes replaced the dinner with its
wine-glasses by the stately and elegant reception. Perhaps while
men rule the state in their government "of the minority, by the
minority, for the minority," its highest expression will still be
the dinner-table with its clinking glasses and plenty of tobacco-
smoke afterward, but when men and women both come into
the kingdom for the glad new times that hasten to be here, the
gustatory nerve will be dethroned once and for evermore. . . .
Doubtless in the outworn and stereotyped forms of society where
material pleasures still hold sway, we do "descend to meet,"
but when a philanthropic purpose determines our companion-
ships, and leads to our convenings, then we climb together into
purer and more vital air. The "coming women," nay, the women
who have come, have learned the loveliest meanings of the
word "society." Indeed, some of us like to call it "comradeship,"
instead, this interchange of highest thought and tenderest aspiration, in which the sense of selfhood is diminished and the sense
of otherhood increased. . . . If a new woman's face appears in
church we wonder if she won't "come with us" in the W.H.M.S.,
the W.F.M.S., the W.C.T.U., or some other dear "ring-around-
a-rosy" circle, formed "for others' sake." If new children sit beside her in the church pew, we plan to win them for our Band
of Hope or other philanthropic guild where they will learn to
find "society" in nobler forms than this poor old world has ever
known before. . . .

At a London dinner where I was the guest of English friends,
and seven wine-glasses stood around my plate, I did not protest
or abstain—so easily does poor human nature fall away, especially
when backed up by a medical prescription. But beyond a flushing
of the cheek, an unwonted readiness at repartee and an anticipation of the dinner hour, unknown to me before or since, I came

under no thralldom, and returning to this blessed "land of the wineless dinner table," my natural environments were such that I do not recall the use of intoxicants by me, "as a beverage" from that day to this.

Thus much do I owe to a Methodist training and the social usages of my grand old mother church. Five years in Oberlin, Ohio, in my childhood, also did much to ground me in the faith of total abstinence and the general laws of hygiene.

In 1873 came that wonderful Christmas gift to the world—the woman's temperance crusade, beginning in Hillsboro, Ohio, December 23, and led by that loyal Methodist woman, Mrs. Judge Thompson, daughter of Gov. Trimble and sister of Dr. Trimble, the oldest member of the last M. E. General Conference. All through that famous battle winter of Home *versus* Saloon, I read every word that I could get about the movement, and my brother, Oliver A. Willard, then editor of the *Chicago Evening Mail,* gave favorable and full reports, saying privately to me, "I shall speak just as well of the women as I dare to"—a most characteristic editorial remark, I have since thought, though more frequently acted out than uttered! Meanwhile it occurred to me, strange to say, for the *first time,* that I ought to work for the good cause *just where I was*—that everybody ought. Thus I first received "the arrest of thought" concerning which in a thousand different towns I have since then tried to speak, and I believe that in this simple change of personal attitude from passive to aggressive lies the only force that can free this land from the drink habit and the liquor traffic. It would be like dynamite under the saloon if, *just where he is,* the minister would begin active work against it; if, just where he is, the teacher would instruct his pupils; if, just where he is, the voter would dedicate his ballot to the movement, and so on through the shining ranks of the great powers that make for righteousness from father and mother to Kindergarten toddler, if each were this day doing what each could, *just where he is.*

I was teaching rhetoric and composition to several hundred students of the Northwestern University and my eyes were opened to perceive that in their essays they would be as well pleased and would gain more good if such themes were assigned as "John B. Gough" and "Neal Dow" rather than "Alexander the Great" and "Plato the Philosopher," and that in their debates they would be as much enlisted by the question, "Is Prohibition a Success?" as by the question, "Was Napoleon a blessing or a curse?" So I quietly sandwiched in these practical themes to the great edification of my pupils and with a notable increase in their enthusiasm and punctuality. Never in my fifteen years as a teacher did I have exercises so interesting as in the Crusade winter—1874.

Meanwhile in Chicago the women of the Churches were mightily aroused. . . .

Events moved rapidly. . . .

It is my nature to give myself utterly to whatever work I have in hand. . . .

With several new friends I went to Old Orchard Beach, Me., where Francis Murphy, a drinking man and saloon-keeper recently reformed, had called the first "Gospel Temperance Camp Meeting" known to our annals. Here I met Neal Dow and heard the story of Prohibitory Law. Here I saw that strong, sweet woman, Mrs. L. M. N. Stevens, our white ribbon leader in Maine almost from then till now; and here in a Portland hotel where I stayed with Mary Hartt, of Brooklyn, and wondered "where the money was to come from," as I had none, and had mother's expenses and my own to meet, I opened the Bible lying on the hotel bureau and lighted on this memorable verse: Psalm 37:3, "Trust in the Lord, and do good; so shalt thou dwell in the land, and verily thou shalt be fed. . . ."

One day in September, 1874, a few ladies assembled in one of the Young Men's Christian Association prayer rooms adjoining Farwell Hall [Chicago], and elected me their president. . . . So with no financial backing whatever I set about my work, opened the first "Headquarters" known to Woman's Christian Temperance Union annals—the Young Men's Christian Association giving me a room rent free; organized committees for the few

lines of work then thought of by us, started a daily three o'clock
prayer meeting at which signing the pledge and seeking the Lord
behind the pledge were constant factors; sent articles and para-
graphs to the local press, having called upon every editor in the
city and asked his help or at least his tolerance; addressed Sunday-
schools, ministers and mass-meetings and once in a while made
a dash into some town or village, where I spoke, receiving a collection which represented financially "my little all. . . ."

When in Italy I had been greatly moved by the study of
St. Francis d'Assisi, whose city I had visited for this purpose,
a nobleman who gave his life to the poor and who was so beloved of Christ that legends say he was permitted to receive
the stigmata.

Thinking of him, my small privations seemed so ridiculously
trivial that I was eager to suffer something really worthy of a
disciple for humanity's sweet sake.

*In the days of American optimism, when inventions poured
from the Patent Office and installations of revolutionary import
were overnight occurrences, when mass production was still a
novelty and the markets of the world seemed ours for the asking,
it was bad form to speak of "classes" in the United States. The
very idea was scoffed at as an importation from monarchies,
anarchist-inspired and "un-American."*

*Nevertheless the idea persisted and fascinated women of leisure
if it was less attractive to women of labor. For the leisured it
became a grand adventure to explore the landscape looking for
class phenomena and discovering "how the other half lives."
Disguises were donned, investigators posing as domestic servants,
laundry workers, factory hands, or shop girls in order to bring
back to the society, which was their own, news of the economic
underworld.*

*Among the explorers of this bent were Mrs. John Van Vorst
and her sister-in-law, Marie Van Vorst, who published an ac-*

count of their experiences in THE WOMAN WHO TOILS.[1]
Mrs. Van Vorst's Introduction to this book lifts the curtain on
their act.

Any journey into the world, any research in literature, any
study of society, demonstrates the existence of two distinct
classes designated as the rich and the poor, the fortunate and
the unfortunate, the upper and the lower, the educated and the
uneducated—and a further variety of opposing epithets. Few of
us who belong to the former category have come into more than
brief contact with the labourers who, in the factories or elsewhere,
gain from day to day a livelihood frequently insufficient for their
needs. Yet all of us are troubled by their struggle, all of us
recognize the misery of their surroundings, the paucity of their
moral and esthetic inspiration, their lack of opportunity for
physical development. All of us have a longing, pronounced or
latent, to help them, to alleviate their distress, to better their condition in some way, in every way.

Now concerning this unknown class whose oppression we de-
plore, we have two sources of information: the financiers who,
for their own material advancement, use the labourer as a
means, and the philanthropists who consider the poor as objects
of charity, to be treated sentimentally, or as economic cases to be
studied theoretically. It is not by economics nor by the distribution of bread alone that we can find a solution for the social
problem. More important for the happiness of man is the hope
we cherish of eventually bringing about a reign of justice and
equality upon earth.

It is evident that, in order to render practical aid to this class,
we must live among them, understand their needs, acquaint ourselves with their desires, their hopes, their aspirations, their fears.
We must discover and adopt their point of view, put ourselves
in their surroundings, assume their burdens, unite with them in
their daily effort. In this way alone, and not by forcing upon
them a preconceived ideal, can we do them real good, can we help

[1] Reprint obtained through the courtesy of Doubleday, Doran and Company.

them to find a moral, spiritual, esthetic standard suited to their
condition of life. Such an undertaking is impossible for most.
Sure of its utility, inspired by its practical importance, I determined to make the sacrifice it entailed and to learn by experience
and observation what these could teach. I set out to surmount
physical fatigue and revulsion, to place my intellect and sympathy in contact as a medium between the working girl who
wants help and the more fortunately situated who wish to help
her. In the papers which follow I have endeavoured to give
a faithful picture of things as they exist, both in and out of the
factory, and to suggest remedies that occurred to me as practical. My desire is to act as a mouthpiece for the woman labourer. I assumed her mode of existence with the hope that
I might put into words her cry for help. It has been my purpose
to find out what her capacity is for suffering and for joy as
compared with ours; what tastes she has, what ambitions, what
the equipment of woman is as compared to that of man; her
equipment as determined,

> 1st. By nature,
> 2d. By family life,
> 3d. By social laws;

what her strength is and what her weaknesses are as compared
with the woman of leisure; and finally, to discern the tendencies
of a new society as manifested by its working girls.

After many weeks spent among them as one of them I have
come away convinced that no earnest effort for their betterment
is fruitless. I am hopeful that my faithful descriptions will perhaps suggest, to the hearts of those who read, some ways of
rendering personal and general help to that class who, through
the sordidness and squalor of their material surroundings, the
limitation of their opportunities, are condemned to slow death—
mental, moral, physical death! If into their prison's midst, after
the reading of these lines, a single death pardon should be carried,
my work shall not have been in vain.

In choosing the scene for my first experiences, I decided upon

Pittsburgh, as being an industrial centre whose character was determined by its working population. It exceeds all other cities of the country in the variety and extent of its manufacturing products. Of its 321,616 inhabitants, 100,000 are labouring men employed in the mills. Add to these the great number of women and girls who work in the factories and clothing shops, and the character of the place becomes apparent at a glance. There is, moreover, another reason which guided me toward this Middle West town without its like. This land, which we are accustomed to call democratic, is in reality composed of a multitude of kingdoms whose despots are the employers—the multi-millionaire patrons—and whose serfs are the labouring men and women. The rulers are invested with an authority and a power not unlike those possessed by the early barons, the feudal lords, the Lorenzo de Medicis, the Cheops; but with this difference, that whereas Pharoah by his unique will controlled a thousand slaves, the steel magnate uses, for his own ends also, thousands of separate wills. It was a submissive throng who built the pyramids. The mills which produce half the steel the world requires are run by a collection of individuals. Civilization has undergone a change. The multitudes once worked for one; now each man works for himself first and for a master secondarily. In our new society where tradition plays no part, where the useful is paramount, where business asserts itself over art and beauty, where material needs are the first to be satisfied, and where the country's unclaimed riches are our chief incentive to effort, it is not uninteresting to find an analogy with the society in Italy which produced the Renaissance. Diametrically opposed in their ideals, they have a common spirit. In Italy the rebirth was of the love of art, and of classic forms, the desire to embellish—all that was inspired by culture of the beautiful; the Renaissance in America is the rebirth of man's originaliy in the invention of the useful, the virgin power of man's wits as quickened in the crude struggle for life. Florence is *par excellence* the place where we can study the Italian Renaissance; Pittsburgh appealed to me as a favourable spot to watch the American Renaissance, the en-

livening of energies which give value to a man devoid of education, energies which in their daily exercise with experience
generate a new force, a force that makes our country what it is,
industrially and economically.

So it was toward Pittsburgh that I first directed my steps. . . .

The whole problem in mechanical labour rests upon economy
of force. The purpose of each, I learned by experience, was to
accomplish as much as possible with one single stroke. In this
respect the machine is superior to man, and man to woman.
Sometimes I tried original ways of doing the work given me.
I soon found in every case that the methods proposed by the fore-
woman were in the end those whereby I could do the greatest
amount of work with the least effort. A mustard machine had
recently been introduced to the factory. It replaced three girls;
it filled as many bottles with a single stroke as the girls could
fill with twelve. This machine and all the others used were run
by boys or men; the girls had not strength enough to manipulate
them methodically.

The power of the machine, the physical force of the man, were
simplifying their tasks. While the boy was keeping steadily at
one thing, perfecting himself, we, the women, were doing a
variety of things, complicated and fussy, left to our lot because we
had not physical force for the simpler but greater effort. The
boy at the corking-table had soon become an expert; he was
fourteen and he made from $1 to $1.20 a day. He worked ten
hours at one job, whereas Ella and I had a dozen little jobs almost impossible to systematize: we hammered and cut and
capped the corks and washed and wiped the bottles, sealed them,
counted them, distributed them, kept the table washed up, the
sink cleaned out, and once a day scrubbed up our own precincts.
When I asked the boy if he was tired he laughed at me. He was
superior to us; he was stronger; he could do more with one
stroke than we could do with three; he was by *nature* a more
valuable aid than we. We were forced through physical inferiority
to abandon the choicest task to this young male competitor. Nature had given us a handicap at the start. . . .

My first experience is drawing to its close. I have surmounted the discomforts of insufficient food, of dirt, a bed without sheets, the strain of hard manual labor. I have confined my observations to life and conditions in the factory. Owing, as I have before explained, to the absorption of factory life into city life in a place as large as Pittsburgh, it seemed to me more profitable to centre my attention on the girl within the factory, leaving for a small town the study of her in her family and social life. I have pointed out, as they appeared to me, woman's relative force as a worker and its effects upon her economic advancement. I have touched upon two cases which illustrate her relative dependence on the law. She appeared to me not as the equal of man either physically or legally. It remains to study her socially. In the factory where I worked men and women were employed for ten-hour days. The women's highest wages were lower than the man's lowest. Both were working as hard as they possibly could. The women were doing menial work, such as scrubbing, which the men refused to do. The men were properly fed at noon; the women satisfied themselves with cake and pickles. Why was this? It is of course impossible to generalize on a single factory. I can only relate the conclusions I drew from what I saw myself. The wages paid by employers, economists tell us, are fixed at the level of bare subsistence. This level and its accompanying conditions are determined by competition, by the nature and number of labourers taking part in the competition. In the masculine category I met but one class of competitor: the bread-winner. In the feminine category I found a variety of classes: the bread-winner, the semi-bread-winner, the woman who works for luxuries. This inevitably drags down the wage level. The self-supporting girl is in competition with the child, with the girl who lives at home and makes a small contribution to the household expenses, and with the girl who is supported and who spends all her money on her clothes. It is this division of purpose which takes the "spirit" out of them as a class. There will be no strikes among them so long as the question of wages is not equally vital to them all. It is not only nature and the law which demand protection for women, but society as well.

In every case of the number I investigated, if there were a son, daughters or a husband in the family, the mother was not allowed to work. She was wholly protected. In the families where the father and brothers were making enough for bread and butter, the daughters were protected partially or entirely.

There is no law which regulates this social protection; it is voluntary, and it would seem to indicate that civilized woman is meant to be an economic dependent.

Yet, on the other hand, what is the new force which impels girls from their homes into the factories to work when they do not actually need the money paid them for their effort and sacrifice? Is it a move toward some far distant civilization when women shall have become man's physical equal, a "free, economic, social factor, making possible the full social combination of individuals in collective industry"? This is a matter for speculation only. What occurred to me as a possible remedy both for the oppression of the woman bread-winner and also as a betterment for the girl who wants to work, though she does not need the money, was this: the establishment of schools where the esthetic branches of industrial art might be taught to the girls who by their material independence could give some leisure to acquiring a profession useful to themselves and to society in general. The whole country would be benefited by the opening of such schools as the Empress of Russia has patronized for the maintenance of the "petites industries," or those which Queen Margherita has established for the revival of lace-making in Italy. If there was such a counter-attraction to machine labor, the bread-winner would have a freer field and the non-bread-winner might still work for luxury and at the same time better herself morally, mentally and esthetically. She could aid in forming an intermediate class of labourers which as yet does not exist in America: the hand-workers, the *mains d'œuvre* who produce the luxurious objects of industrial art for which we are obliged to send to Europe when we wish to beautify our homes.

Mary Heaton Vorse, in MEN AND STEEL,[2] opened up for the general public one of the darkest recesses of industrial America and helped to set questions of social policy.

Principalities in America do not exist as geographical areas. In America principalities exist by industries.

The principality of Steel is young. It has the despotism and the power of youth; its power rests only on wealth and dominion. Power without responsibility. Power which throttles among its subjects all efforts at self-government. Power brutal, young, riotous, lusty, driven by the force of steam. Power which treats men's lives as commodities. A creative thing made of fire and iron and taking no account of the lives of men. Smoke, fire, iron and human lives are its substances. Gain and greed and the sullen discontent of men are the stuff from which the unthinking despotism is made.

The men who have iron prevail. The iron masters have always had power. The smiths have always been the aristocrats of the artisans. America of the Indians might yet dispute the civilization of Europe, as does North Africa, had the Indians had iron. Iron and Steel began the life of moderns. Iron and Steel still rule.

No industry is as imposing as Steel, no industry so knocks at the door of the imagination. There must have been a time when that piece of molten metal made from a stone seemed magic; it still is so.

The magic has grown.

The might of Steel has increased.

This industry has progressed mightily. There is no prouder achievement in American industry than Steel. In manufacture of Steel we surpass the world. Sheffield is an old man in his dotage. Newcastle sleeps. Pittsburgh is To-day making To-morrow.

The steel towns make all the raw stuff of life as we know it. Here are our great forges. Here is the core of our civilization. They make steel cars in Lyndora. They make rails in Monessen.

[2] Reprint obtained through the courtesy of the author and Horace Liveright.

In all the world there are no such tubing works as in Youngstown and McKeesport.

In the steel towns they make the raw material for all the swift moving things; the wheels of great machines, the engines which move trains and vessels and airships, the frame-work of high buildings. Our civilization is forged in the steel towns.

A rampart of mills lines the river bottoms near all steel towns. These mills stretch in a mighty frieze miles long. The men who go in mornings and come out nights, who go in nights and come out mornings, seem like processions of ants.

Smoke belches perpetually from the black mill chimneys, which rise like the pipes of black organs, three chimneys, five chimneys, seven chimneys in a row. Chimney and furnace follow one another along the rivers.

The fires of these mills burn night and day. Night and day, steel is made by the men who live huddled around the flanks of the mills.

Through the work of these men Pittsburgh grew strong and built high towers. Town after town made steel; one mill bred another. Youngstown, Johnstown, Wheeling, Steubenville made steel and iron, or things that were made from steel and iron.

Steel grew powerful and great. Steel blackened the skies of South Chicago; Steel built Gary and the towns in Calumet Basin. Steel was made in Joliet; Allentown grew rich on Steel, and Steel was made in Colorado and Alabama.

A great industry flung itself across a continent. Through the ceaseless energy of the steel masters and through the unfailing faithfulness of the men who went to the mills every morning and every night, a principality was built.

If these men stopped working our civilization would stop. Between them coal and iron hold America in their hands. Coal and iron and steel rule our civilization and are its masters. . . .

In the steel towns the mills are surrounded by high walls. The gates are guarded by uniformed guards. You must have a permit to go in. A man may live years in steel towns and see no more of the mills than smoke and steam.

The yards of the steel mills are surrounded by tracks. Engines puff up and down through the twenty-four hours. Mountains of ore, mountains of coke, trains unloading, scrap engines unloading ore and coke, trains carrying off steel bars. Magnets everywhere are loading and unloading steel ingots into cars. Men moving in unhurried fashion. No one moves rapidly; every one has time. There is a never-ending quality to all this. . . .

Three things impress you when you go into the mills: the size, the absence of men, the absence of haste. Here a tremendous work is in progress. Here is being manufactured the steel skeleton of our monstrous civilization. Here before your eyes you may see it being made from fire and iron with the help of great machines. That is what you think first.

Later you say, "Oh, men are helping too!" This is an afterthought. . . .

When the workers in important industries strike, it is customary to hold a Senate investigation.

During the first ten days of the strike, fourteen people had been killed. All of them were strikers. Fanny Sellins had been murdered. The number of wounded was not known. People nursed their wounds in silence. Gary was under martial law. There were no civil liberties in Pennsylvania. A million dollars a day was the loss in wages to the steel workers. The loss to the steel companies was not calculated. The industries dependent on steel were slowed down.

Mr. Gary's eighteenth century principles, which give a man control over his own business, were at stake.

The Senators inquired into these facts. The investigation took place in a courtroom in the Post Office Building in Pittsburgh. In the center of the room is a square enclosure. Here sat the middle-aged-to-elderly gentlemen, the Senators. One came from the South, one from New England, one from the Southwest, and one from the Middlewest. The lawyer for the steel corporation and the lawyer for the workers sat within the enclosure. A small group of steel operators sat with them.

The investigation was only interesting to the steel workers.

They had come in numbers. They stood quietly, filling one side of the court house allotted to them, while the "general public" sat in a sparse row at the far end of the hall.

Before the Senators flowed a ceaseless stream of people. These were all dressed in their best clothes. The men were shaved. They came before the Government in their best. Few spoke English well. Many of the women testified through interpreters.

They told before the Senate the stories of violence which one could not escape in Foster's office or in the offices of the local secretaries. They told without emotion the stories of beatings and arrests. They seemed resigned. They did not seem surprised or indignant. For days one found before the Senate decent respectable folk telling fantastic stories of abuse. Their defenselessness and respectability were what one remembered of them.

A Slovak woman from Dinora, with dark hair and pink cheeks, testified. This is my memory of what she said:

"My husband and my children were in bed. I go to the store before they get up. I must go to the store early and get what they need. I go on street walking to the store. Some one behind me call 'Scab.'"

She was caught in the picket line between the picketers and the scabs. A negro took hold of her arms. He pointed a gun at her and arrested her.

"He called me bad names, too," she said. She was taken to jail and told to pay a fine. She said she would not pay—she was not guilty; but because she had a six-months-old baby she finally paid. But they kept her in jail all day and into the night while her husband looked for her. She testified there were colored strike-breakers and that negroes were deputized. While she was in jail, terribly beaten men were brought in.

"My wife and children were sick," said a man from Monessen who worked in the wire mill. "I was going for the doctor. Some one said, 'Don't go down there. The State Constable is there taking people to jail.' I had to go back—they got clubs."

The State Constable with a horse rode him down. He was arrested and held for $500 bail. He pleaded with them to send the doctor to his wife and children. He worked eleven hours a day and thirteen at night. He worked through a long shift Sundays, and was striking for better conditions and for eight hours. He had taken out his first papers, but had never had time to become a citizen.

He was young and full of high vitality, and he told his story of his arrest with an air of naïve surprise as though he were asking himself, "What the devil did the State Constable pounce on me for when I was just going to the doctor? And they searched me too—that's queerer yet."

A Croat, who makes wire in Monessen, was an angry witness. They had arrested him, found him unarmed, and told him: "If you don't go to work, you must go to jail."

He was a strongly built young man and his fury streamed out in his answer. He was not polite to the Senators. The representatives of the higher government of the United States did not impress him as they did the other workers. To most steel workers the government is an august thing which they respect. He had been in America thirteen years. They asked him why he was not a citizen and he flung at them with passion:

"Cause I don't get time!"

Later he told them, still rudely, and with anger:

"I'd like to learn. If I'm going to work eight hours I'm going to learn. I like this country. I like America. If I take a day off I have no money to pay board. Sure, I like to learn about the government of this country."

But his manner said, "You fools! How do you expect me to learn when I work half the time nights and twelve hours?"

As a final proof of his fatigue he flung at them that he hadn't been to a movie for over a year.

Not every one was bewildered and not every one was resigned. Now and then a conscious young fellow would tell you all you wanted to know about the strike, like a young man who said he worked in the Mayo Mill at 17½ cents an hour in 1914. He was in the Sixth Engineers during the war. He came back March, 1919, and was demobilized in April.

"I had a mother to support. They offered me a shoveling wheelbarrow job. I turned it down. I got a job in the steel works on September 3rd. Clothes cost six or seven dollars a week. You can't keep on wearing your clothes. They get soaked with oil. Your shoes don't last. The heat burns the soles off your shoes."

"Did many men strike in your mill?"

"They all struck." His answer was like a sharp salute.

"Why did you strike?"

"I thought it was my duty because I couldn't get any satisfaction from the Company. They patted me on the shoulder and said, 'We will give you a good job.' They urged the men to come to work and then the Company gives them guns. We were told the Superintendent carried in whiskey to the scabs."

"What are you striking for?" they asked him.

"Eight hours, more pay, better conditions and more safety devices," he rapped out on them, barking it like a command on parade.

There were called as witnesses some odd men who were not strikers. Such as the man from the grocery store in Homestead, with a greenish pale face and a long plaster on his head. He had been an American citizen for three years. He was standing in the doorway of his store when a State policeman came in and knocked him down and beat him. He never knew what he was charged for, but was held in $300 and fined $6.35. He gave his testimony in a low tone, unassertive, almost apologetic. He seemed to be questioning the Senators and the crowd at large as to why this strange fate should have overtaken him. The hotel keeper from Homestead has been an American citizen for ten years. He was a pufly, inoffensive man, not accustomed to asserting himself. He, too, seemed puzzled like the man of the grocery store. He had come from Germany and had his hotel for six years. He was beaten up and arrested. They chased him into the hotel and tried to ride the horses in after him. He was asked whether they often rode their horses into the houses.

"They rode their horses into the women's houses," he answered.

Later some one explained the case of the hotel man and the grocer to me. "Most likely they gave the strikers credit or let them come to their places. Any one sympathetic to the strikers is liable to get beat up."

It was the matter-of-factness of this that is its most fantastic element. Every one had accepted the troopers; every one had accepted the facts that strikers get beaten. The Constabulary and beatings had become part of the strikers' lives in Allegheny County.

There are plenty of satisfied workers, plenty of people who have nothing against the United States Steel Corporation.

There was one gentle old fellow who testified a long time. He spent thirty-three years of his life working in the mills. An old man, gray of face, gray of hair. He seemed very tired. He seemed dim and bewildered. He works twelve hours a day and doesn't think it is too much. He has worked twelve hours for thirty-three years. He got 17 cents an hour when he started and now gets 33 cents. He has nine children, five boys and four girls. All but one are married. Life has given him all he desires. He owns his home. He thinks he is glad to work twelve hours a day. He is the perfect product of the system of the Steel Company. There would be no disturbance in the steel mills if all were like him. He is an Englishman, and he doesn't know what they want to go out making trouble for. He accepts twelve hours of work like a law of nature.

Another witness like him was a man, thirteen years in this country, now making $4.32 a day. He had no complaint against the Steel Corporation. He shoveled coal ten hours a day.

"What was the strike about?"

He shook his head. He did not know.

Would he like to learn English? Yes, but he was too old.

"If I go to school now some one laugh at me," he said deprecatingly. He intends to go on all his life shoveling coal for ten hours a day. He thinks he is content.

There were many witnesses like this, slow old men, long in the service of U. S. Steel, old men without complaint. They did not know what the strike was about. They did not want to know. Dim, patient people, uncomplaining, men whose desires did not transcend a steady job.

After a few weeks of deliberation, the Senators turned in the report of their investigation. They recommended a shorter work-day; they admitted the Constabulary had overstepped the bounds in some cases. Americanization of the workers, they felt was what they needed.

I was discussing this question of Americanization with a striker standing on the street corner of Braddock. The smoke rolled up in a mountain of gray and white before us. A flicker of sulphur-colored flame blossomed for a moment at the summit of one of the mill chimneys. The street was empty but for an old woman with her hair tied up in a black kerchief, dragging some wood along, and another carrying groceries.

"Being a citizen," he said, "that means first of all loving your country, don't it? You have got to love it to begin with."

Two state troopers turned in at the far end of the street and paced slowly up.

"That's hard to do," he said, "when you live in the town with them fellows."

The other side of adornment and power was abundantly evident in the slums of great cities where none of the golden shower fell, where the scene was not even gilded, where the minds of poverty-stricken men and women were prepared to heed the disciples of Bakunin and Marx. In the midst of one such social desert, in Chicago, Jane Addams planted a Social Settlement and in TWENTY YEARS AT HULL-HOUSE[3] she gives an account of her early experience with the classes and the masses.

The Hull-House residents were often bewildered by the desire for constant discussion which characterized Chicago twenty years

[3] Reprint obtained through the courtesy of The Macmillan Company.

ago, for although the residents in the early Settlements were in many cases young persons, who had sought relief from the consciousness of social maladjustment in the "anodyne of work" afforded by philanthropic and civic activities, their former experiences had not thrown them into company with radicals. The decade between 1890–1900 was, in Chicago, a period of propaganda as over against constructive social effort; the moment for marching and carrying banners, for stating general principles and making a demonstration, rather than the time for uncovering the situation and for providing the legal measures and the civic organization through which new social hopes might make themselves felt.

When Hull-House was established in 1889, the events of the Haymarket riot were already two years old, but during that time Chicago had apparently gone through the first period of repressive measures, and in the winter of 1889–1890, by the advice and with the active participation of its leading citizens, the city had reached the conclusion that the only cure for the acts of anarchy was free speech and an open discussion of the ills of which the opponents of government complained. Great open meetings were held every Sunday evening in the recital hall of the then new auditorium, presided over by such representative citizens as Lyman Gage, and every possible shade of opinion was freely expressed. A man who spoke constantly at these meetings used to be pointed out to the visiting stranger as one who had been involved with the group of convicted anarchists, and who doubtless would have been arrested and tried, but for the accident of his having been in Milwaukee when the explosion occurred. One cannot imagine such meetings being held in Chicago to-day, nor that such a man should be encouraged to raise his voice in a public assemblage presided over by a leading banker. It is hard to tell just what change has come over our philosophy or over the minds of those citizens who were then convinced that if these conferences had been established earlier, the Haymarket riot and all its sensational results might have been avoided.

At any rate, there seemed a further need for smaller clubs,

where men who differed widely in their social theories might
meet for discussion, where representatives of the various economic
schools might modify each other, and at least learn tolerance
and the futility of endeavoring to convince all the world of the
truth of one position. Fanaticism is engendered only when men,
finding no contradiction to their theories, at last believe that the
very universe lends itself as an exemplification of one point of
view. "The Working People's Social Science Club" was organized at Hull-House in the spring of 1890 by an English
workingman, and for seven years it held a weekly meeting. . . .
The enthusiasm of this club seldom lagged. Its zest for discussion
was unceasing, and any attempt to turn it into a study or reading club always met with the strong disapprobation of the
members.

In these weekly discussions in the Hull-House drawing-room
everything was thrown back upon general principles and all
discussion save that which "went to the root of things" was impatiently discarded as an unworthy, halfway measure. I recall one
evening in this club when an exasperated member had thrown
out the statement that "Mr. B. believes that socialism will cure
the toothache." Mr. B. promptly rose to his feet and said that it
certainly would, that when every child's teeth were systematically
cared for from the beginning, toothache would disappear from
the face of the earth, belonging, as it did, to the extinct competitive order, as the black plague had disappeared from the
earth with the ill-regulated feudal régime of the Middle Ages.
"But," he added, "why do we spend time discussing trifles like the
toothache when great social changes are to be considered which
will of themselves reform these minor ills?" Even the man who
had been humorous fell into the solemn tone of the gathering.
It was, perhaps, here that the socialist surpassed every one else
in the fervor of economic discussion. He was usually a German
or a Russian with a turn for logical presentation, who saw in the
concentration of capital and the growth of monopolies an inevitable transition to the socialistic state. He pointed out that the
concentration of capital in fewer hands but increased the mass of

those whose interests were opposed to a maintenance of its power, and vastly simplified its final absorption by the community; that monopoly "when it is finished doth bring forth socialism." Opposite to him, springing up in every discussion, was the individualist, or, as the socialist called him, the anarchist, who insisted that we shall never secure just human relations until we have equality of opportunity; that the sole function of the state is to maintain the freedom of each, guarded by the like freedom of all, in order that each man may be able to work out the problems of his own existence. . . .

And yet in the same building adherents of the most diverse religious creeds, eastern and western, met in amity and good fellowship. Did it perhaps indicate that their presentation of the eternal problems of life were cast in an older and less sensitive mold than this presentation in terms of social experience, or was it rather that the new social science was not yet a science at all but merely a name under cover of which we might discuss the perplexing problems of the industrial situation? Certainly the difficulties of our committee were not minimized by the fact that the then new science of sociology had not yet defined its own field. The University of Chicago, opened only the year before the World's Fair, was the first great institution of learning to institute a department of sociology.

In the meantime the Hull-House Social Science Club grew in numbers and fervor as various distinguished people who were visiting the World's Fair came to address it. . . . The club at any rate convinced the residents that no one so poignantly realizes the failures in the social structure as the man at the bottom, who has been most directly in contact with those failures and has suffered most. I recall the shrewd comments of a certain sailor who had known the disinherited in every country; of a Russian who had served his term in Siberia; of an old Irishman who called himself an atheist but who in moments of excitement always blamed the good Lord for "setting supinely" when the world was so horribly out of joint.

It was doubtless owing largely to this club that Hull-House

contracted its early reputation for radicalism. Visitors refused to distinguish between the sentiments expressed by its members in the heat of discussion and the opinions held by the residents themselves. At that moment in Chicago the radical of every shade of opinion was vigorous and dogmatic; of the sort that could not resign himself to the slow march of human improvement; of the type who knew exactly "in what part of the world Utopia standeth."

During this decade Chicago seemed divided into two classes: those who held that "business is business" and who were therefore annoyed at the very notion of social control, and the radicals, who claimed that nothing could be done really to moralize the industrial situation until society should be reorganized.

A Settlement is above all a place for enthusiasms, a spot to which those who have a passion for the equalization of human joys and opportunities are early attracted. It is this type of mind which is in itself so often obnoxious to the man of conquering business faculty, to whom the practical world of affairs seems so supremely rational that he would never vote to change the type of it even if he could. The man of social enthusiasm is to him an annoyance and an affront. He does not like to hear him talk and considers him *per se* "unsafe." Such a business man would admit, as an abstract proposition, that society is susceptible of modification and would even agree that all human institutions imply progressive development, but at the same time he deeply distrusts those who seek to reform existing conditions. There is a certain common-sense foundation for this distrust, for too often the reformer is the rebel who defies things as they are, because of the restraints which they impose upon his individual desires rather than because of the general defects of the system. When such a rebel poses for a reformer, his shortcomings are heralded to the world, and his downfall is cherished as an awful warning to those who refuse to worship "the god of things as they are."

And yet as I recall the members of this early club, even those who talked the most and the least rationally seem to me to have been particularly kindly and "safe." . . . In the discussion of these themes, Hull-House was of course quite as much under the suspicion of one side as the other. I remember one night when I addressed a club of secularists, which met at the corner of South Halsted and Madison streets, a rough-looking man called out: "You are all right now, but, mark my words, when you are subsidized by the millionaires, you will be afraid to talk like this." The defense of free speech was a sensitive point with me, and I quickly replied that while I did not intend to be subsidized by millionaires, neither did I propose to be bullied by workingmen, and that I should state my honest opinion without consulting either of them. To my surprise, the audience of radicals broke into applause, and the discussion turned upon the need of resisting tyranny wherever found, if democratic institutions were to endure. . . .

I also longed for the comfort of a definite social creed, which should afford at one and the same time an explanation of the social chaos and the logical steps towards its better ordering. I came to have an exaggerated sense of responsibility for the poverty in the midst of which I was living and which the socialists constantly forced me to defend. . . .

In the meantime, although many men of many minds met constantly at our conferences, it was amazing to find the incorrigible good nature which prevailed. Radicals are accustomed to hot discussion and sharp differences of opinion and take it all in the day's work. I recall that the secretary of the Hull-House Social Science Club at the anniversary of the seventh year of its existence read a report in which he stated that, so far as he could remember, but twice during that time had a speaker lost his temper, and in each case it had been a college professor who "wasn't accustomed to being talked back to."

He also added that but once had all the club members united in applauding the same speaker; only Samuel Jones, who afterwards became "the golden rule" mayor of Toledo, had been able to overcome all their dogmatic differences, when he had set forth a plan of endowing a group of workingmen with a factory plant and a working capital for experimentation in hours and wages, quite as groups of scholars are endowed for research. . . .

Trade-unionists, unless they were also socialists, were not prominent in these economic discussions, although they were steadily making an effort to bring order into the unnecessary industrial confusion. They belonged to the second of the two classes into which Mill divides all those who are dissatisfied with human life as it is, and whose feelings are not wholly identified with its radical amendment. He states that the thoughts of one class are in the region of ultimate aims, of "the highest ideals of human life," while the thoughts of the other are in the region of the "immediately useful, and practically attainable."

The meetings of our Social Science Club were carried on by men of the former class, many of them with a strong religious bias, who constantly challenged the Church to assuage the human spirit thus torn and bruised "in the tumult of a time disconsolate." These men were so serious in their demand for religious fellowship, and several young clergymen were so ready to respond to the appeal, that various meetings were arranged at Hull-House, in which a group of people met together to consider the social question, not in a spirit of discussion, but in prayer and meditation. These clergymen were making heroic efforts to induce their churches to consider formally the labor situation, and during the years, which have elapsed since then, many denominations of the Christian Church have organized labor committees; but at that time there was nothing of the sort beyond the society in the established Church of England "to consider the conditions of labor."

During that decade even the most devoted of that pioneer church society failed to formulate the fervid desire for juster social conditions into anything more convincing than a literary statement, and the Christian Socialists, at least when the American branch held its annual meeting at Hull-House, afforded but a striking portrayal of that "between-age mood" in which so many of our religious contemporaries are forced to live. . . .

Chicago thus took a decade to discuss the problems inherent in the present industrial organization and to consider what might be done, not so much against deliberate aggression as against brutal confusion and neglect; quite as the youth of promise passes through a mist of rose-colored hope before he settles in the land of achievement where he becomes all too dull and literal minded. And yet as I hastily review the decade in Chicago which followed this one given over to discussion, the actual attainment of these early hopes, so far as they have been realized at all, seems to have come from men of affairs rather than from those given to speculation. Was the whole decade of discussion an illustration of that striking fact which has been likened to the changing of swords in "Hamlet"; that the abstract minds at length yield to the inevitable or at least grow less ardent in their propaganda, while the concrete minds, dealing constantly with daily affairs, in the end demonstrate the reality of abstract notions? . . .

At any rate the residents at Hull-House discovered that while their first impact with city poverty allied them to groups given over to discussion of social theories, their sober efforts to heal neighborhood ills allied them to general public movements which were without challenging creeds. But while we discovered that we most easily secured the smallest of much needed improvements by attaching our efforts to those of organized bodies, nevertheless these very organizations would have been impossible, had not the public conscience been aroused and the community sensibility quickened by these same ardent theorists.

As I review these very first impressions of the workers in unskilled industries, living in a depressed quarter of the city, I realize how easy it was for us to see exceptional cases of hardship as typical of the average lot, and yet, in spite of alleviating philanthropy and labor legislation, the indictment of Tolstoy, applied to Moscow thirty years ago, still fits every American city: "Where-ever we may live, if we draw a circle around us of a hundred thousand, or a thousand, or even of ten miles circumference, and look at the lives of those men and women who are inside our circle, we shall find half-starved children, old people, sick and weak persons, working beyond their strength, who have neither food nor rest enough to support them, and who, for this reason, die before their time; we shall see others, full-grown, who are injured and needlessly killed by dangerous and hurtful tasks."

As the American city is awakening to self-consciousness, it slowly perceives the civic significance of these industrial conditions, and perhaps Chicago has been foremost in the effort to connect the unregulated overgrowth of the huge centers of population, with the astonishingly rapid development of industrial enterprises; quite as Chicago was foremost to carry on the preliminary discussion through which a basis was laid for like-mindedness and the coördination of divers wills. . . .

I am inclined to think that perhaps all this general discussion was inevitable in connection with the early Settlements, as they in turn were the inevitable result of theories of social reform, which in their full enthusiasm reached America by way of England, only in the last decade of the century. There must have been tough fiber somewhere; for, although the residents of Hull-House were often baffled by the radicalism within the Social Science Club and harassed by the criticism from outside, we still continued to believe that such discussion should be carried on, for if the Settlement seeks its expression through social activity, it must learn the difference between mere social unrest and spiritual impulse.

The group of Hull-House residents, which by the end of the decade comprised twenty-five, differed widely in social beliefs, from the girl direct from the country who looked upon all social unrest as mere anarchy, to the resident, who had become a socialist when a student in Zurich, and who had long before translated from the German Engel's "Condition of the Working Class in England," although at this time she had been read out of the Socialist Party because the Russian and German Impossibilists suspected her fluent English, as she always lightly explained. Although thus diversified in social beliefs, the residents became solidly united through our mutual experience in an industrial quarter, and we became not only convinced of the need for social control and protective legislation but also of the value of this preliminary argument.

This decade of discussion between 1890 and 1900 already seems remote from the spirit of Chicago of today. So far as I have been able to reproduce this earlier period, it must reflect the essential provisionality of everything; "the perpetual moving on to something future which shall supersede the present," that paramount impression of life itself, which affords us at one and the same time ground for despair and for endless and varied anticipation.

From Hull-House emissaries went into the industrial field bearing the gospel and the practice of humanism, notably Florence Kelley, the first factory inspector in Illinois. Later she devoted her energies to the work of the Consumers' League, a national organization which undertook to improve the conditions of manufacturing. For the mercantile policy, "Let the Purchaser Beware," it took as its slogan, "Let the Employer Beware."

Laws of a protective character were demanded of society in addition to care in buying. The basis of this legal attack on poverty is described by Mrs. Kelley in ETHICAL GAINS THROUGH LEGISLATION.[4]

The more closely the rights of purchasers are scrutinized, the more clearly it appears that they are social rights. However much they may present themselves to the mind as individual, personal rights, the effort to assert them invariably brings the experience that they are inextricably interwoven with the rights of innumerable other people. In the last analysis they cannot be asserted without the previous assertion of the claim of the weakest and most defenseless persons in the community.

[4] Reprint obtained through the courtesy of The Macmillan Company.

It has been suggested that the most obvious rights of the purchaser are to have his goods as they are represented, and to have food pure and garments free from poison and infection when bought of reputable dealers at the price asked; and, finally and most important, to be free from participating indirectly, through the purchase of his goods, in the employment of children and of the victims of the sweating system.

Before, however, these fundamental rights of any purchaser can be established as a matter of course, it occurs incidentally that the lives of infants must be safe from the poison of unclean milk and adulterated foods, and the consciences of the wage-earners cleansed of the degradation implied in preparing impure foods for the market. In the process, honesty must be forced upon the poisoners (by means of adulterations in food and germs in apparel) who now thrive upon the ignorance and credulity of the buying public.

Before the individual purchaser can vindicate his own personal rights, the whole body of purchasers are constrained to save childhood for the children, and home life for the workers who dwell in tenements. The garret of the humblest widow must be safe from invasion by the materials and the processes of industry. The childhood of the dullest orphan must be secure from the burden of toil. On no easier terms can the conscience of the citizen as purchaser be freed from participation in the meanest forms of cruelty, the sacrifice of the weak and the defenseless to the search for cheapness.

These ends can be accomplished, however, only by comprehensive statutes sustained by decisions of the highest courts, and enforced by endless effort of the purchasers and the wage-earners defending their interests together. Under the pressure of competition, the highest ethical level possible to our social life can be reached only through legislation in this, its highest and finest sense.

These truths find an illustration in the history of a disastrously unsuccessful effort of the cigarmakers to protect by statute their own exclusive interests, through the enactment of a measure prohibiting the manufacture of cigars and the manipulation of tobacco in tenement houses in the state of New York. In 1884, when this effort was made, tenement-manufacture was of relatively slight extent compared with its subsequent development, and was confined almost exclusively to the materials mentioned. The sweating system, as we know it, was then in its earliest infancy, and the manufacture of garments and other articles under it was so slight as not even to suggest to the cigarmakers the inclusion of the needle-trade workers in the struggle for the statutory prohibition of work in the tenements.

When the law prohibiting the manufacture of cigars and the manipulation of tobacco in the tenements had been in force less than a year it was pronounced unconstitutional by the Court of Appeals, in the decision of the case of in re Jacobs.

Had that earliest statute been sustained by the Court of Appeals of New York it is safe to assert that the odious system of tenement manufacture would long ago have perished in every trade in every city in the Republic.

Because it was undeniably class legislation, applying only to those tenement-dwellers who were employed in producing the commodities including in some form tobacco as ingredient, and omitting all others, it is impossible to defend the statute. But the deplorable results of the decision of the Court of Appeals, which its defective form called forth, are of such far-reaching ethical, industrial and social character as to deserve careful consideration.

The framers of the law described it in its title as "An Act to Improve the Public Health," by prohibiting certain narrow lines of manufacture in the tenements. But the court held that its title did not properly describe it,—that it was not, in fact, a measure calculated to improve the public health.

On this last point the court was clearly in error as to the facts. The proof of the pudding is in the eating; and, since the annulment of the prohibition, tenement-house manufacture has developed enormously, has produced disease unceasingly by overcrowding not merely individual tenements, but whole districts of every city in which it has existed, and has distributed disease in the communities into which the manufactured goods have carried germs emanating from infected tenements.

Physicians, nurses, inspectors of numerous kinds, friendly visitors of divers charities, residents of settlements in districts in which the sweated industries are carried on, all testify to the impossibility of preventing the spread of disease in the general public where this system of manufacture continues. In 1885, however, this was not yet the case. The germ theory was not yet so thoroughly a part of the public consciousness as it has since become. Nor was the present body of evidence as to the close connection of the diseases of the tenement-dwellers with epidemics in remote parts of the country, whose inhabitants wear tenement-made garments, then available.

A startling proposition contained in the decision in re Jacobs is that the health of the employees is not the public health! "What possible relation can cigarmaking in any building have to the health of the general public?" asked the Court of Appeals of New York in 1885.

It is not long since a visiting nurse among the tenements of New York found a dying consumptive licking the tips of cigarettes which he was manufacturing. This is but one of thousands of observations which have been made and recorded since the decision in re Jacobs embodied that cynical question. During the intervening twenty years the fact has been imprinted upon the public mind that the whole system of manufacture in the tenements does involve a degree of danger to the public health such that it is no longer to be tolerated; that this danger is not confined to the employees in the tenements themselves, but that it is shared by them with the whole purchasing public.

It is not now needful to prove that the health of the workers is an important part of the health of the public. Every epidemic during the years since 1885 has proved that the disease of the workers in the tenements becomes, with certainty and precision, the disease of the public, transmitted in the textures of the goods worked upon in the sickrooms of the invalids of the tenements.

A comparison of the text of this New York decision of 1885 with the decisions of the Supreme Court of the United States in the cases of Holden *vs.* Hardy in 1898, and of Lochner *vs.* New York in 1905, shows the vast transition which has taken place in the space of twenty years in the judicial view of the public health.

Says the court in the decision in re Jacobs: "To justify this law, it would not be sufficient that the use of tobacco may be injurious to some persons, or that its manipulation may be injurious to those who are engaged in its preparation and manufacture; but it would have to be injurious to the public health."

In the later cases, cited in previous chapters, it has been shown that the whole contention of the United States Supreme Court is that the industry must be injurious to the persons engaged in it, in order that their freedom of contract in relation to it may be restricted by statute.

Because it was class legislation, by reason of confining its prohibition to workers in tobacco, and because it was not, in the opinion of the Court of Appeals, sufficiently obvious a measure for the improvement of the public health, the court pronounced the law prohibiting the manufacture of tobacco in tenements unconstitutional and void, alleging that it deprived the cigar-makers of "some portion of their personal liberty."

But, in sustaining his "right to live in his own house, or to work at any lawful trade therein,"—a right of which the tenement-dwellers had laboriously striven to be rid, in order to gain instead thereof the opportunity of working in factories and workshops furnished by the manufacturer,—the court, in fact, established the "right" of manufacturers to turn the kitchens and bedrooms of the poorest of the poor into workrooms and storage places, a "right" of which the most ample use has for twenty years been made by the manufacturers.

While thus inadvertently defending the undesired "right" of the tenement-dwellers to suffer the invasion of manufacture into the innermost recesses of the family life, the court inadvertently deprived the purchasing public of the power of tracing the processes of manufacture which are carried on, in name at least, for its sake. It thus deprived the purchaser, in effect, of the power to exercise the right to knowledge of his source of supply.

Moreover, by the decision, the right of the workingman who lives in a tenement house to enjoy his home, using it for the purposes for which a home is established and free from the intrusion of his daily bread-winning employment, was inferentially shown to be, like his right to leisure, one which must be achieved by the method of trade organization.

This inference the tenement-house workers drew without loss of time. They abandoned all effort to secure sweeping prohibitions, and have since that time striven to deal with their problem by the twofold method of regulation by statute and regulation by public opinion. Sweeping prohibition being unattainable, the next step was towards partial prohibition. Work upon certain specified articles in kitchens and bedrooms was prohibited to all persons not members of the family. Although a man could not be shielded from the invasion of his dwelling by the materials of his industry, he could at least be spared the presence of strange men and women. An immediate consequence of this was the establishment of workshops in the rear of the tenements, sometimes with steam power, sometimes with foot power; but always with the custom of sending the handwork into the dwellings. The list of articles thus kept sacred to the family, short at first, grew from year to year, and now (1905) includes thirty-four items. Baking bread and cakes, cracking nuts for candy manufacturers, candying fruit for sale to school children, stringing beads for passementeries, pickling cucumbers, and drying macaroni are a few of the items not yet embraced in the list.

By adopting these partial prohibitions, while denying to the purchasers and the workers the protection of a complete prohibition of all manufacture in the tenements, the State has instilled into the minds of its industrially weaker citizens a sense of confusion mixed with contempt for the law. For, where a sweeping prohibition would have been logical and relatively easy to enforce, the petty, teasing restrictions enacted piecemeal have been fruitful of the spirit of evasion. When it was a misdemeanor for a man's sister to sew a cloak in his dwelling, but perfectly legal for his wife to sew it, while his sister could legally sew an apron or a skirt for the same employer, the one impression conveyed to the mind of the newly arrived immigrant was that this law was not intended to be obeyed. And it never has been obeyed; nor is there any prospect, even in its present amended form, that it will be uniformly obeyed. For it is clearly non-enforceable.

In the vain effort to enforce partial restrictions which are in the nature of the case non-enforceable, a provision was enacted in 1899 requiring a license from the factory inspector for every person or group of persons who worked at any process of manufacture of some thirty articles, in any tenement house or in any building in the rear of one. After this provision had been in force for five years the writer one day, in 1904, observed a woman walking along Mulberry street, New York, carrying a huge bundle of knee pants on her head. The burden bearer mounted to the fifth floor of an Italian tenement and threw her bundle down upon a singularly greasy kitchen table. Asked to show her license to work, she brought out, with the friendly smile and courteous manner of the Sicilian peasant woman, a letter from the New York State Department of Labor, dated some seven weeks before, notifying her that her premises were unfit for licensing, and that no more work must be done in them until they had been thoroughly cleansed, re-inspected and licensed! The cheerful needle-woman, unable to read in any language, but reassured by the seal of the state of New York on the envelope, had assumed that this was the license for which she had been told to apply, and had worked away happy in the consciousness of having obeyed the law.

The only gain to any part of the community derived from the licensing law, during the five years in which it retained its original form, was the discovery of the places in which manufacture was carried on. More than thirty thousand licenses were issued, and the ugly fact was brought to light that there were more licensed groups of tenement-workers in the four most undesirable streets of New York City, Mott, Mulberry, Elizabeth and Chrystie streets, than in any other streets.

Since the promulgation of the decision in re Jacobs, in 1885, the state and the trade unions have alike been burdened with the despairing duty of performing the impossible. It is utterly impossible to keep the system of manufacture in the tenements, and to avoid its evil consequences.

Tenement work means the underpaid husband letting his wife earn the rent with her needle, instead of insisting, as it is clearly his duty to do, upon wages enough to maintain his family. It means boys and girls of ten years kept at home from school, in violation of the compulsory education law, to do the housework and take care of the younger children while the mother sews for the market.

Tenement work means the use of foot power in competition with steam power, a ruinous strain upon the health of every man, woman and child subjected to it. Tenement work means an endless working day in the tenement at the foot power machine in the "rush" season, followed by the shutting down of the factory for want of orders.

Tenement work means the steady downward pressure upon the wages of the factory workers, to whom it can always be said: "If you do not like our terms in the factory, we can send the work into the homes." Tenement work means the unavoidable spread of disease and the frequent breaking out of epidemics, not only in the cities where it is carried on, but in all those distant places to which the product may be sent.

In the effort to minimize the inevitable consequences of homework, the state has subjected the dwellers in the tenements to threefold inspection, in addition to the oversight of the federal government whose tax collectors were already charged with the duty of following them up for the purpose of gathering the tax upon tobacco.

Because the personal liberty of a workingman would be interfered with, if his employer were prohibited from requiring him to work at home, the unhappy dwellers in the tenements have seen their homes invaded by all manner of materials, from tobacco leaves and stems, to the bales of paper and tubs of paste required for making paper bags, and by three sets of inspectors, —of the Board of Health, of the Tenement House Department, and of the Bureau of Factory Inspection.

Moreover, in the alleged interest of their "personal liberty" these victims of the sweating manufacturers have been constrained to live within walking distance of their employer's place of business, for the burden-bearer between the merchant tailor and his home-worker is usually a woman or a child, reduced by the smallness of the pay to saving car-fare by living near the "shop." Instead of able-bodied men and girls of the family, walking empty-handed to and from their work, or riding perhaps to a desirable suburb by trolley, the burden-bearing woman or child has determined the distance to be traversed. Thus the tenement-house problem has been artificially intensified and complicated; and by reason of the unlimited competition of the women of the tenements, wages have been kept at such a level that neither time nor car-fare can be spared by an adult for fetching and carrying. Hence some child is sacrificed by being kept from school to serve as beast of burden, whenever the goods are such as can safely be trusted to a child.

Moreover, all this sacrifice of the family leaves the task of the officials a hopeless one. No Board of Health has ever succeeded in knowing, every day in the year, where all the goods are concealed in the tenements, nor where all the children are who may be coming down with diphtheria, or shedding rags and patches of their skin after light cases of scarlet fever.

The decision of the Court of Appeals in re Jacobs virtually turned over to the wage-earners the task of providing, through the machinery of their organizations, for the protection of themselves and the purchasers against the evils of the sweating system. For twenty years the unions have faithfully striven to perform a task which it was, from the beginning, impossible that they should achieve. Just as they long before introduced child-labor legislation and factory inspection, which have come to be recognized as benefactions to the whole people; so they now invented that method of dealing with the sweated trades, by offering the label as a guaranty of conditions approved by the workers which are accepted as the best available under the circumstances, and in view of the conditions imposed by the decision of the Court of Appeals in re Jacobs. It is, of course, out of their power ever to do, with palliatives, what a sweeping prohibition could have done long since.

The public, however, cannot afford to allow the courts to relegate to the labor organizations the duty of protecting the public health against the reckless willingness of manufacturers to take risks. For, if the union is not strong enough to dominate the trade (and no union of garment workers has ever been strong enough to do this), the public must take the consequences in disease and death sent out from the tenement sewing rooms. Or, if a union were not only insufficiently strong but imperfectly honest as well, the public would pay the penalty for every label dishonestly sold to contractors for use in places which fell below the accepted standard of wholesome and clean conditions.

Or, let us suppose that a portion of the public may be honestly opposed on principle to the maintenance of trade unions; and unwilling, therefore, to purchase goods guaranteed by the union label. Such abstainers, if left without other means of discrimination in favor of goods made under wholesome conditions, are in danger, not only of incurring disease and death, but of disseminating them throughout the community.

Finally, a large part of the membership of the unions in the garment trades consists of immigrants so recently arrived from Eastern Europe as to have no adequate standards of wholesome conditions for home and workshop, of persons wholly unprepared to defend their own health, much more that of the general public. Clearly the unions, however valuable to their members and to the community in other relations, cannot, in the nature of things, be a sufficient guardian of the health and safety of all the purchasing public.

While, however, the unions have not achieved the impossible, and have not succeeded in performing a task of protection of the public health which should never have been asked of any voluntary organization, they have been vastly strengthened by the effort to do this. Baffled in the endeavor to do away with tenement work by law, they turned to the development of their label, advertising it, obtaining legal guarantees against infringement, and publishing all the abhorrent facts connected with the sweating system and attached, inferentially, to the goods which bore no label. Their label, whether or not it has always guaranteed satisfactory cleanliness and the absence of disease from the workroom, has announced to the world that the conditions as to hours and wages (the organization of employees being understood, of course), in the factories in which it was used, were satisfactory to the workers in those factories.

This recommendation has gradually come to possess a value such that in some industries the manufacturers pay for the label a price which covers the cost of advertising on a large scale.

Since goods bearing the trade union label commonly cost somewhat more than other goods, the workingmen who take the trouble to pay the price required are stimulated to look sharply after the integrity of the union which offers a label.

What, now is the position of that portion of the public which disapproves of the union and repudiates its guarantee and its label? Except within the narrow limits of the Consumers' League, with its label on women's and children's white stitched underwear, such purchasers have no guarantee whatever. Moreover, only a small fraction of the innumerable industries involved in the preparation of apparel is included among the organizations of labor. While labels may be found in many cities by seekers after men's hats and shoes, outer-wear, neckties, gloves, shirts, etc., none is discernible for woven underwear, on which much handwork is regularly done in homes; while for women the union label is scarcely upon the market outside of the shoe trade.

In the manufacture of garments and apparel of all kinds for women, the workers are chiefly young girls and women who have, hitherto, formed no stable union; who have no funds for advertising on a large scale, and no real power of enforcing any provisions for their own protection or that of the public, which has for twenty years left to them this impossible task.

A community which turns over to the workingwomen the task of assuring to it clean and wholesome workrooms in the tenements, for the production of its wearing apparel, gets exactly what it deserves,—the sweating system upon the largest scale that the world has ever seen.

After the state of New York shall have arrived at some method of doing away with tenement manufacture and sweating, after these twin iniquities shall have been effectually abolished, the trade unions will resume their normal function of guaranteeing to purchasers, who ask for it, the fact that the hours of labor and the wages are satisfactory to the workers in the factory from which the label issues. It is preposterous ever to have asked of them, even inferentially, more than this. They have had imposed upon them, by the indirect working of the decision of the Court of Appeals in re Jacobs, a task which it was clearly the duty of the state to perform; and it is in no wise to their discredit that they have failed to do the impossible. That discredit attaches to the community which imposed this unwarranted and unwarrantable burden.

Thus we have, after twenty years of effort, two ineffectual methods of dealing with tenement manufacture, pursued side by side. The state, by statute, legalizes the manufacture in the tenements of thirty-four articles, and proceeds by a cumbersome threefold inspection (by the State Factory Inspectors, the Board of Health Inspectors and the Tenement House Department) to minimize the danger to the public health, including that of the workers themselves. But, as has been pointed out, the public health is not really safeguarded. The people are merely lulled into a false sense of security.

The unions, meanwhile, have spent untold thousands of dollars in their effort to induce the purchasing public to avoid the dangers attending sweated goods, by the individual method of discrimination against tenement-made products and in favor of goods guaranteed by the union label.

The ethical loss by reason of this decision of the Court of Appeals of New York, quite apart from the loss of money in advertising by the unions and in futile, hopeless inspection on the part of the State, is quite beyond the possibility of calculation.

From the day when this decision became effective, the interests of the purchasing public and of the tenement dwellers have been practically identical, and both have been sacrificed to the convenience and the profit of the manufacturers.

For twenty years the state of New York has proclaimed through its highest court that it cannot protect the homes of its industrially weakest citizens from invasion by the materials of their industry. These materials are owned by rich and powerful employers, strongly organized locally and nationally, and are foisted upon the meager dwellings of the poor solely for the purpose of saving to the employers the cost of heat, light, cleaning and, far more important, rent of workrooms. For the convenience of the powerful, the weakest industrial factors in the community, the widows burdened with young children, the daughters kept at home by bedridden parents, have been invaded by industry and by inspectors. This forcing of industry into the tenements has fostered the belief that work *must* be done by all who live there, particularly if they are poor and sick. Thus devotion to the needle and the pastepot has become a sort of touchstone measuring the "worthiness" or the "helpableness" of the women who have dependent members of the family.

Meanwhile, the manufacturer or the merchant tailor, the owner of the goods, bears no responsibility towards the community, beyond the requirements that he must file with the factory inspectors, when so requested, a correct list, in the English language, of the addresses to which he sends his goods to be made up, and must, before sending goods into a tenement, inquire of the Board of Health whether there is recorded any present case of infectious or communicable disease on the premises.

Before the case in re Jacobs can be reversed, and work in the tenements sweepingly prohibited in the interest of the public health, including the health of the workers, it may be necessary to provide—by way of one more last palliative experiment—for placing the goods-owner under a heavy bond for the literal fulfilment of the requirements of the legal restrictions by all the people to whom his goods are entrusted. This would be less than the manufacturer's equitable share of the burden which he inflicts upon society. Since it is for his own convenience and enrichment that the evil of the sweating system is fastened upon society, he should bear the whole burden of the cost of inspection, disinfection of premises and of goods which have been exposed to infection, prosecution of offenders, etc. . . .

All the restrictions which have been placed upon tenement-house manufacture, during the twenty years since complete prohibition thereof was blocked, have been obtained either by the tenement-house workers, or with their eager help.

It may be urged, however, that they are not judges of what is best for themselves; that their arguments are not sound. It is, therefore, worth while to consider who the tenement-house workers are. They are, first, the able-bodied men whose fathers and sons working in other trades all have workrooms provided for them by their employers, such, for instance, as employees in the printing and binding trades, in wood-working, upholstery, boot and shoe making, and all the other industries in which the use of steam or electricity, or the nature of the goods, makes it advantageous to the employer to have the work done in a factory or a workshop. What possible advantage is gained for these men by working in their kitchens and bedrooms, in the midst of the cooking, washing, scrubbing, and care of the babies? Obviously none!

The second contingent of home-workers are the able-bodied immigrant girls. These suffer the disadvantages of losing contact with the English-speaking employers and fellow workers in the factory or workshop. They use foot power instead of steam or electricity, and thus earn less money with more exertion. They spend the day in the same air in which they had spent the night, losing the change and exercise which would attend travel to and from the factory. They lose the *esprit de corps* which arises from work in a group, and their wages are correspondingly wretched. There is no standard of wages and hours; they take what the employer gives them; and they work until the task is accomplished. For them there is no opening hour, no closing time. When work is done, they cease to drive the machine; not until then.

The children whose school life is sacrificed to the need of being on hand to fetch and carry are losers, pure and simple. So are the wretched little boys and girls who are still too young to fetch and carry, but can be employed in stringing beads and pulling basting threads, in pasting boxes and bags, in wrapping paper around strips of wire to make stems for artificial flowers, in digging the kernels out of nuts, or in cracking the nuts themselves.

Finally, there are the widows with young children, the daughters with bedridden old fathers or mothers,—the women who cannot leave home to work. For these persons, work in the home is an evil and an evil only. Not one of them can really support herself while doing the housework and caring for her dependents, and the community, which requires that a woman so placed shall go through the forms of work for self-support, deserves all the punishment that it receives in the form of transmitted disease. All such women are already in the receipt of charitable aid, and the humane and enlightened thing for the community to do in their case is to make that aid adequate to their needs, absolving them from working for the market, on

condition that they take suitable care of the invalids or the
children who are dependent upon them. In the long run, the
community pays many times over in the form of disease transmitted from the sickrooms, and of reformatory life provided
for the children neglected by their overworked mothers in the
effort to do the impossible, for every economy which it attempts
to make by means of relief withheld from such dependent
families.

The men in the trades afflicted with tenement work have
always maintained that, if they could be freed from their
slavery to their kitchens and bedrooms, and enabled to work
in suitable workshops, they could then organize their trades
in such ways as to command wages sufficient to support their
families, including their sick and dependent relatives.

There is a wide-spread belief that the prevailing cheapness of
ready-made clothing is due to the utilization of the ill-paid labor
of women and children in the tenement homes; that the wage-
earner in the non-sweated trades profits by the sufferings of the
sweaters' victims, and wears better garments by reason of their
poverty and the degradation of this great trade. This is, however, the exact reverse of the truth. The cheapness of our
garments is attained in spite of the sweating system, not because
of it. Indeed, it is doubtful whether the fall in prices of garments
is commensurate with the fall in the prices of the cloth of which
they are made. Certain it is that cloth is vastly cheaper than it
was thirty years ago. The methods of placing goods of all kinds
upon the market (garments and cloth for making garments
included) have been revolutionized in the direction of cheapness within the memory of us all. That part of the work of
making garments which lies outside of tenements has also been
cheapened by the general application of steam machinery to
garment-cutting. These three great modern improvements have
enabled the corporations which control the garment trade to
prolong the life of the foot-power sewing machine and the
tenement-house workroom.

The purchasing public, made gullible, perhaps, by its own

greed for bargains, has willingly believed that in this one set of trades alone primitive machines and petty shops maintaining a multitude of middlemen were really cheaper in the end (because they employ the worst-paid women and girls to be found in the field of manufacture) than well-equipped plants, with power furnished by steam or electricity and conducted by managers of higher intelligence.

It has become an axiom in political economy that high-priced labor stimulates the application of machinery. On the other hand, the presence in the tenements of girls who sew on buttons and run errands for wages ranging from thirty cents to seventy cents a week, and of women who sew at foot-power machines for $3.00 to $5.00 a week from ten to twenty hours a day during the five to seven months which form the busy season, and receive relief from public and private charities during the remainder of the year, distinctly tends to prolong the present primitive and belated equipment of this part of the garment trades. It is perhaps not too much to say that the thousands of women and girls in the tenements present a serious obstacle to the process of lifting the garment trades from their present degradation to the level of the factory trades.

Under the sweating system, the wholesaler or the merchant tailor shifts the burden of rent from himself to the tailor who sews in a tenement-house kitchen or bedroom. The wholesaler or the merchant tailor further avoids the risk attendant upon maintaining a plant equipped with steam or electricity throughout the dull season. He offsets, as far as he can, the added expense of a horde of middlemen, by subdividing the work of the women and girls in the tenements and simplifying it to the utmost extreme, so that skill in the worker is reduced to the last degree, and wages follow skill in the direction of zero. Hence we find in the tenements "hand girls" whose backs grow crooked over the simplest of hemming, felling, and sewing on buttons, and "machine girls" whose exertion of foot power entails tuberculosis and pelvic disorders ruinous to themselves at present and to their children in the future. The foul, ill-ventilated, often damp shops, the excessive speed and intensity of the work, the ceaseless exertion of the limbs throughout interminable days, and the grinding poverty of these workers combine to render consumption the characteristic disease of these trades. The very youth of the workers increases their susceptibility to injury and disease. Young backs grow crooked over the machines, young eyes and membranes are irritated by the fluff and dust disengaged from cheaply dyed woolen goods by flying needles. The eagerness of young workers is stimulated to the highest pitch by ill-paid piece-work and the uncertainty of its continuance.

All this wretchedness, attending this belated survival of primitive organization in a great industry, surely cannot permanently survive in the face of the advantages which mechanical power possesses over foot power. It is only a question of time when the garment trades shall be placed upon the factory level.

This change, however, cannot reasonably be expected of the corporations which control the garment trades, or of the growing intelligence of the sweaters' victims. It will be brought about, if at all, by an enlightened public refusing to wear tenement-made garments, and embodying its will in prohibitory legislation carried much farther than the tentative measures of regulation now in force.

A necessary preliminary to this revolt against tenement goods is a clear perception of the truth that no one (except possibly the wholesaler) profits by the pauperism and suffering of the men, women and children who work in tenement rooms.

Factory labor did not solve every problem either. With respect to the physical strains in factory labor, Josephine Goldmark became an authority, likewise advocating protective legislation. From her work on FATIGUE AND EFFICIENCY,[5] a section is reproduced here to indicate her approach to this study.

[5] Reprint obtained through the courtesy of the author.

Striking as is the unanimity of the world's industrial experience and the testimony of observers in each country as to the need of more complete protection for the workers, such empirical data furnish, after all, no scientific basis for labor legislation. They are arguments, legitimate presumptions in its favor, not scientific proof.

Yet a scientific ground for such legislation does exist and is available today. The fundamental basis for laws regulating the working hours of men, women, or children in industrial occupations—at the spindle or loom, in machine shops or laundries, behind the counter or in the glass-houses—is the common physiological phenomenon, fatigue, the normal result of all human action. For fatigue is nature's warning signal that the limit of activity is approaching. Exhaustion, or over-fatigue, follows when the warning is disregarded and the organism is pushed beyond its limit by further forced exertions.

In this inexorable sequence, subject to countless variations but never failing, we have a broad fundamental basis for the short working day in industry: a physiological necessity inherent in man's structure for allowing an adequate amount of rest. The regulation of working hours is the necessary mechanism to prevent over-fatigue or exhaustion, forerunner of countless miseries to individuals and whole nations.

It is precisely in explaining the normal and abnormal aspects of fatigue, its nature, effects, and relation to all human life, that science can give its authoritative sanction to labor legislation. For, during the last century, unknown to those who saw the practical results of overwork in industry and sought a legal remedy year after year, so often in vain, men of various sciences were studying the same phenomena in the laboratory. The physiologist, chemist, bacteriologist, and psychologist have contributed to the study. The scientific investigations of fatigue in its varied aspects make up a wide and growing literature. In spite of still unverified details, the underlying principles and laws have been agreed upon.

The study of fatigue, as applied to industry, is not an academic nor a remote speculation. It shows why the system of long hours must, physiologically, result in human deterioration and inferior output. It should help, also, to determine what protection is needed in the future for workers under modern conditions of labor, viewing the new conditions and their demand on human energies from the physiological standpoint.

Such a change of front, indeed, from the purely economic to the broadly physiological, is what this study chiefly advocates. Heretofore, the scientifically well-known principles of fatigue have not been utilized in the protection of the workers, just because they have been unknown to those persons who could have benefited most directly: the legislators who frame the laws, the enlightened employers who need legislation to restrain unscrupulous competitors, the trade unions and philanthropic agencies which have promoted legislation, and the judges whose official sanction of the laws must precede enforcement. To all these, in the main, the contributions of science on the subject have been unknown. To the scientist, on the other hand, the industrial world has been an undiscovered country. Even physicians and students of hygiene are to a large extent unacquainted with the vast speed and complexity of processes to which workers are subjected. They hardly know, for instance, how machinery is additionally speeded each year; how, to cite a single example from the needle trades, the newest power machines run by girl operators carry 12 needles instead of one, or set almost 4000 stitches a minute, each thread and needle to be intently watched for breaking as the material is guided on its rapid passage. Changes of which this is typical have added to the strain of industry in a progressive ratio, and, obviously, add also to all the elements which make up the worker's fatigue.

When attention is given to the utmost ramifications of modern industrialism, the thought of women is also found there. Dr. Alice Hamilton, for instance, has specialized in the health aspects of industrial processes from the standpoint of poisons, and presented her findings in a volume called INDUSTRIAL POISONS IN THE UNITED STATES.[6] *In recognition of her competence Harvard University drew her into its faculty as teacher of industrial medicine. Previously she had been a special investigator for the United States Department of Labor.*

It is not my intention to describe in detail the practical measure by which a factory or workshop may be rendered safe from toxic dust and vapors. That is the task of the engineer, not of the physician. All that the latter can do is to make clear the principles on which methods of protection must be based and then leave their actual execution to the experts in the mechanical trades. These principles depend on the character of the poisonous compound in question, above all on its special mode of entrance into the human body. If this is by way of the inspired air, the prevention of fumes and dust becomes the matter of first importance. Whatever money is available for factory hygiene must be expended first on mechanisms to prevent poisoning the air, even if this means a scanty equipment for the washrooms and the lunchrooms.

The physician will sometimes be told that certain processes cannot be carried on without contamination of the air, that the workman must be protected in some other way, by some sort of respirator or mask. This brings him into a field of controversy in which difficulties await him. The experiments now being carried on by the United States Bureau of Mines will doubtless throw much light on the question of the efficacy of such devices against different sorts of dusts and vapors, but at present it does not seem safe to say more than this: no apparatus, respirator or army mask, through which a man can breathe with entire ease and comfort while doing heavy work, will serve to hold back all the poisonous dust or vapor in the air. If such a mask is really efficient it will cause some discomfort and difficulty to the wearer. This means that it is a device for emergency use,

[6] Reprint obtained through the courtesy of The Macmillan Company.

not for use during eight or ten hours continuously, day in and day out, for the best shop discipline would break down under a strain like that, and the foreman would have to pretend not to see the masks worn on the forehead or around the neck.

A mask, carefully selected for the particular poison against which protection is needed, should be provided for emergency use, during short periods only, in all places where there is a danger of fumes or dust, but to place one's trust in masks for the continual protection of men is simply to close one's eyes to unpleasant facts.

If the poison belongs to those that gain entrance primarily through the skin, cleanliness of the premises, of work-benches and apparatus, is essential and in addition it is necessary to furnish clean working clothes and facilities for bathing, as well as for the usual washing of hands and face. This is already accepted as a necessity in connection with the compounds which produce trade eruptions but it is quite as essential for those which produce systematic eruptions without local irritation. If direct contact with the poison cannot be avoided, then every means must be adopted to protect the skin. As much of it as possible should be covered with clean underwear, overalls, socks, and caps, and the surface which is necessarily exposed may be covered with a bland ointment or dusted with powder or washed frequently. It must be remembered, however, that there is a risk in too much washing of the human skin and that care must be taken in such cases to use the least irritating cleansers, to avoid scrubbing, and to restore the lost oils of the skin by inunction with some animal fat.

The consensus of opinion among men experienced in such industries as the production of coal-tar intermediates, where skin absorption is of prime importance, seems to be against gloves as a protection. Gloves make the hands sweat and the skin soft and hot and in excellent condition for the absorption of poisons, and if there is even a small rip or tear in the glove letting the dust or liquid in, it will form what is practically a poultice of poison around the hand.

There are poisonous dusts which not only contaminate the air but also produce poisoning through the intestinal tract if the worker has his hands and face covered with such dust when he handles his food or his plug of tobacco. The protective measures indicated in such cases, provision of a separate lunchroom, only to be entered after thorough ablutions, are too well known to need anything more than a mention.

The factors that favor absorption of industrial poisons, or that heighten their effect, were dealt with in the first chapter. These also come within the field of the physician. Heat from furnaces, steam from tubs and tanks, may seem to be outside his province; long hours and low wages, the employment of young lads and girls, may seem to him questions for the management alone, but the incidence of sickness among his charges is profoundly affected by such factors as these. He should not fail to assume some responsibility for the feeding of the employees at least so far as the noon-day meal is concerned, for if a warm, wholesome lunch is furnished them it will go far to protect them against poisoning.

The industrial physician is entrusted with the ungrateful task of selecting, by physical examination, men and woman whom he considers fit to face the risks of work in poisonous occupations. The textbooks warn him to reject the tuberculous, the anemic, the individual with lesions of the kidneys or heart, and this is doubtless wise, but he is an innocent optimist who believes that after all this is done he has guarded himself against distressing accidents. The management may believe that such a weeding out has rid the force of the over-susceptibilities; the wise physician knows that this is not true and that the most vigorous and blooming men and women may be the ones to develop lead encephalopathy or benzene purpura hemorrhagica and that the only way to guard against this is to keep constantly on the watch for the warning signs and then to remove the victim before serious harm has been done.

To do this, it is best to make a careful classification of the different jobs in the plant, according to the degree of danger in each, and to devote special attention to the employees in the class that heads the list. New hands who are given jobs in this class should be examined at frequent intervals till the physician is able to say whether they have a normal degree of resistance to the poison in question, for, if not, it is only good economy to shift them at once to other work. It will always, however, be necessary to subject all the employees in the dangerous class to routine examination, for at any time some disturbance of metabolism may break down the defenses of one who was apparently immune.

The physician should be the one to whom the education of the employees in personal prophylaxis should be entrusted, or at least he should plan and supervise it, though it may be he will not have enough of factory vernacular to "get it across." But he should insist on the necessity of such instruction. The idea is often held by employers who are using unfamiliar poisons that it is best to say nothing about them for fear of frightening the men away. This attitude on the part of the men in charge of munition works during the war was a distressing obstacle in the way of all who tried to introduce into American plants the safe-guards successfully worked out in the British, which could not be done if the fiction were maintained that trinitrotoluene might indeed explode, but was otherwise quite harmless. As a matter of fact we all know the workmen were not hoodwinked; they were only muddled. They knew perfectly well that something was there that made men ill but just what it was and how it affected them they did not know, so they ended by suspecting everything and promptly quitting the job if they felt ill, regardless of whether the illness were caused by the poison or not. The plants which were under intelligent management, with careful instruc-tion of the men and prompt resort to the dispensary even for light ailments, had a much lower labor turnover than those which followed the policy of secrecy.

The task of education is not easy—it is exhaustive of time and temper alike, but it is a duty which cannot be shirked, espe-cially in unorganized industries. Trade Unionists are to a varying extent responsible for the conditions under which they work, but the great majority of the poisonous industries are unorganized. Much of the dangerous work is done by foreign-born men and women and toward these workers the responsibility of the management and of the physician is far greater. Such people are like children in their readiness to accept the conditions of life, they will work long hours, in heat and filth and poisonous dust, they make no demands for security or comforts, they are quite free from the irritating interference of trade union officials. These are great advantages to the employer but if he accepts them he must accept the accompanying disadvantages. With child-like docility goes childish ignorance, recklessness and obstinacy. The management cannot throw upon such men and women the responsibility of their own health and safety. They are not capable of assuming it. For them the protection must be especially elaborate, it must be "fool-proof," the vigilance of the physician must be unrelaxed.

It may happen that the physician will be asked what to do in a department where all known mechanical devices for the prevention of poisonous dusts and vapors have been applied, and yet, because of the very nature of the process, there is still contamination of the air. In such cases there seem to be but two courses open. The dose of poison may be reduced by shortening the exposure, cutting it down perhaps to only a couple of hours in the day's shift or even less than that. Or the work may be allowed to go on under the watchful eyes of the physician who knows that a certain warning symptom will appear in time for him to order a change of work before real harm has been done. An excellent example of such a system is described in the chapter on tetrachlorethane. With newer poisons, it may be that the physician will have to study for himself the physiological effects in order to discover what sign or symptom can be depended on to give the needed warning of danger.

In closing, let me beg the industrial physician not to let the atmosphere of the factory befog his view of his special problem. His duty is to the producer, not to the product. If measures which he knows to be necessary are declared impossible, because they interfere with production, he may have to yield, but let it be understood that such yielding is against his judgment. A sanitary engineer may be told by a city council that it cannot afford a pure water supply and he may have no choice but to accept the verdict. But he would be greatly at fault if he allowed the city fathers to believe that the half-way measures they plan will safeguard the community against typhoid fever. In the same way the industrial physician may be obliged to abandon his plans for protecting his charges against poisoning because the expense is greater than the management will allow or because a change in the method might make the product less perfect. But in so yielding let him be careful never to sacrifice his own intellectual integrity nor adopt the standards of the non-medical man to whom the proper working of the plant is of first importance. His task is to safeguard the health of the patients who are entrusted to him, often without any volition of their own. The successful production of goods is outside his field. To the physician, always, life is more than meat and the body than raiment.

CHAPTER X

BREAKING INTO PRIVILEGE

As THE social structure of the bourgeois civilization rose higher and higher with the expansion of industry, the increase of property to be divided, and the multiplication of white-collar occupations, the legal barriers to women's economic advance became obsolete or at all events obsolescent. Inevitably, forceful and intelligent women demanded the full right to share in the golden profits of capitalism and attacked the legal and social restrictions that stood in their path.

Before their determined assaults, masculine privileges yielded to married women's "property rights." The stronghold of the law broke down before the invasion of women advocates. Women physicians and surgeons were admitted by license to the practice of medicine. The stern guardians of "learning" permitted women to teach in faculties and become presidents of colleges, at least for women. With these trenches carried, full political enfranchisement came into sight for women. Taxpayers, social workers, factory employees and professionals, determined to have a share in the governing process, demanded the ballot as an instrument necessary for the attainment and protection of civil liberties for women. Some agitated by appeals to masculine reason on the assumption that man was a reasoning animal and when that operation did not prove swift enough to suit their taste, other women led by Alice Paul and Lucy Burns turned to man's historic method—militancy. Then the movement for political enfranchisement, which had lagged behind vocational movements, gained a rushing impetus. Con-

gress passed and the country ratified the Nineteenth Amendment to the Constitution establishing complete political equality
in 1920.

*How the tabu against women lawyers was removed is related
by Ada M. Bittenbender in WOMAN'S WORK IN AMER-
ICA,[1] edited by Annie Nathan Meyer.*

The history of various ages and nations, since the days of the
prophetess Deborah, who filled the office of judge among the
children of Israel (Judges, IV. 4), records the names of women
distinguished for their legal learning, some of whom were also
successful advocates. Among the latter we content ourselves
with mentioning Aspasia, who pleaded causes in the Athenian
forum, and Amenia Sentia and Hortensia in the Roman forum.
But, alas, the right of Roman women to follow the profession
of advocate was taken away in consequence of the obnoxious
conduct of Calpurnia, who, from "excess of boldness" and "by
reason of making the tribunals resound with howlings uncommon
in the forum," says Velerius Maximus, was forbidden to plead.
The law, made to meet the especial case of Calpurnia, ultimately, "under the influence of the anti-feministic tendencies"
of the period, was converted into a general one. In its wording
the law sets forth that the original reason of woman's exclusion
"rested solely on the doings of Calpurnia."

This exclusion furnished a precedent for other nations which,
in the course of time, was followed. . . .

The first woman since the days of Mistress Brent to ask for
and obtain admission to the bar of this country was Arabella A.
Mansfield of Mt. Pleasant, Iowa. She studied in a law office, and

[1] Reprint obtained through the courtesy of Henry Holt and Company.

was admitted to the Iowa bar in June, 1869, under a statute providing only for admission of "white male citizens." The examining committee in its report, which is of record, said:

"Your committee have examined the provisions of section 2700 of chapter 114, of the Revision of 1860, concerning the qualifications of attorneys and counselors in this State but in considering the section in connection with division 3 of section 29, chapter 3 of the Revision, on construction of statutes, we feel justified in recommending to the court that construction which we deem authorized, not only by the language of the law itself, but by the demands and necessities of the present time and occasion. Your committee take unusual pleasure in recommending the admission of Mrs. Mansfield, not only because she is the first lady who has applied for this authority in this State, but because in her examination she has given the very best rebuke possible to the imputation that ladies cannot qualify for the practice of the law."

At the time of Mrs. Mansfield's début into the profession without opposition, Myra Bradwell, of Chicago, having studied law under the instruction of her husband, ex-Judge James B. Bradwell, was unsuccessfully knocking at the door of the Supreme Court of Illinois for admission. To give an understanding of the case, and line of argument used in denying her application, we extract from the opinion of the Court, delivered by Mr. Justice Lawrence, the following:

". . . This step, if taken by us, would mean that, in the opinion of this tribunal, every civil office in this State may be filled by women; that it is in harmony with the spirit of our constitution and laws that women should be made governors, judges, and sheriffs. This we are not prepared to hold. . . . There are some departments of the legal profession in which women can appropriately labor. Whether, on the other hand, to engage in the hot strifes of the bar, in the presence of the public, and with momentous verdicts the prizes of the struggle, would not tend to destroy the deference and delicacy with which it is the pride of our ruder sex to treat her, is a matter certainly worthy of her consideration. But the important question is, what effect the presence of women as barristers in our courts would have upon the administration of justice, and the question can be satisfactorily answered only in the light of experience."

The Supreme Court of Illinois having refused to grant to Mrs. Bradwell a license to practice law in the courts of that State, she appealed the case to the Supreme Court of the United States, where the judgment of the State court was affirmed. . . . Mr. Justice Bradley, while concurring in the judgment, gave expression to his views in a separate opinion in which he took occasion to say that, "The constitution of the family organization, which is founded in the divine ordinance as well as in the nature of things, indicates the domestic sphere as that which properly belongs to the domain and functions of womankind." The Chief Justice, Salmon P. Chase, "dissented from the judgment of the court, and from all the opinions."

The Legislature of Illinois, in 1872, enacted that "No person shall be precluded or debarred from any occupation, profession, or employment (except military) on account of sex." But Mrs. Bradwell, ever since being occupied with editorial work on the Chicago *Legal News,* which she founded in 1868, and with the publication of Bradwell's Appellate Court Reports and other legal works, did not renew her application for a license to practice law. The sequel is this, copied from the Chicago *Legal News* of April 5, 1890: "We are pleased to say that last week, upon the original record, every member of the Supreme Court of Illinois cordially acquiesced in granting, on the Court's own motion, a license as an attorney and counselor at law to Mrs. Bradwell."

The next case was that of Mrs. Belva Ann Lockwood, of Washington, D.C., who graduated from the Law School of the National University, and was admitted to practice before the Supreme Court of the District, in 1873. The same year a motion was made for her admission to the bar of the U. S. Court of Claims. This Court refused to act upon the motion, "for want of jurisdiction."

At the October term, 1876, of the Supreme Court of the United States, Mrs. Lockwood applied for admission as practitioner of that court. Her application was denied. . . . She continued practicing before the courts of the District and elsewhere, outside of the United States courts, until Congress passed a bill [1879] providing, "That any woman who shall have been a member of the bar of the highest court of any State or Territory, or of the Supreme Court of the District of Columbia, for the space of three years, and shall have maintained a good standing before such court, and who shall be a person of good moral character, shall, on motion, and the production of such record, be admitted to practice before the Supreme Court of the United States." Mrs. Lockwood drafted the bill and secured its passage. She was the first woman to be admitted under the law and to practice before this Supreme Court. . . . Mrs. Bittenbender moved the admission of Miss Gillet, the first instance of one woman moving the admission of another to the highest court in the country. A few days after Mrs. Lockwood's admission, she received word from the Court of Claims that she could now plead before it.

The next State court to be heard from on the subject was the Supreme Court of Wisconsin, in 1875. The matter was the motion to admit Miss R. Lavinia Goodell to the bar of that court. . . . The following extract from that opinion we believe will be read with interest, and remain of historic value as showing the fossilized misconceptions woman combated with in attaining the generally acceptable position in the legal profession in this country which she now holds:

". . . The profession enters largely into the well-being of society; and, to be honorably filled and safely to society, exacts the devotion of life. The law of nature destines and qualifies the female sex for the bearing and nurture of the children of our race and for the custody of the homes of the world and their maintenance in love and honor. And all life-long callings of women, inconsistent with these radical and sacred duties of their sex, as in the profession of the law, are departures from the order of nature; and when voluntary, treason against it. The cruel chances of life sometimes baffle both sexes, and may leave women free from the peculiar duties of their sex. These may need employmnt, and should be welcome to any not derogatory to their sex and its proprieties, or inconsistent with the good order of society. But it is public policy to provide for the sex, not for its superfluous members; and not to tempt women from the proper duties of their sex by opening to them duties peculiar to ours. There are many employments in life not unfit for female character. The profession of the law is surely not one of these. The peculiar qualities of womanhood, its gentle graces, its quick sensibility, its tender susceptibility, its purity, its delicacy, its emotional impulses, its subordination of hard reason to sympathetic feeling, are surely not qualifications for forensic strife. Nature has tempered woman as little for the juridical conflicts of the court room, as for the physical conflicts of the battle-field. Womanhood is molded for gentler and better things. And it is not the saints of the world who chiefly give employment to our profession. It has essentially and habitually to do with all that is selfish and malicious, knavish and criminal, coarse and brutal, repulsive and obscene, in human life. It would be revolting to all female sense of the innocence and sanctity of their sex, shocking to man's reverence for womanhood and faith in woman, on which hinge all the better affections and humanities of life, that woman should be permitted to mix professionally in all the nastiness of the world which finds its way into courts of justice; all the unclean issues, all the collateral questions of incest, rape, seduction, fornication, adultery, pregnancy, bastardy, legitimacy, prostitution, lascivious cohabitation, abortion, infanticide, divorces."

Ah, dear sir, it is largely to "mix professionally in all the nastiness of the world which finds its way into courts of justice," that many, very many women seek admission to the bar. In every case involving anyone of the "unclean issues" or "collateral questions" you have named, some woman must appear as complainant or defendant, or be in some way associated.

What more proper, then, than that some other woman should be in court, clothed with legal power, to extend aid and protection to her sister in trouble, that justice may be done her, and the coarse jest and cruel laugh, so proverbial in social impurity cases before woman's advent as pleader, prevented! And we respectfully call upon the mothers of every land to see to it that in no instance in the future of the world shall a woman be summoned to the bar of justice as a party or witness in any case involving one of these "unclean issues" or "collateral questions" without being accompanied by one or more of her own sex of irreproachable character. When such emergencies are otherwise unprovided for, let the "good mothers of Israel" in the place convene and depute one or more of their number to perform this duty. It is a duty, unquestionably, to be performed in the interest not only of one sex, but of mankind generally; for what affects one sex for good or evil, affects both.

Aye, Mr. Chief Justice, "the profession enters largely into the well-being of society"; and it is because of this fact woman desires and ought to enter it. This is the best of reasons. As to her motherhood prerogatives, experience has shown her able to perform these as the Father of the Universe and Mother Nature would have her, and still not to be precluded from giving the profession the necessary "devotion" to the end that it shall be "honorably filled and safely to society." If "the law of nature destines and qualifies the female sex . . . for the custody of the homes of the world and their maintenance in love and honor," as you say, Mr. Chief Justice,—we say "if" because we believe the male sex to be joint-heir,—that does not mean that all women, or any woman, should stay inside of four walls continually to cook, wash dishes, sweep, dust, make beds, wash, iron, sew, etc. Oh, no! A woman may properly act as the custodian of a home and maintain it in love and honor, and do none of these things. Instead of such "life-long callings of women" being "departures from the order of nature, and, when voluntary, treason against it," as you think, Mr. Chief Justice, we hold that to stifle the longings of an immortal soul to follow any useful calling in this life, to be a "departure from the order of nature, and, when voluntary, treason against it."

A law was promptly enacted enabling women to practice law in Wisconsin, under which Miss Goodell was admitted to the Supreme Court of the State. . . .

Mary Hall, of Hartford, Connecticut, in 1882, after having completed the prescribed term of study and passed the required examination, applied to the Superior Court in Hartford county for a license to practice law. . . .

We have a record showing that there were fifty-six women attorneys in the country at the time this last decision was rendered, in July, 1882, of whom thirty-one had graduated from law schools. . . .

Col. C. K. Pier, his wife, and three daughters, of Madison, Wisconsin, are widely known as "the Pier family of lawyers." The Colonel is a lawyer of long standing. Mrs. Pier and their eldest daughter graduated from the Law Department of the University of Wisconsin in 1887. All three practice together. The two younger sisters, Carrie and Harriet, have nearly finished the course in the law school from which their mother and sister graduated. Miss Kate, in her twenty-first year, appeared before the Supreme Court and won her case, the first to be argued by a woman in the supreme tribunal of the State. A newspaper, commenting on the fact, says: "Her opponent was J. J. Sutton, a veteran practitioner. The gray-haired patriarchs of the profession smoothed the wrinkles out of their waistcoats and straightened their neckties, and then wiped the specks off their spectacles. The audience was one before which any young man might readily have been excused for getting rattled. There were present Gen. E. E. Bryant, dean of the law faculty, ex-Secretary of the Interior William F. Vilas, and a host of visiting legal lights. Even the dignified judges were compelled to affect an extra degree of austerity to conceal their interest in the young attorney. But Miss Pier showed no sign of embarrassment. Her argument was direct and to the point, and, moreover, relieved of the superfluities that frequently characterize the verbose utterances of more experienced attorneys of the male sex. She stated her case unhesitatingly, and frequently turned to and cited authorities, showing an acquaintance with the law and a degree of self-possession which indicated that she was truly in love with her profession. She showed she possessed the true mettle for success, and two week later, when the judges rendered their decision, she had the pleasure of winning her first case. Since then both she and her mother have frequently argued cases before the Court." . . .

Woman's influence in the court room as counsel is promotive of good in more than one respect. Invectives against opposing counsel, so freely made use of in some courts, are seldom indulged in when woman stands as the opponent. And in social impurity cases, language, in her presence, becomes more chaste, and the moral tone thereby elevated perceptibly. But there should be one more innovation brought into general vogue, that of the mixed jury system.

There has not been time enough yet for a woman to develop into an Erskine or Burke, an O'Connor or Curran, a Webster or Choate. But few men have done so, if history correctly records. Woman has made a fair beginning, and is determined to push on and upward, keeping pace with her brother along the way until, with him, she shall have finally reached the highest pinnacle of legal fame.

The first doctors, anthropology warrants our believing, were women. They combined nursing with prescribing and the compounding of remedies. Country women on the successive American frontiers, heirs of the age-old mother lore, likewise served their communities in times of illness and continued to do so until medical colleges and licenses transferred the art of healing to other hands. When, therefore, women in the cities demanded the right to receive equal education with the men who had entered the field of doctoring, they were not departing from feminine tradition but simply seeking greater skill.

Dr. Mary Jacobi was not the first American woman to win a medical degree but she became a physician of recognized ability and her own narrative of the struggle for equal right to heal reveals an opposition scarcely credible today. In WOMAN'S WORK IN AMERICA,[2] by Annie Nathan Meyer, Dr. Jacobi tells this story.

The history of the movement for introducing women into the full practice of the medical profession is one of the most interesting of modern times. This movement has already (1891) achieved much, and far more than is often supposed. Yet the interest lies even less in what has been so far achieved, than in the opposition which has been encountered: in the nature of this opposition; in the pretexts on which it has been sustained, and in the reasonings, more or less disingenuous, by which it has claimed its justification. The history, therefore, is a record not more of fact, than of opinion. And the opinions expressed have often been so grave and solid in appearance, yet proved so frivolous and empty in view of the subsequent event, that their history is not unworthy careful consideration among that of other solemn follies of mankind.

In Europe, the admission of women to the profession of medicine has been widely opposed because of disbelief in their intellectual capacity. In America it is less often permitted to doubt —out loud—the intellectual capacity of women. The controversy has therefore been shifted to the entirely different ground of decorum.

At the very outset, however, two rival decorums confronted each other. The same centuries of tradition which had, officially, reserved the practice of medicine for men had assigned to women the exclusive control of the practice of midwifery. It was assumed that midwifery did not require the assistance of medical art,—that the woman in labor traversed a purely physiological crisis, and required only the attendance of kindness, patience, and native sagacity,—all obtainable without scientific

[2] Reprint obtained through the courtesy of Henry Holt and Company.

knowledge, from her own sex. This being taken for granted, the propriety of limiting such attendance to women appeared so self-evident, that, from the beginning of the world till the eighteenth century A.D., the custom was not seriously questioned. There is an exact parallelism between the relations of men to midwifery and of women to medicine. The limitation of sex in each case was decided by a tradition so immense, as to be mistaken for a divinely implanted instinct, intended by Providence as one of the fundamental safeguards of society and of morals. In each case the invasion by one sex of a "sphere," hitherto monopolized by the other, aroused the coarsest antagonism of offended delicacy. In each case finally, a real basis existed for the traditional etiquette: there *was* some reason for protesting against the introduction of the male accoucheur into the lying-in room, or of the ardent young girl into the medical school. But in each case, whatever reasons for protest existed, they were outnumbered and outweighed by others, to whose greater importance they were finally compelled to give way. Other things being equal, it *was* unpleasant for a woman to be attended in the crisis of her confinement by a man. But when the necessity for knowledge was recognized, when men became skilled while midwives remained ignorant,—the choice was no longer possible; the greater decorum of female midwifery was obliged to yield to the greater safety of enlightened masculine practice. Similarly, it *was* occasionally unpleasant for young women students to find themselves engaged in certain subjects of medical study together with classes of young men. But in proportion as midwifery became enlarged by the new province of gynæcology did occasions multiply on which it was extremely unpleasant for non-medical women to be medically treated by men. The difficulties of educating a relatively few women in medicine were compelled to be accepted, in order to avert the far greater difficulties of medical treatment for a very large number of women.

The history of medical women in the United States, to which these pages exclusively apply, may be divided into seven periods. as follows:

First, the colonial period of exclusively female midwifery, many of whose practitioners, according to their epitaphs, are reported to have brought into the world one, two, or even three thousand babies apiece. The Mrs. Thomas Whitmore of Marlboro (mentioned in the note) is especially described as being "possessed of a vigorous constitution, and frequently traveling through the woods on snow-shoes from one part of the town to another by night and by day, to relieve the distressed." This sturdy woman lived to be eighty-seven years of age, an ironical comment on the theory of necessary deficiency of endurance in the female sex. (Anne Hutchinson began her career as a midwife.)

During this period of female midwifery, the medical profession proper of the colonies remained entirely unorganized and inarticulate. Without making especial inquiry, a superficial observer could have almost overlooked the existence of doctors, as a special class, in the community.

There followed, however, a second period, that, namely, of the Revolution, and the years immediately preceding and following it. During the former, physicians began to travel to Europe for instruction. During the Revolutionary War their public services in the military hospitals, though apparently not very useful to the sick, yet served to bring the profession, for the first time, out of obscurity; and the opportunities afforded for the collective observation of disease on a large scale first breathed the spirit of medical science into the American profession. The first achievement of the newly-born interest in medical art and education was the expulsion of "females" from even the outlying provinces of the profession, and from their world-old traditional privileges as accoucheurs. It was a harsh return to make for the services rendered to the infant settlements by these valiant midwives, who had been tramping through the snow by night and by day to bring into a very cold world the citizens of the future republic.

Third, after this, however, came a period of reaction. In 1848, a Boston gentleman, Mr. Samuel Gregory, began vehemently to protest against the innovation of "male midwives," and opened a crusade on behalf of the women with something of the pathetic ardor of the Emperor Julian for a lost cause. To judge by the comments of the public press, Mr. Gregory's protest against "man-midwifery" awoke sympathetic echoes in many quarters. At the present day the interest in the movement thus roused, at once progressive and reactionary, lies chiefly in the remarkable similarity between the arguments which were then advanced against the intrusion of men into midwifery, and those which were subsequently urged against the admission of women to medicine. . . .

The fourth period of woman's medical history [and man's] was initiated when Mr. Gregory, supported by the popular enthusiasm he had aroused, succeeded in opening a School of Medicine (so called) for women, in November, 1848. The first term lasted three months; a second term began the following April, 1849;—and with the announcement for the second year it was declared that the twenty pioneer pupils had not only followed the lectures, but "had attended above 300 midwifery cases with the most satisfactory success."

In the prospectus issued for the second year of the school, Mr. Gregory brought forward a new set of arguments in its support, in addition to those previously adduced. . . .

To support Mr. Gregory's school, a Female Medical Education Society was formed in Boston, and incorporated with a state charter. Nothing seemed at the outset fairer than the promise of the new college,—but it had one fatal defect. There was no one connected with it who either knew or cared what a medical education should be. . . . It followed that, under the name of a medical education, was offered a curriculum of instruction, so ludicrously inadequate for the purpose, as to constitute a gross usurpation of the name,—in a word, to be an essentially dishonest affair. And still more unfortunately, the same inadequacy, naïvely or deliberately unconscious of itself, continued in greater or less degree to characterize all efforts for the isolated medical education of women for the next twenty years. This, the fourth period of their medical history, deserves therefore to be considered by women rather as a pre-medical or preliminary epoch; where purposes were enunciated that were only to be fulfilled many years later. . . .

In 1849, "Diplomas and advanced courses of study were things entirely outside the intellectual life of women." The pioneer female colleges, the Troy seminary and the Mt. Hoyloke school, had scarcely been founded, and women everywhere received only the most rudimentary education. On the other hand, the medical education of men was, as compared with the objects to be attained by it, in almost an equally rudimentary condition. The intrinsic tests were so shifting and unreliable, the standard of attainments so low, that it was proportionately necessary to protect the dignity of the profession by external, superficial, and arbitrary safeguards. Of these the easiest to apply was the distinction of sex. It was often difficult to decide, in the absence of intrinsic tests, whether a given individual were or were not a competent physician; but it was of course always easy to recognize that he was a man. . . . The principle was well suited to crude and uncultured societies, and became proportionately popular.

Elizabeth and Emily Blackwell were led to the study of medicine in a different manner from Harriet Hunt, their immediate predecessor. While still quite young girls, they were, by the sudden death of their father, unexpectedly confronted with the necessity of supporting not only themselves, but their mother, and a large family of younger brothers and sisters. "Then we realized the infinite narrowness and pettiness of the avenues open to women, and the crowds of competitors who kept each other down in the struggle. We determined that we would endeavor to open a new door, and tread a fresh path,—rather than push for a footing in one already filled to overflowing."

In this determination a new key-note was sounded. The Blackwells, and especially Elizabeth, were less the associates of Harriet Hunt, and of their own immediate successors, than the spiritual daughters of Mary Wollstonecraft. . . .

It was by sheer force of intellect, and of the sympathetic imagination born of intellectual perception, that Elizabeth Blackwell divined for women the suitableness of an occupation whose practical details were, to herself, intrinsically distasteful. . . . For with her, the struggle with bitter and brutal prejudices in the world was not sustained by the keen and instinctive enthusiasm for medicine, which has since carried hundreds of women over impossibilities. Rather was the arduousness of the struggle intensified by a passionate sensitiveness of temperament, which, under a cold exterior, rendered her intensely alive to the hardships of the social obloquy and ostracism which she was destined to encounter in such abundance. . . .

It is worthy of note, that the originality of the main idea was sustained by an almost equal originality of view in regard to the true nature of a medical education. . . . It was at this time that Elizabeth Blackwell recognized that preparation for medical practice demanded the sanction of test examinations at a respectable school; not for a few months, but years of study; and above all, abundant clinical experience. Rather than accept as final the indorsement of little schools established *ad hoc,* or exclusively for women, she applied to be admitted as student at twelve medical schools throughout the country, and among these found one, the school at Geneva, New York, to grant her request. . . . During the term of study at Geneva, she utilized a vacation to seek admittance to the hospital of the Blockley almshouse at Philadelphia, and obtained it by skillful manipulation of the opposing political influences which prevailed among the managers of the institution. After graduating at Geneva in 1849, first woman in America or of modern times to receive a medical diploma, Miss Blackwell immediately went to Europe, and by exceptional favor succeeded in visiting some of the hospitals of both London and Paris. In Paris, moreover, she submitted for several months to the severe imprisonment of the great school for midwives, La Maternité.

Emily Blackwell was refused admission to the Hobart College at Geneva, which had graduated her sister; but was allowed, for one year, to study at the Rush College of Chicago. For this permission, however, the college was censured by the State Medical Society, and the second term was therefore refused to the solitary female student. She was, however, enabled to complete her studies at Cleveland, Ohio, and graduated thence in 1852. During one of her vacations, she obtained permission to visit in Bellevue Hospital, where Dr. James Wood was just initiating the system of regular clinical lectures. After graduation, Emily Blackwell also went to Europe, and had the good fortune to become the private pupil of the celebrated Sir James Simpson of Edinburgh. She remained with him for a year, and when she left he warmly testified to her proficiency and competence for the work she had undertaken.

Miss Blackwell received similar testimonials from several distinguished physicians in London and Paris, in whose hospital wards she faithfully studied. Thus equipped, she returned to New York in 1855 to join her sister, with a fair hope of success in the arduous undertaking before them.

Dr. Elizabeth Blackwell, with the aid of a few generous friends, had opened a little dispensary for women and children,—which after three years' existence and one year of suspension, developed into the New York Infirmary.

This was first chartered in 1854. But when Emily Blackwell returned from Europe, no opportunities existed for either of the sisters to secure the hospital medical work, whose continued training is justly regarded of such inestimable advantage to every practicing physician. . . .

Unable to obtain elsewhere hospital opportunities, the Blackwells resolved to found a hospital that should be conducted not only for, but by women. The New York Infirmary, chartered in 1854, preceded the Woman's Hospital by a year, and, like it, was the first institution of the kind in the world. . . . The second hospital to be conducted by women physicians was founded in 1862—at Philadelphia during the excitements of the great Civil War. . . .

The fifth period for women physicians began with the founding of hospitals, where they could obtain clinical training, and thus give some substance to the medical education they had received in mere outline. The woman's hospital in Boston, the New England Hospital for Women and Children, was also founded during the war. The women who engaged in it were all heavily burdened by the great public anxieties of the time. But the very nature of these anxieties, the keen interest aroused in hospital work and in nursing organizations, helped to direct attention to the women's hospitals. In New York, the first meeting to consider the organization of nursing for the army was held in the parlors of the Infirmary, and at the suggestion of Elizabeth Blackwell. This little meeting was the germ from which subsequently developed the splendid organization of the Sanitary Commission. . . .

In 1865, a fourth hospital for women and children was organized in Chicago, "at the request and by the earnest efforts of Dr. Mary H. Thompson, the pioneer woman physician in the city. Opened just at the close of the war, many of those to whom it afforded shelter, nursing and medical attendance were soldiers wives, widows, and children, and women whose husbands had deserted them in hours of greatest need. There came from the South refugees both white and colored." Thus in the West as in the East, we find repeated for the women physicians of the nineteenth century the experience of the men of the eighteenth; it was amidst the exigencies of a great war that their opportunities opened, their sphere enlarged, and they "emerged from obscurity" into the responsibilities of recognized public function.

The fifth woman's hospital was opened in San Francisco in 1875, under the name of the Pacific Dispensary, by Dr. Charlotte Blake Brown and Dr. Annette Buckle, both graduates of the Philadelphia school (of medicine). . . . Finally, in Minneapolis, a sixth hospital sprang up in 1882. . . .

The sixth period is that of the struggle to obtain for women physicians official recognition in the profession. In the prolonged debate which followed, the women's cause was defended by many distinguished men, with as much warmth as it was opposed by others. . . .

Apparently the first general hospital in the country to confer a hospital appointment on a woman was the Mt. Sinai Hospital of New York. Here, in 1874, Dr. Annie Angell, a graduate of the Infirmary School, was made one of the resident physicians, at the instance of several members of the medical staff. She served three years very acceptably. . . . A special and extremely interesting branch of the struggle for hospital positions for women physicians has related to their appointment in the female wards of insane asylums. . . .

There are horrors in medicine, because there are horrors in life. But in medicine these are overcome or transformed by the potency of the Ideal; in life they must be borne unrelieved. The women, who, equally with men, are exposed in life to the fearful, the horrible, the disgusting, are equally entitled to access to those regions of knowledge and ideas, where these may be averted, or relieved, or palliated, or transformed. . . .

The women physicians of America share, while rather intensifying, the main characteristics of their medical countrymen. They have, as a rule, little erudition; but they have great capacity for bringing to bear all available and useful knowledge upon practical issues. They certainly do not read enough; and there is, therefore, a noticeable thinness in their discussions of medical topics when they meet in isolated council. But they have a resolute helpfulness in dealing with the individual cases entrusted to their care, and a passionate loyalty to those who have put their trust in them. They are possessed of abundant motive power for concrete intellectual action, though they might lack this power, if the work depended exclusively on abstract intellectual interest. And, after all, it is this habit of mind which most distinctively marks the modern practicing physician, and without it the advances in medical science would be of little profit to the sick; indeed, would not often be made. And what is often overlooked, it is precisely these mental habits which have usually been considered as particularly characteristic of women.

Thus the introduction of women into medicine demands no modification of the typical conception traditionally held by women, but only an enlargement of the applications which may be made of this characteristic type.

In WOMAN SUFFRAGE AND POLITICS,[3] Carrie Chapman Catt, surveying her long and varied campaign for women's enfranchisement, describes with the collaboration of Nettie Rogers Shuler, the spear-point of the opposition as she encountered it.

The campaign for woman suffrage in America long since ended. Gone are the days of agitating, organizing, educating, pleading, and persuading. No more forever will women descend on State Legislatures and the national Congress in the effort to wrest the suffrage from State and national legislators. The gates to political enfranchisement have swung open. The women are inside.

In the struggle up to the gates, in unlocking and opening the gates, women had some strange adventures. They learned some strange things. Especially startling became their experiences and their information when woman suffrage once crossed the devious trail of American politics. It is with that point of intersection that this book concerns itself. We have left it to others to write the details of suffrage history. Those details fill six huge volumes. We have left it to others to tell the immortal story of the services of individual suffragists. Here we eliminate names to emphasize work. We have left it to others, too, to synthesize American politics. This book's essential contribution must be sought in its revelation of the bearing of American politics upon the question of woman suffrage.

It is impossible to make that revelation adequately without a summary of the seventy-two years of campaign for the en-

[3] Reprint obtained through the courtesy of Charles Scribner's Sons.

franchisement of women in the United States, together with a survey of American politics for the last fifty-five years of that period. The two are interlocked, neither story is complete without the inclusion of the other, and this story is not comprehensible without the inclusion of both. But our summary of the woman movement will be brief. Our survey of American politics will be brief. Our emphasis will lie where woman movement and American politics met in mutual menace. Our revelations will illumine political crises with which the suffrage cause was closely identified and over whose motivation suffragists had to keep sharp watch.

Throughout the suffrage struggle, America's history, her principles, her traditions, stood forth to indicate the inevitability of woman suffrage, to suggest that she would normally be the first country in the world to give the vote to women. Yet the years went by, decade followed decade, and twenty-six other countries gave the vote to their women while America delayed.

Why the delay?

It is a question that was the despair of two generations of American women. It is a question that students of history and national psychology will ponder through generations to come.

We think that we have the answer. It was, not an antagonistic public sentiment, nor yet an uneducated or indifferent public sentiment—it was the control of public sentiment, the deflecting and the thwarting of public sentiment, through the trading and the trickery, the buying and the selling of American politics. We think that we can prove it. Suffragists consider that they have a case against certain combines of interests that systematically fought suffrage with politics and effectively delayed suffrage for years. We think that we can make that case.

We find it difficult to concede to the general opinion that, because of the tendency to overestimate the importance of events with which they are most familiar, those who have been a part of a movement are disqualified to write its history. We are sure that history would be worthless if it took no account of the observations made within a movement by those who have been a part of it. That is why we, who have had an opportunity to become acquainted with facts which throw light upon the political aspects of the woman suffrage question, feel impelled to pass our knowledge on to others.

The sources of all our information when not otherwise indicated are the archives of the National American Woman Suffrage Association, which contain continuous reports and other data from 1848 to 1922. Documents of this kind decline in interest for the general public as the movement they chronicle recedes into the past, but the facts and deductions drawn from them, and here assembled, should prove of significance to the advocates, perhaps especially the women advocates, of each recurring struggle in the evolution of democracy. . . .

Those invisible influences that were controlling elections; that invisible and invincible power that for forty years kept suffragists waiting for the woman's hour; for forty years circumvented the coming of suffrage; that power that made Republican leaders hesitate to fulfill their promises to early suffragists; restrained both dominant parties from endorsing woman suffrage; kept Legislatures from submitting suffrage amendments; and organized droves of ignorant men to vote against suffrage amendments at the polls when its agents had failed to prevent the submission of the question, was, manifestly, the power that inhered in the combined liquor interests.

The vested interest in human slavery exerted a controlling influence over American politics for more than half a century; but the public was never deceived concerning that fact, for its battles were fought in the open and its political compromises were frankly acknowledged. But when the vested interest in liquor arose to dictate terms to parties and politicians it executed its strategical moves in secret. The political wires, laid with purposeful care to trip the feet of men, were unseen by the public. The action of men, Legislatures and parties had the appearance of being the reflection of public opinion.

Victorious movements record their history; vanquished ones rarely do. The men who buy or sell votes do not confess. Political leaders do not acquaint their own party following with the deals they make. Full knowledge, therefore, of the extent to which the liquor trade exercised a dominating influence over the politics of the United States for a generation will probably never be revealed. But enough indisputable evidence has been accumulated to establish the fact that it did wield that influence and to reveal also much of the general plan by which results were achieved.

In 1862, while the nation was absorbed in the life and death struggle of the Civil War, the United States Brewers' Association was quietly organized. Although other reasons for organizing were afterwards given by the Brewers, the weight of evidence indicates that the main object of the Association was the political protection of the trade. It is a fact that this organization continued to be the chief directing power in the political defense of the liquor interests until the end of the struggle.

At its convention in 1867 the Association boldly warned political parties to take due notice that it would declare war upon all candidates of whatever party who were favorably disposed toward the total abstinence cause. Although no more resolutions of this character were passed, and no pronouncements of this nature were made by the leading brewers in the years that followed, there was no break in carrying out that policy. When the first decision was made to include woman suffrage as an indirect menace to the liquor cause is unknown but, in 1867, when the Kansas suffrage campaign was on, suffragists noted that in all parts of the State local liquor men were conspicuous workers against the suffrage amendment.

It was in 1869 that the Legislature of Wyoming extended the vote to women. It was in that same year that the Prohibition Party was formed. These unrelated but outstanding events may have called the attention of the trade to a possible connection between the two reforms, but far more definite causes for fear of women on the part of the liquor interests soon appeared. In 1873-4 an uprising of Christian women against the saloons of Ohio startled the church, the saloon and the nation. . . . Out of this "crusade" the Woman's Christian Temperance Union emerged in 1874. . . .

Women thus became an unmistakable factor in the movement which was rapidly pressing forward the demand for "total abstinence for the individual and prohibition for the State." Their meetings filled churches, bridged denominational differences, enlisted the clergy and influential churchmen. More than all else, the organization aroused women and trained them for public work as no movement had yet done. . . .

It was doubtless because of these things that the press reports of the Brewers' Convention of 1881 included the account of the adoption of an anti-suffrage resolution to the effect that the Brewers would welcome prohibition as far less dangerous to the trade than woman suffrage, because prohibition could be repealed at any time but woman suffrage would insure the permanency of prohibition. [!] Thirty-two years afterward, President Ruppert of the United States Brewers' Association denied that the brewers had ever taken such action, but suffrage scrapbooks preserved the resolution and the brewers confessed to the Judiciary Committee of the Senate, in 1918, that they had kept no minutes.

Meanwhile, evidence had accumulated to prove conclusively that whether the brewers had stated their hostility to woman suffrage in resolutions or not, they had ceaselessly demonstrated it in practice. Three official investigations into the political activities of the brewers have been made and four large volumes of the evidence have been published. . . .

The press reported that some tons of documents were taken on subpœna from various offices and bureaus. Although the evidence was fragmentary, it made clear that a national political agency, set up by the combined interests, had long existed and that it supervised or was active in both prohibition and suffrage campaigns throughout the United States.

This evidence, combined with the circumstantial and direct evidence supported by affidavits carefully preserved by the National American Woman Suffrage Association during a period of fifty years, shows the liquor interests in active opposition to woman suffrage on the following counts. . . .

We have brought together the evidence that the answer to our question in the foreword to this book is—politics. The evidence that it was politics that made America, the cradle of democracy, 27th instead of first on the list of countries democratic enough to extend the right of self-government to both halves of their respective populations.

That evidence tends to make clear, too, how slowly men as a whole retreated from the "divine right of men to rule over women" idea, and how slowly women rose to assume their equal right with men to rule over both. Long after men's reason convinced them that woman suffrage was right and inevitable the impulse to male supremacy persuaded them that the step would be "inexpedient." The lower types of men have always frankly resented any threatened infringement of the rights of the male and although the higher classes of male intelligence defined the feeling toward woman suffrage in other terms, at source the highest and lowest were actuated by the same traditional instinct.

Men believed what they wanted to believe in believing that women did not desire the vote. In 1916, 38,000 women of Maine signed petitions to the electors asking for the vote; but when the question was put to the men voters at the election, only 20,000 responded with "aye." In 1917, 1,030,000 women in New York said, over their signatures, that they wanted to vote; but only 703,000 men voted affirmatively on the question at election time.

These examples, were there no others, bring into high relief the fact that in the suffrage struggle there were more women who wanted to vote than there were men who were willing to grant them the privilege.

Superimposed upon this biological foundation of male resistance to female aggrandisement was the failure of political leaders to recognize the inescapable logic of woman suffrage in a country professing universal suffrage. On top of this, and as a consequence of it, lay the party inaction which gave opportunity to men who were far from inactive on the suffrage question, because they feared that their personal interests would suffer should the evolution of democracy take its normal course.

Had not the Republican party enfranchised the Negro by whip and bayonet it would have been easier for women to gain their enfranchisement without party endorsement, but suffragists, left to make their own appeal to majorities accustomed to be told how to vote, found that the lack of political endorsement was as effective as a mandate against. Lax election laws and methods often opened doors for corruption, and by, and with, the assistance of party officials, suffrage elections were stolen.

The damage thus wrought to the woman suffrage cause, and the nation's record, was far more insidious than the loss of any election would imply. The alleged rejection of suffrage became to the unknowing public an indication of an adverse public sentiment, and tended to create rather than correct indifference, for the average man and woman move with the current of public opinion. The inaction of the public gave a mandate for further political evasion of the question to party leaders, some of whom were certainly cognizant of and others working factors in the criminal schemes which produced the misleading result. Around and around the vicious circle went the suffrage question. "Get another *State,*" said President Roosevelt, excusing national inaction. "*Congress* has given no indication that it wants woman suffrage," said Governor Pierce of Dakota, as he vetoed the Territorial Bill which would grant suffrage to women. The Congress looked to the States for its cue, the States to Congress, both to the parties and the parties to the various financial interests, which in turn were responsible for the election of a picked list of members of Congress, of Legislatures and of the party leadership.

Had more statesmen and fewer politicians directed the policies of parties, women would have been enfranchised in the years between 1865 and 1880, and American history, along many lines, would have changed its course. Party suffrage endorsement was won in the United States after forty-eight years of unceasing effort, but when the final victory came women were alternately indignant that it had been so long in coming, and amazed that it had come at all. Many men expressed disappointment that women did not at once enter the party campaigns with the same zeal and consecration they had shown in the struggle for the vote. These men forgot that the dominant political parties blocked the normal progress of woman suffrage for half a century. The women remembered.

The Republicans found that the Negro fresh from slavery knew too little to play the "game of politics." All parties may find in the years to come a still more formidable problem in the woman vote, but for a different reason. If women do not make docile partisans, it will be because through the long weary struggle they have learned to know too much. "Wars are not paid for in war time; the bills come afterwards," said Franklin, and so it may be said of the cost of political blunders. American women who know the history of their country will always resent the fact that American men chose to enfranchise Negroes fresh from slavery before enfranchising American wives and mothers, and allowed hordes of European immigrants totally unfamiliar with the traditions and ideals of American government to be enfranchised in all States after naturalization, and in fifteen States without it, and be thus qualified to pass upon the question of the enfranchisement of American women.

The knowledge that elections can be controlled and manipulated, that a purchasable vote and men with money and motives to buy can appear upon occasion, that an election may be turned with "unerring accuracy" by a bloc of the least understanding voters, that conditions produce many politicians but few statesmen, began long ago to modify for Americans the fine pride in political liberty still the boast upon the 4th of July. That this knowledge should have made conservative types of men and women hesitant to extend the suffrage is not strange, nor is it to be held against conscientious men that they had to struggle with real doubts as to the wisdom of adding women to the electorate.

On the other hand, in spite of all weaknesses of the American government, no conscientious man or woman should ever have lost sight of four counter facts: (1) The United States will never go back to government by kings, nobilities or favored classes. (2) It must go forward to a safe and progressive government by the people; there is no alternative. (3) Women have had a corrective influence in department after department of society and the only one pronounced "a filthy mire" is politics where they have not been. (4) The problem of leading government by majorities through the mire to the ideal which certainly lies ahead is one which women should share with men.

Looking backward, however, it is not resentment at the long scroll of men's biological inhibitions and political blunders unrolled in the suffrage struggle that is, for suffragists, the final picture. The final picture fills with the men and the groups of men, Republican men, Democratic men, with a vision of real democracy luring their souls, who in the political arena fought the good fight for and with suffragists. Their faith and loyalty to the suffrage cause, their Herculean efforts, their brilliant achievements, their personal sacrifices, leap out from the record compellingly, riding down all else.

On the outside of politics women fought one of the strongest, bravest battles recorded in history, but to these men inside politics, some Republicans, some Democrats, and some members of minority parties, the women of the United States owe their enfranchisement.

And if we have made here a case for our assertion that American politics was an age-long trap for woman suffrage, we hope that we have not failed to make, as well, a case for these higher-grade American politicians who rescued woman suffrage from that trap and urged it forward to its goal.

As man's last monopoly was being broken down, "Society" women plunged into the fray of "practical politics," attending conventions, publicly supporting candidates, and serving on pub-

lic committees. Thus Mrs. J. Borden Harriman, bent on a "lark,"
attended in 1912 both the Republican and the Democratic con-
ventions only to succumb to the wiles of political action herself.
She became one of Woodrow Wilson's most active adherents.
"Her devotion and loyalty to Wilson never flagged through all
his vicissitudes," writes the daughter, Ethel Borden Harriman.
"During the war, as head of a large division of the American
Red Cross, she went back and forth between France and
America many times. At the end of it all, she had barely sat
down to her first lunch at home when she was notified that
President Wilson had appointed her to an advisory committee in
connection with the Peace Conference. And, with typical en-
thusiasm, in twelve hours she sailed."

Democracy functioning in its great quadrennial spectacle is
etched in Mrs. J. Borden Harriman's FROM PINAFORES
TO POLITICS.[4]

In June, 1912, a party of us decided to go to Chicago for the
Republican Convention, and then back to Baltimore to see the
fun with the Democrats.

There was a time in my life when election year was nothing
to me, but in 1912, I joined that great army of Americans who
drop a stitch in their routine every four years, and give themselves up to backing first a candidate for the nomination and
afterwards a nominee. . . . I went to Chicago a babe, fed on the
orderly blue-print pap that comes in school books about civil
government. It may be, of course, that a national political convention, seen a long way off, is just such an affair of neat democratic selection as the professors analyze. But to me 1912 in
Chicago was a strange phantasmagoric, unbelievable chaos of
sights, sounds and smells, slogans and emotions, that made the
school-book version of the American political system seem
very tame.

"Chicago in 1912" brings back to me a flat, flat lake, sizzling
asphalt pavements, bands circling and zigzagging along Michigan

[4] Reprint obtained through the courtesy of Henry Holt and Company.

Avenue, tooting and booming, "Everybody's saying it, Roosevelt, Roosevelt." [Theodore Roosevelt]

The Coliseum—red-faced, perspiring men—one's frocks sticking to the back of the chair. Monotonous roll-call of states,— "Alabama, Arkansas." Coats off and flashing fists—delegates pummeling each other. The sultry air was charged with dynamite. Rumors flashed like lightning. Delegates talked of drawing pistols and knives over the disputed seats. Everybody jostled, pushed, whispered. Day and night the excitement grew, monotonous, continuous. Savages in the African forest, hearing the distant roll and boom of the tribal drums, could not better have been worked into a furious pitch of expectation than were the Americans who quivered and hoped and feared in the medley of trombones and telegraph tickers, hoarse oratory and shrill battle cries of the Coliseum medicine men. The heat was terrific. The manager of Roosevelt's Indiana contest came out saying the convention would last a month. We groaned and believed him. . . .

I was not a delegate. I was not even a Republican. I was only a spectator, but no one's sympathy could have been more active than mine for the progressive element of that Convention. I was as excited as the rest when the rumor would go around that the Roosevelt leaders planned to seize the convention hall. But I was too much on my way to Baltimore to see the nomination of that even greater progressive, Woodrow Wilson, to be really one of them. The two men, Wilson and Roosevelt, were very different, but in their followers there was often the identical thing, the same passionate yearning for better times for the whole people. . . .

Almost I left this chapter out. Then, as I looked over an old letter that I had written during odd minutes at the 1920 Democratic Convention out in San Francisco, I was surprised to find myself living it all over again. I dare not include the names. Don't ask me who is who, who M. really is and which man I call R. My letter-writing style at San Francisco wasn't calculated to please anybody but the friend to whom the letter went.

Thursday, July 1st. Yesterday was a perfect day, as Conventions go. The nominating speeches were excellent and the demonstrations amounted to pandemonium! When Al Smith had been nominated in a masterly speech by Bourke Cochran, it was such fun singing all the old songs: "Tammany," "The Sidewalks of New York," "Maggie Murphy," "Daisy Belle," etc., accompanied by an organ and an orchestra—the latter one of the biggest in the world. Al Smith is the greatest governor New York has ever seen, and he was a fish peddler in his youth! Of course, his religion (R. C.) bars him from the Presidency, at least for the present.

When McAdoo was put in nomination I really believe there was more spontaneous enthusiasm for him than for any one. The S. F. papers are poisonous about him, and I suppose most of the N. Y. ones are too, but that only proves that the Republicans are afraid of him. I am working hard for him and even with the "Crown Prince" taint believe him our best candidate, as Davis hasn't strength enough.

Today I am assigned New York, New Jersey, Delaware and Connecticut to do lobbying on the floor, when the balloting commences.

Last night I went to a delightful café for a fish dinner with Sir Arthur Willert and General Bethel and then to a McAdoo caucus at the Palace Hotel. There is much about S. F. like Marseilles or other French seaport towns. It is really one of the most delightful cities in the world—such people, so hospitable! There is nothing they don't do for us.

I have cheered and waved my arms so long for McAdoo that I am quite stiff and voiceless.

Thursday, July 1, 11:10 a.m. Jim Ham Lewis has just come onto the platform stroking his faded pink whiskers; the band is playing the "Sidewalks of New York"—a warmed-over inspiration from yesterday's Al Smith demonstration. It has now changed to "Dixie" and amidst the roars of the delegates an old man from Kansas is dancing a jig in the center aisle.

11:15 a.m. Mrs. Antoinette Funk, principal feminine McAdoo backer, climbs to the platform and whispers mysteriously to other McAdoo boosters. Organ playing "Dear Old Pal."

11:30. Now to soft organ-music a man is reciting verses of the "Battle Hymn of the Republic." A beautiful soprano voice floats from the far-distant corner of the top gallery singing the air of the chorus. Then the whole twelve thousand people (there is not an empty seat) join in singing the chorus.

It is grand and impressive and gives one chills up and down one's spine.

12:00. They resume calling the roll of states for nominations. Oregon and Utah unanimously second the nomination of McAdoo. Virginia nominates Glass. He is the third man so far given sole credit for the Currency Bill!!!

The delegates seem mussy-tempered this A.M. There have been three fights—or near fights—already, and we have been in session only fifty minutes.

Just been sent to lobby with a woman from Porto Rico who can't make up her mind whom she is for! Think I won her for McAdoo.

12:15. West Virginia nominates John Davis. Would that he were better known. The McAdoo boom has lost strength a little today.

12:30. Mrs. Brown, of West Virginia, seconds Davis' nomination. She is very good looking and has a charming voice. She tells a funny story of the creation which brings the delegates roaring to their feet. The band plays "You Great Big Beautiful Doll." The most finished and perfect speech I have ever heard a woman make.

12:50. Irving Cobb is now standing up in the press seats and minutely estimating the claims to his notice of the individual cherubims in our organ loft. His profile is uniquely conspicuous.

1:00. One poor woman from the Philippines is now putting Burton Harrison in nomination. Thank goodness her voice is such that one can't hear her.

1:05. The secretary has just reported that Senator Glass says that the Resolutions Committee won't be ready to report until 8 P.M.

Adjourned until eight tonight.

Evening session. 8:00. Large crowd. All seats in balcony taken; so I am perched on organist's bench. The organist is playing "Song of Songs." Rumors are flying madly about "there will be no session"—"there will be," etc. Jim Ham Lewis and Senator Robinson are embracing. Franklin Roosevelt is shaking hands on the platform to "Rose of Washington Square" played by the band.

8:05. Word has just come up that the Resolutions Committee won't be ready to report until 9 P.M., and then the session will last until 5 A.M. I wish I had taken a nap this afternoon instead of talking so long to Mr. Heney and doing some work among the doubtful delegates for McAdoo.

8:35. Band and organ play "On the Banks of the Wabash," and Indiana delegates jump to their feet and cheer.

8:40. Chairman calls to order.

Singing of "Star Spangled Banner."

8:45. Resolutions Committee not ready to report.

Sergeant-at-Arms Martin has appeared tonight in a full Colonel's U. S. A. uniform! Dear old soul, he looks so proud.

George Creel is laying down the law to a chosen few back of the chairman's seat. He is working hard for an Irish plank. The sub-committee of the Committee on Platform and Resolutions, that has been sitting twenty-two hours out of the twenty-four for two days, are Senator Glass, Chairman, Secretary Colby, Senator Walsh of Montana, Vance McCormick, etc. They are all powerful.

9:15. Band plays "How Dry I Am," and the New York State delegates go wild!

Governor Al Smith has just appeared in the aisle amidst local applause from New York.

Mrs. Castleman, silver-haired National Committeewoman from Kentucky, 78 years old, is standing up and singing "My Old

Kentucky Home," with a rapt and inspired expression. Dear thing, she is for McAdoo. Oh! I wouldn't have missed this convention for anything! It is wonderful.

9:23. The wife of Dr. Jenkins, the editor of the Kansas City *Post,* has just asked me what paper I write for, and says that she wants to put me in touch with her husband, as she is sure my notes would be valuable to their paper. I make my most professional bow and say, "I will be glad to consult with him."

A National Committeewoman from Washington, on Mrs. J's right, leans across and asks me if I will tour the Northwest, speech-making for the Democratic candidate. I give an evasive answer.

9:30. Mrs. Bass, Chairman Women's Bureau, introduced to address the convention, tells the story of the triumph of woman's suffrage in Congress.

Governor Smith is sitting smilingly beside Miss Mills from "Up State"; her other side is substantially buttressed by Bessie Marbury, who has chewed gum consistently ever since the convention convened on Monday.

9:45. The crowd is yelling for Jim Ham Lewis, and the Chairman has sent for him! Jim Ham refuses to speak. The delegates are tired and restless and want to be amused.

10:20. Howls for Bryan, "We want Bryan," from all over the house. Chairman raps hectically for order; the yells increase.

10:22. Committee on Resolutions not ready to report. Convention adjourns until ten o'clock Friday morning.

Friday, July 2nd. The Commoner in the same old alpaca coat, Carter Glass, Bourke Cochran, and other members of the Resolutions Committee appear on platform; so their labors must be over. Howls of "Bryan." Prayer; then "The Star Spangled Banner."

10:50. "We favor the League of Nations." Enormous applause.

11:05. Ray Baker, bechecked and bediamonded as usual, leads his wife, draped in sables, triumphantly to the platform.

11:45. Suffrage plank brings on a great demonstration. All states join in procession except Maryland and South Carolina.

12:05. All the planks of the League of Women Voters included in the platform.

12:23. Glass says, "Nearly through," which brings applause. He is very human and lovable. His voice is nearly gone, and he must be near a collapse after sitting up for three nights.

12:40. Ireland. "I have to read the plank in my own 'brogue,' and this is the American 'brogue.'" Great applause.

12:50. Reading of platform concluded.

Senators Robinson and Glass standing on the Speakers' platform surrounded by heavy ropes like the principals in a prize fight waiting for the referee's "GO."

12:55. Bryan steps out to present minority report. Convention in an uproar. Bryan wants dry plank.

1:10. Bourke Cochran comes on platform with another minority report. He wants wines and beer!

1:40. Bryan opens debate on amendments. He speaks with all his old-time vigor except that his voice seems a little husky. He is a great exhorter, and to me what he says has a perfectly sincere ring, although I don't think that the dry and wet question should be touched on in the platform. It is a dead issue. Bryan makes very kind allusions to the President. He is altogether very kindly toward everyone, notwithstanding the belligerent tone of his newspaper articles after he was not included in the subcommittee on Resolutions.

2:10. Hobson, the much-kissed, comes on to speak for five minutes. The audience is impatient with him—he hasn't Bryan's magnetism.

2:20. Mrs. Peter Oleson, of Minnesota, makes impassioned appeal for Bryan's plank.

2:30. Bourke Cochran begins his address with the invocation with which Mrs. Oleson left off, "God speed the right." He "sure is" a silver-tongued orator!

Hiram Johnson is sitting in one of the Press seats looking deeply interested in the debate. Bainbridge Colby, Vance McCor-

mick and others of the sub-committee of the Committee on Platform are holding their hands to their heads and look about a
foot from a fit!

3:20. Senator Walsh, of Massachusetts, pleading for a plank
for Irish freedom.

3:55. Several minor speakers who can be passed over. Bryan
has come on again to speak about a National Government Bulletin. Great and prolonged demonstration for Bryan. Largest
personal one there has been.

4:55. Secretary Colby arguing for the platform as presented by
the Committee. He makes a most masterly speech full of very
subtle sarcasm, but perfectly courteous.

5:05. Ovation for Colby.

5:15. Carter Glass speaking. Alas, my dear Senator is laying
into Bryan unnecessarily harshly it seems to me. Colby said
everything without giving offense. It seems a pity to alienate the
old man completely.

6:20. Voting on amendments. All lost.

Have just been down on the platform. Overheard Bryan say
to himself, "I never thought they would beat me so badly." I felt
like crying. At times this afternoon he seemed to me to have the
look of a fanatic.

Platform accepted as a whole. The delegates have voted just
as they chose, notwithstanding the applause they gave Bryan.

The League of Nations is a terribly difficult plank to determine.
I do hope that they will make a compromise possible. They
can't get it through just as President Wilson brought it home,
even if they have a majority in Congress next year; so why try
to deceive the country?

On the surface this isn't at all a characteristic Democratic
Convention. The Auditorium is beautiful and there is no confusion or disorder of any kind—and no perspiring delegates in
shirtsleeves.

Saturday. Nobody knows anything, and everybody lies every
minute! McAdoo has dropped behind. I have been down on

the floor trying to induce three women on the New York delegation, who came to San Francisco favorably disposed toward McAdoo and have now dropped to Cox, to reconsider.

Miss M., who was sent by the women of the Tenth District as an antidote to J's machine affiliations, has become her shadow, never moves without her, sits next to her in the convention and is obviously voting under instruction. With her mouth full of sandwich and her face screwed up as if afraid of dropping a hint of the truth, or a piece of bread and butter, she has just said to me, "No, I won't be coerced—no one but McAdoo people have tried to influence me since I have been here—I am voting as my conscience dictates, and my conscience says, 'Cox.'" That pretty D. has also succumbed, but I think to the wiles of Foxy Grandpa R. or Bourke Cochran's facile tongue. She says: "I've heard things since I have been here that have weaned me from McAdoo; they are so unfortunate that as you are his friend I can't tell you about them!" "All lies!" I retorted.

Mrs. O'Day has also slipped. The men will too. Marbury calls insinuating remarks across to me as I hold a colloquy with Al Smith. "You's better jump on, you'll be sorry you opposed Cox," etc. She annoys me so that I call back to her, "All right, Bessie, I bet you one hundred dollars against the field that McAdoo will be nominated." She takes me up at once and makes a great show of passing two fifty dollar bills to someone telling him he must be stake holder. "My bag is in the organ loft; so I'll put up my hundred dollars later." I don't add that I am more likely to have a hundred cents in it than a hundred dollars. I tell Al Smith he is so sure of reëlection that he can afford to have any Presidential candidate on the ticket and he will slip through with him. He says, with a knowing smile, "I would like to discuss that with you further." He is a corker. How in the world did Tammany ever produce him?

In the aisle I meet G. and L. B. waiting for my report. "Hopeless," I sigh. G. throws a scornful look over the delegation and says, "And to think I am paying that woman's board and expenses! Good-night!" One can't suspect either.

A little woman in a white shirt-waist draws me aside and whispers in a tearful voice, "I hope you will tell Mr. McAdoo, when it is over, that I stood firm through it all, and it's been a nasty business too; such gibes as Mrs. J. has thrown at me—we women are so embarrassed by her. You should hear her talk. At our state delegation meeting the other morning, Bessie Marbury announced she was 'going to the mat' with Bryan on the prohibition question before the convention closed. Why, I hear of teas and entertainments that California women are giving all the time and our state is never invited."

Mrs. Bass calls me on to the platform. Your old friend is there, sinister and jubilant, because McAdoo has lost ground to Cox. He keeps muttering: "What did I tell you?" and "I did it." "Alas, poor Yorick, I knew him well, etc." Senator Robinson turns around and says, "It is too soon to crow; he may come back and surprise you."

Senator Glass says he thinks Chairman Robinson is for Cox. I wonder. Anyhow, Walsh of Montana, Pittman, Henderson, Glass, Gerry, are for McAdoo. —— seems to hate him. Ex-Senator Saulsbury comes up to me and says: "Why are you alienating all your friends by so conspicuously backing McAdoo?" I asked him since when he had changed his mind, as in 1913 at a dinner in Washington, he said to me, "After Wilson, McAdoo should be our next President." "Yes, but I have learned better since then." Everyone seems to be personal in his political opinions—what can McAdoo have done to Saulsbury?

3 p.m. Senator Walsh asks me to take a walk and we stroll about outside for an hour. It is a relief to get into the fresh air for a little and not to hear that continual repetition of "Alabama, Arizona, Arkansas," etc. I shall dream of that roll call for weeks.

6:30. It is a deadlock, no less, with Cox a little ahead. I've just been down to talk to the Texas delegation, which has never varied from forty votes for McAdoo. Thank goodness! And they want a recess as Cox is forging too much ahead. They asked me to go to Senator Glass and suggest an adjournment. I did so and he says he thinks it is a good idea. Vance says that the Palmer people will vote with the McAdoo crowd, so that will carry it.

6:40. Demand for a roll call. Taken. Vote to adjourn carried. Dined hurriedly at Palace Hotel.

Evening Session. Very little change in lineup. Where, oh, where, are those states that were coming over solid to us? As time goes by, it will be more and more difficult to nominate one of the leaders. Senator —— says, "How can a sensible man like McCormick go on holding delegates for Palmer and so complicate this situation still further? Palmer has no earthly chance of winning. Why doesn't he release them?"

He isn't the only one that could help matters. If Bryan would advise Senator —— to let his corporal's guard of votes go, it might put McAdoo over.

11 p.m. My head is woozy with listening to roll calls and trying to keep a record of them. So many deluded ones think they are going to be the dark horse.

Midnight. Adjournment until Monday.

Later. Senator Walsh took me up to the Fairmount. When I began asking him about Vice-Presidents, he said, "Let's get McAdoo nominated first."

Sunday night. Went to Senator Phelan's most beautiful place in the Santa Clara Valley for luncheon. It is five miles from San Francisco. There were eight or nine motors in line like those used at funerals. I went in one with Senators Pittman, Walsh of Montana, Gerry, and a Mrs. Gardner. A luncheon for one hundred people was served at small tables on the terrace. I sat between Senators Jones and Beckham. Others at that table were the host, Mrs. Marshall, and Mrs. Jones.

The Vice-President made a clever, short, and fitting Fourth of July speech. Senator Jones told Mrs. Marshall that if the deadlock continued he wouldn't be at all surprised to see her husband nominated. She replied, "He doesn't want it, but I can tell you that the party hasn't anyone as good a vote-getter as its Vice-

President." There was a lot of Marshall talk today. Mr. Woolley told me after luncheon that McAdoo was a sure thing, as he went over with me the votes that are coming to him eventually.

July 5th. Well, it's all over. Now we must be good sports.

A McAdoo woman on the platform has just handed me this intellectual ditty:

> I couldn't dream—I couldn't know
> That I would have to swallow Crow.
> I have an awful tummy ache.
> Perhaps the Crow will turn to cake.
> Just now it's like a ton of rocks,
> This swallowing of Jimmy Cox.

All of this seems a great deal of excitement in behalf of the goal we never reached. It was surprising how as soon as Cox was nominated, we accepted him and forgot that we had done our best to keep the Ohio man from getting it. I think that Cox's offish attitude toward Prohibition accounts far more than the politicians will admit for the Democratic failure in 1920. It would have been much safer to choose a candidate to stick drouth out.

CHAPTER XI

CARRYING ON IN AGRICULTURE

IT was perhaps inevitable that the countryside should be almost forgotten by the "intellectuals" who flourished, for a time at least, in the new American civilization. As the clamor and uproar of the machine increased, as cities spawned and sprawled, creating "palaces" and slums, the minds of the "asphalt flowers" became more and more intensely occupied with urban interests as if they were eternal and could stand alone. In the "great enlightenment" farmers became "hicks," or to use the slick phrase of the self-anointed prophet, Henry L. Mencken, "prehensile monkeys," or boorish "populists" who disturbed the fair and perfect pageant of industrialism.

But even superficial students of any history extending beyond day before yesterday knew very well that superstructures of civilization had always rested at bottom on the land and that, when they had crumbled, social life had always been renewed in homestead and field, amid the ruins of temples, aqueducts, forums, amphitheaters, and villas. Whatever the future might hold for the skyscrapers of New York City or the marble houses of Newport, it was written in the stars all along that agriculture was, as always, the basis of life and the one secure refuge in time of social storm. And in fact, all through the age of enrichment, adornment, and urbanization, American agriculture, amid many vicissitudes, with serfdom increasing, had been carried on—as always —with the indispensable help of women, the original inventors and promoters of the agricultural arts, if the general verdict of modern anthropology is to be accepted.

Woman at the center of a changing farm management in America is made a creature of flesh and blood by Mary Meeks Atkeson, in an article entitled WOMAN IN RURAL LIFE AND RURAL ECONOMY,[1] printed in the "Annals."

The woman on the American farm has been considered, by those who have studied the position of farm women the world over, to be in a very happy situation. However hard her lot might be, she has been protected, at least, against working outdoors in the fields and against actively directing the farm processes. Except in some few foreign settlements, a farmer could not hold his position in the community if he allowed his wife or his daughters to labor in the fields. Even the foreign communities have tended to get away from field work for the women in the second or third generation as they have become Americanized. In other words, outdoor work in the fields for women has been taboo, and that has been the pride of the American farmer.

Furthermore, no American hired man, however low his station, would take orders for farm work from a woman. And a woman was never supposed to know anything about field crops like wheat and corn, or about live stock.

The American farm woman has been constantly reminded that in some European countries the peasant who tills the soil not only allows, but expects, his wife and children to toil daily with him in the fields, and that the farm woman is sometimes yoked with the family cow to drag the plowshare through the soil—the peasant, presumably, doing the driving. Perhaps this is true, but the American farm woman has generally not been to Europe to see those sad conditions with her own eyes. She is inclined, therefore, to be a bit skeptical about some of the tales. She is not sociologist enough, perhaps, to realize that the taboo against outdoor work and the management of the money-making farm crops, however much she disliked it as an individual, had through the years saved her, as a class, from much exploitation and too heavy labor.

[1] Reprint obtained through courtesy of the American Academy of Political and Social Sciences.

In fact, the American farm woman has looked directly at her individual problem and her individual farm. She has seen that, although she was not allowed to ride the disc-harrow or the reaper in the fields, no one objected to her working long hours over a steaming washtub, or cleaning the chicken house, or handling the deadly heavy cans of milk in the dairy, although this was a part of the heaviest work done on the farm. Effective labor-saving machinery for work in the fields has been developed a whole generation ahead of effective labor-saving machinery for work in the farm home.

Although it has been considered improper for the farm woman to handle wheat-money or corn-money, she has observed that often it has been her egg-money and butter-money that have kept the family going and sometimes even paid off the mortgage on the farm. So it happens that the farm woman is very generally breaking away from the old standards and taking over the easiest work in the fields, and, at the same time, shifting some of the heavier housework to the shoulders of the men of the family, or else to effective mechanical appliances.

This new tendency will amount, in some neighborhoods, to a real revolution among the farm people, who are disposed to be conservative in social matters. But it is happening, and the American farmer may as well take the new woman-farmer into account. She will soon be a real rival to him, as more women become farm foremen, and more and more young girls enter the state universities for agricultural courses. It is true that the change may lead sometimes to an exploitation of women on the farm and may bring a hardship upon some women, but the traditions are being broken, whether for good or ill, and it is a condition to be reckoned with.

One thing that the farm woman has noted in her survey of things as they are, is that the apparent prosperity of American agriculture in the past has resulted chiefly from two things: first, the steady rise in land prices, and second, the unpaid service of the women and children. Even the most inefficient farmer, if he succeeded in holding his bit of land, left a good inheritance to his family because of the rising value of the land. It was like money piling up in the bank. The farm operations did not need to yield more than bare living expenses. But now, when falling land values are the rule, the farmer must make much more than bare living expenses or he will become bankrupt.

In the old days the farm processes were carried on by the common effort of the family. It was almost impossible for an unmarried farmer to manage a farm, and the woman without a family, in the farm business, had no chance to survive. The field crops and live stock carried the farm—its mortgage, equipment, improvements, repairs and the like—but it was the work of the women and children which provided most of the living expenses. Thus, most of the prosperity of American agriculture has rested squarely upon the backs of the women and children who worked without pay, and unless prices of farm crops advance greatly there it will continue to rest.

It is little wonder that the American farm woman feels that she should, at least, be given a chance to manage the farm in part and be allowed to choose the kind of work she shall do. She likes the custom of the whole family working together in the business of farming, and takes pride in being a real help to her husband. She is even willing, or so it seems from the letters that come to the writer, to work very hard and to accept a somewhat lower standard of living than is common in the towns, for the sake of that great end.

Dependable figures showing the amount of work performed by women on the farms of America are not available, since most of the agencies computing women's work neglect the farm workers, or else employ such varied bases that the results are not very conclusive.

The States Relations section of the Home Economics Division of the United States Department of Agriculture reports that in 1913-14, on seventeen crop farms of Central Illinois and Indiana, women averaged less than one hour's work a day in the fields, even in the growing season. Later figures, in 1921, the results of a survey of 900 farms in Nebraska, showed only 12½ per cent of the women working at all in the fields, and about 3 per cent of the children. This survey was made by the Division of Farm Population, Bureau of Agricultural Economics, United States Department of Agriculture. Probably the least outdoor field work is done in the corn belt and wheat-raising states. States more generally given to the raising of truck crops, sugar beets, and other crops requiring much hand culture, and to live stock and dairying, would show a much higher average of work by the women and children.

A survey of 300 farms in South Carolina, in 1921, also conducted by the Bureau of Agricultural Economics, showed an average of 55 per cent of the white women working in the fields for about four and a half months a year. The average number of wives of farm tenants, working in the fields, was nearly twice that of the wives of farm owners, indicating that a rise in the social scale brought along with it the usual American taboo against field work for women. The average number of children working in the fields was about the same for farm owners and farm tenants.

The population tables of the 1920 census report, showing the women engaged in gainful occupations, give a better idea of the large part which women are now taking in the agricultural industry. In 1920, there were 247,253 women listed as general farmers. This does not include, of course, the farm wives, who are listed as of "no occupation." In the same year, 13,764 women were listed as foremen of general farms. Even assuming that many of these are widows or elder daughters carrying on after the death of the father and husband, it is evident that many women are already taking active management of farm affairs. In fact over 1,000,000 women are listed as gainfully employed on the farms of the United States. More than half of these, however, are working on the home farm.

Next to general farming, gardening and fruit-growing engage the women workers, according to the 1920 census report. Over 18,000 women are employed in these pursuits, 176 being greenhouse foremen, and 163 orchard foremen. There were 140 women foremen on dairy farms, and ninety-four on stock farms, nearly 11,000 being engaged in the live stock industry as a whole. This, also, does not include the great amount of unpaid dairy work done by the farm women. Poultry raising as a gainful occupation engaged 3,336 women in 1920; unpaid poultry raisers would undoubtedly total several million, as nearly every farm woman has her flock of chickens.

An even greater activity in the management of the farm business will probably be forced upon the farm women in the next few years, because of increasing economic necessity. The standard of living in America is steadily rising and the farm income shrinking, or barely holding its own, so that in many cases, the only hope for the farm family to maintain proper standards is for the farmer and the older children to engage in other pursuits for a part of the time. If the family remains upon the farm, the farm woman will take over much of the farm management and perhaps help with the work in the fields.

What effect these changes will have upon the social and economic life of the American country people, no one seems to know. Farming must be done by some one, and if we are to maintain American standards of living on the smaller holdings of land, at present prices for farm products, a considerable part of the family income must certainly come from sources off the farm. Otherwise the family will either be forced out and away from farm life, or forced down to peasantry and a very low standard of living.

Coöperation has long been held up as the sure cure for the farmer's ills, but like most other patent nostrums it will probably cure only in those cases in which the patient would have survived anyway. In most instances the small farmer will continue to stand upon his own feet and meet his economic problems as best he may.

Although making money upon a farm under present conditions is one of the most difficult of tasks, the American farm woman knows that spending this money, for a proper value in return, is almost as difficult. One of her chief duties is to turn the hard-earned money into a living for the family, and to secure goods, of the style and durability she desires, is very difficult under present conditions.

The average village store does not adequately supply the needs of the cultured family upon the farm, and yet they are largely dependent upon it for supplies. In a recent statement, Dr. C. J. Galpin of the United States Department of Agriculture showed that some 20,000,000 rural people are dependent upon 39,000 small towns, hamlets and villages for their buying. In other words, they are divided up into buying communities of about 500 persons—and the several stores in each village split up these units to an infinitesimal degree. Thus a competition is set up between these stores, so destructive, that often their chief task is fighting each other, rather than rendering service to their customers. City business has greatly improved its methods in the past few years, but rural town business has been at a standstill. Thus the wide-awake farmer, who has gone far in recent years in the scientific production of crops and live stock must deal with a business system that belongs to the days of the ox-cart and the flail.

Some people think that goods can be bought more cheaply in the villages, because of the low rents and low wages. But it is quite otherwise. I do not know of any country store which furnishes groceries as cheaply as do the chain-grocery stores of the cities. Many of the commodities run as much as 25 per cent higher in the village stores, and, of course, in the variety and freshness of the stock carried there is no comparison. The same thing is true of the "variety" store of the little town, which furnishes its class of goods much less efficiently and less cheaply than does the ten-cent store of the city. Likewise, the clothing and piece goods of the average village store are both high in price and low in quality.

All this is not the fault of the village storekeeper, particularly. It is simply that both he and the farmer are in the grip of an antiquated and wasteful system, and both are suffering from the ill effects. It is a bad situation, nevertheless, that the farmer, whose income is probably the lowest in America, in comparison with the service he renders to society, pays a higher price for the things he buys than does any other class.

One grievance of the farm woman is the difficulty she experiences in buying goods which the village store does not carry at all, and which the advertisers and mail-order houses do not offer in such a way that she can find what she wants and secure it.

It is true that the woman on the farm is a rather poorly trained buyer. At least this is indicated by figures recently compiled by the United States Department of Agriculture, showing that the woman on the farm who had previously lived in the city was a somewhat more efficient buyer than the country-reared woman. It must be remembered, however, that the country woman has not had the day-by-day education in buying as has her city sister. She has been deprived of the "window-shopping," and leisurely shopping about among many stores for an article, with the opportunity to inspect the materials, before making a choice. All this is a liberal education in buying which stands the city woman in good stead in choosing values and styles, and in getting the full worth of her money.

The country woman, even if she makes a trip to the city for her buying, is hurried and disturbed by the din and confusion. She does not know the lines of goods carried by the different stores, or what are the best styles, and she frequently ends by buying things which she does not care for, at a higher price than she should pay.

Or perhaps the woman on the farm buys her clothing from a mail-order catalog, in which five-dollar dresses and fifty-dollar dresses look much the same on the pictured figures, and materials of both are described by trade-names with which she is unfamiliar. She has no basis of discrimination except the price, so she chooses the cheaper article, and then feels cheated and ill-dressed when it quickly loses its attractiveness after wear.

Yet good-quality clothes are a necessity for the farm family, particularly, because their clothing is subjected to exceedingly hard wear, for in the active country life all the seams must stand a strain, the material may become muddy or wet, causing it to shrink or spot, or otherwise show its cheapness very quickly. Cheap shoes fall apart when wet, or completely lose their shape and attractiveness, and cheap furs soon look bedraggled and ugly.

Another serious difficulty for the rural woman is the buying of her house furnishings. There is so much cheap, ill-made furniture upon the market, and much of the cheap furniture finds its way into the village store. Few people realize what a difficult job it is for the woman on the farm to have a tasteful and harmonious home, unless she has the time and money for a protracted stay in the city to do her buying. She is fortunate, indeed, when she can fall back upon some local craftsman in hand-made chairs or in hand-woven rag rugs.

It is true that the women's magazines come to the farm homes, full of beautiful pictures of house-furnishings, but when the eager woman has read the alluring advertisement through, she finds at the end—"at all dealers"! The advertiser, apparently, does not know that in fact those goods are not at the dealers of these 20,000,000 farm people, and that they are helpless to secure them without making a long and expensive trip to the city. No wonder that the farm woman sometimes feels that the boasted efficiency of American business, in quantity production and quantity selling, is quite equalled by its lack of efficiency in handling those smaller units in which she, unfortunately, finds herself.

Another reason why the farm people find fault with the quality of the factory-made articles which they buy is that, especially in the eastern sections of the United States, they come into direct comparison with articles made by hand labor. For instance, one farm woman wrote that, after using one wash boiler for thirty years, she replaced it with one which, under exactly the same conditions, lasted scarcely six months! Yet this was not the cheapest wash boiler listed in the catalog from which she ordered. It was sold at a good price and recommended for its durability! To replace it, she will have the annoyance of doing without it for a considerable time, the trouble of re-ordering it, the expense of the money order, and the express or freight charges, as well as the expense of the new boiler. Naturally she feels much more concerned about it than would a city woman, who would find replacement both cheap and easy.

The modern furniture, which sometimes falls apart in a short time, is used alongside old local-made furniture which has stood the test of rough wear for nearly a hundred years. And cheap, edgeless garden tools replace those which have come down through the family for two or three generations. This may be an unfair comparison between the goods of that past age and of this age of quantity production, but it is inevitably made upon the farm.

Another difficulty in country living is the lack of service for repairs on all mechanical appliances. When the farm family has a water system and something gets out of order, there is no plumber to be called. They must either do their own plumbing, or wait for weeks and pay out much money for a plumber to come out from the city. They repair the family sewing machine. If they have an electric light system they must do electrical repair work. The gasoline engine which charges the batteries is managed by the farm woman engineer. And more than that, as one farm woman writes, she must "mind the baby and keep up the fire in the kitchen stove, and answer the telephone and get dinner" all at the same time. She not only drives the car, but makes repairs upon it. At best, she has only her husband or the village blacksmith, who has turned over night into a garage keeper, to depend upon for nice adjustments.

Hence, it is more important that all automobiles and mechanical conveniences bought by country people be well made and simply constructed, with parts easily replaceable when breakage occurs. Otherwise they are out of use much of the time, are a continual annoyance, and the repairs soon equal the purchase cost of the article. In fact, the one great reason that there are so few conveniences in the country homes is that farm people have seen them tried under country conditions and have found that they did not render service as they should.

One of the chief reasons for the great shifts in population from country to city, during the past few years, has been that the country family could not adequately change their money income into the comforts of life which they desired. It is natural that the country woman should want a home such as the city woman has. Under present conditions on the farm this is difficult to achieve, and, rather than endure the continual annoyance and expense of the conveniences when installed in the farm home, she gives up the struggle and moves to town.

Much has been said about the low economic status of the farmer who "retires" to the country town when he is scarcely past middle life, but few have remarked that one reason for his retiring is that, in the country, he cannot buy the things he wants to buy. He does not want his wife to work so hard. He wants her to have running water in her kitchen and electric lights and a well-heated house, so he spends as little as possible while he is on the farm, and puts aside his money so that he can later move to town where dependable home conveniences are to be had for a reasonable outlay.

Indeed, the present situation on American farms is in many ways discouraging. American farming is certainly in a period of transition. To what? Nobody seems to know. The farm women will probably do their work and their spending as best they can where they are. But it will be some years before farming reaches an economic plane equal to that of other occupations requiring the same amount of skill and energy.

Yet, even at its worst, the farm has much to offer in the way of health and happy living. And, in spite of all obstacles, this new American farm woman may eventually find her way to economic independence and as high a standard of living as that prevailing in the towns.

The utter incapacity of urban intelligence—mechanized, stand-ardized and thinking in terms of mathematics—to comprehend the biological and cultural realities of agrarian life is impressively discussed by Caroline B. Sherman, of the United States Depart-

ment of Agriculture, in an article called RURAL STANDARDS OF LIVING,[2] *published in the "South Atlantic Quarterly."*

Standard of living studies among city dwellers have been watched with equanimity and interest for many years. Now that investigators are beginning to make such studies of farm families, many of us among the rural-born laity pause and think. We feel like making some restraining gesture until we shall have ascertained just how these studies are to be made, just how the results are to be interpreted, and just what kind of advice or readjustment plans are to be built upon them.

To a very limited extent only can the methods and interpretations that have served for city families be used successfully with families on the farms. So far as actual income and expenditure go, the same methods will probably suffice, but when it comes to dealing with all those intangible and psychological factors that go to make up a satisfactory standard of home life, we who grew up in them feel rather strongly that the measures for farm homes should be rather different from those used in measuring satisfactions in the towns.

Fortunately, we have among our professional investigators a few who are fully alive to the fact that the term "standard of living" has never yet been accurately defined to the satisfaction of all students, and that a device for measurement which satisfies all students has not yet been found. Perhaps a series of measurements including different kinds for the tangibles and the intangibles will be one of the solutions. Even then it is not likely that entire agreement and exact methods of measurement and evaluation will be reached, for we do seem to have at least tacit agreement that the element which makes life really worth living is usually something too illusive to isolate or to name.

Just how far farm income and expenditure help toward securing the psychic satisfaction—the mental and psychological atmosphere of home—is debatable, and will always vary as between families. The ability to realize or achieve it sometimes seems to

---

[2] Reprinted through the courtesy of the author and the Duke University Press.

be a quality or ability inherent in the family, or in certain individuals in the family, more or less regardless of income or expenditure.

For the present, expenditure is rather generally recognized as the best single measure of standard of living we have yet devised and the closer this expenditure is analyzed the more satisfactory it is as a measure. Particularly is this true in the case of the analysis of that part of the family expenditure that goes for items other than the necessities of food, shelter, and clothing. These other expenditures, which in earlier studies were often classed as sundries or miscellanies, are the items that vary most as incomes increase or decrease. The objectives of these expenditures and the proportioning of funds among them are often significant indications of standards of living. In recent studies these expenditures for the intangibles and for the more minor items are given more discriminating attention than was usual in earlier days.

By those who are fully aware of the significance of the quality in home life which we usually designate as atmosphere, the standard of living studies that are based chiefly on expenditure, or even on income and expenditure, will be regarded as foundation studies only. As such they are of undoubted value and are welcomed by all who have rural welfare at heart. Before any discussions of any subject, no matter how abstruse, can be constructive, certain basic facts must be known and reckoned with. Until recently we have not actually known what was spent by the average farm family in the average farming community of a fair number of states during the course of a year. Much less did we know about how it was spent or for what. Now that the Department of Agriculture has given us the figures, closely analyzed, we are in a better position to go into the more debatable realms. But, thoughtful studies though they may be, the investigators are not yet venturing far therein. Carefully they are feeling out the ground step by step. Not content with knowing the basic figures for the average farm family, they are now busy on similar studies of farm families in sub-marginal districts—of farm families at the very bottom of agriculture. Farm families of exceptionally large incomes, in exceptionally favored localities, will probably come in for attention before our economic basis for the more social phases of the study is complete.

Another important phase of the economic basis is the relation of expenditure to income. This is a many-sided feature, the adequate study of which requires men and women of different kinds of training and outlook. . . . The coöperation necessary to secure the facts and to work toward definite knowledge regarding this relationship in farm families and farm communities is now going forward.

For, contrary to the usual opinion, it cannot be taken for granted that increased farm earnings mean higher standards of living. Many economists and many lay observers believe that traditional habits, education, and general intelligence are as large a factor as earnings in deciding how well farm families shall live. There are many examples that seem to show that the tendency among farmers, as their income grows, is to buy more land, build larger barns, and increase their farm equipment, rather than spend the additional money for family comforts and pleasures. But most of us are relieved and not surprised to find that the preliminary studies apparently establish the fact that a fairly close relation does exist between the farm income and the farm standard of living. As among wage earners, when farm incomes increase, the families begin to spend a larger proportion, according to these studies, for purposes other than the necessities of food and rent. More is spent for non-material value, like education, recreation, books and magazines, travel, and church and philanthropic subscriptions.

The question naturally arises, "How permanent are these standards of farm living if they are based on increased income only?" It is the belief of many economists that only when an increased income is used to improve the conditions of everyday life and work on the farm, that such increase can be counted upon to continue as a permanent addition to the farmer's income, and hence is a safe basis for an improved standard of living. They point out that unless farmers insist upon holding tenaciously to a satisfactory standard of living, once it is attained, that standard will shift and fluctuate with the fluctuations of farmers' incomes; and so long as farmers compete with each other on the basis of an unsatisfactory standard of living, they cannot hope for a permanently enlarged share of agriculture in the national income. Higher land values and cheaper prices for farm products will absorb it. They must decide definitely as to the number and character of the advantages upon which they must insist if they are to continue to farm, and they must adhere to this decision. This argument does not seem to take into consideration those exceptional families whose inherent abilities and personal aspirations will maintain a certain desirable atmosphere or "standard," regardless of how low the actual cash income falls. But it is probably applicable to farmers as a group, and those exceptional families are probably the very ones who could be most effective in their communities in helping to demand conditions that make generally possible a satisfactory standard of life.

Based on this reasoning of the necessity for insistence on satisfactory standards, the relationship that investigators seem to detect between farm income and farm standard of living is encouraging. It indicates that farmers in general are tending in the right direction, and that an increased share in the national income would mean improved standards of farm life. On such reasoning it is, to a considerable degree, apparently up to the farmers as a group to make permanent any satisfactory standard of living that they are once able to establish.

So far, so good. As long as we stay this near to the economics of the question, we are on fairly safe ground. But the thoroughly interested student is not going to be content to limit his work to this safe and measurable territory. He is ever tempted by, and probably eventually must examine, that illusive phase of the standard of life which, to some of us, counts for much more than money income or money expenditure.

This is where our layman's reluctance comes into play. Are we ready yet to go into those realms? Just what is the magic combination of delicately adjusted social antennæ, of infallible sense of real values, and of mystic mastery of words, which will make it possible for us to detect, measure, evaluate, and reduce to terms these precious imponderables? And who among us will possess this vital combination, once its adhering abilities are decided upon?

As yet the tentative entries into this phase of the subject have been made with due caution, and as yet but little interpretation of the facts disclosed has been attempted. One or two studies have included the important item of leisure time. We have the carefully checked disclosure that, in a comprehensive study, little or no relationship was found between the average length of the work day of the homemaker and the "average value of goods used in a year." Apparently, the heads of the families "using more goods" do not find the corresponding leisure to enjoy the satisfactions that these things might bring, for the average working day was eleven hours out of the waking thirteen. This gives pause to those who are inclined to believe that improvement in methods and machinery is setting free much time that was previously given to farm production and farm housework. It would seem to indicate that increased production has been the more evident result. But along with this realization should go the more intimate one, that this business of farming and homemaking is, usually, a joint family enterprise. Some farmers' wives who put in eleven hours a day are comparable to the business woman who owns her own business or is one of a partnership owning the business. Such owners or partners expect to devote many more hours to their work than they would if they were employed on a salary basis. They are more interested in it than in anything else, and often they regret any diversion that takes them long away.

This economic solidarity of the farm family is among the inherent factors that serve to differentiate farm family conditions from those of the city family. And because of its secret implications, in a more closely knit family life, it is frequently one of the greatest satisfactions of the farm householders. The farm and the farm home constitute one economic unit. Not only is much of the food produced on the farm, but frequently the farm wife and the farm children have joyfully aided to produce it with no consciousness of the mooted questions of woman and child labor. The thrifty farm flocks, whether of chickens or of turkeys, or even of sheep, are often the playmates of the family. They add materially to the family resources both in money and in food, but they frequently have cost the head of the family little in either planning or labor. This is a type of family coöperation of which the harassed money-maker of the city family usually knows nothing.

In fact, the farm and the farm home constitute a coöperative enterprise in which is found a blend of work and home atmosphere which is not inherent in any other business. At its best it suggests to the discerning a sense of solidarity, security, and peace of mind which probably approximates, as does no other business, the state of harmony in which men were meant to live.

Then when we are considering the amount of leisure time a family has at its disposal, we must also consider how this leisure is spent. This is fundamental to a true determination of the standard. The cotton-chopper, who leans five minutes on his hoe for every minute that he chops, is not conscious of having any leisure, and our schedule would show him as working all day in the fields. The one who lolls in the hallway of the log house through the hottest hours of the day might be said to be occupied in idleness rather than possessed of leisure.

And what of those who spend their leisure consciously? Who is to be the judge of whether they spend it wisely or well? By what is he to judge? The day should come again, we fully believe, when a family standard will be judged, not by the number of associations with which its members are affiliated or the number of events and affairs in which it "participates," but by the number of evenings per week the family is *satisfied* to spend at home, happily occupied with books and pen and needle, with freedom and fireplace and family. Whenever a carefully compiled table of "family participations" greets my eye in our sociological bulletins, which seems to suggest that organization is worth while just for organization's sake and that "going" is worth while just for the sake of going, my mind turns with deep gratitude to memories of long evenings spent under the lamplight or before the fireplace of a quiet country home. Here dwelt with us the characters of all ages and here we knew the experiences of all climes. No club suppers or programs or parties remain in my mind or color my later consciousness or thought as do those long, quiet, uneventful but fruitful evenings of family companionship, discussions, reading, writing, and study.

Such differentiating factors that are not economic and are not usually recognized as having any money value are difficult, indeed, to evaluate. But they play an important part in this sense of harmony with the great forces of life and are usually rated high in any list of advantages of farm life. They must be recognized and reckoned with in the adequate farm standard of living study. Nature and circumstances give to the usual farm family abundance of air, light, space, and shade, and the blessing of quiet nights. In fact, to the worker in the city slum a decade ago it seemed that there could scarcely be a rural social problem. The study of standards in city living must take account of every window in the house, but two windows opening almost against a brick wall and adjacent to several chimneys do not compare with one window thrown wide to unobstructed breezes blowing across a field of many acres. The house in town that has no bathtub and is lighted only by kerosene lamps is either a shanty or a tenement, but, difficult as it may be to believe, in many a fine old spacious country home, set deep in its wide fields and shaded groves, a life of gracious dignity still exists without benefit of faucet or tank, electricity or delco.

In a home like this, redolent with thought, meditation, tradition, and courtesy, of what use is the investigator's bag of trusted measurements? What is the cost of food compared with the way it is prepared and its flavor, the serving and the surroundings— the spirit of hospitality? The sheens of long-polished mahogany, of ancient damask, of time-worn silver; the glow of mellow candlelight and a few well-chosen flowers; the adumbrations of a courtesy and a culture that no man can measure—these, we maintain, connote a standard of living that few new families and new houses can equal, no matter what the income and the expenditure.

Nor do we need to go to the homes of established tradition to find a depth of satisfactions that cannot be sounded by the plummets of modernity. There are few of us who do not know homes of approximately the same money level in which the difference of standards is very marked. Here we find a home, perhaps only one or two years old, in which the suggestions of background, of traditions-to-be, of daily mental and spiritual life lived within its walls, are so definite as to be almost tangible. There we have a house, long occupied, wherein the restlessness, the shifting ideals, the lack of any mental or spiritual family objective, results in a lack of standard so obvious as to be almost painful.

Does all this mean that standard of living studies should cease when the tangibles of the matter have been charted and evaluated? How is the thorough student to work his way on through the other factors that go to make up the whole? Naturally the laity have no solutions to offer and no criticisms to make of those who are devoting years to this work. We wish but to warn against ready-made methods and judgments, and urge deep thought and careful evaluation. And who knows? Perhaps that essence and fragrance and texture that make up the flower of family life may ultimately survive such analyses by the sociologists as well as our blossoms of field and garden have weathered the dissections of the botanists.

CHAPTER XII

CARRYING ON IN BIG BUSINESS

SINCE women were enmeshed in the whole process of transforming a virgin soil of continental proportions into an industrial society, it is not surprising to find that one of the first systematic treatises dealing with the growth of this huge industrial organism was written by a woman, Professor Katherine Coman of Wellesley College. Her "Industrial History of the United States," a pioneer in the field, was for a long time the chief compendium and guide for the exploration of the "dark continent" of industrial relations. Since it was published in 1912, other women and men have filled in the outline and have written, often out of the fullness of personal experience, on phases of great business enterprise as it advanced.

Advertising became the accepted "intellectual weapon" of capitalism and at that art Helen Woodward was an adept. THROUGH MANY WINDOWS[1] she looked out upon the world of business in which she directly participated, and revealed secrets relative to buying and selling which render more comprehensible the vagaries of the market.

It is a relief to turn from this story of confusion to another which from beginning to end was harmonious. This story came

[1] Reprint obtained through the courtesy of the author and Harper & Brothers.

from Massachusetts, too, from the Boston Manufacturing Company, makers of Gilbrae ginghams and other cottons in Waltham. I knew the treasurer of these mills slightly. It occurred to me that I could build up an [advertising] account there, and one day I asked him, "Why are all ginghams always the same tiresome little red and white or blue and white checks? Isn't it possible to make something more beautiful and original?"

"Rather!" he replied. "It certainly is mechanically possible; and we have a designer whose business it is to plan new patterns. But so far we've found them hard to sell. Buyers in the big stores say that women want the same little checks year after year."

"I don't believe that," I said. "I don't believe that at all. I think it's the buyer who hates to change. That makes him think it's the customer. I'm sure that if women could see the ginghams in new good designs they would like them better than the old ones."

"Nothing would please me more." Mr. Sweetser was encouraging. "I should like to introduce new designs for very good reasons. If we could manage that, we might get rid of many of our labor troubles, cut down dull seasons, and make more money all around. And—" I was surprised at the reverberations brought forth by my small questions—"don't you think that if we had new designs, we might also make a finer gingham and get a higher price?"

"Yes, you could. American women look for pattern first, not quality. There are almost none who can judge the quality of a material."

"Our experience shows that is so, too," he agreed. "It wouldn't do just to make a better gingham—we'd never get the money for it."

"You're perfectly right," I continued. "You'd have to make the better gingham with new designs, and if a woman got interested in the pattern, then she'd perhaps discover by experience that the quality was better."

The positive tone of my remarks did not come out of the air; I had a close friend who was then on the editorial staff of *Vogue* who had been telling me much about the planning of fabrics and clothes, and by this time I had acquired such experience in selling various things to the public that I often could tell with something like certainty how that public would act. Part of this was intuition; part of it was experience piled up little by little. Such intuition and experience combined give us in the advertising business a feeling about the public that can be easily understood by editors and politicians.

Mr. Sweetser and I were pleased with each other's point of view.

He went on, "If we can sell our ginghams steadily at a uniform price, we'll be able to keep our labor employed continuously. That way we'll get rid of labor troubles that are bound up in short time running and that sort of irregularity."

"And there's another aspect to it,"—I was growing enthusiastic. "You know women want something different all the time."

"They certainly seem to," he laughed.

"Now you give them each year the same old checks—naturally year after year passes and women will not buy ginghams except for aprons because they've already got all the checks they want. If you had new designs each year, really new and interesting and in tune with the fashions, I think you wouldn't have so many bad years. You could make gingham a staple fashion; because it really is the most comfortable material to wear in the summer. It doesn't crumple like linen and it is cooler than silk."

"That sounds reasonable," he said. "But you said something just now that I don't understand exactly. You said 'in tune with the fashions.' "

"Yes. Your designers can make the most beautiful ginghams that ever were, and if they don't make up attractively, in the straight or bouffant lines that are in fashion that year, they're of no use."

"Of course," he said. "Of course. I don't think we've given enough consideration to that, although we have tried to be careful about colors—to keep them the right ones for the year's styles. I don't think we've done it, though, as a matter of fact."

"It all sounds good to me," he went on. "But I don't see any way of making the better gingham and selling it in this country without some extra help. Women have a habit of paying twenty-five cents a yard for American ginghams and from sixty-five cents to a dollar and a quarter for Scotch ginghams. Now to get them into the habit of paying fifty-five and sixty-five for American ginghams, you can be sure is no easy matter."

"Let me think about it a while," I asked. "I have an idea, but it's a little vague."

He was interested at once. "Why don't you work it out and let me know?"

"Love to," I answered. "Of course it's just a plan I'd show you. I don't want to prepare any advertising or show any sketches on speculation."

He agreed.

"Anyway," I remarked, "you will see that the advertising will prove to be a small part of this plan."

I then sat down with this problem. To get American women interested in new designs in gingham; to persuade them to pay more than they were used to paying for it; to get department-store buyers to buy the gingham for their women customers; to design new and striking patterns; to make gingham a permanent rather than a temporary and changeable fashion.

But this is the wrong order. With the American buyer you have to put over a fashion first; once that is done, price doesn't matter. First would come the designs, because it takes a year to plan and make these before they can be delivered to the trade; then new and permanent gingham fashions; then the department store buyer, then the woman who wears the clothes, and last the price.

First, knowing my own limitations on matters of fashion, I made an arrangement with Lotta Alger, then one of the editors of *Vogue,* who supplied all the technical ideas and knowledge. Then I tried my own hand at designing. This was a new toy and I got some ideas which might never have come if I had spent my life doing that kind of work. One day, playing with a piece of gingham, I pulled out a few threads lengthwise and cross-wise, making squares that looked like hemstitching. I was sur-prised at the result! The bit of fabric in my hand looked as light and delicate as voile, but was as strong as gingham. Here was a new design, if it could be made on gingham machinery—and we found that it could. On pieces of gingham without any pat-tern Mrs. Alger drew thin black lines up and down and across. These two basic changes in pattern we turned over to the design-ers of Gilbrae ginghams. They had meantime also been working on new patterns and new combinations of color, which were charming. Where the old-plan ginghams had been always one color, now they made the warp, for instance, blue, and the woof yellow, so getting a soft green. Even the little checks were trans-formed by changes in sizes and color and arrangement.

It took months to make these new ginghams, as the machines had to be rigged up for each pattern, and only about a hundred yards were made of each so that we could try them out.

We had decided at the very beginning that we could not put this plan through without the help of Paris. We can talk of American-inspired fashions as much as we like. I have heard it charged that Patou, the French dressmaker, comes to the United States to get ideas and then goes back to Paris to make them up and adapt them to the American trade. What he really does is probably not that; he sees what Americans have done to modify the original French ideas, and what they like; then he goes back to Paris and gets up his new designs to fit in with that knowl-edge—that is, he works to please American taste. Many of the big French dressmakers do this much more reluctantly.

No fashion can be introduced successfully in the United States by the *haute couture* of Paris unless American women want it. Each year out of the workrooms of the famous French dress-makers come hundreds of new models, even thousands. The American buyers for the big department stores and specialty shops look these over and pick out what they think their cus-customers will like. From these the customers make a further selection. These buyers so completely represent the American woman and her taste that she usually likes what they bring over. But not always. Any large shop at the end of the season sells off original French models that have been failures. So that while the Paris dressmaker does the original thinking, the American woman does the deciding. And the pressure of her deciding is beginning to change French work.

But more powerful than the reality is the American woman's idea of French fashions. She likes to think that her clothes are planned in Paris. For years there have been patriotic drives in the United States for American-inspired clothes. They have been failures, not because we cannot design clothes, but because American women do not want us to. The American woman is convinced that the Frenchwoman knows more than she does about charm and allurement. Whether she does or not, certainly the French *grand couturier* is already highly trained in the making of lovely things. So why not let him go on? What exactly is the good of trying to do it at home? We have enough other things to do. Why not take advantage of this precise French talent? Anyway, whether our pattern makers and manufacturers like it or not, we are still taking our fashion inspiration from France.

So we knew that in order to put over our ginghams we had to take full advantage of this French idea as it was understood in the United States. The Boston Manufacturing Company had rushed through a small quantity of the new designs in the new quality. I had to go to Paris, anyway. When I got there I was told at once that my idea sounded beautiful but was impractical. It couldn't be done.

"Why not?" I asked the great fashion expert to whom I was talking.

"My dear lady,"—his English was precise and his gold-link bracelet contrasted oddly with his powerful figure,—"don't you know that all *les grands couturiers* have an agreement among themselves not to push American-made fabrics? More than that, they refuse even to use them?"

"Why?"

"Because of the great French fabric-makers like Rodier and Bianchini. These people make only a small quantity, you know, of each fabric, and make it by hand; and they are always putting out new and beautiful designs."

"But," I objected, "our mills are making better quality silks than are made over here." I learned later that many of the famous French dressmakers are financed by the great French weavers and jobbers, who thus control the dressmakers. But they do create fabrics with a lavish gift of beauty.

"That is so," he agreed, "but the designs are still not so beautiful or so original. You see a great dressmaker has to get inspiration from new fabrics. You will agree with me that there has been no really new idea in line in fashions for many years; that we all keep turning back to history for the lines of women's clothes. . . ."

"Yes, that is so, but there have been many new materials and new patterns and colors."

"Exactly,"—the arbiter of style was gracious,—"and it is this novelty to which the great dressmaker turns for inspiration. Without it they feel helpless. They depend on Rodier and Bianchini. And so you see, my dear madam, if they made up the American gingham they would antagonize the French maker of new fabrics. It is quite impossible, what you want to do."

"Will you pardon me a moment?" He turned to the telephone and spoke to a maid at his home. "Marie, will you have some one start at once with my gray outfit for the races? It is now twelve o'clock and I must be there at twenty minutes to two, as you know. I shall have to eat luncheon in the interval, so you must hurry. See that the tie also is gray. . . . Yes, you know what shoes. That's right. Thank you."

As he hung up the telephone he explained to me why the French rarely wear cotton dresses. Summer in France is not warm enough except on the Côte d'Azur, and no fashionable people go there in summer. Everywhere else silks and even woolens are worn the year round. Cotten dresses are made mostly for the American trade, because these lend themselves to embroidery and handwork. Although gingham as a fabric was invented at Guingamp, it is almost never worn except as aprons in the kitchen.

What to do? I had no connections with big dressmakers and knew little about clothes in a technical sense. So I did what I always do in such a situation—went to some one who did know all about it, to an able American woman, who knew all the dressmakers and for whom they were eager to do favors. She understood every technical detail of making and selling clothes. Without any friction or any trouble on my part, she had sets of dresses made for me within two weeks after I had been told on every hand that the whole thing was completely impossible. The dresses were beautiful, they cost little, they were made by four of the most famous French dressmakers. Very good names to use in the United States.

We put these dresses on manikins and photographed them in the Bois de Boulogne, and on the Champs Élysées, being careful to include the Arc de Triomphe or some fashionable restaurant in the picture for atmosphere. We had hats and parasols made to match. And dolls—impudent, smart French dolls dressed in pert little gingham dresses, with gingham hats and sunshades.

But I had had another idea about which I was much in doubt —to photograph our gingham dresses on French noblewomen. It was important that they should belong to distinguished families, that they should be rich and of good social position. Rich women of title who have no position in French society are common enough. These would not do for our purpose. The plan might have seemed a flighty one if I had not already secured so many indorsements from well-known people at home for one product or another. They are easy to get. But never before had we had to use the actual photograph of any woman of social prominence, and I had been told that the Frenchwoman of good position wouldn't dream of allowing her name, much less her photograph, to be used for publicity.

When you see pages advertising creams or what not, each one praised by some actress or social leader, you think perhaps that these commendations are paid for. Sometimes they are, but often they are not, at least not directly. We had a dozen ways of getting them. Sometimes they were given for the sake of publicity, even by some social star. Sometimes an actress or social leader has a poor friend who acts as a sort of intermediary between herself and the advertiser, in which case she permits her name to be used simply through kindness and good nature. To help such a friend to earn a hundred dollars she is willing to say the most generous things about products of which she knows nothing.

We never paid more than a hundred and fifty dollars for a name. There are advertisers who pay from five to ten thousand dollars apiece for such names. But the method is different. The advertiser in that case works with a society collecting funds for some public movement. To this society they say: "We've got a good product. Your members would like it if they used it, and we'd like their endorsement. We'll contribute five thousand dollars to your funds for each well-known name among your members that you will allow us to use in publicity."

The secretary of the association, who has had a hard time raising funds, takes this proposition to its members, and the job is done.

I put my plan up to some representatives of American magazines in Paris. They were discouraging. I had told them that I not only wanted the photographs of these society women for the ginghams, but also their indorsement without photographs for a perfume I was advertising.

"We'd like to help you very much, but it is a hopeless thing you ask. Frenchwomen of standing will hardly allow their photographs to be used in society news, much less in advertising!"

But by exactly the same methods used in the United States we had within three days commendations from women of the highest social rank, all of them wealthy, both for the perfume account and for the dresses. And we photographed them in their homes wearing our gingham gowns. They made only one stipulation, that the advertising should appear only in the United States and Canada, not in Europe. And we had at our disposal, though we did not use them, the names of several women of high rank in England.

So then we had our material: a number of dresses from famous French houses; some equally charming dresses from French wholesalers; we had our dolls, our parasols, our hats; photographs of the titled women in their own homes; photographs of manikins in the Bois.

Meantime the mills in Massachusetts were making up the new patterns of ginghams in quantity. We were ready to fire our guns, and then we found that we did not know exactly at whom to fire. Ginghams had always been sold to big jobbing houses, who in turn sold to retailers. It is well known in the advertising and selling world that it is harder to put through a new idea with a jobber than it is with retail shops. This is easy to understand: the jobber gets his profit from enormous quantity—he does not depend so much on salesmen, and he therefore falls back on staples. We knew that it was going to be hard to put over our new patterns with the jobbers and it did not look promising even with the retail-store buyers. Although we had kept our plans and work more or less secret, we had shown some of our new designs to a few of the largest shops in New York.

The buyers of dress goods said, "Yes, they're pretty, but we can't sell them. Ginghams should be a staple."

"That's why you never sell ginghams except for children's dresses and aprons."

"That's all right. We've got a good sale in them. Don't like to disturb a good thing."

"But," we argued, "you do sell new patterns in Scotch ginghams."

"That's different. The public is used to that idea. Your patterns are a lot more unusual than the Scotch ones. You've got this new drawnwork thing, too—it's practically a new material. You can't put over a brand-new thing so suddenly. Got to change fashions and patterns gradually. It's no use showing women this stuff. They'll be afraid to try it."

In this they bore out our own opinions. It will not do to show a new fabric suddenly to the public. No matter how much it is admired as a work of art, it will not be bought unless women can see how it will look as a dress. But all the material we had brought from France served this purpose.

I found the dress departments in the stores more open-minded. I showed these new things myself to Franklin Simon & Co., who welcomed them before they saw any of the French work.

Though we had to sell to the jobbers and the retail stores, we could not rely on either to resell to the consumer without our help. They had too many other things to handle. So it was part of our plan to make the consumer go to the nearest shop to buy Gilbrae ginghams, after we had persuaded that shop to buy from the jobber or from us. We were not yet ready to do this, although we had been working for nine months on Gilbrae.

Instead, our next step was to arrange an exhibition for the jobbers who were then about to come to New York for their annual buying of cotton goods. We made a display in the selling offices of the mills in New York—of our dolls, our dresses, our photographs. And when the jobbers came in to buy we would say: "We have picked out a few of the leading jobbers in the country—about a dozen of you can have this display. You may be one of them if you want to." With everything so clearly before them, they were only too eager. So we shipped the display in specially made trunks from one jobber to another.

When this was over it was time for department stores to begin to sell gingham to customers. We divided our display into several windows, with little drawings in color to show how these windows should look, and with engraved cards containing advertising material. These we loaned to the best store in each of the larger cities for a week. Since the season for gingham varies in different parts of the country, this was feasible. The displays traveled all over the country.

When the woman had been attracted by the window to go to the dress goods department and see the ginghams close at hand, she found there colored folders with photographs of the dresses and samples of the materials attached, which she could show to her dressmaker; or she found copies of the gowns themselves in the dress section of the store. At the same time we had a little advertising in women's magazines, in which we used our material from Paris.

The newspapers were glad to print the photographs of the titled French ladies and even of the manikins, because it was really fashion news. The dresses we showed were new. It is easy to get publicity from the newspapers if you have something with news value to their readers. The photographs were also shown in moving-picture news reels and in the magazines. . . .

The first thing that happened was that we sold our goods. The second was that the commission house which handled the selling end for the mills sold more of every other gingham which it carried. The commission house, seeing the effect of new designs in the Gilbrae line, made all their other gingham mills likewise put out new designs. That is the way such things usually work. And if you have what is called a "leader" to give your salesmen—something that goes well and stands out from your other goods—it pushes everything else along.

With the Gilbrae ginghams we set a new fashion in women's clothes. The restless desire for a change in fashions is a healthy outlet. It is normal to want something different, something new, even if many women spend too much time and too much money that way. Change is the most beneficent medicine in the world to most people. And to those who cannot change their whole lives or occupations even a new line in a dress is often a relief. The woman who is tired of her husband or her home or her job feels some lifting of the weight of life from seeing a straight line change into a bouffant, or gray pass into beige. Most people have not the courage or the understanding to make deeper changes.

Yet to-day this plan has become worthless. It was copied as quickly as possible by other manufacturers. As a consequence there were competitive demands for dealers' windows and for jobbers' displays. Each manufacturer planned a more expensive show than his competitors; each was willing to pay heavily for parts of the plan which had cost us nothing. So the whole thing became impracticable. And it became necessary to think up a new idea for the client. In the advertising business it is necessary always—always—to think of a new plan.

Nowhere is the interweaving of ideas and interests more strikingly illustrated than in the managerial experiments made by JOSEPHINE ROCHE, INDUSTRIALIST,[2] described in Nancy Cattell Hartford's sketch for the November, 1932, issue of "The Independent Woman," organ of the Business and Professional Women's Clubs.

The concrete results of one woman's activities in the industrial world—in an industry which few women have entered—may be studied in the career of Miss Josephine Roche, of Denver, Colorado, who, since 1929, has been president of the Rocky Mountain Fuel Company, one of the largest coal companies of the west.

In January, 1927, after the death of her father, Miss Roche succeeded to his interest, and soon found herself the controlling power in the second largest coal company in Colorado. She might easily have delegated her power to others, and lived a life of luxury and ease. But she saw an opportunity to put into practice some theories which she had long been harboring. For years she had been a student of economics and sociology, and her research work along those lines had already brought recognition.

The Colorado coal fields—like the coal fields of Kentucky and Illinois—have been an industrial battleground for almost a half century. Labor disputes have been the cause of a bitter resentment, keeping the coal operators and miners in a state of siege amounting almost to civil war. Machine gun and rifle fire have taken many lives; troops have been sent into the mine areas to quell riots; homes have been destroyed and women and children left destitute by prolonged strikes.

[2] Reprint obtained through the courtesy of *The Independent Woman.*

Although many serious battles have been waged in these fields, the Ludlow strike of 1913 and 1914 was one of the most fatal. The whole nation was aroused when a tent colony of strikers was burned and women and children, taking refuge in the pits, were suffocated. The Columbine mine of the Rocky Mountain Fuel Company suffered a severe setback only four years ago, when a conflict between labor agitators and local deputies resulted in six dead and thirty-five seriously injured.

At that time, Miss Roche was merely a stockholder in the company, powerless to cope with a situation that stirred her deeply, and that remained unsolved by the men who held a controlling interest in the company. She had inherited her father's interest —the largest minority holding—but it was not enough to give her a voice in the conduct of the business. A year later, through the purchase of another large block of stock, she found herself the controlling power, as she had wanted to be for years.

Her first move was a reorganization of the official personnel which enabled her to gather about her men of vision, experience, and education, who believed, with her, that the problems which had heretofore been solved with such bitterness and violence would in time disappear under a more humane régime.

Her next step was to invite the miners to unionize the property. At her first conference with the mine workers, it was difficult to make them believe that she was acting in their interests and with no selfish motive. But after this unprecedented move, she appointed as manager of the company one John R. Lawson, who for thirty years had been the miners' leader against the "Big Three" Colorado coal companies. Lawson had been indicted on thirteen murder counts in the Ludlow disturbance, convicted and sentenced to life imprisonment. When a gubernatorial pardon was offered him, he refused it, but was finally freed by the Supreme Court. With this advocate of the mine workers in her employ, Miss Roche was able to convince the men that she was acting from a sincere desire to better their conditions. This conviction was strengthened when she appointed as general counsel

Edward F. Costigan, now Senator from Colorado, who had been counsel for the miners in 1913 and 1914.

At her first miners' conference, Miss Roche asked the men what she could do for them immediately to improve their conditions, and their reply was, "Give us more pit cars!" When this request was granted, the first victory was gained in her fight to win the loyal support of her workers. Now they are unanimously united in favor of the new régime under a feminine head—Communists, Industrial Workers of the World, and adherents of the American Federation of Labor, all actuated by a desire to further her interests and by so doing to further their own. They are getting a square deal.

The new policy which Miss Roche inaugurated was based on recognition of the public interest involved in mining and marketing coal; on fair market practices; and on union labor contracts, under which coöperation has been substituted for hostility and waste. Long years of warfare between coal operators and miners have been the history of Colorado's coal industry; work has been at a standstill, and striking miners and their families have suffered starvation. When the Rocky Mountain Fuel Company in 1928 took this action of union recognition it marked a complete reversal of the company's previous stand, which had been the same wasteful and anti-social attitude so prevalent in the industry.

Meeting with the coal miners' union delegates, the company signed with them the document under which it has since operated, the preamble of which reads:

"We, the signers of this document, seeking a new era in the industrial relations in Colorado, unite in welcoming this opportunity to record the spirit and principles of this agreement.

"Our purposes are:

"To promote and establish industrial justice;

"To substitute reason for violence, confidence for misunderstanding, integrity and good faith for dishonest practices, and a union of effort for the chaos of the present economic warfare;

"To avoid needless and wasteful strikes and lockouts through the investigation and correction of their underlying causes;

"To establish genuine collective bargaining between mine workers and operators through free and independent organization;

"To stabilize employment, production and markets through coöperative endeavor and the aid of science, recognizing the principle that increased productivity should be mutually shared through the application of equitable considerations to the rights of workers and to economic conditions affecting the operators and the business of the company;

"To assure mine workers and operators continuing mutual benefits; and consumers a dependable supply of coal at reasonable and uniform prices;

"To defend our joint undertaking against every conspiracy or vicious practice which seeks to destroy it; and in all other respects to enlist public confidence and support by safeguarding the public interest."

The outstanding results of putting her theories to work during the three years of union-management coöperation have been the safeguarding of workers' earnings at an annual figure of approximately $1,800, an amount several hundred dollars above the earnings of miners in other mines of Colorado; an increase in production and sales of coal; and a decreased operating cost due to the improved working relations and increased production.

No less important than the fair wage scale as a factor in the results of the Rocky Mountain Fuel program is the recognition of mutual rights. Meeting together as equally free parties, but with the same end in view and a joint task, the frequent conferences held between miners' union committees and company officials, superintendents, department heads, and salesmen, have resulted in suggestions for improved operating methods and for extension of markets. Rocky Mountain Fuel Company miners are not only producing coal—they are helping to market that coal. They are telling their communities what union-mined coal means to the miners and the community; that their union wage scale means nearly one and a quarter million dollars a year to be spent in their communities; and they and the company jointly have endeavored to prevent the general unfortunate and wasteful reduction of miners' wages and consequent decline of purchasing power which has had such dire effect in other parts of the state and in other states in the country.

A story is told of Miss Roche which illustrates that from early childhood she had imagination and sympathy which provided the foundation for the humanitarian outlook of maturity. At the age of twelve, she begged her father to let her go down into the mines. When he replied that it was too dangerous for her, she said, "If it is so dangerous, why are the men allowed to go down?"

Her interest in the social sciences grew, and when she graduated from Vassar in 1908, she took a master's degree in economics at Columbia University. Her career began with the post of probation officer in Denver, and she was the first policewoman appointed in that city. Later she became director of the Girls' Department in the Juvenile Court, and from 1925 to 1927 served as referee clerk. During the war she was special agent on the Commission for Relief in Belgium, and was the organizer of Belgian Relief in New York State.

A key to Miss Roche's attitude toward human problems may be found in the following incident:

During a stormy session with a lawyer who was explaining the seriousness of a petty infraction of the law, he became irritated with her apparent lack of indignation.

"Don't you realize," he exclaimed, "that this is a serious situation? The law and the observance of the law are the most important things on earth!"

"Oh, no, they're not," Miss Roche replied calmly. "People are the most important things on earth."

And this expresses very aptly the whole attitude which has made her such a unique figure in the world of industry to-day.

Out of labor agitation and humanistic concern about the social conditions that shadowed big business enterprise came a body of protective legislation applicable particularly to women, such as minimum wage requirements, restrictions on night work, and the limited working week. After considerable experience with this kind of legislation, one of the liveliest industrial disputes arose as the result of protests by feminists demanding equal opportunity in industry—protection for both sexes or for neither.

This issue Professor Elizabeth F. Baker, of Barnard College, discusses in an article captioned AT THE CROSSROADS IN THE LEGAL PROTECTION OF WOMEN IN INDUSTRY,[3] written for the "Annals."

Why are there special laws for women in industry and to what extent have they accomplished their aims? These have been seething questions since the World War—a far cry from those days at the turn of the century when pitying friends of overworked women pleaded with legislatures to pass bills for their relief. Year after year, as women poured into store and factory, these pleadings were heard. Laws were enacted in one state after another reducing inhumanly long hours in the working day, limiting or forbidding night work or all employment in mines, saloons, and certain other specific occupations, demanding seats and decent dressing rooms, and, in a number of states, minimum wages. Public sentiment was aroused in favor of these laws and they largely stood the tests of the courts.

Any who wish to know vividly and at length the basis for this crop of laws can do no better than to pore over the Federal report in the nineteen volumes on "The Condition of Women and Child Wage Earners in the United States," published in 1915, and summarized in Bulletin No. 175 of the United States Bureau of Labor Statistics. This and, in England, Hutchins' and Harrison's "History of Factory Legislation" and those delightfully written volumes of the Hammonds', "The Town Labourer," "The Village Labourer," and "The Rise of Modern Industry."

[3] Reprint obtained through the courtesy of the American Academy of Political and Social Sciences.

In works such as these one learns of the suffering among workers which the introduction of power machinery wrought. All workers were victims but protection was urged for women much more than for men. The reasons for this sex discrimination are well known by now, at least those which lie on the surface. The phrases, "physical inferiority" of women, their "potential motherhood" and the "welfare of the race" suggest them. It was these concepts which threw into relief the ugly facts of employment that prompted special legal protection for women.

Important facts are that employed women are young—over 41 per cent of them in 1920 being less than twenty-five years of age, and about one-half of these under twenty. One-fifth of all employed females are married, and many are mothers of little children. Morbidity studies show that women suffer some 50 per cent more sickness than men. These conditions have kept women's union membership smaller than that of men and their bargaining power weaker, so that they tend to be more particularly the prey of unscrupulous employers. This is destructive to women's health and to the health of their children.

The desirability of these laws for the special protection of women was rarely questioned in the earlier part of this century. In fact, the custom of having them was established then. The great remaining task appeared to be their extension and perfection.

However, after full suffrage was won for women and through women's revealing work experiences during the war, opposition to these laws arose. The objection has been not to the theory of protection for workers, but to its exclusive application to women. The protestants explain that these laws do not always protect— that they too often shackle instead. They urge that women have small chance before their profit-seeking employers to secure desirable occupation when there are restrictions placed upon what they can offer, while men can give their services on their own terms. Other things being equal, they say, men will always be preferred if these laws prevail, leaving women to earn a scanty living out of the left-over jobs—a part of the luckless mass of underpaid, unskilled and unorganized workers who toil long and hope little.

If society is to be protected against the raids of power-driven machinery, the critics of discriminative legislative protection say, *all* of the human victims must be guarded—the men as well as the women, the fathers as well as the mothers. All of those who cannot protect themselves, whoever they may be, must be guarded. In this way only can weaker bargainers, men or women, have an equal opportunity before employers.

Closer inquiry into the sources of this protest reveals the fact that women in the wage-earning classes are most often pressed into industry by the economic defeat of their husbands and fathers, by their illness or death from exposure and overwork, or their inability to bargain for a living wage. Studies of the Federal Children's Bureau, for example, show high correlations between the low earnings of fathers and infant mortality—the number of infant deaths falls sharply as fathers' earnings increase. Furthermore, while we hear much of the strength and pugnacity of trade unions, wage-earners in this country are at the very most only 25 per cent organized. That is one in every four. Thus there are many more men than women who are unable to demand human and economic justice before their employers.

This fact is recognized in the minimum wage laws of England and all European countries in that they apply both to men and to women. These laws are designed to protect the low paid wage-earners, their sex being considered beside the main point.

In the matter of health, while women have more illnesses than men, the physical disabilities of working men are enormous. Tuberculosis, because it is peculiarly a disease of industry, may almost be considered a man's disease. Although young women between 15 and 19 years of age are from three-tenths per cent to 60 per cent more tubercular than young men, males from twenty years of age to the end of their lives are all the way from twenty to 300 per cent more tubercular than females. During the twenty-five years from forty-five to seventy, three times as many men have tuberculosis as women.

Men victimized by industry in this way are a menace to their families and associates, economically, physiologically, socially. The evils of their position should be attacked directly. To work for protection of the women and children who are affected by the ill health of men seems to be giving disproportionate attention to the symptom, to the neglect of striking at the source of the trouble.

It appears to be true also that while employment in lead-poisoning occupations is much more harmful to mothers and their offspring, than to men, there is sharp danger for the children of fathers who are so employed, and inguinal hernia is the greatest single frailty of the American male worker.

These facts have commanded attention from those interested in industrial workers; they have made at least more understandable the contention that the welfare of society cannot be promoted by laws for the protection of women alone.

This view has been accepted by many of the special protectionists who have urged, nevertheless, that, since women need protection more than do men and since it is easier to get laws for women, these laws should be enacted as a step in the direction of legally protecting all workers who need it.

For the sake of perspective, let us review, specifically, reasons why some women oppose this theory as unfair to them—as inducing laws which have cost them their jobs. These complainants are not the millions who form the rank and file of women in industry. They are some of the minorities who, through superior skill or opportunity, have found their way to places seldom filled by women, and who therefore find sex-discriminatory laws endangering their economic security. . . .

And so there has brewed a conflict between those who have sought protection for the masses of women, with the theory that in the end all workers would be benefited, and the minorities who have suffered therefrom. The case of these minorities has been expanded and championed in recent years by the National Woman's Party in a broader political program for the equal rights of men and women "throughout the United States and in every place subject to its jurisdiction." Aside from this political combat, a solid contention is that these minorities are important to the progress of women in blazing new trails in industry, and that their gains should in some way be encouraged instead of ignored. Whether such encouragement should bring a shift in the theory of protective legislation is a question which has persisted but which has remained unanswerable because of the paucity of ascertained facts as a basis for appraisal. But now we have new material which makes an answer more nearly possible than ever before.

An important out-post has just been planted in this controversy, and toward the further adjustment of women to industry. This appears in the form of a 500 page report by the Women's Bureau of the United States Department of Labor on "The Effects of Labor Legislation on the Employment Opportunities of Women." Here is the first inclusive attempt to discover first hand the effects of these laws—to see to what extent during this quarter century they have been hitting the mark or falling short of it. It is a masterly effort to drive into the heart of the question and to fetch out the truth whatever it may be. The resulting story deserves to be read by all who are genuinely interested in women's economic problem. It is a mass of orderly material assembled by a new and skillful method which establishes a pattern for further analysis and greater refinement of points. . . .

To summarize adequately in this paper a report of these proportions is impossible. More important for this discussion perhaps is the essence of the report. In the light of ascertained knowledge, what showing does special legislation make? Has the requirement of these standards for women so restricted their employment that their opportunities are limited and they are placed at a disadvantage in competing with men for the chance to work? Is this worried question settled at last to the satisfaction of all? What are the lights and shadows in the findings, and where do they fall? . . .

Ballasted by scores of carefully presented tables and pages of explanation and direct report these summaries of the Federal Bureau's findings leave no doubt that laws restricting the hours of labor of women have had broad beneficial effects. They have reduced the hours of thousands of women and also of thousands of men, because of the frequent interdependence of the occupations of men and women. In the five woman-employing industries not many cases were reported where women were actually displaced by laws for their protection.

On the other hand, the revolt against those laws by some women in less wonted occupations, on the ground that they are harmful instead of protective, appears now to have solid and authoritative foundation. . . .

Let us be as concrete as is possible in the examination of the nature of these handfuls of women. Some sampling was done in Massachusetts in the course of the investigation of the Women's Bureau, and there among woman-employing factories an estimated 500 more women would have been employed had the law permitted them to work longer hours. Five hundred as compared with some 10,000 employed women—about 5 per cent. Samples were also sought of new occupations which would have been open to women but for the forty-eight hour law. Some dozen occupations were discovered in which groups of from six to one hundred women would have been making their way as operators of mesh-making machines, light lathes and drills, and rubber foot-wear cutting machines, in work on metal parts, comb-tending, wire-testing, textile machine tending, weaving and cutting, knitting surgical appliances and corsets. The displacement in these occupations was estimated as between three and four hundred women. In stores in New York, "a very few cases" among women in supervisory positions were those of dislodgment by the law, as was true also of elevator operators. Perhaps some 10 per cent of New York's night waiters in hotel restaurants would be women were they permitted to work at night. And among ninety-four women pharmacists who were interviewed sixteen had received a setback from the impact of the law.

The widespread existence of these minorities of women would seem therefore to be certain, but we can only estimate their extent. Doubtless they amount to a few thousands among the approximate 3,000,000 women covered by special laws. If 2 per cent of 3,000,000 fell into this group, it would make some 60,000 women whose occupational opportunities are cramped or cut off by laws which may be directly benefiting all the others.

To be sure this seems a small number when one speaks in quantitative terms, although when measured by other values the emphasis appears to shift. It is defensible to think of these openings, denied through the law, as little industrial frontiers for women which must be taken in the course of their advance to full economic enfranchisement. That the few women who take these frontiers must make the way for the many to follow. That this is one way to break prejudice down—the abiding enemy of women.

Women's experience in the metal trades offers a still more concrete example of what is meant. Their entrance into automobile factories has been spectacular, as has been the growth of that industry itself. From under 1,000 ten years before, women operators in 1920 numbered nearly 13,000, an increase of some 1,400 per cent. They jumped from a ratio of one woman to fifteen men to one woman to eight men, the increase for men having been less than 500 per cent. It was ever-potent economic pressure that brought this about. The "labor vacuum" which the war created and the heightened demand for metal products then being turned out in these factories brought women into machine shops handling castings and forgings of steel and iron. They worked on lathes and milling machines and they welded.

After the return of the men from the war, however, the number of women in automobile factories fell off. In Michigan, where their status was especially examined, the number of women decreased by one-half between 1919 and 1927. But it had increased in automobile-accessories-and-parts factories—from 615 to 2,111, or 250 per cent. Here, in 1927, women formed 45 per cent of the total working force. Only one of the plants examined had reduced the number of women, and this was a steering-gears factory where work is heavy.

Thus, if Michigan is representative, it appears that women have suddenly become an integral part of the working forces in metal trades. And yet they are meeting a sea of obstacles in the effort to hold their ground. . . .

We know too little of what wages women receive for their work in the Michigan metal trades; as for the fifty-four hour law it appears that it has given them a shorter day than they would otherwise have had. But here again have some women forfeited possible opportunities for advancement. For example, one manager said he would sometimes like to ask the women to work extra time but he could not do so because of the law; and furthermore his president was one of those who opposed both overtime and night-work for women.

This tiny incident is worth notice in passing, for, like those mentioned above, it could be many times duplicated, and it suggests a more subtle influence of special laws upon women's opportunities at their industrial frontiers. Weighing in the atmosphere of prejudice against women's being in the metal trades at all was the law which encouraged this prejudice. Picture an actual occasion on which this plant or some other finds itself in critical need of extra labor, with women and not men available. The employment manager would nine times out of ten run the risk of incurring his president's disfavor by being prepared to show that production schedules were thereby met. The women taken on make more money, and perhaps one per cent of them drops into a permanent job better than they had before. In this case one per cent might mean one or one hundred women, but this is the way hundreds in the aggregate, when they have been free to do so, have risen out of their low-paid industrial ruts. . . .

To the protectionists these minorities of women who are hurt by legal protection have been unimportant. Their loss of opportunities is but the usual sacrifice made for the optimum good. To the anti-protectionists, these minorities are at women's industrial frontiers. They are so valuable to the advance of the majorities that their need for greater freedom from the law must be met.

Here, then, is a question of emphasis the crux of which may be largely a matter of time. Advocates of special legislation have been distressed by the oppression of working women and have striven to relieve it at almost any cost. They were concerned with immediate results, which they have largely attained. The opponents have risen to protest that this cost is too great for the future of women. They ask that present relief securable for women alone be forfeited in order to hasten a more permanent and solid emancipation for women.

Until now, these conflicting theories of procedure have seemed to present an *impasse*. But in the new light shed by the Women's Bureau a horizon opens ahead. May it not be that instead of conflict these two viewpoints now suggest a sequence of action? For to link present with past a great change emerges. The conditions under which women work today, with hours "not excessive for the majority," as compared with those a score of years past which were intolerable, are a basis for agreeing that women's sharp need for protection has abated.

Moreover, in this country there is little question that the days of widespread, degrading exploitation of labor are behind us. . . .

Now if combined forces have lifted the level of working conditions of women to a place where women are no longer severely exploited, and to a plane more favorable to all workers, may it not be desirable to arrest further legislation for them and work with a wider purpose? May not the time now be ripe to seek relief by legislative action for all who still labor at a sublevel—men as well as women? There is no opposition in theory to a move of this nature, except by laggard employers who always fight legal protection of their employees, and some of the less enlightened trade unions. Moreover, we have sufficient precedent framed by our highest courts.

It is impossible to estimate the value which would accrue to the workers in this country if a program such as this were to be seriously drafted. The present trend toward a better work life for all wage earners would take a fresh start, and backward employers would be forced into line. The minorities of women who are now restricted by special laws would gradually be absorbed into their respective groups with opportunities strengthened for equality with men—at least so far as the law is concerned. Labor law would discourage prejudice against women wherever it has fostered it before. Those who are striving for the future of woman would find common cause with those who have made gains for women workers of today. With forces united the progress of women, in the next twenty-five years, would hold promise greater than we dare now to prophesy. . . .

Is not our direction, then, clear? Let the present statutes for women remain for the present at least, with some necessary exceptions for the victimized minorities. Drive hard for the extension of these laws to include men as well. Aim as rapidly as possible to wipe out sex discrimination in the labor law by raising the status of all sub-level workers to the level of those better off. Present a program of legislation for men and women workers with solid economic foundation, one which is abreast of the time. Let this program be developed by an informed and industrious commission with the progress of women at heart. Those who think freely agree that our tariffs, in a world of interlocked nations, must have scientific adjustment away from vested interests and in line with present economic needs. Just so does this vexed question of the legal protection of women workers require scientific adjustment. If we sincerely desire to advance the position of women in industry, is not this the road to take?

CHAPTER XIII

WORLD WAR AND WORLD PEACE

Having flung its interests around the globe, American business enterprise, which had transformed a rural culture into a capitalist civilization, undermined the traditional work of men and women, and scattered wealth with one hand and industrial slums with the other throughout the land, was inexorably caught in every disturbance introduced by revolution and war—in the Far East, in Latin America, and in Europe. When the imperialist rivalries of the Old World, sharpening historic conflicts, burst into the World War, American capitalism, pushing into all markets, and American agriculture, largely changed from a self-sufficing economy into a single-crop economy, were drawn into the conflagration. When the ruins were examined after the holocaust and efforts were made to reconstruct a stable and tolerable life for the earth's weary multitudes, the necessity of a return to first principles became widely evident.

Meanwhile in this vast tumult of promotion, excitements, propaganda, ideas, interests and values, the heedless and the thoughtful alike, including women, took part.

At her strategic post as wife of the American chargé d'affaires in Mexico during the chaotic period which succeeded the despotic Diaz régime that collapsed in 1911, Mrs. Edith O'Shaughnessy wrote a trenchant account of American aggression in that region,

443

entitled LETTERS OF A DIPLOMAT'S WIFE.[1] Having familiarized herself with the Spanish tongue and Mexican history, she was able to appreciate the background of the neighboring country as few Americans have done. At the same time she was sensitive to the conditions of life and labor in modern Mexico and deeply troubled by the methods which her countrymen employed in dealing with the Mexicans. Rare in books on Latin-American politics is her sympathetic treatment of the women affected by the policies and purposes of men.

Though the events recorded in these letters are known to all the world, they may, perhaps, take on another significance seen through the eyes of one who has loved Mexico for her beauty and wept for the disasters that have overtaken her.

The time has not yet come for a full history of the events leading to the breaking off of diplomatic relations, but after much pondering I have decided to publish these letters. They were written to my mother, day by day, after a habit of long years, to console both her and me for separation, and without any thought of publication. In spite of necessary omissions they may throw some light on the difficulties of the Mexican situation, which we have made our own, and which every American wishes to see solved in a way that will testify to the persistence of those qualities that made us great.

Victoriano Huerta, that central figure of these letters, is dead, and many with him; but the tragedy of the nation still goes on. So above all thought of party or personal expediency, and because of vital issues yet to be decided, I offer this simple chronicle. The Mexican book is still open, the pages just turned are crumpled and ensanguined. New and momentous chapters for us and for Mexico are being written and I should be forever regretful had courage failed me to write my little share.

It is two years ago today that diplomatic relations were broken off between the two republics. It is more than two years since

[1] Reprint obtained through the courtesy of the author and Harper & Brothers.

the Constitutionalists under Villa and Carranza have had our full moral and material support. The results have been a punitive expedition sent into Mexico to capture Villa, and very uncertain and unsatisfactory relations with the hostile *de facto* government under Carranza. As for beautiful Mexico—her industries are dead, her lands laid waste, her sons and daughters are in exile, or starving in the "treasure-house of the world." What I here give forth—and the giving is not easy—I offer only with a trembling hope of service. . . .

The history of Mexico is without exception the most fascinating, the most romantic, and the most improbable in the world; and the seed of Spanish civilization implanted in this marvelous land has produced a florescence so magnetic, so magical, that the dullest feel its charm. All that has been done for Mexico the Spaniards did, despite their cruelties, their greeds, and their passions. We, of the north, have used it only as a quarry, leaving no monuments to God nor testaments to man in place of the treasure that we have piled on departing ship or train. Now we seem to be handing back to Indians, very like those the Spaniards found, the fruits of a great civilization, for them to trample in the dust. Let us *not* call it human service. . . .

Great Britain will be very polite, but will not depart one hair's breadth from what it has decided on as its Mexican policy, involving big questions, not alone of prestige, but oil, railways, mines, etc. In fact, the British reply to Mr. Bryan in today's newspaper quite clearly says that England will be delighted to follow any policy from Washington as long as it does not interfere with what the British Foreign Office has decided to do. They simply can't understand our not protecting American lives and interests. Their policy here is purely commercial, while ours, alas! has come to be political. . . .

All the foreigners here have nerves. What would be peaceful, dove-like households at sea-level, become scenes of breakage of all description at this altitude, and all sorts of studies might be made on the subject of "air pressure" on the life of man and woman. . . .

Last night came what is practically an ultimatum from Washington to Huerta. He is to get out, he, and all his friends, or—intervention. N. was at the palace until one o'clock in the morning. It is asking Huerta to commit political suicide, and he, unfortunately, does not feel so inclined. Also, he has a conviction that he is a sort of "Man of Destiny" who can bring peace to Mexico. N. tried to convince him of the complete impossibility of standing up against the United States, and urged him again and again to give way. I was troubled during the night by visions of intervention, further devastation of this beautiful land, and the precious blood of my own people. . . .

If we come in, the military part is, perhaps, the least of it; a huge administrative job would follow—Cuba and the Philippines are mere child's play to it.

There was interesting conversation at lunch, only we four being present. Mr. Lind repeated to von Hintze what he has, curiously enough, said to many people here—his opinion that the crux of the matter was the Anglo-American relations, and that the United States would never allow the dominance of British interests to the injury of American or Mexican ones; von Hintze, though he listened attentively, was non-committal and most diplomatic in his answers. It is always of absorbing interest to Germans to hear of possible difficulties between England and other nations, and *vice versa*, too, for that matter. A light springs into the eye; and I dare say von Hintze made a report to his home government on returning to the Legation. He told Mr. Lind he thought we had not sufficiently respected the *amour propre* of the Mexicans; that we were wrong in trying threats when what they needed was skillful coaxing. Mr. Lind volunteered the surprising statement that it didn't suit us to have the elections held, anyway, as there would be concessions granted and laws passed that would render the Mexican situation difficult for us for fifty years. I really felt quite embarrassed. . . .

Mr. Lind said, in a convincing manner, as he departed, that he would arrange rooms for us in Vera Cruz. He knows it is N.'s right to conduct any business connected with the breaking off of relations, which he seems sure will be decided on at Washington, and he realizes that N. has borne the heat and burden of the Mexican day. He seems more understanding of us than of the situation, alas! I said Godspeed to him with tears in my eyes. Vague fears of impending calamity press upon me. How is this mysterious and extraordinary people fitted to meet the impending catastrophe—this burning of the forest to get the tiger? . . .

The ineradicable idea among all foreigners is that we are playing a policy of exhaustion and ruin in Mexico by non-recognition, so that we will have little or no difficulty when we are ready to grab. One can talk oneself hoarse, explain, embellish, uphold the President's policy—it makes no difference: "It is like that." . . .

I have been reading accounts of the deportation of the Yaquis from Sonora to Yucatan, the wordless horrors of the march, the separation of families. I can't go into it now; it is one of the long-existent abuses that Madero, at first, was eager to abate. . . .

It sometimes looks as if the whole situation could be summed up in the one word, "oil." Mexico is so endlessly, so tragically rich in the things that the world covets. Certainly oil is the crux of the Anglo-American situation. All the modern battle-ships will be burning it instead of coal—clean, smokeless, no more of the horrors of stoking—and for England to have practically an unlimited oil-fount in Mexico means much to her. . . .

The position here gets more curious every day. Public opinion, as we understand it, is non-existent in Mexico. It is always some despot who brings some sort of order out of chaos by means unknown (though they may be suspected) to the public, who judge his worth entirely by the peace and prosperity that follow. . . .

The Mexican men are often put in the shade by their handsome wives, who would be lovely anywhere. The difficulties of bringing up young boys here are, for obvious reasons, so great that both Mexicans and foreigners send their sons away at an early age. The men we know have most of them been at school in England (Beaumont or Stonyhurst); and their English is as good as ours—sometimes better. There is a sort of resigned irritation, veiled by perfect courtesy and unfailing amiability, on the part of these people toward our policy, which seems to them cruel, stupid and unwarranted. I can only hope it will soon bear testimony to itself, for this close watching of the means to an end—if it be an end—is very wearing. . . .

The foreign Powers used to think that, though extremely annoying, our Monroe doctrine was respectable. Now they seem inclined to think it is an excuse for monopolizing the New World for our own benefit. We may come into Mexico with glory. Can we get out with credit and not too high a bill? . . .

I find that the Mexicans are constantly studying us, which is more than we do in regard to them. They look upon us as something immensely powerful, that is able and, perhaps, if displeased, willing to crush them. They are infinitely more subtle than we, and their efforts tend more to keeping out of our clutches than to imitating us. Our institutions, all our ways of procedure, are endlessly wearisome to them, and correspond to nothing they consider profitable and agreeable. . . .

We can put in any sort of government in Mexico—but can we keep one in? We encouraged the powers of dissolution around Diaz, recognizing and aiding Madero. The world knows the result. History always repeats itself here, and the writing on the wall is always in blood. . . .

If only poor old Huerta could have begun in some other way than by riding into the capital in a path of blood spilled by himself and others, he would probably have been able, with recognition, to do as well as any one, and better than most. As it is, he is like a woman who has begun wrong. The neighbors won't let her start again, no matter how virtuously she lives. . . .

A quiet day, but we are distressed beyond words at the renewed reports of a lifting of the embargo on arms and ammunition for the rebels. I feel as if I couldn't stand it, and N. even felt that he ought to resign if it happens. The ship of state is going so inevitably on the rocks. He will make some sort of protest to Washington against the advisability of this move. Villa's cry is "On to Mexico," and he may get there, or rather, here. . . .

Gamboa's answer to Mr. L [ind] last August, though not satisfactory to *us* when laid by Mr. Wilson before Congress, remains a dignified, clever, and unimpeachable *exposé* of the Mexican situation from *their* point of view, which is that the United States, by every international law, is unwarranted in interfering in their interior affairs, as these, however unfortunate, are those of a sovereign state. They never got over the fact that the communications Mr. Lind brought with him were respectfully addressed to no one in particular, and referred to the government as "the persons who at the present time have authority or exercise influence in Mexico." They consider that if they even once allowed such counsel from the United States they would compromise indefinitely their destinies as a sovereign state.

As for the phrase, "the United States will not hesitate to consummate matters, especially in times of domestic trouble, in the way that they, the United States, consider best for Mexico"—it is graven on the mind of every Mexican who can read and write. Concerning our professions of friendship, which left them decidedly cold, Gamboa neatly said that never could there be a more propitious time for displaying it, that we had "only to watch that no material or military assistance of any kind be given to the rebels who find refuge, conspire, and provide themselves with arms and food on the other side of the border." He further quietly states that he is greatly surprised that Mr. Lind's mission should be termed a "mission of peace" as, fortunately, neither then nor today had there existed any state of war between Mexico and the United States. The document is the tragic, bootless appeal of a weak nation to a strong. . . .

Tonight has come the long-feared cable from Washington stating that the President intends to raise the embargo on arms and ammunition. The note was for Nelson's special information, not for delivery to the Foreign Office yet, but the hour will come when he will have to gird himself to do the deed. It has been sent to every chancery in Europe, where it will raise a storm, to blow hard or not, according to the amount of material investments in Mexico. We scarcely know what to think; we are dazed and aghast. . . .

We are aghast at the resignation of Mr. John Bassett Moore as counselor to the State Department. He is learned, perfectly understanding, and very experienced in a practical way about Latin-American affairs. . . .

The mad dance of death goes on, and I feel as if we were the fiddlers. Mr. Lind has so idealized the rebels in the north that he has come to think them capable of all the civil virtues, and he is obsessed by the old tradition of north beating south whenever there is an issue. His deduction is not borne out by facts, as in Mexico it is the south that has produced the greatest number of men—"the governmental minds"; the south has come nearer to loving peace; the south has shown the greatest degree of prosperity and advancement. Vera Cruz is the poorest possible vantage-ground for a study of conditions; it is a clearing-house for malcontents of all kinds, mostly rebels, fleeing from the consequences of *some* act against *some* authority. My heart is heavy at the grim fatality that has permitted our policy to be shaped *from there.* . . .

This is largely an agrarian revolution, and Huerta was the first to realize it. He says that everybody has made promises to the people, and nobody has kept them. I wonder, if the people ever get a chance to make promises, will *they* keep them? *Quién sabe?* However, all this is not a question of taking sides, but of stating facts. . . .

I am not keen about the confidential agent system, anyway. With more standing in the community than spies, and much less information, they are in an unrivaled position to mislead (wittingly or unwittingly is a detail) any one who depends on them for information. Apropos of Mr. Lind, one of the foreigners here said it was as if Washington kept a Frenchman in San Francisco to inform them concerning our Japanese relations. For some strange reason, any information delivered by confidential agents is generally swallowed, hook and all, but, unfortunately, the mere designating of them does not bestow upon them any sacramental grace. . . .

Huerta said he would apologize for "the Tampico incident."

N. indicated that his government would not consider that sufficient. Huerta asked, squarely: "What do you want?" N. answered, "The salutes," saying he might arrange the matter quietly, giving the salutes some morning at sunrise, for instance. The President began to ponder the matter; whereupon the secretary, thinking his chance had come, broke in upon the silence with the remark that it would be derogatory to the national honor to salute, and that there was no guarantee that the salutes would be returned, that Mexico's sovereignty was in question, and the like. The President immediately stiffened up.—So can a nobody turn a nation's destinies! . . .

There is going to be a lot of trouble about the Tampico incident. The "Old Man" is recalcitrant and feels that the public apology by General Zaragoza should be sufficient. What we will do can only be surmised. Recently, one of the newspapers had a cartoon of Mr. Bryan speaking to "Mexico." Under the picture was this pleasing caption, "I may say, I am most annoyed; and if you do not immediately reform, I hesitate to say what I may not be inclined to decide, perhaps!" . . .

Had this war been induced by a great incident or for a great principle, I could bear it. But because the details of a salute could not be decided upon we give ourselves, and inflict on others, the horrors of war. . . .

We are at war. American and Mexican blood flowed in the streets of Vera Cruz to-day. . . . It has been many a year since American blood flowed in the streets of Vera Cruz. General Scott took it in 1847. The endless repetitions of history!

It is the deep-lying urge of women to associate themselves with war that seems to fascinate Margaret Deland in SMALL THINGS,[2] while she studies the modern character of that affiliation.

[2] Reprint obtained through the courtesy of D. Appleton and Company.

"Well, *I'm* just plain scared!" a Y.M.C.A. girl said: "Let's have some jam and Educators."

"Educators! Where did you get Educators?" said the other Y.M.C.A. girl.

"Oh, from home," the girl said. She brought out the Educators and some strawberry jam, and then they both sat down on the floor to eat them, pausing once in a while—a spoonful of jam in mid-air—when the bang of the barrage was a little louder, or when there came the terrific detonation of an exploding bomb.

"Jam from home, too?"

"You bet! Do you think you could get stuff like this over here?"

Then, by the light of a candle leaning sidewise in a tumbler (for all the electric lights had been turned off), and with the consolation of a cigarette, these two girls talked over their day in the canteen,—interrupted from time to time by those sudden BANGS! It was a quarter to twelve. The sky was velvet black, and the stars were very faint, but there was no mist. "So," said the Educator girl, judicially, "it's a bully night for a raid."

"I don't mind raids as much as shelling," said the other. "That scares me stiff! Give me a light, will you?"—they put their young heads together, and a glimmer leaped from one cigarette to the other—then *Crash!* The windows shook. "Ooow!" said one of the girls, *"that* was near."

The town in which these two workers were stationed had been shelled for several days, and the last three nights there had been air raids. Both of the girls were tired; one had come in from her canteen at 11:30—about fifteen minutes before the raid began; the other had just crawled out of bed, where she had been for two days with a temperature of 102, from pure fatigue. "No bug," she said, calmly. She was the one who had said that she was "plain scared."

While the raid was going on, they huddled together on the floor, ate jam and Educators, smoked, planned their work for the next day, and discussed the psychology of Fear. . . . *"Why* is being shelled nastier than being bombed?"

"Don't you think," some one said, "that it may be because a bomb from an airplane seems a *little* more accidental? It hits any place. A shell is supposed to be accurately aimed, so when it blows you up, your annoyance is more personal."

"Well," said the owner of the can of Educators, *"I'm* not crazy about either of 'em."

"Makes the U. S. A. look sort of good, doesn't it?" the other girl inquired maliciously.

After that they talked about their work.

The significant thing about this scene, which might (except for the bombs) have taken place in any woman's college in America at twelve o'clock at night, was that, though "plain scared" and "scared stiff," the idea of leaving their job never occurred to either of these girls. And this, I think, sums up very accurately the work of American women in France just now.

Endurance.

There wasn't any pose of heroism in eating Educators, and jumping at the crash of a bomb. These two girls were hungry and tired; they were scared, and said so. And they both agreed that, in an air raid, "home looked sort of good" to them.

But they had not the slightest idea of going home.

Their conduct was not what you would call "showy"; it was just the expression of an age-old characteristic of their sex; the quality which mothers have, and always will have. It was the Everlasting Feminine which is rooted in the most elemental instincts. . . .

Some two months ago I was asked to write a paper about Y.M.C.A. women over here. It was to be called "The Startlingly Heroic Work of Women in France." It seemed a simple enough thing to do; so, like Dr. Syntax, I began my "search for the picturesque."

I did not find it.

I found something which seems to me very much better. I found an infinite capacity for toil; I found patience, and quick understanding of other people's feelings (meaning by "people," "soldiers"). I found a ready friendliness, and extraordinary executive ability; I found good housekeeping, good cooking, and good courage. I found these things in every canteen. Of course I found the reverse of these qualities, too; I found a few indolent women who could not drudge, and who wanted excitement; a few flirtatious women, who made eyes at everything in trousers; a few bad-tempered women, who would not take orders, and did not know what obedience meant. Far be it from me to deny the existence of these unpleasant ladies! But where, if you please, on this distracted terrestrial ball are such persons *not* to be found? Of course, these women ought not to have been allowed to leave their own country and quarter themselves on poor France, but their presence here only reflects on the efficiency of the Y.M.C.A. War Council in choosing its personnel—both men and women; it does not, as some people seem to think, stigmatize the Y.M.C.A. workers as a class among the women. On the contrary, these undesirables were a very small minority; it was among the majority that I looked for instances of heroism. But just as I thought I was about to pick a fine, rosy apple of the "startlingly heroic," I found a prosaic slice of bread and butter!—merely the old business of "enduring."

I confess to having been, just at first, a little surprised, which was unreasonable in me, for the prosaic is what Nature has arranged for women ever since the Race began to stand on its hind legs. Perhaps before that, for when the male apes banged each other on the head, the female apes probably grabbed the babies, and watched the scrap from the tree tops! In other words, when it comes to the "Unusual," men have *done* it, and women have *endured* it.

But who is going to deny that "enduring" needs any less nerve than "doing"? Not I,—for I have seen our women in France!

And as I watched them, I realized that their main value in this poor, terrified, crazy Europe is that what they are doing is rooted in the ordinary and the elemental, instead of in the unusual and the spectacular. Their work is not bucking Nature! It could only fall down if it did,—if things were turned around, and women were placed on the firing line, and men poured out

chocolate behind canteen counters, the result would be very up-
setting to civilization. Which is only a rather long way of saying
that the overseas War Work of American Women is, generally
speaking, fine, but not spectacular. Our girls in France are rarely
in the limelight. They are not Deborahs, nor Joans of Arc.
Which is just as well, for if women should ever turn into the
exceptional woman, the race might cease. It is the normal
women who keep up steady. And look at the "normal" things
which our girls are doing over here!

They are standing, red-faced and perspiring, over the most
exasperating stoves you can possibly imagine,—stoves which often
"simply won't draw!" They are making enormous quantities of
chocolate, and then handing it over counters which it takes continuous efforts to keep clean,—for the men "do slop so!" They
are sorting out passionately desired American mail in Y.M.C.A.
post offices. They are at desks, and at typewriters, and at tele-
phones, in the various headquarters of the Association. They
are scrubbing floors, and playing games, and putting up turkey
red curtains in chilly huts. They are washing stacks of dishes
(how they used to hate dish-washing at home!), and peeling
potatoes, and selling chewing gum, and jollying homesick
soldiers. They are getting up vaudeville shows, and dancing,
and singing. They are offering maternal advice upon stomach
aches, and promising to write home and tell his mother just how
he looks, and how much he has gained in weight, and that she
must not worry about him, because that worries him!

Our girls, Red Cross girls, Salvation Army lassies, Y.M.C.A.
workers, are doing all these things, occasionally under dangerous
conditions, very frequently under conditions of great discomfort.
They live in cold, damp, dirty places; they eat ill-cooked food,
and sometimes not quite enough of that! In other words, they
are doing all the things that all the women of all the generations
(except a few shirkers and parasites) have done all the time, since
the world began! As a result, one looks on, and says:

"Thank God that woman's part in this dreadful business of
war is still *normal*."

For man's part is not, and cannot be. Man's part is often—
terribly often!—"spectacular," as well as necessary and splendid.
But it is not normal for men to spend their time killing other
men in the awful limelight of the trenches. So I come back to
what I said in the beginning: I found, in my search for the
"startlingly heroic" in the Overseas work of our women, something much better than the startling; I found the ordinary, glori-
fied by its own high purpose.

Of course there have been individual instances of the "startling," individual instances of superb heroism on the part of
women. I could tell you things done by the Salvation Army
girls,—simple, honest, wonderful lassies,—I think, perhaps, the
most wonderful of all our women workers; I could tell you of
the heroism of the Smith unit; of women driving ambulances
under fire, of girls directing convoys of soldiers in the hell of a
bombed district; splendid deeds, all of them!—but occasional.
Not the deeds by which the Race lives; not that prosaic bread
and butter of conduct, which feeds Humanity. The steady, regular work in American women overseas has been just the old, old
race-work of endurance.

How is the following for endurance? I went to see a Canteen
rather near the front and stayed in a hotel,—well, as a French
hotel can be the best on earth, so also it can be the worst! This
was the worst. I have tried many hotels in my native land,—
traveling from Alaska to Florida, and from Kennebunkport to
Santa Barbara, to say nothing of Europe,—so I may fairly claim
to have seen a pretty good assortment of hotels, and to be qualified to express an opinion. They are, all of them, Waldorf-
Astorias, compared to this terrible place of dirt dampness and
evil food. In it, all last winter, lived, worked, and enjoyed life, a
Connecticut girl (her people came from Old Chester, so I feel a
personal affection for her); here she lived without any way of
keeping her room warm, though it was so damp that at times
water trickled down the walls; here, in the freezing darkness of
winter dawns, she broke the ice in her water pitcher, and dressed;
then ran, shivering, through snowy mud, to her canteen (which

was at least warm, thank Heaven! The U. S. A. sees to that.)

In the canteen, which is a big hut covered with tarred paper, on which the nail heads glisten in the sunshine like decorations, —in this hut she worked from eight A.M. until eleven P.M. I need not speak of the work in detail; it is pretty generally known, and it is practically the same thing in all the Y.M.C.A. posts and canteens. It is not the detail that counts, it is the endurance,— the gay, friendly, uncomplaining, *un-self-conscious* endurance, which never flagged,—and was never spectacular!

But when you come to think of it, she was only doing the work her grandmother did (I speak generically), only doing the work of the Race Mother. She, the Race Mother, has always been sleeping any way and in any place, if circumstances made it necessary; she, too, has risen in the winter darkness, and given food to her house and a portion to her maidens; she has often given pretty poor food—though if she could cook it herself she did her best to have it good. And she has worked from that early rising until "anywhere from eight to eleven."

So the dark-eyed, smiling, tired girl from Connecticut has been living the Race Life, for the sake of our soldier boys. And they love her, not because she is spectacular, but because she is normal! And how they do love her,—hundreds of her,—for she has come from almost every state in the Union. (Which is one of the cheerful things about this dreadful moment in the world; just because our men and girls come from every state, our country is ceasing to be "states," and is becoming a State.) She—this Y.M.C.A. worker who is helping in the work of the national amalgamation—is displaying many other kinds of endurance than the cold, dirty, hotel type; some of them harder, I think, than the hotel. Endurances just as fine and necessary but even less "startling" than canteen work.

I know one girl who sits in an office of the Y.M.C.A. head-quarters in Paris, and pounds on a typewriter all day long. "I never had touched one of these old machines till I came over here," she told me; "of course I was crazy to go to the front; but they said they were wild for typewriters, so I just buckled down and learned how to do it. I hate it like the devil," she added, sighing; "but what was the good of fussing? It seemed to be up to me—for *somebody* had to do it. So I just said, 'Oh, damn! I guess it's my job.'" (I can imagine how that expletive, from Y.M.C.A. headquarters, will make some people at home jump!)

Just think of all the generations of women who have come head on against the realization that "somebody's got to do it!"—and, by the grace of God, have been able to add, "It's my job" (personally, I prefer to omit the expletive). Sometimes I think the girl who does this particular sort of job (there are hundreds of her, too) is even more necessary than the woman who washes dishes until she nearly drops, or tries to control her temper when the men secretaries are particularly stupid and trying and religiously narrow-minded! The girl who pounds out: "Your letter of the 14th instant duly received. I would say in reply that the consignment of Fatimas shipped by you on the S.S.——is not yet to hand," etc., etc.—this girl may not realize that the comfort of a thousand men is being aided by her pounding fingers; she may not have the particular kind of imagination which would illuminate her task for her and show her what she is really doing; but if she is a woman of sense (and so far as I have met her over here she distinctly *is!*) she must know that the business of the whole Y.M.C.A. would stand still without her; that the girls who are doing the "spectacular," interesting work of making doughnuts on the firing line, or scrubbing floors near the front, could not fry or scrub unless she poked up some slow transportation office to send the lard and the scrubbing brushes. She ought to know that the chief cook and bottle washer of the whole Y.M.C.A., the grave, burdened, steady executive himself, would be brought to a dead standstill if she (or her kind) preferred to be or tried to be startlingly heroic. The Y.M.C.A. girls in Paris, and in the large or small headquarters all over France, who endure the drudgery of clerical work, fill one with just as great admiration, just as true reverence for duty well done, as any canteen worker stationed (as they are all crazy to be) "at the front." I do wish they could know how fine and how necessary is the old feminine quality of endurance, which makes them stick to their typewriters! But apparently most of them don't know it; most of them are rather dismal about it. They seem to be half ashamed of it. "We're in no danger," some of them say, with gloomy self-contempt—which is very funny, but perfectly sincere. They say they do nothing but "sit tight" at their desks, when they might be handing out chocolate under shell fire, or racing a motor ambulance to a Poste de Secours! So they might, —but what would happen to the Y.M.C.A. if they did only what they liked? I wish these steady, necessary girls, a few of whom smoke (never publicly, I think), and who love to make sober folk jump with their occasional "bad word"—I wish they knew that we are just as proud of the courage of their endurance of the dull job, as we are of the courage that meets shell fire with composure.

Apropos of that occasional and rather self-conscious "bad word," and the childlike satisfaction of flourishing a cigarette case, as if to say, "See what a bad boy am I!"—I am struck by the fact that mentally and temperamentally there seems to be a great gulf between the men and the women workers. Many of the former are dismayingly narrow-minded (they call it being religious); a few of the latter are,—well, we'll say "wide-minded"; I suppose they call it being *free*. The narrow men represent the Past—and the lost opportunities over here of the Y.M.C.A. The "wide" women represent the future—full of danger and beauty and bad taste and hope! Or you might put it that the men stand for Faith, and the women for Works. (Of course this is a generalization: the majority of the workers stand for both. But unfortunately it is the minority which can give any movement or organization a black eye.) Naturally the difference in the mental processes of such men and women makes it sometimes a little hard for them to appreciate each other. I heard a man say, with a significant roll of his eye toward a group of petticoats: "I don't see how any human creature, man—*or woman*—can smoke, and preserve his—*or her*—self-respect. For my part," he added, "I believe that I received my body, beautiful, from God, and I must return it to Him as beautiful as when He gave it."

He was not very beautiful, this little man, but he was *very* good, and honest, and devoted, and hard-working—for religious narrowness does not interfere with work! But the effect of his remark upon that group of petticoats can be imagined. . . .

One of the women, also rolling a significant eye, said: "I don't see how any one can want to close the Canteen on Sundays, so he can attend divine service. For my part, I believe there is no diviner service than waiting on the soldiers!"

Of course these excellent workers are boring to each other; but from the soldiers' point of view, the "wide" girls do less harm to the reputation of the Y.M.C.A. than the "narrow" men, some of whom are so concerned with the mint, anise, and cumin of sectarianism, that they overlook the weightier matters of service and freedom of opinion,—thereby laying the Association open to the charge of considering itself wiser than its Master, and holier than its Lord.

But I must go back to the normalness of the girls' service. There is another race-old loveliness in their work in France, which has impressed me very much. It was particularly in evidence in one of the large Leave Areas, where several thousand men came together for a brief rest after months of the strain of the trenches. This service started in with being exciting and stimulating and full of enthusiasm; but it merged gradually into what somebody called, wearily, "dead horse." It was the work of entertaining the soldiers.

"It is dreadfully dull to be funny all the time," one girl said, simply.

It was the dullness which women have endured since first there were babies in the world, or worn-out husbands, or little growing brothers and sisters.

"I *must* amuse them!" tired, bored women have been saying for—how many thousand years? It isn't spectacular to pile up blocks on a nursery floor,—nor is it to get up shows in a Hut, day in and day out, pull off "sing-songs," or play baseball with a lot of fellows until you are tired enough to drop. It is not showy to do things like this, but it is blessedly useful. Consequently hundreds of our girls are in the "Entertainment" bureaus. And the gratitude of the soldiers, put into preposterous slang, or quite inarticulate, is touching to a degree.

Just here is a very interesting and significant thing about our men; in all the intimacy which is inevitable in games, "freshness" on their part is practically unknown. It is the rarest thing in the world that a man has to be snubbed. "I would rather dance with these boys than some of the men in our set at home," a charming girl told me.

There is another "endurance" which is to be seen here, as well as all the world over in offices and shops and factories and schools and homes. I mean the toil of planning other people's work, the drudgery of the executive. There is power with it, and power is, of course, interesting; but take it day after day, and it is not exciting. It is a heroism of the boy-stood-on-the-burning-deck type, but it isn't "spectacular."

There is still another way in which our girls are doing wonderful, and not showy work; namely, *holding their tongues*. That doesn't sound like anything remarkable, but you just try it! Try working in a canteen with other girls who have nothing in common with you but the English language, and the Purpose which has brought you all to France! Try taking orders from a "secretary" of possibly different manners and probably different theological views! Try seeing your little job suddenly taken out of your hands by a soulless Paris office, and given to somebody else, and you obliged to get a move on for another job! Do you think it would be easy to hold your tongue? "If you think so, heaven is your home," said one girl morosely. Certainly this nervous, wracked, irritable, fermenting world does not foster such self-control. I don't mean to say that our girls are angels of sweet temper; they are not. They are very human, and some of them make it extremely hard for that same "soulless," frequently blundering, but really well-meaning Paris office. But on the whole, they *do* hold their tongues, keep at their work, and endure—each other! I am inclined to think this is the hardest and the least showy thing our women are doing over there.

But it, too, is an ages-old domestic quality. Think of all the generations of women who have held their tongues in the family circle! And it doesn't come easily; it has to be cultivated. It isn't easy for human creatures, whether at home or abroad, to forget themselves, to be gentle, to be courteous, to "suffer fools gladly" (and the person who doesn't agree with us is, I have noticed, always "foolish"). No, it isn't a usual thing, such endurance; it is the Great Achievement; it is not commonplace,—it is divine.

And it is "heroic"; but just in proportion as it is true and good, it is not spectacular. . . .

So this is why I never wrote the paper upon the *"Startling Heroic Work of American Women in France!"*

Remembering Clara Barton's nineteenth-century outburst against the idea of war as glorious, we turn to another war nurse in a world war in the twentieth century with eagerness to know her attitude. Mary Lee's preface to her report of experiences in IT'S A GREAT WAR,[3] *is the key to her reaction.*

A book with the war as a background cannot be a short book. For those who are in it, War is interminably long, and only a long book can create the impression of interminable length. Those who lived through the war in Europe have lived two lifetimes: one the lifetime in France; the other, that connected existence which took place before they went and resumed its pace after they came home. A book about War cannot move smoothly, swiftly. War moves in jerks. Jerks which consist in moments of intense excitement punctuated by hours and weeks and months on end of boredom. A book which would picture War faithfully must not fail to give that alternating sense, first that living has

[3] Reprint obtained through the courtesy of the author and Houghton Mifflin Company.

become more real, more vivid, and then that the whole pace of life has been made suddenly sluggish and dull. Nine tenths of War is Waiting. A book which eliminates the waiting, eliminates nine tenths of what the people who go to War live through.

A book about War cannot be a romance built about an organized and neatly thought-out plot. War is not a romance. There may be romances in it, but the Chief Protagonist is always War itself, with its stupidity, its carelessness of human life. The aims, the desires, the emotions of the thousands of separate individuals who make an army are sacrificed in the enormous welter of uncontrolled events. Therefore a novel of the war cannot be a coherent romance, moving logically to an unforeseen end. People there were in France who conducted such short, coherent romances, but such people were inevitably sent home. The chief characteristic of War is that human beings are powerless to achieve their ends. War is a Spectacle in which millions of lives are jostled about by mental and moral forces not their own.

There cannot be an organized plot, yet there must be a rhythm swinging through the book which portrays War. There is a certain rhythm about War which penetrates the consciousness of those who live through it, which goes on after it, still singing in their souls. A book which would re-create War, must re-create this Rhythm of war-time life.

A book with the background of war should not be written in war slang, nor use too many of those technical and military terms which were so vivid in the language of the army of the time. War jargon will be unreadable for the generations to come. And it is important that the generations to come should be able to find out about the last war. The parents of the rising generation, perhaps, will not find it easy to explain to their children everything they did.

A book about the war must not stop with the Armistice. For the army, the war went on for nearly a year after the Armistice. And the causes, for which the members of that army were sent to war, were not settled till two years after that.

Neither must a book about the war deal entirely with soldiers at the front. For every day spent at the front, some three or four days were spent behind the lines. For every man at the front, some seven or eight men were occupied in other sorts of positions at the rear. To tell of the one man at the front, is to tell only one eighth of the story of War.

A book about the war may not, perhaps, be written by a man. A man who goes to war, unless he be a member of the high command, sees only one small corner of the army. He sees the Infantry, or the Artillery, or the Air Service, or the Medical Corps, —but he sees little of the whole, great welter of human activity and inactivity which is an expeditionary force. Furthermore, men, during a war fought in a foreign country, are under a constant moral and emotional strain. So great is that strain that they can, perhaps, neither see clearly and impartially events that occur while they are there, nor can they remember them clearly after they return home. Emotion blurs the picture. Emotion sets up complexes which interfere with the intellectual analysis and recollection of events. And it is only when one looks back with a certain intellectual clarity, free from the blurring of emotional enhancement, that one can see through the heterogeneous, chaotic stream of separate events of War towards the Truth.

To be of value to the world, a book which deals with War should be built up of Truth. As long as romances are fabricated about War, it will remain a noble, worthy, beautiful adventure for Youth. As long as War is made romantic, it will go on.

To the bellicose of 1915, Peace was just a fit theme for "molly-coddles." To practical persons after the war, Peace seemed the fundamental objective of all intelligent citizens.

According to the preconception of the judges, "misguided" or "inspired" women undertook during the second year of the struggle among the nations to bring the war to an end. They met at The Hague under the presidency of Jane Addams of the

United States, who was accompanied to the assembly of women by 46 other delegates from her own country, including the distinguished Dr. Alice Hamilton and Professor Emily Balch. Sweden sent twelve delegates, Norway twelve, the Netherlands had one thousand, Italy one, Germany twenty-eight, Denmark six, Canada two, Belgium five, Austria six, and Great Britain three. One hundred and eighty representatives were on their way from England when the closure of the North Sea for military purposes halted them.

The principles laid down by this international congress were forerunners of the Fourteen Points made famous by Woodrow Wilson and the resolutions which it passed also called for a Society of Nations to handle issues on a basis of reason. But there was added a demand for woman suffrage in order that the path to the future might be shaped by all the people.

After this congress had convened, its envoys bore to all the nations at war and to neutrals its conclusions. Thus, like every other head of a nation, President Wilson in 1915 received a copy of these early proposals for international coöperation.

In a volume called WOMEN AT THE HAGUE,[4] written soon after their meeting, Emily Balch presents the motives and purposes of this international assembly.

There is a widespread feeling that this is not the moment to talk of a European peace. On the contrary, if we look into the matter more deeply, there are good reasons to believe that the psychological moment is very close upon us. If, in the wisdom that comes after the event, we see that the United States was dilatory when it might have helped to open the way to end bloodshed and to make a fair and lasting settlement, we shall have cause for deep self-reproach.

The question of peace is a question of terms. Every country desires peace at the earliest possible moment, if peace can be had on what it regards as satisfactory terms. Peace is possible whenever the moment comes when each side would accept what the

---

[4] Reprint obtained through the courtesy of The Macmillan Company.

other side would grant, but from the international or human point of view a satisfactory peace is possible only when these claims and concessions are such as to forward, not to hinder, human progress. If Germany's terms are the annexation of Belgium and part of France and a military hegemony over the rest of Europe, or if the terms of France or England include "wiping Germany off the map of Europe," then there is no possibility of peace at this time or at any time that can be foreseen, nor does the world desire peace on these terms.

In each country there are those that want to continue the fight until military supremacy is achieved, in each there are powerful forces that seek a settlement of the opposite type, one which instead of containing within itself the threats to international stability that are involved in annexation, humiliation of the enemy, and competition between armaments, shall secure national independence and respect for rights of minorities, and foster international coöperation.

In one sense the present war is a war between the two great sets of belligerent powers, in another and more significant sense, it is a struggle between two conceptions of national policy. The catchwords, "imperialism" and "democracy," indicate briefly the two opposing ideas. In every country both are represented, though in varying proportions, and in every country there is a strife between them.

The overriding of the regular civil government by the military authorities in all the warring countries is one of the too little understood effects of the war. The forms of constitutionalism may be undisturbed but as *inter arma silent leges* so military power tends to control the representatives of the people none the less really because unobtrusively. Von Tirpitz, Kitchener, Joffre, the Grand Duke Nicholas have tended to overshadow their nominal rulers.

Another effect of war is that, as between the two contending voices, one is presented with a megaphone and the other is muffled if not gagged. Papers and platforms are open to "patriotic" utterances as patriotism is understood by the jingoes; the moderate is silenced not alone by the censor, not alone by social pressure, but by his own sense of the effect abroad of all that gives an impression of internal division and a readiness to quit the fight. In our own country during the tension with Germany loyal Americans who believe that the case of the United States is not a strong one (and a hundred million people cannot all think alike on such an issue), those who loathe the idea of going to war, cannot and will not seek any commensurate expression of their views for fear this may make it harder for our Government to induce Germany to render her naval warfare less inhuman.

Thus everywhere war gives an exaggerated influence to militaristic and jingo forces and creates a false impression of the pressure for extreme terms as a basis of settlement.

Each side, of course, would like to make peace when the struggle, which is in a rough general sense a stalemate, is marked by some incident favorable to itself. Germany would like to make peace from the crest of the wave of her invasion of Russia; Russia and England from a conquered Constantinople. If the disinterested neutrals, who alone are free to act for peace, wait for the moment when neither side has any advantage, they will wait long indeed. The minor ups and downs of the war are shifting and unpredictable, but their importance is much less than it appears. The gains that either makes are as nothing to its losses. The grim unquestioned permanent fact, which affects both sides and which is to the changing fortunes of battle as the miles of immovable ocean depths are to the waves on its surface, —this all-outweighing fact is the intolerable burden of continued war.

This fact is that which makes a momentary advantage comparatively unimportant. All the belligerents want peace; though they none of them want it enough to cry "I surrender," they all want it enough to be ready to treat.

This making of peace involves not only the questions of the character of the terms, of demands more or less extreme—it also involves the question of the principle according to which settlements are to be made. Here too there are two conflicting conceptions.

On the one hand there is the assumption that military advantage must be represented *quid pro quo* in the terms,—so much victory, so much corresponding advantage in the terms. There is even the commercial conception of war as an investment and the idea that the fighter has a right to indemnity for what he has spent.

On the other hand, starting from the fact that the war has thrown certain international adjustments into the melting pot, the problem is to create a new adjustment such as on the whole shall be as generally satisfactory and contain as much promise of stability as possible.

The gains won by force have no claims that any one is bound to respect. The expenditure of blood and treasure is no basis for a demand for reimbursement, no one has contracted to render any return for it, and it is to the general interest that such expenditure, undertaken on speculation, should never prove a good investment. Admitting these things, yet since the arbitrament of war is an arbitrament of force, this fact is bound to tell in the resulting adjustment. But a fact that it is important to understand is that with a given balance of relative strength as between the two sides, an equilibrium may be reached in more than one way, as there are equations which admit of more than one solution. The equilibrium of peace might be secured by balancing unjust acquisition or by balancing magnanimous concession against magnanimous concession.

A mediator or mediating group, without throwing any weight into the scale of one or the other side, can help to find the equilibrium on the higher rather than the lower level. We find a parallel in the economic sphere when there is a choice between a balance based on low wages and low efficiency and one based on high wages and high efficiency and when the state, not interfering with the economic balance, yet helps to secure that balance by the socially desirable method.

On the basis of military advantage or on the basis of military costs the neutrals have no claim to be heard in the settlement.

The soldier is genuinely aggrieved and outraged that they should mix in the matter at all. Yet, even on the plane of fighting power, unexhausted neutrals are capable of throwing a sword into the scale and on the plea of costs suffered they have good claim to a voice. It is however as representatives of civilization and the true interests of all sides alike that those who have not been in the thick of the conflict can and should be of use in the settlement and help to fix it on the higher plane.

The settlement of a war by outsiders—not their mere friendly coöperation in finding acceptable terms—is something that has often occurred, exhibiting that curious mixture of the crassest brute force with the most ambitious idealism which frequently characterizes the conduct of international dealings. The fruits of victory were refused to Russia by the Congress of Berlin in 1878, Europe recently denied to Japan the spoils of her war with China, the results of the Balkan wars were largely determined by those who had done none of the fighting. While mere physical might played a large part in such interferences from the outside, there is something besides hypocrisy in the claim of the statesmen of countries, which had taken no part in a war, to speak on behalf of freedom, progress, and peace.

A peace involving annexation of unwilling peoples could never be a lasting one. The widespread sense of irritation at all talk of peace at present seems to be due to a feeling that a settlement now would be a settlement which would leave Belgium, if not part of France, in German hands. Such a settlement would be as disastrous to Germany as to any nation. It might put an end to military operations, but it certainly would not bring peace, if we give any moral content to that much-abused word. Europe was not at peace before August, 1914, nor Poland for long before, nor Ireland, nor Alsace, nor Finland. Any community which, if it could, would fight to change its political status may be quiet under coercion, but it is not at peace. Neither would Europe be at peace with Germany in Belgium.

The question is, then, what sort of peace may we hope for now—on what terms, on what principles?

We may be sure that each side is ready to concede more and to demand less than appears on the surface or than it is ready to advertise. The summer campaign, in which marked advantages are most likely, once over, the belligerents are faced with a winter in the trenches which will cost on all sides, in money and in suffering, out of all proportion to the gains that can be hoped for. It must be remembered, too, that the advantages hitherto won are not all on one side, but that each side has something to concede. The British annexations of Egypt and Cyprus may be formal rather than substantial changes, but the conquest of Germany's colonies, large and small—Southwest Africa, Togo Land, Samoa, Neu-Pommern, Kaiser Wilhelm's Land, the Solomon, Caroline, and Marshall Islands, to say nothing of Kiao-Chao—and probably Russian gains at the expense of Turkey in the East, give bargaining power to the Allies. So, even without success in the Dardanelles, does their ability to thwart or forward German enterprise in Asia Minor and Mesopotamia or possibly in purchasable parts of Africa or elsewhere. Friends of Finland and of Poland must see to it that the debatable lands of the Eastern as well as of the Western front are kept in mind. From the point of view of Poland the main thing to be desired is the union of the three dismembered parts—Russian, German, and Austrian Poland—and their fusion in some sort of a buffer state, independent or at least essentially autonomous. Something like this appears to be the purpose of both Germany and Russia, with the difference that this Polish state would be in the one case under Teutonic, in the other under Russian auspices. No one knows, as between the two, which would be the choice of the majority of the Poles concerned. Concessions to Germany, in Finland and in Poland, especially if coupled with adequate security from nationalistic oppression, might prove to be in the ultimate interest of European peace, and would render it easier for Germany to make the concession on her side of complete withdrawal in the West. Very important too are the concessions in regard to naval control of the seas that Great Britain ought to be willing to make if the safety of her commerce and her intercolonial communications could be secured otherwise, and this would seem to be the natural counterpart of substantial steps toward disarmament on land.

But all this is speculation. The fact, obvious to those who look below the surface, is that every belligerent power is carrying on a war deadly to itself, that bankruptcy looms ahead, that industrial revolt threatens, not at the moment but in a none too distant future, that racial stocks are being irreparably depleted. The prestige of Europe, of the Christian Church, of the white race, is lowered inch by inch with the progress of the struggle which is continually closer to the *débâcle* of a civilization.

Each power would best like peace on its own terms, although our common civilization would suffer by the imposition of extreme terms by any power. Each power would be thankful indeed to secure an early peace without humiliation on terms a long way short of its extreme demands. There is every reason to believe that a vigorous initiative by representatives of the neutral powers of the world could at this moment begin a move toward negotiations, and lead the way to a settlement which, please God, shall be a step toward a nobler and more intelligent civilization than we have yet enjoyed.

The armistice was announced on November 11, 1918. Immediately the ultimate purposes of the war came into clearer review, and among the citizens who insisted on knowing what had been gained and whither the victors and vanquished were heading was Harriot Stanton Blatch, habituated to thinking in social terms.

In A WOMAN'S POINT OF VIEW; SOME ROADS TO PEACE,[5] Mrs. Blatch reports on a visit to Europe made with the idea of observing the outcome of a "war to end war," and a "war for democracy."

[5] Reprint obtained through courtesy of the author and The Womans Press.

Late in the armistice The Womans Press asked me to write a book on the constructive outcome of the Great War. The enterprise seemed to me to promise only success. During four years the idealists had been waging war to end war, and had had visions of a new world rising from the wreckage of the old. Humanity was promised a rebirth when peace should again spread over the earth its sheltering wings.

When I sailed to Europe to gather material for the book, I was full of confidence that I should find the roots if not the leafage of strong growths of sound constructive policies. The lessons of the war, we had been led to expect, had been taken to heart and had borne fruit. As a reflex of war needs we supposed there would have developed in civil life greater attention to sanitation, greater generosity towards education, greater hospitality towards all efforts for the salvage of the race, and above all, a larger spirit of justice and fellowship. In short, I had been bitten with the propaganda of the war idealists, and went forth an optimist on a voyage of discovery. I was not a foolish optimist, expecting to see no sorrows and hardships, but amid the ruin I felt certain had been planted promises of future good.

My book is finished. . . . Circumstance honestly faced has changed a book, which was to have shown constructive results of the Great War, into a contribution of a volume to the library against all war. . . . Women shook my optimism, and experience forced me to disbelieve in the possibility of good coming from conflict. . . .

The constructive contribution of the Great War in the eyes of a woman [the report itself says] must be the lesson of war's futility. The greatest argument against war is the Europe of to-day, in disrepair if not devastated, with progress arrested if not destroyed, staggering under taxation if not bankrupt, underfed if not starved, morally broken if not in lawless barbarism.

The new world that was to spring from the inspiring ideals for which humanity was supposed to have waged the Great War is forgotten. Europe, with eyes of infinite sadness, negates the expectation. War-spent Europe is war-spent in heart and mind.

She is not thinking new thoughts, nor forwarding old ones with driving energy. If many of the seeds of reform planted before the war are not left unwatered to die, that is the most weary humanity can hope for.

Nothing does Europe need more than a fresh and vigorous new population, but her children are still meeting undernourishment. Here would seem to be appeal as by a trumpet blast to national self-interest. If the nation is to hold its own then the young generation must have vigor. Europe is intellectually aware of the situation, but it is emotionally stunned and responds to stimuli in but a dull way. Now new and startling reform is demanded; the salvaging of child life by clinic and milk station, by school meal and district nurse, was in a measure achieved before the year 1914. Wholesale devotion of wealth to destruction through years has but curtailed such endeavors, and peace has not broken the bonds of unwise economy. War bent men to its purposes; now men will bend peace to their desires. Self-indulgence takes the place of discipline. The Zeppelin, says London, hangs above us no longer; let us light our lamps, and be merry. In the restaurants wine is seen at every table (1920) and men quaff champagne as they inveigh against a higher school rate. Instead of giving all children the needed portion of milk during the morning school hours, the local wiseacres in England, for instance, examine and question and consider whether this child has fallen low enough to get the portion allowed free, and whether that one may not hold out a little longer without aid. Meantime, women revel in extravagant dress as never before, tilt themselves on high heels, and men, in their parliaments, vote huge sums for the upkeep of warships.

The centers for community care of mother and baby and the trained health visitor still exist, but they are not one whit less grudgingly supported than in pre-war days. It is common knowledge that the children are nervously spent, it is common knowledge that each population needs new foundations laid, but effort tends to volubility rather than achievement. War has trained the world to a lurid and somewhat unscrupulous use of propaganda.

Even government reports seem to hide facts from all but the most careful reader. In discussing health visitors one public document tells the inquirer that half the County Councils of England and Wales appoint only whole-time health visitors, but by comparing table with table it is ascertained that only 430 of these officers are employed and of these 355 are giving part-time service. Talk makes the people think the weighing of the baby, the confinement allowance to the mother, are general and adequate, while the fact is that all such work, ceasing to grow during the years of ravage, is most limited and is supported in miserly fashion. In speaking of that very interesting venture, the open-air and camp school started some years ago in the crowded district of Deptford, one of its backers said: "The year 1914 was a dark one for all social workers. Gifts and subscriptions dried up suddenly." Needed economy compelled curtailment of this work.

War is a destroyer worse than pestilence. It not only kills the human being by wound and disease, but it seizes the well and strong, and putting half of them at direct destruction, shuts the other half in workshop and factory to fashion the implements used by the destroyers. Having built nothing useful, having repaired nothing since 1914, the world finds itself short of shelter and food and clothes. In the towns the visitor notes the unpainted doors and window frames, the unpointed brickwork, the broken panes of glass held in place by patches of paper. In the country one remarks the dilapidation of cottage and villa, the untrimmed hedge, the untilled field. Europe talks of schemes of rehabilitation. The housing plans are drawn on generous lines, but poverty stretches out a detaining hand. It is not unsuggestive that the British schemes laid before parliament do not try to dislodge prejudices. Everyone knows, having suffered from the condition, that cold is one of the most depleting of ills for the human creature, everyone knows that the world is short of coal, and yet coal-saving methods of heating are ignored in the new building proposals. I visited exhibitions of plans for housing, and centers where "model dwellings" had been put up, but found no practical attempt to solve the problem of central heating. The extravagances of the old generation are not to be supplanted by wise economies in the new. Human nature has not the courage to venture out of old grooves. It is easy to think and to act in the same old way. The new world of promise threatens to be the old world in fulfilment.

Whole populations have learned the appalling lesson that toil may end in poverty. Barbarism gives that lesson; slavery gives it with dire reactions on the individual. Learned tomes have developed the thesis that the worst side of slavery is that it trains humanity to irresponsibility, laziness, lack of initiative. Well, peoples put forth intense and prolonged effort from 1914 to 1919 only to find themselves in the end with food, clothes, shelter at a premium and taxes resting as a heavy yoke upon their necks. Labor ends in destitution; that is what war has proclaimed to Europe's populations. Work has not meant accumulation, has not meant riches to spend in leisure and joy. Toil more exacting than human beings have ever had, toil more continuous than humanity has ever submitted to, ends not in promise and beauty but in bitter realities and ugliness. And to the workers, raw under the disillusionment, statesmen say: "Work harder, faster than ever before, or our commerce will die, our civilization be lost. Work."

The reaction is the same in France, in Germany, in Great Britain, the same everywhere; the fruits of toil having been denied, toil itself has no attraction. Unemployment rests in determination not to work. Why work when the return is gall and bitterness? Work calls for initiative, and in war time, obedience, not initiative, is required of the mass of men. Men must not think, must not originate; they must forget and follow. The soldier demobilized does not lay off his military training with his uniform. He was trained to be willing to risk his life to perform a difficult and horrible task, to efface his will, to submit himself to discipline. The task accomplished, he is expected by thoughtless leaders to take up his civil work with the old-time push and enthusiasm. A vain hope. He is a different man. Snap has turned to mere touchiness. His finger finds the trigger quickly. He was trained to kill, trained to defend the flag. He argues that an offense to him is an offense to his country. In short, he is lawless as well as slothful.

And those who worked at white heat to supply the army with gun and shell are not unlike the soldier. They worked under abnormal pressure. Patriotism lashed their muscles, they obeyed, they abandoned trade-union agreements, and made heavy sacrifice to fight for a new world. Their effort ends with less to eat, less comfort and less freedom than in the sordid old world. Why work? In Germany the returned soldiers refuse employment, in Great Britain idleness is seen in all ranks, and France keeps her armies largely mobilized to prevent them from joining the discontented. Work which brings nothing but debt and disaster instills, just as certainly as slavery, its lessons of irresponsibility, of dishonesty, of lack of initiative.

But perhaps the most soul-killing reaction of war is the denial of the right to think and to express thought freely. A nation desiring to put forth its whole effort to meet its enemy with brute force cannot and will not tolerate any weak links in its armor. It fights to win and must force itself into a fury of fear, of determination, of concentration. It exaggerates its danger, for that puts drive into effort and shortens the days of the combat. It cannot argue. Argument implies doubt, and doubt confuses the issue. The nation has an enemy, it buckles on its armor for a fight, there being no international way to assuage our animosities by argument. A nation cannot parley with its foe, and it will not parley with its friends. The nation becomes a car of Juggernaut to crush free speech. The nation is centering on one idea, war. War precludes peace. Peace develops liberty, freedom, the right to think; war destroys the habits. Through fear of contempt, ostracism, police surveillance, imprisonment, persons take on what is called in industry, "repetitive processes"; they repeat phrases, imitate jingles of words. They cease to think; they prattle. War cannot tolerate freedom of opinion. A people at war must act as a unit, think as a unit. The minds of men are forced into a groove; they invent, they sing, they argue, they

philosophize to the one end,—war. To die in war is not so great
a tragedy as to live for it. War sears the heart and mind of
the world.

In one of the branches of the Thompson-Houston engineering
works in Paris, I visited the division set apart for employees who
had lost their sight at the front. Over the department was an
officer who had been formerly one of the leading engineers of
the company. He came each day to advise about the work of his
brothers in darkness. He had lost his sight at the very end of the
war, was still under treatment, and was attended by a nurse.
The employees were all among the most skilled, in happier days.
They worked now at simple processes, and the head engineer
had suggested checks and guards making the work safe and
possible. They did not speak at their work. It seemed as if
they scarcely breathed. Nearly all sat with head thrown back,
looking up towards heaven. But pray as they might, their future was unalterable. Perhaps it was that thought which led
my guide, who had himself served throughout the war, but had
escaped unscathed, to say with an emphasis I had not heard before and did not hear again from any man: "We must find a way
out. The nations must unite to save men in the future from
all this."

Not a man who had seen the actualities of the battle front—
not even among the American soldiers whose experience had
been so short—not a man did I meet but declared he would himself never go to war again. Many talked wildly of what they
would do to escape, if another call came in their time. They
would change their names and hide, they would do this or that,
and if driven to the wall and forced to make choice they would
choose suicide. And yet to the suggestion that war might be
ended, that nations could find another way to settle difficulties,
came the invariable response from the young and virile, "Oh, no,
the world can't escape war." The worst heritage of war is its grip
on the male mind of its inevitability, a grip that will never be
loosened until the diametrically opposed conviction of the mothers
of the race has full and free outlet. . . .

Admirable and highly necessary as the leading paternal characteristics may be for the evolution of any species, a simple and direct instinct of protecting the young is feeble if not lacking. This is painfully illustrated in the Covenant of the League of Nations. In Articles XVI and XVII the "severance of all trade or financial relations" is to be the weapon to enforce peace. A conference solidly male substitutes the economic blockade for military action, instituting in that way the most deadly attack upon children. The adult male of the future proposes to fight with an instrument which hits the child first, last and always.

CHAPTER XIV

TAKING NEW BEARINGS

In the smooth era of "prosperity" for the United States, which followed the World War, generally accepted thinking took on the nature of the automatic machine. In the Coolidge formulation of policy, adopted as sound by President Hoover at the beginning of his administration, lay the pleasing assumption that the economic system would operate flawlessly, shedding its golden blessings in every direction—provided nothing were done by the government to interfere with its divinely appointed mission, save possibly in minor details. If any slight modification of the almost perfect order should be made, sentiment was not to rock the boat. At every point the "scientific method" was to be brought into play to direct change. President Hoover himself devised the engineering recipe: get the facts in the case, draw only the conclusions which they authorize, and then proceed cautiously and in harmony with those findings—a recipe which exactly fitted the trend in education.

In this spirit the reputable "thinking" was done and won the popular plaudits, as long as nothing of a crucial nature was required of it; that is, until the crash of 1929 cast doubts on existing perfection and its intellectual shadow. Then, suddenly, with the force of an earthquake or tidal wave, suspicion of imperfections arose in all quarters and engines of skepticism and criticism were wheeled into position.

Having worked their way into every department of the political and social structure and having a long tradition of feminine criticism as encouragement, women shared in the tempest of discussion which blew at the close of "the perfect day." Accustomed to the exercise of insight rather than to refurbishing the refinements of logic, they broke into the press with their reflections on the supposed excellence of scientific fact-finding as the sole way to social understanding, on the position and responsibility of women in the technological order, on the assumption of basic superiority in American provisions for the masses, on the utility of the "political game" as played according to historic rules, and on projects for planning a better society.

What happened to the tons of material relative to economic and social facts so diligently collected by researchers? This question was asked by Lillian Symes in the February issue of "Harper's Magazine," in the year 1932, and answered in the thesis that we were enjoying THE GREAT FACT-FINDING FARCE.[1]

He was the principal of a little grammar school in one of the bituminous coal districts—the school attended by children from the various company "patches" within a radius of five miles—and he had, by begging, borrowing, and threatening, kept the children alive with bean-soup lunches all during the terrible winter months just past. He knew more about "conditions," I was told, than any other man in that part of the country. He looked very tired and, unlike the mine officials, he did not ask for my credentials.

"Another investigation? That makes the third in the last two months. First the State Labor crowd, then some welfare group, now Washington. Oh, I know. You want to get the facts and you can't take one another's word for them. Lady, we've been surveyed to death down here. What we need is a little action. I've been here since 1916—through most of the investigations.

---

[1] Reprint obtained through the courtesy of the author and *Harper's Magazine.*

You've seen the U. S. Coal Commission report? Eleven months' work with a whole army of experts and two years to get the results published. Well, they said all there was to say about coal in 1925. The things that were wrong then are worse now, just as they knew they'd be. More men out of work, more kids starving. Too bad we can't feed them reports."

His tired smile took the edge from his words, but I should not have blamed him if he had thrown an inkwell at my head.

That was last spring. Recently I heard that the State Administration had been so moved by the various reports on the coal fields that it has ordered—another investigation.

"Ye shall know the truth and the truth shall make you free."

Like the words Liberty, Equality, and Justice that fall so quaintly upon our post-war ears, the term Truth has lost much of its significance to our pragmatic modern minds. Truth is, in the light of our experience, a jade who may be all things to all men—or like God in the late World War, an ally to every combatant. Nevertheless, the Biblical injunction has that quality of terse finality combined with noble sentiment of which our great slogans are made, and in adopting it as our own we have translated it into a form more in keeping with the national temperament—"Ye shall know the facts and the facts shall be sufficient."

Since we became "sold" on what we believe to be the scientific method, the accumulation of facts as a substitute, rather than as a basis, for collective action has become a national gospel. To it we have transferred that faith which once reposed in Heaven, the Constitution, and American Womanhood. The intensity of our conviction that the sum total of a sufficient number of facts is wisdom is equalled only by our reluctance to do anything about the facts once they are found. In a period in which it has become possible to acquire high academic honors by the patient collection of data on matters of interest to no one—including the acquirer—the practice of fact-finding in our social, political, and industrial life is rapidly assuming the aspects of a pure science, undefiled by vulgar, practical application to the common weal. As a result, our public, like our academic life, is suffering not so much from lack of vital information as from a psychic autointoxication induced by masses of unassimilated data with which we have neither the wisdom nor the courage to deal.

If anyone doubts this let him cast an eye at the history of the official fact-finding expeditions of our national, state, and municipal departments, bureaus or special commissions, and at the unofficial activities for the past twenty years of the thousand and one foundations, welfare councils, federations, associations, leagues, societies, boards, unions, and what not, constantly engaged in surveying our situations. Let him consider the public and private archives fairly bursting with valuable but dust-gathering data which, had they been studied, coördinated, pursued to their logical conclusions and applied to the problems on hand would have enabled us to meet our present situation with some degree of preparedness and wisdom, and might even have obviated its more serious complications—a subject to which I shall return later.

It would be unfair, of course, to insist that all this well-meaning activity has been so much wasted effort. In those fields where it has not run afoul of any of the passionate prejudices and entrenched privileges by which we operate, the process can boast of certain successes. In the realm of organized philanthropy and the social services, for example, sentimentality and hit-or-miss aid have given way very largely to scientific administration which is based upon careful surveys and which goes about its business in an effective and economical fashion. The obnoxious Lady Bountiful is disappearing, and it becomes increasingly difficult for the undeserving poor to put anything over on the fact-fortified case worker who considers "pauperization" a worse scourge than hunger; all of which may be hard on the undeserving poor but no doubt redounds to the benefit of the deserving "underprivileged."

There are other fields of successful operation in which the application of scientific principles involves no fundamental change in social outlook, personal prejudices, or private interests. In a volume published last year by the Russell Sage Foundation—one

of our most effective and best endowed fact-finders—is presented
a classified list of two thousand seven hundred important social
studies and surveys made up to 1928. Unpublished reports are not
listed and their name is legion. The bibliography covers a range
of subjects, from sight conservation to regional planning, from
deportations to unemployment. To trace the ultimate outcome
of each study would be in the nature of a life-work, and to question the value of much of the information obtained would be
foolish. But we need only to look about us in the year 1931 to
realize that, however rich may have been the fruits of research in
such fields as sight conservation, mental deficiency, child marriages, and regional planning, current practice in such vital but
controversial matters as deportation, trade fluctuations, unemployment insurance, and industrial planning shows an almost total
unawareness of either past experience or accumulated data. For
on subjects such as these we are satisfied to juggle a few statistics
and then revert to those emotional biases of which psychiatry
can tell us more than sociology. To the office-holder a realization
of this fact is the beginning of political wisdom. As a result, the
fact-finding investigation is becoming increasingly popular as a
safety valve for public indignation, a short circuit for possibly
dangerous discontent. By the time the pros and cons are accumulated, the conferences held, the reports carefully edited, and then
—a year or two later—finally published in a form that no one but
a professional statistician can possibly understand, the public will
be gnawing at a new bone of contention.

The practice of fact-finding had a legitimate and respect-worthy
origin in a period in which we were somewhat more naïve about
the mainsprings of human conduct. It was born of the application of the scientific method to the realm of our social economy
and it was intended to supersede guess-work, good intentions,
prejudice, or sentimentality as a basis for political and industrial
action, intellectual leadership, social reconstruction. At a time
when the older professions were becoming unbearably crowded,
it created a new one which helped to absorb that surplus of
earnest young A.B.'s, M.A.'s, and even Ph.D.'s spawned each

year by our institutions of learning. The questionnaire and the case card supersede the muck rake of less scientific and more colorful days; and an army of research workers, trailing degrees like clouds of glory—and too frequently in terror of drawing an unqualified conclusion—were turned loose upon a lethargic world to gather mountains of unrelated data from which we hoped political and social wisdom would be distilled. The prestige of the profession was derived largely from the success of research in the physical and mathematical sciences, it being assumed that a method of procedure which could disclose a bend in space, enable us to fling music across the ether, develop antitoxins and Drinker respirators and spin silk out of cellulose could also find the solution to poverty, unemployment, juvenile delinquency, and the liquor problem. Supplemented by sincere purpose and sufficient cerebration, it undoubtedly could. As one who has been at various times professionally engaged in the fact-finding industry, I have no desire to quarrel with that premise. I am concerned here with its application in a world of big and little vested interests—intellectual, political, financial.

It has been argued that the results of privately endowed fact-finding on important matters involving conflicting interests must be discounted even as a supplementary basis for public action because they can never be wholly disinterested. It is true, of course, that aside from the mere collection of statistical data divorced from any interpretation (and statistical data divorced from interpretation are necessarily sterile), private research may not be relied upon to publicize facts subversive of its original purpose. One does not expect the National Industrial Conference Board, with its imposing array of experts, to discover that the factory workers of New York State are grossly underpaid, the National Child Labor Committee to conclude that child labor develops sterling citizens, the Labor Research Bureau to assure us that Henry Ford's employees are over-indulged, or the Committee on Social and Religious Surveys to announce that the church has failed of its Christian duty in the Southern textile districts. Social science, unlike mathematics and chemistry, is neither a pure nor an exact science, as anyone who has listened to the testimony of experts on debatable subjects can testify. It is possible to find some facts to sustain almost anything. Nearly all organizations have a point of view to sustain, and when that point of view is involved in an investigation, the paid investigator, even with the utmost sincerity of purpose, can usually find the facts that will sustain it. If he does not, the fate of his report is doubtful. His findings will either be so emasculated—otherwise known as "edited"—as to render them fairly innocuous, publication will be postponed until the facts gathered have become irrelevant, or complete suppression will be rationalized—in all honesty perhaps —on the grounds of untimeliness, insufficient evidence, inefficiency or prejudice on the part of the investigator, etc.

For example, the conclusions of a preliminary survey into the desirability of free lunches for school children in a Middle-western city were disregarded because they seemed too "socialistic" in tendency. The report of an honest investigation by a well-known research economist for a privately supported research group never saw the light of day because his findings did not bear out the contentions of those who subsidized the investigation that the cost of living had so declined that "real wages" had increased, and that, therefore, a wage cut was in order. Recommendations made by paid and impartial investigators for organized relief work in a group of starving industrial communities were disregarded because of the presence of a few Communists in those communities. Few experienced fact-finders have been without one or more such experiences; and while professional ethics and a desire for continued employment usually forbid them to air their grievances in public, when two or three are gathered together in friendly safety their indignation can become profanely vocal.

The situation of many professional investigators was ably described by Professor John R. Commons of the University of Wisconsin in an address of a year ago, in which he said: "The economic investigator is usually permitted to investigate no more than a small part of the whole institution. He is controlled by somebody higher up. He is not like the physical scientist who hurts only the theologians. He hurts or helps politicians or business or labor or agriculture. Hence the insistence that his investigations must be colorless. He is forbidden to investigate purposes or policies, and even some practices. These indeed give life and color, but they are invidious, secretive, and they deal with living persons. It is safer to investigate them *post mortem.*"

All of this, however, by no means invalidates all those mountains of social data, the finding of which has been paid for by persons with a large stake in the *status quo.* There are many troublesome fields in which investigation does not endanger the *status quo,* or at least that section of it upon which the large donor depends. A public-spirited millionaire whose fortune derives from electric power may contribute enthusiastically to a thoroughgoing investigation of the milk business even though he holds that such public utility inquisitors as Senator Norris are possessed of horns and a forked tail. The soundest and most courageous criticism of the Rockefeller "company union" plan (in Colorado) emanates from the excellent department of industrial studies of the Russell Sage Foundation. One would scarcely expect it to emanate from any fact-finding division of the Rockefeller Foundation. But even if one disregards all social conclusions drawn from private research as consciously or unconsciously prejudicial, there remains a valuable residue of factual information which, had we the collective wisdom to sift and sufficient non-specialized intellectual leadership to coördinate, could serve at least as a basis for that constructive thought and action so sorely needed and so conspicuously lacking in our national affairs.

If the results of private research in the social sciences are not always wholly disinterested, official and governmental fact-finding, on the other hand—representing as it does that amorphous thing called "the public interest"—is ostensibly "above the battle." In respect to the routine collection of facts by its various governmental divisions, this last is undoubtedly true, although even bare figures thus collected may be "interpreted" to fit a political formula—as witness last year's juggling of the Census

Bureau's unemployment figures. But to expect a fact-finding commission appointed by Herbert Hoover to report back in favor of a federal "dole" would be as naïve as to expect a commission appointed by Al Smith, if he were president, to find the Noble Experiment a howling success.

As I write this, a senatorial committee is investigating the subject of unemployment insurance and its possible application in America. If there is any doubt about the redundancy of these hearings, let us recall the remarks made a few months ago by Senator Hebert, who somehow got to be chairman of the Committee in place of Senator Wagner who proposed the measure. It was Senator Hebert who disclosed the state of mind of the average political fact-finder on controversial issues when he announced to reporters: "I still have an open mind and I hope to hear exhaustive testimony on this vital subject. However, I have about reached the conclusion from interviews I have had abroad that *any* system of unemployment insurance will lead to the dole." [Italics mine.] The Senator undoubtedly could have learned more about the subject if he had stayed at home and read a book—such a book, for example, as Paul Douglas' and Aaron Director's recently published study.

Because of the publicity, caustic and otherwise, bestowed upon our twenty-seven presidential commissions, particularly the Wickersham Commission, there is a popular tendency to associate the whole gospel of "pure" official research with the present administration. This is not altogether just. If during the difficult past two years the national policy has seemed to be "In the midst of a crisis, be nonchalant, make a survey," that policy is not altogether without its precedents. The practice of surveying embarrassing situations, that have already been super-surveyed at a time when they cry aloud for vigorous and decisive action, is a time-honored device for which the Romans undoubtedly had a word.

Since 1880, our Federal government has been the country's largest fact-producer and, in the words of one of its documents, "the greatest of all modern publishers." Many of the publications of its various departments contain mere routine statistics of interest only to specialists, and are the result of investigations undertaken in response to some specialized need for information, public or private. Many more are on technical subjects which have no relation to public policy and are, therefore, fairly certain of practical application. But others embody the results of exhaustive research upon situations which contribute to our present national pain and bewilderment. Upon the more recurrent of our social and economic difficulties, mountains of valuable data have already been accumulated—and forgotten. To illustrate, let me return to that outstanding example of a desperate industrial situation about which information is limitless and nothing has been done—the coal industry.

Coal is, and has been for many years, a sick industry. In periods of general depression, sick industries are points of focal infection dangerous to the whole weakened industrial structure. If the social revolution ever comes to America its first sparks, I feel sure, will be lighted, not in Union Square, New York City, but in some obscure patch in the coal counties. Even before the industry became a victim of technical progress in other fields and its own *laissez-faire* industrial policy, its history was replete with violence, bloodshed, public discomfort—and investigations. From the Report to the President on the Anthracite Coal Strike made by Carroll D. Wright in 1902 down to the latest investigation of 1931, no problem in the country has been so industriously studied in all its aspects. Reports on wages and conditions in the coal fields have been made by various bureaus of the Department of Labor in fifteen of the thirty years since 1902. In 1914 the Commission on Industrial Relations went deeply into the problem of industrial unrest in the coal fields, and in 1915 the President's Colorado Coal Commission made a special investigation of the situation in that State. In the decade between 1913 and 1923, inquiries into various aspects of the coal problem were made by nine separate Senatorial and by eight separate House committees, and from these inquiries eleven thousand printed pages or between five and six million words resulted. In 1919 a Bituminous Coal Commission was appointed by the President, to be followed in 1921 by an Anthracite Commission. In 1923 even Mayor Hylan of New York appointed a commission to investigate the bituminous coal strike, and the committee's final recommendation was nationalization of the coal mines. State commissions have contributed their quota of facts. The Russell Sage Foundation has contributed two studies of employee-owner relationships and an excellent analysis of the insecurity of the coal miners' lot that goes deeply into one of the fundamental causes of the unceasing conflict in this field.

But most exhaustive of all was the report of the U. S. Coal Commission—to which my school principal referred. The Commission was headed by John Hays Hammond, and its report, filling five fat, closely printed volumes, was obviously no revolutionary document. But the report was made by disinterested experts and while it called, of course, for still more fact-finding, it closed with a long list of definite recommendations. These recommendations, conservative as they were, have never been acted upon. The report was a monument of industrious fact-finding and was dedicated to the proposition that "guided by facts rather than rumors, by information rather than prejudice, the people will be able to exercise wisely the powers of government over this type of private business." The people, as usual, did nothing. But we should have learned enough about coal, it would seem, to have been prepared for the present débâcle in that field. To see, to-day, the final tragic fruits of our rugged individualism run riot in a great national industry in Pennsylvania, West Virginia, Kentucky, and Ohio; to see dull-eyed, weazened, half-naked children drooping at their school desks because they are too starved to be able to sit erect (industrial chaos and resultant unemployment being no "act of God") is to see the public fact-finding investigation for the farce that it is.

And what are we going to do about it? That facetious paragrapher, Mr. Howard Brubaker, recently remarked: "A conference has been called to discuss the desperate situation in the soft coal industry. We begin to feel a Hoover Commission coming on." By the time this is printed that intuition may have justified itself. At the moment the efforts of Secretaries Doak and Lamont to evoke a spirit of sweet reasonableness in the coal fields have resulted in little more than some figurative nose-thumbing on the part of the operators. It would be sardonically in keeping with past performances to meet the situation with another fact-finding commission.

Perhaps all of our great national expeditions in the pursuit of Truth have not been quite so barren of consequences as the coal investigations. I am aware of the claims made for the Iron and Steel Investigation of 1911–13. But it is impossible to measure the extent of its contribution to the eventual abolition of the twelve-hour day and the seven-day week. The existence of these conditions as late as the great steel strike and the Interchurch World investigation of 1919 indicates that something more than the facts about steel making was necessary to impress the need of reform on corporate sensibilities.

I am inclined to think that the Commission on Industrial Relations which functioned from 1912 to 1914 served a valuable purpose. It fathered no specific legislative action and produced no tangible results, but it did much to educate a generation in the cruder realities of the American scene. By the simple process of rubbing genteel noses in the muck created by thoughtless industrial policies, it undoubtedly helped to develop some of the outstanding cases of social consciousness among our great national philanthropists. It had its staff of experts to hold up the scientific end, as one of its members put it; but probably because its chairman, Frank P. Walsh, had sufficient political sophistication to realize that facts have no motivating power in politics, and that the best he could accomplish was the dramatization of "industrial relations" for the American public, each session became an absorbing social drama in which corporation heads, strikers, experts, labor leaders, social workers, and saboteurs followed one another on the witness stand. Its eleven-volume report is not yet dated. Its contribution to the literature of unemployment— the result of a study directed by Professor Commons—might still be read with profit by the members of our latest unemployment committee.

Too much discussion has already accompanied the work of the Wickersham fact-finders, and it is unnecessary to dwell at any length here upon that famous effort. The man in the street did not need a commission to tell him—after nineteen months' work at the cost of half a million dollars—that prohibition does not prohibit, that the third degree is practiced in our best police stations, and that poverty is a fertile source of crime—the last so daring a conclusion that only one member would definitely commit himself to it. On the explosive subject of prohibition the famous ambiguous report was, of course, inevitable. Even on such a non-political issue as police brutality, however, the Commission could not stand as a unit behind its trained investigators when regional sensibilities became affected. The city in which I live is one of those in which the police were accused—and quite justly —of using third degree methods. When civic indignation—not at the police but at the Commission—began to simmer, at least one member of the Commission hastened to explain that the Commission did not vouch for anything in the report. It was all the work of hired experts.

"We made no attempt to verify the information or the conclusions," said Commissioner MacIntosh of Seattle. "It isn't a Wickersham report at all."

The lengthy Stern-Pollak report on the Mooney-Billings case, an important item in the Commission's findings on legal lawlessness, would undoubtedly have been explained away in the same manner if it had not already been suppressed. Certain contributions of value, such as the Van Waters report on the treatment of children in Federal prisons, undoubtedly came out of the Commission's activities. It remains to be seen what will be done about these. The Commission, however, is inevitably associated with the prohibition question. Ignoring all conclusions or lack of them on this issue, has the opinion of a single individual undergone any revision as a result of the facts found? Will any party program be altered or any political candidate revise his attitude in the next election on the basis of the Commissioners' work? The questions are merely rhetorical. We know the answers.

To cover the whole history of official fact-finding would be to repeat, very largely, the story of the coal investigations. The job, in its entirety, awaits a Super-commission on Commissions which will deal not only with such fact-finding whales as the Wickersham body but with such minnows as the Hamilton Fish Commission on Communist Propaganda (whatever became of the "facts" it found?) and Presidential Commission No. 13, engaged at the moment in surveying our "national trends." It would need to consider the continuous fact-finding efforts of our Departments of Commerce, of the Interior, and especially of Labor, with their thousands of bulletins and special reports; for it is from these that some of our most significant social data may be gleaned—data which bear directly on our present national crisis. Had they been read and digested by an intelligent public as issued, many of our political and business slogans of the past ten years would have been laughed off the billboards and out of the headlines. Had we paid any attention to these facts when they were found many of our frantic current investigations along the self-same lines, with their enormous waste of time and money, would be unnecessary.

Could any candidate of any party, for example, have won an election on the slogan of "continued prosperity" if at any time during the past eight years we had paid the slightest attention to the discovery that the average family income in our sixteen major industries was just about one-half of what social experts have estimated as the minimum family income required for the bare necessities of life? Could anyone have talked about our "universal high-wage standard" when official investigation disclosed the fact that many unskilled laborers—such as the railway-track repairers in some of our States—were receiving the princely wage of seventeen cents an hour during the years of Coolidge prosperity? Or when our Bureau of Labor Statistics revealed an army of at least 1,800,000 unemployed at the peak of

our greatest business activity? Or could anyone, with the remotest notion of economic cause and effect and a willingness to
look facts in the face, have failed to realize that the above facts,
together with concurrent international developments, made a
period of so-called over-production and resultant depression a
practical certainty in a mass-production world in which there are
limits to even the conspicuous waste of the wealthy and in which
a man who is underpaid must necessarily underbuy? Or, if we
had acted upon any of the facts found in 1921, should we need to
be re-investigating the same subjects in 1931? How many members of Congress have read the statistical study of the causes and
extent of industrial unemployment in 1921 issued by the Department of Labor?

During and after the last depression, the Federal Children's
Bureau—the researches of which are among our most valuable
governmental activities—made a sound and exhaustive survey of
the effect of prolonged unemployment upon the health of the
nation's children. The picture was not a pretty one, and its implications were obviously tied up with our whole industrial
problem. Corrective action would have involved something more
than May Day speeches on child health over the radio. One
might think, however, that the facts found would be as eloquent
for 1931 as for 1921. But it has been necessary in the very midst
of the present crisis to gather more brand new data on this subject in order to convince State and national politicians that there
is a vital connection between lack of jobs and undernourished
youngsters—and that some ameliorative action is in order if we
are not to develop a physically and psychically stunted generation. Undoubtedly the same thing will be repeated in 1941 with
the same lack of effect.

Or, to return for a moment to the field of commissions and conferences, the Unemployment Conference called by President
Harding in 1921, presided over by Mr. Hoover, then Secretary of
Commerce, and attended by a hundred leading citizens (many of
whom are now functioning on unemployment committees), left
behind it a Sub-Committee on Unemployment and Business

Cycles to prepare a comprehensive report on this subject. The report was published in 1923 and was based in part on an admirable study made by the National Bureau of Economic Research with the coöperation of well-known experts. The Committee's report ignored many of the more fundamental remedies proposed by the Bureau's experts. It did, however, recommend definite means of industrial stabilization and large-scale public-works planning which, if acted upon, might have saved us the past two years of national muddling on this subject and might have ameliorated, at least, the present crisis. Proposals based upon this program had been recommended by the Senate Committee on Education and Labor a few days before President Hoover's inauguration. But it was only recently and after much bitter opposition—on the ground that it was now too late for large-scale public work to help the present situation—that a permanent organization to regulate such public work in accordance with business conditions was passed. That organization will probably spend the next five years re-finding the facts about business conditions.

There is every indication that, in spite of our passion for statistics and our commitment to the expertising of public affairs, we are as ready to ignore expert testimony as we are the fruits of investigation when it conflicts with private interests or political policy—a process which Professor James Harvey Rogers has described as "hiding expert findings behind a false front of political expediency." Professor Rogers used these words in connection with the dismissal of Dr. Ray O. Hall, financial expert of the Department of Commerce, but the Hall case was not unique. The increasing dismissals and indignant resignations of experts, as well as the complete indifference displayed toward recommendations made by the nation's leading economists, indicate how superficial is our belief in the scientific method of conducting our public affairs.

All of this redundancy of effort, this failure to utilize the facts so relentlessly pursued, this ignoring of expert testimony is not, of course, typical of all fields of federal investigation. The researches of our Department of Agriculture into the problems of hog cholera and wheat rust, the analysis by its Food and Drug Administration of proprietary products, the findings of the Department of Labor on the subject of phosphorus necrosis in the manufacture of fireworks—all may be relied upon, as a rule, to be translated into action and to achieve their purposes. But the uncovering of an odorous social situation that grows out of an untenable national policy, the discovery that selfish and unenlightened industrial management can involve us all in insecurity and misery, and that children in several States have been *literally* starving while other children a few miles away have been fed because their fathers were drought-stricken farmers instead of unemployed miners—all these merely serve to illustrate the growing conviction among research workers that in the social sciences, at least, facts, like virtue, are their own reward.

The practice of fact-finding as pure research is not confined to national politics. Harried New York State legislatures have used the method to dodge responsibility on more than one important issue. In other States departmental investigators have served somewhat similar purposes. The Federal Children's Bureau once made a study of child labor in a certain industrial community and revealed the fact, known to everyone in the community, that child labor was rampant. But the local industrialists sputtered with righteous indignation, and a State department made another investigation. It found no child labor.

Does political expediency deserve to bear all the blame for the obvious sterility of the great bulk of social research? I doubt it. Our social practice is rooted in the sacredness of private enterprise, and even when there is an individual official willingness to do something, this tradition acts as a brake upon public correction or the application of scientific principles. An apathetic and gullible public must be held responsible, for, on the rare occasions when public apathy has given way to rage, things have happened. Most of us can remember a minor example of what fact-finding, backed up by an aroused public conscience, can accomplish. Its results may be found in that bulk of factory legislation which, even with inadequate enforcement, makes the State of New York one of the most enlightened commonwealths in the world in this field. But it took the ghastly tragedy of the Triangle Shirtwaist Factory fire to arouse the public to a pitch of indignation that resulted in the appointment of the historic Factory Investigating Commission and the enactment of these reforms.

Part of the blame for public apathy, however, lies with the fact-finding profession itself, with its distrust of popular sentiment and the publicity that can create it; its tendency to address itself exclusively to its own narrow, professional audience, to develop the same sort of professional jargon and to surround itself with the same sort of mystical hocus-pocus that already characterize the legal and medical professions. The fact-finder has become too acutely aware of his professional standing and too little aware of his public responsibility. He is developing a standard of purely "professional" ethics which forbids the disclosure of socially important information which conflicts with private or political purposes. He is not always to blame for this. In times such as these, he must look to his job with as jealous an eye as any bookkeeper, reporter, or automobile mechanic. But even if he is under no economic pressure, the fetich of objectivity which seizes upon the fact-finder when he sits down to write his report usually robs 't of four-fifths of its value.

This is no plea for "colorful" reporting. But I feel sure that if a small fraction of the passion and actual mental suffering I have seen manifested by investigators when confronted by some intolerable and heartbreaking condition "in the field" could be translated into simple, direct English and substituted for one or two of the repetitious tables in the average professional report, the results of such efforts would be more commensurate with the time and labor involved. I am inclined to think that all fact-finders should be recruited from the ranks of experienced journalists with noses for the relevant and a knowledge of how to state it, or from the ranks of such poets as Miss Clinch Calkins, whose *Some Folks Won't Work* told more truths about unemployment than all the Department of Labor reports rolled into one.

Recently I heard a well-known research worker who is also an appointive official express the opinion that even the most sterile and purely political of our fact-finding activities have their social value because the process of large-scale investigation necessarily focuses public attention upon the problem investigated. In other words, that a commission's activities have immense publicity, in an age when a cause without publicity value is as unfortunate as a woman without sex appeal.

This last analogy is undoubtedly true, but I question the conclusion he rests upon it. To focus public attention upon a certain problem and then mislead it is as reprehensible as letting public attention slumber on in the midst of danger. To create an impression of having done something about a disease-breeding situation, when actually nothing but a few statistical tables have been formulated, may lend a profound and scientific aura to political programs that are actually bankrupt and futile, but it will do nothing to prevent social and economic contagion. It may create a false and dangerous sense of safety, but it will not stave off a final day of reckoning.

That that day of reckoning, a day when we shall need to think seriously and act quickly, is rapidly approaching, no one can doubt who reads the international signs of the times. As I write this, Los Angeles is conducting its Community Chest campaign on the slogan, "Communism, the Dole, or Personal Sacrifice?" While other communities may choose to be less melodramatic than the Screen Capital in such matters, it is obvious that we consider it expedient just now that the public should be a little alarmed. Perhaps one more boom and another decade of purely academic "investigation" will restore our confidence in the workability of the *status quo;* but unless the next crash is to be the final one, we had better start to do something with the facts we have found about this one.

We know enough now about the starvation- and violence-breeding anarchy of the coal fields, the futility of *laissez-faire* competition in the oil business, the possibly permanent break-down of the cotton market, the inability of our present industrial organization to guarantee steady employment or prevent depressions, and the need of some sort of insurance to meet this situation. We know now that prohibition does not prohibit, that politicians are afraid to admit this, and that we are financing the criminal world by its personal nullification. We know now that we want peace, that no other nation can afford to attack us, but that our combined military and naval costs are the highest in the world. We know, in short, that whatever else may ail us, we are not suffering for lack of information.

How much more must we know before we can act?

To Eunice Fuller Barnard, woman as consumer was one key to developments. Symbolism had always reflected economy. So she transformed "Mother Earth" and "Liberty Enlightening the World" into THE GODDESS OF OUR ECONOMIC MACHINE.[2] *Her observations appeared in the "New York Times Sunday Magazine" on June 12, 1932.*

Matriarchy, our more sensitive—or timid—literati have recently been telling us, is just around the corner in America. And for the first time in a century, when that recurrent threat has been made, the Main Streeter has failed to respond absently, "Oh, yeah?" It is an odd paradox. Here we are with an excess of 1,499,115 males in what is still probably the most prosperous nation in the world, virile with self-confessed, rugged individualism, and obviously run both politically and industrially by men. Yet somehow of all countries we are singled out for suspicion, until now we are half fearful ourselves of petticoat government.

To the European indeed our subjugation has long been axiomatic. To him quite casually America is the land where woman

[2] Reprint obtained through the courtesy of the author and the *New York Times Sunday Magazine.*

permanently retains much the same relative importance compared to man as does the bride to the bridegroom at the conventional wedding ceremony. Indeed, of all the stock characters with which European tradition has peopled the American scene none probably has been more assiduously cherished than the dominant American woman. Almost indistinguishable from the Goddess of Liberty, she still stands in the European imagination a pampered, pedestaled figure, over-topping the Indian, the gangster and the wild Westerner—a kind of Amazonian colossus.

Every lineament of hers, every gesture has become almost as standardized in his tradition as those of Punch and Judy, though her habits are admitted to change slightly from decade to decade. Before the war it was the custom to depict her dragging a more or less protesting husband through the art galleries, the opera houses and the dressmaking establishments of Europe. One has only to glance at C. D. Gibson's early drawings of the "Education of Mr. Pipp" to grasp the symbol of a whole American era, borrowed from the European interpretation. Today she is perhaps more often shown sampling life on her own in the cafés of Montmartre—without her trailer. But the idea is the same. She is out disposing, after her own fashion, of the dollars piled up by her more or less careworn provider.

At home woman is presumably always in the parlor eating bread and honey with the visiting foreign lecturer while her spouse is in the counting house counting out the money to pay him. Concert and matinée goer and more and more serious patron of the arts and sciences on the instalment plan of the lecture and the one-man show, she is supposedly the maintainer of a pseudo culture in which her silent partner has little interest or share. This is the picture which Count Keyserling touched up when he was last here, asserting that America is a two-caste country, with women forming the higher caste. "The tradition of culture, linking one generation with another," he said, "is maintained solely by the women, the men forgetting their education as soon as they go to work."

One can see, of course, why this belief might be cultivated by foreign lecturers. It gives at once an opportunity to flatter the American woman, the fount of fat platform fees. But enhanced by wishful thinking or not, there is evidence that the American woman's dominance has come to represent in the European mind an almost scientific hypothesis.

Last summer a German medical journal carried an article to prove that the subjugation of the male in this country is probably due to our climate or our diet. Endemic influences in certain parts of America, the author argued, modify the thyroid. Why, then, may there not be other influences here acting on the sex hormones, sufficiently at least to change masculine psychology? Some such theory was necessary, he held, to explain the phenomenon of a healthy man kneeling before a woman to put on her overshoes. But the more popular European theory traced feminine dominance to Yankee pioneer days when women were scarce. Thus supposedly grew up an obsequious cult, handed down from father to son, whose slogan was perforce not alone *cherchez* but *tenez la femme*.

In the midst of all this foreign smoke and outcry, however, like a fire chief summoned by a false alarm, the American man up to now has maintained a practically unheeding composure. In everything he has cared about, America has been, to his complete satisfaction, a man's country. And if he has spent the days and sometimes the nights of his vacationless life in counting house and factory, it was usually because it was the game he liked best, as the European might crave polo or baccarat. Commerce, industry, government were all his thrilling, if sometimes brutal and heartrending, games to play.

A chief bogy indeed of the old-fashioned American business man was of the day when he might have to retire to that life of leisure and culture in which his wife presumably reveled. In the meantime if his wife wanted to take over the non-essential and somewhat distasteful task of putting up a presentable family façade in the social world, he was glad enough to have her do so. It was—to change the figure—only so much more gilding on his prow. It increased his prestige and advertised his success.

In this view of the relative advantages of their rôles, the American woman has been prone to agree with her husband. Typically she has not shared or presumably even understood the feeling of the king's mistress in Bernard Shaw's "Apple Cart," to whom government apparently was rather like dishwashing—something one didn't do if one could possibly get any one else to take it over.

Indeed, up to recent years the American woman has frequently had the slight pout of one from whom the jolly plums of power hung just a trifle out of reach. A seat, she recognized, might occasionally be proffered her in the subway, but virtually never in the Senate, on the Bench, the Stock Exchange or a gilded board of directors. Increasingly she has shown her envy of these prerogatives to be in good earnest by leaving golf course and bridge table to learn man's sport of business from the bottom up —or rather out, from behind the counter or the typewriter into the more Olympian realms of the private office.

And now, just as woman has toilsomely learned some of the plays and found an occasional place in man's producing and managing game, at least on the scrub team, a cataclysmic thing has happened. For the first time the American man's lusty belief in the game and his own self-sufficiency begin to waver. Suddenly in her place on the side lines he recognizes the woman in the home as being the mainstay of that powerful public by whose gate receipts the game is supported. That all-important Ultimate Consumer, on whom any producing game inevitably depends, has turned out to have silken shirts and a permanent wave and the familiar features of mother.

In times when every dollar takes on the aspect of a life preserver, the knowledge that women do 80 per cent of the retail purchasing in this country is less casually dismissed. On the cover of a popular magazine recently appeared a drawing of a troubled, slim-walleted Uncle Sam being dragged acquiescently forward by a determined young woman with her arms full of parcels. "It's up to the women!" read the accompanying slogan. It was part of a national campaign to end the depression by mobilizing the tightly gripped dollars, in the hands of woman, the great American purchasing agent.

As a symbol of the dawning suspicion that woman after all works the stop-and-go signals of our economic machine, it deserves preservation as a historical record. The lightning flashes, so to speak, of the current financial storm have revealed the strategic economic position into which the American woman has more or less unwittingly been shoved by the machine age. Her erstwhile hard and confining home work of garment making and food preparation the factories and the automatic household machines have largely taken over, making her rôle increasingly that of selector of ready-made goods and therefore a more and more powerful, if unconscious, controller of man's world of industry and commerce.

One reason perhaps why America has been reputed a matriarchate is that industrialization and urbanization have progressed faster and further here than in any other country, yet without taking a majority of women out of the home. Less than anywhere else probably is the home in America a producing agency, yet 73 per cent of our women remain in it. They, as the president of Stevens Institute remarked recently, present the most acute cases of technological unemployment.

Yet their control of industry through their power as consumers increases directly with that unemployment. Today it is taken for granted in America. Recently, as part of a nation-wide survey of consuming habits, canvassers have been going through the city of New York, interviewing every twentieth housewife. Not a man was scheduled to be approached. Yet the survey, when completed, is expected to give an accurate picture of what 80 per cent of the population eat, drink and wear; what kind of automobiles, radios, furniture and houses they have, and how they invest and save.

Similarly, last Winter a great department store made all its wholesale purchases with a view to meeting the detailed specifications of the wants expressed by 20,469 women whom its canvassers interviewed on the point. Here were women recognized in practice by a powerful commercial organization as the controllers of the outward aspects at least of our civilization.

Another metropolitan establishment proceeds on the assumption that women do up to 90 per cent of the retail purchasing, if one counts in the things bought by men at women's behest. Moreover, in the great shops nowadays, it is said, the department heads —those who select the stock from which women buy—are themselves on the distaff side in the ratio of about six to one. Behind the counter, too, stand largely women, trained to sell to a feminine public; at the advertising desks sit others turning out the glamorous copy intended to ensnare the pocketbook of their sisters. To women, indeed, a large block of newspaper advertising is addressed. As for the women's magazines, they have become a kind of national mart in which manufacturers vie to display their goods from catsup to cabriolets.

No longer merely in graceful theory but in hard pragmatic fact, woman sets the physical stage of existence. From cradle to deathbed, for most of us, our intimate and personal world is woman created, or rather assembled. From breakfast cereal to midnight coverlet practically all children and most men live among the objects and according to the pattern chosen by some woman.

To suit her taste counters are stacked and factories rumble, magazines are published and plays and motion pictures produced. All along the far-flung line of modern business, from the trappers on the snow fields of the North to the perfume distillers of the rose fields of the South, thousands of toilers starve or flourish at her whim. And most of the complicated machinery of industry—not alone the spindles and the motors—but the salesmen, the designers, the stenographers and the great executives—speed or stand idle as she pulls the purse-strings.

Where she economizes, in other words, the whole economic shoe pinches. And a main objective of the business race today is to catch and keep her fancy. Should she, for instance, turn suddenly against lipstick and powder and rouge, a $750,000,000 industry would be blown into space. Or should she decide that cotton would be an agreeable change from silk, Japan's trade with us—more than a third of its exports—might go a-glimmering. And there would be an economic boycott in more potent fact than any governmental fiat probably could manage.

More and more frequently, too, women are not spending merely their husbands' or fathers' cash, but their own. Hoarded in socks, or invested in bonds and mortgages, more American wealth every day is passing directly into feminine hands. Already, it has been recently revealed, women own 40 per cent of our capital, constitute about half of our millionaires, our income taxpayers and our stockholders in corporations. If the trend continues, in which women are the beneficiaries of life insurance, of 70 per cent of men's estates and 64 per cent of women's, the time may not be far off when they will dominate the investment field as they do that of retail purchasing.

With this press-the-button rôle of purchasing agent rather than producer has come to millions of American women a mass leisure unknown in the world before—a leisure also which has been used to an amazing extent for education as well as amusement. The woman's club, it has been symbolically suggested, came on the heels of the sewing machine. And so, we might add, did the woman's college and the extension course, so largely woman-supported. While the machine age forced man to become more and more narrowly a specialist, shut up all day in office and factory, it gave woman her first opportunity to become mentally a citizen of the world. She became, intellectually as well as economically, the ultimate consumer.

The reason why the typical American middle-class husband is still apt to prefer the college glee club while his wife frequents concerts of chamber music lies largely in the discrepancy in their sum total of leisure. The man stays collegiate in his tastes because he has never had enough free time since college to develop any others. Upon feminine supporters all the arts and most of the philanthropic and social reform movements have come in America automatically to depend. Women unquestionably dominate, as the foreign lecturer has shrewdly recognized, the market of ideas as well as that of goods.

Yet this is still probably a man's country. For woman's growing power, vast as it already is, economically and intellectually, stops just short of effectiveness. It is still scattered among millions of isolated individuals with no coherence except that blindly imposed by fashion and custom. If and when American women ever do become organized, self-directing users of their new power as consumers given them by the machine age, then indeed men and the world may well beware.

OUR AMERICAN STANDARD [3] *of living, much-vaunted, was never "too high," Christine Frederick declares.*

It was before the depression struck us so heavily that a governor of a state and an officer of an association of bankers both declared, almost simultaneously, that American standards of living were too high. The banker declared they were too high because of the "dangerous" contrast they afforded to foreign standards of living. The governor said they were too high because we were "living beyond our means."

It is not only President Hoover—he promptly combated the banker's statement—who regards such criticism of our American living standards as spreading a sapping and destructive doctrine. The women of America, as with one voice, would surely condemn and contest any tendency to lower those standards. Such controversy must proceed from a lack of comprehension as to what a living standard is, and what the purpose of the machinery of civilization is.

A "living standard" is the level of necessity (as well as comfort and luxury) which, in a given place and period of civilization, is regarded as a requirement for the welfare and happiness of the average family. It has never been interpreted, when ap-

[3] Reprint obtained through the courtesy of *The Independent Woman.*

plied to a country as a whole, as meaning extravagance or profusion of goods or wasteful indulgence. Indeed, it has nearly always meant, as we have applied it in the United States to our whole nation, a level that was barely above what we would call the common decencies of life. We do not, in this country, regard as extravagances a bathtub, toothpaste, a new suit or a new dress once a year, or even silk stockings, electricity, steam heat or a refrigerator. Such things are at the base, not at the peak, of our ideas of a standard of living. Consequently, when our economic experts have talked of "the American standard of living," they have meant the family which is supported on a salary of about $2,000 a year. Any budget which might be made up within this limit, as representing the details of such an American standard of living, would show very little extravagance, because such an income comes close to the subsistence level.

A year and a half ago, in *Selling Mrs. Consumer,* I presented a tabulation of the ten levels of society in the United States, as follows:

Crœsus level: $50,000 a year and upwards; .125% of our population.

Super-Liberal level: $25,000 to $50,000; .268% of our population.

Well-to-do level: $10,000 to $25,000; 1.08% of our population.

Liberal level: $5,000 to $10,000; 3.58% of our population.

Moderate level: $3,000 to $5,000; 8.92% of our population.

Comfortable level: $2,000 to $3,000; 7.154% of our population.

Minimum Comfort level: $1,500 to $2,000; 35.37% of our population.

Subsistence level: $1,000 to $1,500; 22.76% of our population.

Bare subsistence level: $500 to $1,000; 13.93% of our population.

Poverty level: below $500; 6.78% of our population.

Here we see a picture of the United States as our living standards actually operate in relation to income. It shows precisely how many people had attained to that level where they could afford the minimum American standard of living of 1930; that is, when they could afford the common decencies of life—the moderately varied diet, the health care, the sanitary living conditions and precautions; the self-respecting outward appearance of an upstanding American family—with not more than a few dollars left for extras or indulgences. Just how do matters stand, when we examine these figures?

We should be rendered thoughtful, not to say startled, to realize from these statistics that 70 per cent, or over two-thirds of our population, even before the depression, lived below the recognized American standard of common decency and minimum comfort, that is, below $2,000 a year. Even in boom times, the number of families with incomes above $5,000 comprised only a little over 5% of the total.

Surely it is evident to anyone that it would be fantastic to attempt to achieve "extravagant living" on an income up to $5,000. Raising and educating a family with fair comfort and a little luxury on less than $5,000 is only accomplished nowadays either by a very able housewife-manager, by cutting down the size of the family, or by depriving that family of its just share of education, comfort and welfare.

In rural and semi-rural districts, it is true, an income can be stretched much further than in the larger cities; but the figures I have quoted serve to indicate how groundless must be the idea that our American living standards were ever "too high"!

The National Industrial Conference Board in 1926 made a survey of the cost of living in New York City. This survey was significant because New York is the one city in the United States where living standards are conceded to be the highest. Even the factory workers have a higher standard of dress and as a rule do not go home in working clothes, as they are in the habit of doing in mill towns.

Research has proved that the "average minimum cost of maintaining a fair American standard of living for an office worker, with a family of three, in 1930, was $2,156. For one child it was only $1,565, but as we must calculate on a family basis, the three-child basis is soundest. This budget was divided as follows: housing, $516; fuel and light, $40.70; food, $762.32; clothing, $298.20; sundries, $479.44.

Some idea may be gained as to what is regarded as a "fair American standard of living" when we examine the sundries classification. This is based on the sum of $9.22 weekly; out of which $1.27 goes for transportation; 85 cents for recreation (movies, et cetera); 50 cents for reading matter, stationery, postage, telephone, et cetera; a dollar for medical care, and sick benefits; $1.05 for candy and tobacco; $2.00 for cleaning supplies and toilet requisites; 90 cents for furniture and furnishings. Is it possible to see any particularly "high" standard of living here, in the home of a New York City office worker's family?

Even the working girl who earns $1800 a year ($150 a month), and without family responsibilities, cannot be classified as living in pampered luxury. The Chicago Home Economics conference worked out her budget several years ago. Statistics showed that she paid $37.50 a month rent and $3 a week board. Her lunch expenditure was 35 cents a day. Recreation (two movie tickets or one theatre ticket) cost her $1.75 a week. Doctors and drugs totaled $30 during the entire year; cosmetics, $27 (about 50 cents a week); beauty treatments, $24.50 a year.

As for her clothes, $84.12 went for lingerie; $102 for dresses; $36.25 for hats; $182.69 for coats (two or three per year); $51.60 for shoes; and $24.90 for accessories.

Is this extravagance? The American girl very vehemently replies *no*. Even if she may be criticized for spending an appallingly small proportion of her income on food, it may be added that in this she is discriminating, preferring good food, even if little of it.

I have purposely presented here the facts about the New York family and the unattached business girl with a fair salary, both of whom are likely to be singled out as examples of high living standards. Yet, as we have seen, there is very little leeway for criticism of their extravagance.

Among the majority of the 95 per cent of people below the $5,000 a year income level, there has not been (and certainly is not now, in the depression period) even a realization of the *accepted minimum American standard of living*. Out of this 95 per cent, only 25 per cent have actually attained this accepted minimum standard of living—*making a total of not quite 30 per cent of all American families, under normal conditions and in normal times, able to boast of living at the minimum standard.*

The small towns of America have surely no claim to extravagant or riotous living. In a survey made by *The Literary Digest* a few years ago, taking Zanesville, Ohio, as a test town, it was established that only 61 per cent of the homes had plumbing systems (which means that 39 per cent had—and probably still have—the old form of "outhouses"). Less than half of one per cent had electric refrigerators, and only 48 per cent of the homes had any central heating plant (which means that the other 52 per cent still heated their homes with coal stoves); only 28 per cent of families had electric washing machines; only 52 per cent had vacuum cleaners; while, as for other "luxuries" among electric devices, only 58 per cent had electric irons, only 19 per cent had toasters, and only 4.7 per cent had electric percolators. Only 2 per cent of Zanesville families had regular servants, and 92.4 per cent never used even part-time servants.

That Zanesville is a good test town is demonstrated by the fact that 70.5 per cent of the homes there had incomes of $2,000 or less; which is just about the status of the country as a whole. Despite the theory (which is statistically true) that there is an automobile for every family in the United States, 49.2 per cent of Zanesville families did not own an automobile; 84 per cent did not own a radio set; and 56.7 per cent did not have a piano.

I will not go into the matter of the rural districts, but the well-known complaints of the farmer about his standard of living, so much lower even than that of people in cities, is evidence enough that we have not yet attained that "American standard of living"; not even the level of comfort and decency which by general agreement and knowledge of nutrition, hygiene, safety and sanitation, is called "civilized." Certainly it is rather ridiculous to refer to our living standards as being too high, if we have not yet attained such a living standard to a degree of 30 per cent; for the standard accepted allows for little that is not considered as necessary as toothpaste and toothbrush—and that is a paradox, for only about 30 per cent of American people brush their teeth!

Now, finally, let us attack the underlying assumption of the critics of our supposedly high standard of living, the assumption that the higher our standard of living climbs, the more materialistic and sodden we become. This is a pure myth, a hangover, doubtless, from our penurious Puritan ancestors. The peak periods of prosperity in history have always been peak periods of art, literature, and culture. Such high living standards do not arrive automatically with increased income; often a generation or two elapses before their mellowing influences can infiltrate. But there is little room for doubt that the equivalents of Greek, Roman, French Empire or Elizabethan culture cannot occur again until there is, as in those periods, a high living standard.

Standards of living are tremendously real to women, for woman, rather than man, bears the brunt of the daily ordering of family life on the material plane, and low standards of living literally crucify her. We see heartrending examples of what women suffer under poor living conditions, throughout the world, even in such supposedly civilized countries as France, Italy and England, where an astoundingly large proportion of homes have no water above the first floor and no central heating or modern laundering facilities. Such living standards age a woman cruelly; and a point of view that considers any standard of living too high, or high enough, can only be classified as backward, inhuman and uncivilized.

There can be no progress, no civilization, without a constantly climbing standard, such a standard as I should like to specify as the genuinely American standard of living, and which as yet is enjoyed by no more than three per cent of families in this country. Such a standard is gracious, kindly and stimulating; to the great majority of women it brings genuine dignity and opportunity, and to men a far greater pride in women, their homes and their families.

Such progress can only come about during a peak period, and

we have not yet reached the peak period of our American civilization, as the statistics quoted endeavor to show. The difficulties facing us today are, by general agreement, problems of putting the vast production the United States has proved itself capable of into the hands of consumers. It is a problem of transportation, credit, distribution of wealth, retailing, tariff.

When the men who are masters of these factors succeed in finding the key log in the economic jam, the dammed-up production will come downstream with a roar. It is not the time to talk of a reduction of the lumber output because there is for the moment a log jam!

Human muscle, steam, then electricity, shaped the course of industrial and social progress in the New World. Over the sway of steam, women had less to say than later over the sway of electricity. Aware of Giant Power as an agency of human welfare, the League of Women Voters began, early in its career, to wage a campaign for public control in the interests of the people at large. One of its publications for the year 1929 supplied "An Introduction to the Study of the Regulation of Public Utilities," written by Julia M. Hicks. Already, however, in 1926, the subject had come before the national convention of the organization. In that year Ann Dennis Bursch delivered the following address dealing with women's special interest in electric power, under the head of ELECTRIC POWER AND THE PUBLIC WELFARE.[4]

The Living Costs Committee of the League of Women Voters has added to its recommendations for study:

"The most effective utilization of the electric resources of the country from the standpoint of the public welfare."

That women should be showing such an interest in the way in which electric power is being developed, engineered, and financed

[4] Reprint obtained through the courtesy of The League of Women Voters.

seems to cause some surprise—and, shall we say, some amusement. The ablest engineers, the cleverest financiers already have power development well in hand. Why should we concern ourselves about it?

Because, we answer, here for the first time in history is something that can do household drudgery better than we can! Electric Power is a servant that we can put to the hardest household tasks with a clear conscience. Women have revolted against domestic service. We wish to employ Electric Power in their stead, provided it can be hired at a wage we can afford, and can be persuaded to take a place in the country.

Therefore women have a definite expectation of benefit from the electric revolution now in progress, which they never reaped from the revolution that brought about the Age of Steam.

The steam revolution was purely industrial. It replaced man power with the power of steam-driven fly-wheels, belts, pulleys, and shafting. It had a great effect upon domestic and agricultural life, but that effect was destructive.

Before Steam came, weaving, spinning, tanning and baking were household occupations, carried on at home and on the farm. Mary's little lamb furnished Mary with a coat and the family with shoes and blankets between its school days and the day when it became leg of mutton and tallow dips—all without leaving the place of its birth.

But the steam-engine arrived, with mechanical power to turn all the looms that could be harnessed to its fly-wheel by leather belts. Weavers and spinners followed their machines perforce into the mill. Hand industries became lost arts. Mass production became the rule. Great mill towns grew up, in which there was work for all the family,—old, and young, and very young. So the family left the farm for the town.

Mill-town living conditions were, still usually are, bad. Social engineering had not been considered by any but the dreamers when Steam began to rule. People's lives were caught and whirled around in the machinery by the burly, crippled old giant with whom they worked. For Steam is, at best, only a deformed giant with very short arms and legs. Its work has to be carried to it. Its helpers must live huddled close up to it.

Therefore we call steam a centripetal force. The social results of steam power are crowded factories, congested industrial cities —and outside, a depopulated country.

Imaginative engineering minds (the dreamers again) began to play with the idea that Electricity too might be made to work, instead of playing around the horizon as heat lightning, or roaring in the heavens as it struck blindly at houses, men or trees. Finally they caught *that* giant—a much more nimble and versatile giant than Steam! They transformed its energy first into the power of many home-dipped candles. The Kilowatt Hour became a new light unit.

It was only the cities that got the benefit of this, first in sputtering arc-lights, then in rows, and later in patterns and flowing streams, of brilliant incandescent bulbs that turned the city night into another day, lined the streets and roofs with gaudy signs, brought the moving picture industry up to its present appalling hugeness and attractiveness. Since then, there has been no keeping the growing children and the "hands" on the farm.

Presently the engineers found that electricity was power and heat as well as light. They made it turn wheels, just as steam did. Then the revolution began in earnest.

Still, however, the motion was toward the center. Power plants were installed as part of the factory they served. Electric light plants were inside the city. Congestion increased. This was the situation when the war began, and war conditions made it worse. These conditions still exist to a considerable extent. The cities grow on. The improvement in working conditions in electric factories, no longer cluttered and dusty with overhead shafting, pulleys and belting,—the tremendous attractiveness of the night lights and movies,—still draw the young folks away to the city from the country.

The steam revolution did little for the farmer, nothing for his wife, except to take away the industries that kept her family at home. It took away the farm-hand but gave little applied energy to replace his muscle. Over most of the country the farm energy unit is still horse-power, man-power, woman-power, child-power. The Kilowatt Hour is coming to the farm, but it is not there yet, except on an experimental basis. There is still good reason for any big boy or girl, looking at Mother's broken figure and seeing what farm life has made of Father, to drop the hay-fork and milk-pail and start for the city—"Me for the bright lights!"

Now, one thing seems to me the message of all civilizations to ours: that this country cannot long endure without agricultural prosperity.

The culture of the cities, which we must have—music, the arts of painting, drama and sculpture, our thrilling new architecture —can not long go on, unless it is matched by the culture of the fields. Conditions are not sound if, during such a time of industrial prosperity as exists today, there are such abysses of despair as these into which some of our farming regions have fallen.

We can get along without more big cities. We need many scattered little cities, surrounded by cultivated fields, worked by comfortable farmers whose families love their homes the better because they can reach the city easily for culture, recreation, or work. The farmhouse must be a comfortable modern home to which they love to return, not merely a synonym for drudgery and boredom and isolation.

Rightly directed, electricity can accomplish much of this change. It can replace the vanished farm-hand. It can make the farm kitchen a comfortable, well-equipped work-shop, can lighten the work and increase the productivity of the dairy and henhouse. It can give the housewife the leisure that is her right. Whether it will do this on terms that the farmer can afford will depend upon the terms that society makes with the new power.

This vision of help for the country from electric power could not have been seen ten years ago, when it was drawing people into the cities, offering light and power there and ignoring the outer darkness. But within the past ten years, a movement in the contrary direction has begun. Overcoming the inertia of direction which steam had set up, electricity has now shown that its force is centrifugal. Under the right guidance it can scatter the population again over the land, can break up the congestion, rehabilitate the farms, and plant industries on the roads that lead to the farms.

The new development that turned the tide of the power industry toward the open spaces was long-distance power transmission; that, and hydro-electricity. It has been made practical to build power plants far from the consumers of power. They may be erected wherever water falls, wherever coal can be carried, wherever condensers can be supplied with cold water. At any point in a drive through the open country, one may come upon a huge power house, developing as much current as twenty sizeable plants produced in 1900. And from each power house, the tall supports for high-voltage transmission wires stalk across the fields, carrying tremendous volumes of current to far-away towns and cities.

Electric current flows uphill, steps across the river on stilts, never stoops to look at a State line. It runs over mountains or across prairies to its objective two hundred, even three hundred, miles away, arriving there as quick as winking, fresh as a new-laid egg. Electricity is one thing that can not be adulterated, though it may be weakened by the long journey. However, transmission losses on long lines rarely exceed 10 per cent and on the larger systems are estimated at 5 per cent. Greater distances become practical every year.

So far, American steam-generation plants are being located with more regard to the presence of a cold water supply than the proximity of coal. But it is to be hoped that a technique will be worked out that will make it possible to put the power plants at the mouths of coal mines. This will free the railroads of endless trains of coal cars. It will utilize low-grade coal that cannot economically be transported. It will lead to the saving of valuable chemical by-products of coal that are now entirely wasted in combustion.

Many engineers are devoted to the present technique, based on unlimited water for condensing steam. They view the idea of generating power at the mine-mouth as the dream of mere theorists. They point out that from 400 to 600 pounds of cold water must go with every single pound of coal, in operating the condenser of a steam turbine. Where, they ask, is that amount of water to be found at a coal-mine mouth?

But one may find, in the report of the Pennsylvania Giant Power Survey (made by Morris L. Cooke, the noted industrial engineer, and a corps of technical engineers), accounts and pictures of mine-mouth plants now functioning successfully in England and Germany. There the "dreamers" have learned to cool water artificially in "cooling towers" built close to the mine. They have also devised ways of using the water of a small stream over and over before letting it escape.

I have faith that our engineers will not lag behind those of Europe, when they are once convinced that this problem must be solved. American engineers do not easily say of any problem, "It can't be done," if they are given a reason for doing it. . . .

"Giant Power" is a term invented by certain conservationists who, being dreamers, have visualized the effect upon our civilization of this stupendous and rapidly developing new force. They want us to see it *whole,* as a great national issue, and so have personified it as a "giant," capable of great power for good or evil or both. It is no longer a collection of forty-eight separate state problems. It runs together into an entity as long and as broad as the United States. What is this giant going to do, *to* us or *for* us, when it is full grown? Will it serve the nation, or master it for the purposes of masters of its own?

Psychologists are telling us that the life-long characteristics of a child are established by the time he is six years old. Giant Power is already that old, and we have not yet decided what we want him trained to do, or by what methods. This the Super-power people might deny. His character is already fixed. He is serving industry, manufactures, commerce, transportation, and therefore the Nation.

The Giant Power students think he can be trained to do much

more; not that he should serve business less, but that he should serve the Nation in more ways. To remain healthy, they say, the Nation must be strengthened in every part, like an all-round athlete. Its agriculture must grow in proportion to its commerce. Its homes are even more important than its factories. In other words, the farmer must reap as much benefit from the services of Giant Power as does the miller. The housewife must receive as much help in forming the next generation's standards as does the amusement park.

They remind us that Giant Power could not exist today if it were not fed by the people—fed upon our national and state resources of water-power sites, the privilege of condemning land, the use of public roads, the monopoly privilege of supplying the people—privilege granted by *all* the people, of town and country, and not, as used to be the case, by the people of the cities for the cities alone.

So, they say, the people of the country are reasonable if they demand service for the country places as a right. They insist that power districts should include the thinly settled rural regions on equitable terms with the close-packed towns. They would enforce the farmer's right to demand service from the trunk lines that cross his fields or to be given rural extensions, because the Nation's welfare demands that the farmer be helped to stay on his farm, instead of being forced to abandon it and increase the congestion at the centers of population. And, either in town or in country, domestic rates and service should give the home an even chance.

They do not say that the power industry should be despoiled or so impoverished that investors would not put money into it; but they point out that when electric current was being newly introduced to manufacturers and applied to city and suburban business, concessions were offered to consumers which ensured the rapid adoption of electric power, with the consequent building up of a profitable volume of business. They say the public welfare must be served by similar concessions to farmers and domestic users.

The farm extension may be so planned that in time it will pay a reasonable profit. But those progressive farmers who are willing to start the fashion by experimenting with a thing new to them and buying the needed equipment, at considerable cost, must not be over-burdened with installation charges and rates figured for immediate profit. The power companies must "take the overhead" of inaugurating a branch of public service whose social need and economic value are both factors of importance.

The advocates of Giant Power say also that the present and future welfare will be served best by putting steam power plants more and more at the mine-mouth and sending power into whatever districts need it, conserving transportation, conserving coal, conserving chemicals, all wasted by present practices.

These are the ends, according to the Giant Power idea, toward which the power revolution should be turned by "effective public regulation."

This is the controversy over *aim*. Another controversy rages over *method*. How to get effective regulation? When power projects were local, municipalities made their own regulations. As they grew, State public utilities commissions took over their control, each State developing its system and fixing its standards, according to the preponderance of interests awake to the issue. Some States are still trying to keep Giant Power inside the State line fence. But even now he is too big for any such confinement. Financial Superpower is nationwide already. Its lines show blacker across the map than the State lines which they cross at every angle. Questions continually arise which cannot be settled piecemeal by State commissions. What shall be the method of control, and by whom?

Interstate commissions, representing all the States within one defined power pool, are urged by Dr. Felix Frankfurter, basing his plan in the Compact Clause of the U. S. Constitution, which gives any State the right to enter into agreements or compacts with any other State with the consent of the Congress. Mr. Hoover thinks that voluntary inter-State agreements, added to State control, will be as much of a safeguard as will ever be needed.

Navigable rivers, water-power sites within the national public domain, and projects involving the water-power sources of more than a single State are Federal responsibilities, some of long standing, some created by the Federal Water Power Act of 1920, which forbids leasing for more than fifty years, and stipulates that preference shall be given to public corporations over private companies. By virtue of this statute, 85 per cent of our potential water-power sources come under the control of the Federal Power Commission, consisting of the Secretaries of War, Agriculture, and the Interior, and making use of the engineering forces of those three departments. This means, of course, a one-party Commission, subject to political changes and reversal of policy.

Some sort of Federal regulation for all power questions of inter-State scope is urged by many economists who fear the results of nationwide financial combinations presenting a united front of opposition to forty-eight State commissions or to loose federations of adjoining States. They say that "united we stand, divided we fall" is as good and patriotic a slogan on work-days as on national holidays. Mr. Philip Cabot considers it practical to separate transmission from production (which is carried on in separate spots, each of which might be regulated by its own State) and from distribution (which can be done through power districts confined to one State). Great "electric highways" could be thus developed as are our national roads, placed where public welfare required, and under Federal control. This is only one of many suggestions for securing Federal unity of policy without sacrificing State independence.

When power was a local concern, many municipalities engineered and financed their own plants, which now produce between 3 and 4 per cent of all power generated. There are over 3,000 municipal power systems operated for the benefit of the citizens and not for private profit. In some of the States, home rule gives these plants independence of the State Public Utilities Commission, so it is difficult to compare their statistics; and private companies sometimes consider that statements of relative costs and benefits are computed with too much emphasis on social welfare, and with too little on efficiency and the financial balance sheet.

Here is a subject for careful study by the local League of every city or state owning its own power plant. It is a question how long these cities will be able to maintain independence against the ever stronger pressure of the Superpower combinations. If, because of the greater economy of operating large scale power plants, cities are able to buy private power cheaper than they can produce it at home, the distribution problem is still open for discussion. Cities in such cases are having to decide whether to buy power at wholesale and retail it as a public service at cost, or to pay another profit to a private corporation for local distribution.

Public opinion in many places, especially in the western States, strongly opposes giving up a public necessity like power or water to private exploitation. The present administration at Washington has shown its understanding of the strength of this feeling by recommending to Congress that the Federal government construct and operate a great dam and power plant at Boulder Canyon on the Colorado River, and that under the provisions of the Federal Water Power Act the power generated be sold by preference to States and municipalities and other governmental units; next to private utility companies and, last, to industrial corporations.

The question of the duty of a State to develop and operate her own hydro-electric resources is at this time in active controversy in New York State, and the current New York newspaper record of the diverse opinions of engineers, politicians, and publicists is voluminous.

The development or disposition of our property and interests at the great Muscle Shoals dam in Alabama has been studied by the League of Women Voters for four years. Muscle Shoals is therefore entitled to a publication of its own, and I shall refer to it here only to quote from the last article published from the pen of a disinterested economist, the late Walter Durand.

Mr. Durand called attention to the "need for public yard-sticks," by which public and private ownership of power enterprises might be measured. The Muscle Shoals, Boulder Canyon, Seattle and St. Lawrence projects were pointed out as able to provide, under public operation, bases for comparisons that would be a real test—"of results, not of propaganda and counter-propaganda."

The homely word "yard-stick" is a woman's word. The slide rule (or, as irreverent students call it, the "slip-stick") is beloved of the engineers. It saves them years of figuring; but it looks like mystery and confusion to home folks. The involved power rates with which consumers struggle could be simplified. The bases for calculations should be understandable by those who pay the bills. If the engineers show impatience with our inability to grasp technicalities, we may be similarly impatient with their failure to grasp the importance of our viewpoint.

The great importance to us of the way in which power will develop in the next two or three years, and the positive fascination of its top-speed progress, make it probable that women will think a good deal, and may have a good deal to say, about the purposes and methods of the power promoters. We may sometimes express our opinion with pen or voice; we may have opportunities to express it by our votes. Let us not grow weary with such well-doing—and let us not go off half-cocked. We have the right to the service of cheap power in our homes. And we claim it in the name of the common weal.

"Defeated and chastened, the financial kingdom realizes, as it never has before, the force of public opinion," Anne O'Hare McCormick, one of the leading American journalists, announced soon after the crash. She then turned to politics on the eve of the 1932 national campaign, when the country was showing itself "increasingly distrustful of politics, while the politicians were everywhere beset by confusion and uncertainty," and discussed

*the situation in an article called THE NEW ORDEAL OF
DEMOCRACY.*[5]

This is a story in two parts. The first is written in the Middle
West, home address of America, and generalizes the talk to be
heard almost anywhere in the United States during this highly
conversational, politically heated and financially frigid campaign
year of 1932. The second is written in Washington, the only place
in the country whose business is in full production, and reports
the outlook there in a time constantly spoken of but not yet
recognized on Capitol Hill as an hour of national emergency.
Thus it glances at the same picture from two angles, both pretty
obtuse, one that of the representatives of the people, the other
that of the people represented.

Together the two views form a commentary on the whole
scheme of representative government, in principle so simple, in
operation grown so complex that many begin to think it is un-
workable in a crisis. At any rate the principle is now at test
throughout the world. It is not too much to say that its vindica-
tion, not to say its survival, peculiarly depends on the decisions
to be made in this country in the next few years, perhaps in the
next few months.

We are the oldest existing democracy. No nation has enjoyed
universal manhood suffrage so long as ours. None has been so
free to develop without outside interference, to shape its own environment, to create a system of government under the uniquely
favoring circumstances of geographic security, economic independence and modern political ancestry. We have not been circumscribed by poverty of natural resources, by encroaching
neighbors, by the fibroid traditions of old societies, by the compromises required of nations living in a crowd, like the nations
of Europe. We have not been circumscribed at all. We voided
the past by beginning late, with a century which gave birth to a
new kind of civilization. We laid our own patterns in fresh soil.

[5] Reprint obtained through the courtesy of the author and the *New York
Times Sunday Magazine.*

Industry is our contemporary and lent us speeds unknown before in exploiting the wealth of a rich continent. To this point, in a word, we have governed ourselves, arrived where we are in our own way and under our own power. Our progress has been automotive, almost automatic, and loudly touted as the progress of democracy.

Now the question is: Where are we? Nobody seems quite sure, least of all the masters of our political fate currently engaged in nominating the contending candidates for the Presidency of the Republic and building platforms designed to be indistinguishable one from the other and to contain no plank not broad enough for every voter to stand on. This year's conventions are, like all conventions, splurges on the grand scale of competitive salesmanship, yet they are held in one of the real crises in human history, a crisis not only economic but political.

For ten years and more we have been hearing about the crisis of democracy. Until a few months ago, however, that particular crisis did not hit the mass mind of America. Our democracy has been rather like one of our automatic devices, as much a part of our regular equipment as the telephone, taken for granted as available whether used or not. But lately, from the grass roots to the glass towers, the attention of the country has been focused on government. Everything has piled up together—taxes, tariffs, the crushing cost and corruption of local machines, congealed credit in State and Federal banks, unemployment, snow-balling relief budgets, hunger and thirst, rackets and panic—to fill the valley of depression with a mountainous exhibit of our dependence on politics.

At last we discover that government manages our lives; we wonder if what we suffer is not first of all a crisis of democracy. If it is not a failure of productive or consumptive power, of supply or demand, as obviously it is not, then it must be a failure of the democratic intelligence embodied in political institutions. To point to the simultaneous break-down of other governments or systems of government is no comfort or no answer to the rudely awakened American. He insists that democracy fostered our famous spread of prosperity and that it must be proved equal or unequal to the stresses of adversity.

To a country beginning to face that radical fact, the Congress now adjourning seems feeble and frivolous. The conventions seem frivolous. The whole political bag of tricks looks as cheap and useless as a deposit box stuffed with stock certificates or a counter piled with goods reduced for clearance. During this strange interlude when the national slogan is "No business as usual," repeated everywhere with a certain grim gayety, the nation's business is government. For the first time to anything like the present extent, the eyes of all the States are glued on their political representatives. Under the unflickering gaze of this new and once indifferent gallery, the political show appears something like a costume party, quaint, pre-war, full of Spencerian flourishes, of eternal gestures, of nimble side-stepping, the "à la main de" left and right of the old quadrille. "Actually they are behaving as they always behave!" gasps the audience—embittered because it cannot do the same!

The multitude does not blame the politicians for the depression. The guilt for that has been firmly fastened on the bankers. What is resented in the men of politics, and resented with a unanimity that may unseat them all, is their solemn levity, pussyfooting, resourcelessness, the unbreakable habit of "playing politics." Observe how the slump has multiplied ballyhoo magazines; watch what people read on trains and buses, in the long Summer evenings on the porches of the suburbs and the small towns. Then you will understand why 7,770 Texans telegraphed Congress to adjourn and why Iowa expressed a violent preference for a "chicken-stew" candidate as against "the same old boloney" of Senator Brookhart.

On the most metropolitan main streets today people stop to talk. One of the strange signs of the times is the little groups on the downtown sidewalks exchanging rumors, views, echoes of views on the state of the nation. There is a lot of echo; for once the talk is the same in industrial city and country town; for once both have plenty of time to talk. There is also an air of leisure long absent from the American scene. Turned colloquial, the urban streets become village-like and friendly, and the colloquies themselves bring back the lost flavor of the cracker-box, a ghostly cracker-box overwhelmed by motor traffic but essentially the same old mourner's bench of the country store.

Ten to one the talk goes straight to the new question of America: "What's the government going to do?" The tone is not tragic. It runs around in circles, as in a labyrinth without an exit, but the habit of optimism is strong in us; it never stops in despair. It is not revolutionary. The contemporary models of revolution are mentioned often enough, but as bogeys rather than as beacons. "I'd as soon be in Russia as here." "If Congress keeps on fiddling, we'll be saddled with a Mussolini yet." These are common remarks, but delivered in the accent of Little Orphan Annie referring to the goblins.

Nobody yet believes in such alternatives, and none would be more surprised than the few who seriously predict communism or fascism, if their words were to come true. Such prophets of doom as there are speak without conviction. America would be more reckless if it had any real fear of doom; now it presents the novel paradox of a people saving not for a rainy but for a sunny day. The talk is seldom without humor, wisecracks and sallies of heavy sarcasm. As often as not the huddles break up in a laugh, sour but hearty.

The general tone, however, is one of exasperation, directed particularly against the politicians. Wherever two or three citizens gather together, there is a political convention. In these private conventions, however, the keynoter has no encomiums for any candidate or either party. Four years ago the manœuvres at Kansas City and Houston were followed with a mild sporting interest mixed with shrugging cynicism, the usual attitude of prosperous America toward politics; such heat as developed in the 1928 campaign was kindled from fires going deeper than politics. In normal times we are spectator citizens as well as spectator sportsmen. Now the interest is intense to the point of anger, not a dynamic anger driving toward action but a vague irritation, mostly against hokum and cowardice, which may spend itself in turning out most of the present officeholders and replacing them with names drawn from the same hopper, by the same methods, and promising no change except a greater inexperience.

The elector does not rationalize this resentment. He is not consistent. He curses Congressmen in general for logrolling, for obstructing and delaying national measures in favor of local interests, in the same breath in which he demands from his own Congressman nothing but local representation. If there are no national representatives, neither are there any national citizens.

From the beginning the country has looked to the economy program as the real test of the sincerity of its official representatives. Here, too, it is unreasonable, since the establishment it now rebels against was built to the specifications of the voters, always calling for more government service. Nevertheless, the failure to slash costs is viewed with something like despair, as the final proof of political stupidity.

Can democracy function in an emergency? More and more this question worries the congresses of the street. It is a question I have heard many times, but not in crowds, and not in this temper, except during those fumbling preludes which in other countries lead to dictatorship.

But America is not like other countries. The reporter who has made the international round feels that strongly as he circulates among his protesting and bewildered countrymen. Something destructive has happened to us in the past few years, the same thing that happens to people under dictatorships. Here it is the combined effect of government increasingly concentrated, of mergers and chains and corporate ownership, of ownership without effort, of easy money and paper profits and losses. We were fast becoming a nation of clerks, deputies, high-priced hired men. The sense of responsibility atrophied, the sense of values was corrupted; after the gaudy 1920s we were flabby and a little the worse for synthetic gin and synthetic prosperity.

That shows up now just as Congress shows up now. This

session has been better than most, anxious, laborious, less partisan than usual, more coöperative. When one turns at last from the represented to the representatives, it is only to meet in Washington a group of tired, harassed and baffled men, up against problems too big for them and unhappily aware of it. Was Congress aware that it was under scrutiny more close and critical than ever before, that the public was sick and tired of old stratagems, of stale campaign speeches, of flag-raising on top of a volcano?

Washington remains strangely secluded on its smokeless river, an Olympus hiding in clouds of talk, but I have never seen it so exposed to the harsh weather outside. It is fully cognizant of the mood of the country. Every Representative and Senator I questioned made these three points: first, that Congressional mail was never so heavy as in this session, nor so peremptory; second, that newspapers everywhere now publish daily the record of the local representatives on each roll-call and increasing pressure is brought to bear to make them mere delegates for their constituencies; third, that for two months there has been a concerted campaign of propaganda against Congress, in behalf of the business and banking interests seeking to hasten adjournment, in behalf of the administration seeking to gain prestige at the expense of the legislative body, or in behalf of both. That they are victims of a planned attack of ridicule and misrepresentation is firmly believed by both houses and members of both parties. In this session the persecution complex, so called, has moved from the White House to the Hill.

"Why should we be the scapegoat?" asked a distinguished member of the Senate. "If we had rejected some inspired plan for national recovery, any plan, in fact, we might reasonably be damned. But not a single group in the country, business men, industrialists, bankers, labor leaders, not a single individual, from the President down, has yet come before us with a real program, a constructive suggestion. No, the country pretends it expects nothing of Congress and now condemns us for not doing what nobody can do. We are blamed if we act and if we don't act.

Having led us to ruin, the great business brains of the country can think of nothing but to berate this contemptible body for not pulling them out."

For years all honest Congressmen have lamented that there is no counterweight against the pressure of lobbies representing special interests; the people as such, they say, are never heard from. In this session the people have been heard from again and again, but in such confusion of counsel and demand and protest that they have but added another element to the general bewilderment. The truth is, of course, that democracies cannot act as democracies when there is vital need for quick and disinterested decisions. Representative government gives satisfaction but not efficiency. One reason for the St. Vitus dance of Congress is that it is too representative, pulled by too many strings.

Emergency shows us up, shows up our system of government, and shows up with complete clearness certain processes that have been going on for a long time without much remark. One is that for twenty years we have been electing our public officials on the prohibition issue, making a candidate's sentiments on the liquor question practically the sole test of his fitness to deal with the most intricate problems ever put up to legislators. Another is that our great popular reforms, such as the direct primary and the referendum, as worked out by a heretofore wholly indifferent electorate, have weakened party responsibility without giving us better officers or fairer laws. A third is progressive centralization of power and function in Washington that has neither relieved nor simplified State establishments, but has radically disturbed the original balance between the executive and legislative branches of the Federal Government and turned every session of Congress into a struggle of the waning against the crescent power.

Most important is what has happened to the party system. Under our rigid two-party system, with power and responsibility in the hands of the majority, there is no provision for those legislative sessions, like the last, in which no working majority exists. Usually such sessions are sterile or stormy. But aside from that,

it is perfectly evident that the two parties have long since ceased
to have any sustaining principles or vital points of difference.
Every tariff and taxation bill proves that we are divided not into
parties but into economic sections, so that the parties themselves
have degenerated into little more than rival machines for electing a President and controlling Federal patronage. For effective
government under our charter, the parties have to function as
such, strongly led and unified. Much of our present confusion and
impotence arises from the fact that we are organized under one
system and operating, or trying to operate, under another;
nominally we have two-party rule, but actually we have rule by
group, bloc, section, lobby.

We have an unorganized economic parliament without the
legal machinery to regulate it.

America is not like other countries. It has not even so much
logic as England, which hates formulas but moves pretty steadily
in one direction without them, while we love formulas, and with
them manage to proceed in any direction. Thus you cannot
predict of America what you might of really rational countries
that follow premises to conclusions; you cannot say that because
we are in a mood to welcome it that there is the least likelihood
of a dictatorship.

Our government is not like other governments. It may be
doubted if any other could ride along with so many wheels within
two wheels. That feat supports the hope that even democracy
might work in a modern State if it were tried. Representative
government breaks down in times of stress mainly because it has
never been adjusted to the facts.

This is a time of great decisions. Among the greatest questions,
because it involves the future of the democratic principle in government, is whether we can revitalize the parties and make them
mean something by giving them fighting programs, new names,
new aims, modern machinery, and then whether we have intelligence and courage enough to build up another and more honest
system of representation, strengthened by some sort of economic
council, appointive, non-partisan, non-local, of such intellectual

calibre and practical experience that it can function as a brain for the body politic.

No ordinary political campaign is this on which we now embark. It may be our last chance to prove that there is initiative enough left in democracy to make it worth saving and spirit enough left in America to turn this abstract, sentimental, agitated but unfocused Americanism into positive and adventurous citizenship. It is our representatives, after all, who personify and indict us. "I consider myself a poor Congressman," one the wisest said to me, "abdicating most of the time my own fairly informed judgment. But you know why, don't you? I am a poor Congressman because I want to continue to be a Congressman."

That an efficient distribution of wealth, balancing plant extension and buying power, would help to solve the problem of stabilizing economy was long ago advanced by economic thinkers. But the issue which it presented received little serious attention by the public in general during the period of "prosperity." Here and there, however, it was recognized and the idea of an effective distribution was nurtured. Today one of its widest known champions is Mary Van Kleeck, of the Russell Sage Foundation, whose views Gertrude Gordon summarized in an interview for "The Independent Woman," in December, 1931, headed, BETTER DISTRIBUTION IS THE WAY OUT.[6] Miss Van Kleeck points out international implications.

Is there a solution of the economic tangle in which the world finds itself today? Can business and industry be stabilized? Can a higher degree of social justice be achieved? Mary Van Kleeck, director of the department of industrial studies of the Russell Sage Foundation, who is a profound and earnest student of social problems today, believes that it can be done. A higher standard of living for people in general, beginning with those who have the *least* in all nations, a sense of security that this

---

[6] Reprint obtained through the courtesy of *The Independent Woman.*

standard will be maintained—and their corollary, a more equal distribution of what the world has to offer—these are in Miss Van Kleeck's opinion the way out of the present chaos.

To sound a note of optimism in a period of pronounced depression is unusual. To suggest a higher standard of living when millions of people are finding difficulty in maintaining the standard to which they are accustomed sounds almost revolutionary. But the suggestion comes from a woman who has a wide background of knowledge of world conditions. Not only has Miss Van Kleeck served as director of the department of industrial studies at the Russell Sage Foundation since 1910, but as chairman of the committee on program of the World Social Economic Congress, held in August in Amsterdam, Holland, and as vice president of the International Relations Association of The Hague, she has had an intimacy of contact with the leaders of social and economic thought which gives extraordinary weight and authority to any opinion of hers, no matter how modestly stated.

And Miss Van Kleeck is modest, though none the less definite, in what she has to say.

"What is the 'way out' of this economic tangle in which we find ourselves?" She repeated my first question with a smile. "That is too complicated to answer offhand. It makes me think of the very, very young wife who said to her husband, 'My dear, when you have ten minutes or so to spare, do explain to me all about the Einstein theory.'"

Then her eyes grew grave. "It can't be answered in a sentence nor in a moment," she said, "but the World Social Economic Congress, in which, by the way, women participated equally with men [1931], has clarified the problems and pointed the direction in which to look for the way out.

"Just at present, we are all in danger of being confused by big words, such as Economic Depression, Over-Production, the Machine Age, Over-Population, Capitalism, and Communism. Instead of all these generalizations, we should begin to look at the simple realities of the situation.

"Those realities, as the Amsterdam Congress pointed out, are the world's wealth in the raw materials, and the land, which technological invention and human skill have made more productive than ever before in the world's history. In fact, the world's productive capacity has actually increased faster than the population. Yet in all the countries where modern industry is most highly developed, by some strange paradox, more wage-earners are today unemployed than at any time since statistics of unemployment have been kept.

"The problem is to find the way to get the world's primary resources and the products of modern industry used. That means raising standards of living in proportion to the increase in productive capacity. But it cannot be done by one nation alone. At the very moment when we need to sell our goods, the nations are erecting barriers through tariffs, war debts, expenditures for armaments, and policies of economic self-sufficiency. The paradox will continue unless we look at the world as a whole and act coöperatively.

"The United States, for instance, has almost every natural resource; we have machinery and electric power and the skill and business leadership to develop them; and no country has developed the principles and practice of scientific management more fundamentally than has ours. We have plenty of space. We have a people who are energetic and coöperative in spirit. We have everything a nation could want or need—plus a surplus to exchange with other countries. Is it not senseless that with all this we have men, women and children destitute of the barest necessities of existence, workers unable to find work, children and old people suffering?

"Why is this? The answer is in two words—faulty distribution. Purchasing power is not equal to production. The income of our own people has not been secure or steady enough to maintain a steady market. Our foreign policy—tariffs and war debts —has put obstacles in the way of our selling to other countries, and they, like us, have failed to produce purchasing power simultaneously with the production of goods.

"This is a problem of organization, involving governmental policy, finance and business leadership. The first step to be taken towards the solution of this or any other problem is to possess the will to solve it. Clear the atmosphere of the confusion of words, which, after all, are not realities. Think of the actual standards of living of the workers—food, housing, clothing, opportunity—as the reality towards which all economic activities must be directed. Unless those standards be secure, modern industry cannot sell its goods. Each unemployed worker, unable to buy, creates more unemployment.

"Now I know," she raised her hand to stop the arguments she saw coming. "I know all that has been said about the danger of developing a nation of spendthrifts. I know the usual remark that during the war, when wages were higher, pianos and silk shirts and automobiles were bought recklessly, along with thousands of other things for which pianos and silk shirts and automobiles are a symbol. But why not? If modern industry produces these articles by the methods of mass production, they must be sold by the methods of mass distribution.

"Edward A. Filene, the Boston merchant, pointed this out very emphatically at the Amsterdam Congress. He advocated mass production and mass distribution, by which he meant low unit costs of production, low prices, and high wages with which to purchase the low-priced output of mass production. He profoundly believes that this 'beneficent circle' means greater total profits. The present depression results, he believes, from the faulty thinking of business men and financiers who have not put these ideas into practice. In the Bible, something is said about not muzzling the ox which treadeth out the corn. The worker must receive adequate wage, comfort and enjoyment for the labor he gives. Unless he does, his whole scheme of existence seems futile.

"The truth is that we have permitted the idea of 'over-production' to frighten us. There should be no such thing as over-production so long as one person in the world actually needs what is being produced. Standards should keep pace with production. That is the one big necessary lesson we have not learned —to balance production through buying power.

"The simple law of economics must here be kept in mind, however. Buying power can come only through past production. As we restrict production, so do we restrict wealth. A progressive society must bend all its efforts towards expansion, not contraction. Restriction upon production of the necessities of life —unless all people have already enough—produces poverty.

"But though general over-production is not possible in a world in which there are great lacks in food, shelter and clothing, nevertheless it is entirely possible to over-develop one branch of industry when something else is needed more. And there the element of planned production comes in.

"The subject of the World Social Economic Congress was Social Economic Planning. 'Social' signifies that the planning should be directed towards raising the standards of living. 'Economic' means that all branches of economic life would be integrated by a commonsense analysis of what we have called the problem of organization: namely, how the world's productive capacity can be fully utilized. The latter can be achieved by increasing and distributing the power of consumption. But there must be planning. And in so far as planning must be international, it suggests the need of research to find out how to solve this problem of organization.

"So we come to the idea of a world research center, to study these problems and find the best answer to them; to be the central distribution point for the dissemination of knowledge of the way the nations can coöperate in world commerce, and to be such an authority on the subject that suggestions, advice, answers to problems emanating from it, would be heeded by the whole world.

"But, after the center is established and the problems studied and answers found, there is another difficulty—that the great public, the peoples of the world, should heed what is told them; and—most difficult of all—that their governments should act wisely in economic matters.

"When one hears today the amazing suggestion that only another war can lift us out of depression, despite the economic lessons which the last war should have taught; when nations are establishing higher tariffs, despite the obvious fact that they are already paralyzing commerce; when you hear the suggestion that railroad workers' wages be lowered in order that investors may receive dividends, although we know that purchasing power through steady, high wages is already too low, in comparison with investments in more production of unsalable goods and services; when you see the gap between the knowledge of what ought to be done and the actual proposals for action, you realize that the Voice which would speak of a solution of world problems, in tones which would be heard and heeded by all the nations in the world, must be a Voice with knowledge and wisdom behind it. Such a voice would emanate from the world research center, and its task would be the education of the peoples of the world in economic questions.

"Meanwhile, of course, we have our pressing problems, of which unemployment is by no means the least. It is deplorable that it should be necessary in America to raise funds to feed hungry people and to shelter them, when what they want is an opportunity to work. But funds must be given with the utmost generosity. At the same time it must be recognized that all this giving is only the demonstration of our failure to plan our economic system. Instead of relief funds we ought to have reserves to take care of part of the unemployment. Yet this unemployment insurance again is solely a relief measure and cannot take the place of adequate wages for continuous employment."

It sounded in part like a futuristic dream. "Do you think"—the question was put a little timidly—"that in time the whole world really could come to a point when everyone would be fed, everyone possessed of enough necessities to make him comfortable, everyone sheltered and protected against want? It sounds like Utopia."

But Miss Van Kleeck smiled, "It is the present, not the future, which is a paradox. If the world is capable of producing enough for everyone, why should anyone be in want? A rational system will not come tomorrow or next week or next year, but there is no logical reason why such a state of progressive balance could not be attained."

As might be expected, Miss Van Kleeck considers it a primary necessity to keep up the wages of the working population. "Every other means of reducing costs should be tested before the wage rate is reduced, and the probability is that the companies which are well enough managed to try all other methods first will be wise enough to raise wages instead of reducing them. For every wage cut is a blow struck against stability and security.

"The man or woman whose wages are reduced immediately begins to retrench, to save, to lay aside for the storm. It does not take a technician to see the result of this. The employers themselves suffer in the end, as, with buying halted, production pyramids on itself until there is an economic crash which deprives capital as well as labor of its wage. Planned production, directed towards increased consumption, should replace wage-cutting and restricted output.

Miss Van Kleeck believes that the World Social Economic Congress made real progress in clarifying the present economic situation and pointing out the general road to a satisfactory future. She stressed the constant emphasis on planning. "Though economic planning is a technical subject, the attitude which makes it possible is a positive constructive force needed to free individuals and nations from their present fears. The trouble with so many individuals today—and I mean now many of the leaders as well as the rank and file—is that they are bewildered, suddenly stopped, having come unexpectedly to the end of the road without seeing what is coming next. Confidence is gone, hope is being stultified, and worst of all, young men and women are utterly discouraged at the beginning of their careers. However long the task of a more rational organization may take, the important thing is to begin to think about it, so that intelligence may be released instead of thwarted.

"If public opinion can be brought to bear with increasing force upon the tasks which confront the governments of nations; and if that public opinion can be animated by the social will to apply to all policies the test of the effect upon standards of living, then it will be possible at once to make use of technical skill in its bearing upon these problems. In other words, the immediate aim of political action needs to be redefined in terms of its social effects, and the technical procedures for achieving the end desired must be worked out by technicians.

"Social economic planning is no simple concept. Those who are beginning to study it need a common center. It is of the utmost importance that there be close contact between those who are seeking to establish national planning in different countries. All national planning should be conceived and administered in the light of international and world points of view, for the reason that national planning cannot cover its whole subject without taking account also of international factors.

"To this end a World Research Center is needed to coördinate the efforts of technicians, to direct their attention to common problems, to agree upon uniformity in statistics bearing upon economic planning, and to develop greater precision in the methods of economic and social research.

"Business and professional women of America have a real place in such world planning. To study the problems of consumption, the raising of standards of living of families and individuals, should be a congenial task for them. First they should study the problems in their own branches of economic life and then expand into wider fields. The common center which their organization gives may enable them to see the inter-relations of their vocations. They can have great influence in policies. But may a word of caution be given? Is it possible that the business woman of America thinks of herself too often as an isolated individual, responsible alone for her own success? Certainly the danger is that the general spirit of America has put this emphasis upon individual success. John Dewey said recently that education to-day must develop independence of thought and coöperation in action. The principle is applicable to woman's place in economic life. Inventiveness and constructive ideas which grow out of independent thought must be brought to bear upon our economic problems. We must not merely accept the world as we find it. We must be ready to make sacrifices for the common good.

"It may be that America can only fulfill its destiny by a period of sacrifice and deprivation. But if we are to make our contribution to the world, we must see to it that the burdens are not allowed to rest upon those who have the least. Those who have the most must prove themselves capable of learning to live more simply and freeing themselves from the love of possessions. In that spirit, the essence of which is the capacity to coöperate, America may discover that true individualism thrives best only in the most highly developed coöperation."

When Edith Wharton pondered on the stuff of thought with reference to the art of writing fiction, the social clash which stirred her most was the conflict of a seasoned urban culture in New York and other cities with the urban culture of industrial parvenus. But Ellen Glasgow of Virginia was affected by two American social upheavals amounting to revolutions: one, the collapse of the Southern rural aristocracy in the middle of the nineteenth century; the other, the collapse of the Northern urban aristocracy, old and new, in the panic which opened in 1929. Viewing from her high tower—no ivory tower—the ruins of two powerful systems, Ellen Glasgow, in "The Nation" of April 12, 1933, under the title, WHAT I BELIEVE, seeks an eternal amid the ephemeral—the real amid the nominal.

To begin with my start in life, since all of us who are not converts for an advantage bring a measure of our belief into the world with us, I was born with a nonconformist mind at a time when being a rebel, even an intellectual one, was less exciting and more uncomfortable than it is nowadays. By temperament I was on the side of the disinherited, a position which is neither commendable nor the reverse, but simply a matter of the thickness of the skin over one's nerves. The world I lived in as a child was, in part at least, the world of Dickens, and he, as Santayana has said, "was a waif himself, and utterly disinherited." Even now, I cannot tell whether I loved Dickens because he had compassion for "the deformed, the half-witted, the abandoned, or those impeded or misunderstood by virtue of some singular inner consecration," or whether the early influence of Dickens made me pity these unhappy creatures.

Although I was different from other children whom I knew, I excelled only in imaginary adventures, and I could never, no matter how hard I tried, learn to do sums. But a thin skin and over-sensitive nerves made my childhood unhappy. I saw painful sights that did not distress other infants or even the adult minds that surrounded me. For I had come into the world hating cruelty as Voltaire hated superstition (though, of course, Voltaire hated, too, the cruelty in superstition), yet I saw the needless suffering of human beings and especially of animals wherever I looked. I was a delicate child, and, perhaps for this reason, the tragedy of life and the pathos which is worse than the tragedy worked their way into my nerves and through my nerves into my beliefs. Yet, even at this tender age, my sense of humor was an adequate defense against the more destructive winds of doctrine.

In the first of my books I was moved to speak for the despised and rejected; but the raveled sleeve had not become a fashion in literature, and the disinherited was less welcome in that year of grace than he finds himself in an epoch that prefers the style of illiteracy to the language of romance. "The Descendant," an honest, defiant, and very immature book, bearing as its motto Haeckel's phrase, "Man is not above Nature, but in Nature," and softened here and there to satisfy the reluctant publisher's demands for "a moral or at least a pleasant tone," records, in words that are hot and crude and as formless as the revolt of youth, many of the things I believed passionately as a girl and believe reasonably as a woman.

For it does not alarm me to hear that an economic system must be revised or discarded. I had heard this as a schoolgirl—though in a republic which was still watching the Rockefeller fortune with admiration and envy, it was not at school that I heard such opinions. My own special interests were in the direction of history and literature; but it was my privilege to study economics (it was all political economy when I was sixteen, and Mill had not ceased to be a major prophet) under the guidance of a brilliant and fearless mind. A profound thinker and student, at least thirty years ahead of his time, my friend died at the age of twenty-six, crushed by physical pain, and crowded out of a world which required not brilliance, and certainly not fearlessness, but conformity. Yet wherever I look today I see his prophecies coming true. Though he did not predict the World War, he did predict other wars and a period of social evolution which would either overthrow our economic structure or result in a more equitable distribution of wealth under the present system. He said to me the first time I heard of Karl Marx, "The economists of the future will have to reckon with that force." There were other predictions, though he was never a convert to any theory; but, after all, I was asked to write an article on what I believe, not on how I came to believe.

To return, then, to my creed, I believe that the quality of belief is more important than the quantity, that the world could do very well with fewer and better beliefs, and that a reasonable doubt is the safety-valve of civilization. So I believe what I believe with an open mind. I am, I hope, ready to reject anything or to accept anything that does not embrace the old infamy, cruelty. I am not frightened by systems. I am not frightened even by names, since I have been called by almost every name, except the right one, as far back as I can remember. When I was one and twenty, it was all very exciting for one and twenty is the proper age for revolt. One is still young enough then to have faith in some miraculous system which will abolish cruelty and greed, and change the primary instincts that have made civilizations so uncivilized. One has not learned that systems are made by human nature, not human nature by systems, and that the ancient evils may still flourish in any social order. Nevertheless, if I firmly believe anything in later years, these are the things I believe:

Since I have no superstition concerning an economic structure, I believe that our system should be revised by economists with an eye for facts, not by prophets with the gift of visions. As a general theory, leaving the ways and means to specialists, I believe that the private ownership of wealth should be curbed; that our natural resources should not be exploited for individual advantage; that every man should be assured of an opportunity to earn a living and a fair return for his labor; that our means of distribution should be readjusted to our increasing needs and the hollow cry of "over-production" banished from a world in which millions are starving; that the two useless extremes of society, the thriftless rich and the thriftless poor, should be mercifully eliminated by education or eugenics; that human progress cannot be weighed in noise and measured by many inventions; that the greatest discovery of the mind was neither fire nor electricity but the power to share in another's pain; that self-pity, the favorite vice of a generation too "hard-boiled" for compassion, is the softest and most primitive form of sentimentality; that art is older, as well as younger, than propaganda, and less subject, therefore, to the processes of change and decay; that freedom in literature should mean freedom not for the bawdy word alone but for the honest word also, freedom not only to be the "tough guy" in letters, but freedom even to wear, without rebuke, the white flower of a blameless speech; that civilization may include a chicken in the pot for every peasant but it includes something more; that if man were really civilized, any system ever invented might usher in the millennium; that fear of the end is an ignoble delusion; and that, to return to Santayana, writing now of the Homeric Age, "nothing can be meaner than the anxiety to live on, to live on anyhow in any shape."

Furthermore, I believe that a change is approaching; whether for better or for worse, who would dare prophesy? Change is not necessarily progress; evolution does not imply evolving upward. I should like to think that a fairer social order might be attained in an orderly way, through some third party with high principles; but is it probable, I ask myself, that the selfishness and greed of political parties can be overthrown by high principles and an appeal to right reason? It would be pleasant to imagine that the American people may experience, within the next hundred years, a great social and moral awakening, and begin ardently but intelligently to make over the world, that the citizens of this Republic may sweep away the cobwebs, old wasps' nests, and dead issues of politics, and reaffirm a noble faith in democracy. It would be pleasant, but is it not also incredible? Incredible, it seems, so long as the mass of human beings everywhere can find an escape from social injustice and cruelty, not in resisting, but rather in the thrill of inflicting, however vicariously, injustice and cruelty upon others. Thus I believe that the approach to a perfect state lies not without but within, and that the one and only way to a civilized order is by and through the civilization of man. "Blessedness," Spinoza has said, "is not the reward of virtue, but virtue itself." And, surely, the greatest menace in an epoch so noticeably deficient in "blessedness," is the menace of material power which has outstripped philosophy, and placed the dangerous machinery of life and death in the grasp of an impatient and irresponsible child, with a child's instinctive worship of savagery and a child's contempt for the sober merits and counsel of adult wisdom.

Economists, believing naturally that economics can make or mar a world, tell us in many books that we are speeding to disaster, and I, for one, am inclined to believe that the prediction is true. Yet I believe also that, before we have reached the last turn on the way to disaster, we shall apply the brakes just in time to avoid the full force of the shock. Or, even if we fall, we are obliged to fall somewhere; and both history and anthropology assure us that we can never fall so low that the discredited will-to-live cannot pick us up, shake us well, and start us off again on our uncertain road between two eternities.

Still other observers insist, with a share of truth also, for truth is many-sided, that the crisis we are enduring is one of character, not of economics at all, and that men will not be saved until they have found a new religion. These prophets forget that men do not find a religion, but a religion finds men. It may or may not be true that the nearest approach to a vital religious impulse is embraced in the Russian experiment. Yet, granting this and much more, can anyone alive today imagine the American mind in a posture of adoration before an idol of government? The more Asiatic Russian temperament may not miss the luxury of a public criticism it has never possessed. To the American, however, the liberty to scoff is an inalienable right, protected by the law and the Constitution; and is it possible to picture the farmers of the South and West and the industrial workers of the North and East uniting in the worship of any powers assembled at Washington? The very force that would prevent our making a religion of any social system is, I think, the same imponderable agent that would defeat a violent revolution—that red hope of the left wing in politics. For the strongest power in our United States is, in my opinion, the relentless pressure of mass, not class, consciousness. The social divisions are too shallow; the classes feel and look too much alike either for reverence or for hostility.

Those zealous converts who are enriching our language with long foreign words will have trouble, I predict, not in persuading the American workingman that he is oppressed, but in convincing him that he is a "proletarian." For it is more agreeable to assign than to accept classification, and the restless proletarian may inquire in his turn, "But what are you?" Since we have lost, happily or unhappily, even the semblance of an aristocracy, there remains only an enormous public composed of self-centered individuals, each living for himself but all thinking in mass-consciousness. The scattered groups that we still call, more from habit than politeness, "the best people" are continually replenished by the upper levels of the order we are learning, boldly but not without embarrassment, to speak of as "the proletariat." It is this essentially fluid nature of our social divisions that makes a violent class struggle appear to be less a disaster than an absurdity.

Let an American workingman of active intelligence change places with an American banker, also of active intelligence, and in a few weeks neither the workingman nor the banker could be sure of the class in which he belonged. The gulf between an unwashed peasant and a perfumed aristocrat may have been too wide for a touch of nature to bridge; but even the most earnest revolutionist would hesitate, one imagines, to display on a pike a head that so nearly resembled his own. Yet, even so, and however mild the reversal, it would seem that, in a time of unrest, of intellectual defeat, of spiritual destitution, it is safer to examine our structure and make the necessary repairs. It would seem, too, wiser to profit by the past than to ignore or deny it; and the most superficial glance back into history will prove that more social disorders have been prevented by common sense with bread than have ever been put down by desperation with bayonets.

At this point we may stop long enough to ponder the changing fashions of intellectual revolt. Twenty-five years ago, when I remarked that it made no difference whether or not a man had stepped out of the gutter if only he had stepped out, I was taken to task by several of the deep young men of the period. For the deep young men of that day were not investigating the gutter. Instead, they were straining their muscles in the effort to write of the American plutocracy or the English aristocracy after the best manner of Henry James or Oscar Wilde. It is amusing, nevertheless, to remember that the word "gutter" offended the sensibilities of an earlier decade quite as severely as the phrase "well bred" shocks our hardened nerves nowadays. Yet it seems not only embarrassing but absurd to be obliged to explain to adult persons one of the first lessons every Southern child is supposed to learn at his mother's knee, or, failing a mother's knee, when he passes through kindergarten, and this is that the term "well bred" does not mean either well dressed or wealthy. It has, in fact, as little to do with gentility or respectability as writing a book has, and all of us know, I assume, how very little that is.

Many ill-bred persons have been the children of royalty; many others have been, no doubt, sons or daughters of bishops. For good breeding may go in rags and often has gone in rags; it may step into the gutter; but it does not belong in the gutter and usually contrives to step out again. The first time I heard the words, I remember, they were used by my mother to describe an old colored man who came to clean out our hen-house and do other work on the farm befitting his years. "Uncle Will is so well bred," she told me, "I like you to be with him." He was not servile. Only a person who considered Epictetus servile could have charged Uncle Will with servility. What he had learned was the old Greek acceptance of fate, or better still, superiority to adverse fortune; all the qualities that lend needed dignity to human nature and appear on the surface of life as fine breeding—courtesy, restraint, forbearance, consideration for others. This is what Ortega y Gasset means when he speaks of "the nobly disciplined mind," and he adds discreetly, "It is not rare to find today amongst workingmen nobly disciplined minds."

And so, believing in, as well as sympathizing with, the nobly disciplined mind wherever it is stranded in an age that scorns discipline, it follows naturally that I prefer the spirit of fortitude to the sense of futility. It follows, too, I suppose, that I prefer, among other things, civilization to savagery (though, if we must return to the wilderness, I should choose the noble savage of Rousseau as my neighbor rather than the "sophisticated barbarian" or sentimental sadist of Franco-American fiction); that I prefer good manners to rudeness, especially toward the weak, the defenseless, and all those who are placed in what we call inferior positions; that I prefer, not new and popular alignments of the persecutors and the persecuted, but a social order in which nobody may be persecuted for his opinions.

Other things also I believe, and these other things are bound up with what I feel to be permanent issues. I believe in the evolution of life on this planet, and though I think that evolution does not imply evolving upward, I do believe that humanity has groped its way out of primeval darkness. I believe, as well, that on this long journey upward from lower forms man has collected a few sublime virtues, or, more accurately perhaps, a few ideas of sublime virtues, which he has called truth, justice, courage, loyalty, compassion. These ideas, and these ideas alone, seem to me to justify that bloodstained pilgrimage from the first cannibal feast, past the *auto-da-fé* of too much believing, to the moral and industrial crisis of the twentieth century.

Because the church has evaded these issues and imprisoned its faith in arbitrary doctrines, I think it has failed to satisfy the intellectual and spiritual needs of the modern world, in which primitive consecrations and barbaric symbols have lost, for many of us, their earlier significance. Yet I think, too, that the mass of men will not be content to live entirely without religion or philosophy as a guide.

And, finally, beyond this, I can see only the vanishing-point in the perspective, where all beliefs disappear and the deepest certainties, if they exist, cannot be comprehended by the inquiring mind alone, but must be apprehended by that inmost reason which we may call the heart.

After 300 years of pioneering, working in field, homestead, shop and factory, dividing into classes, participating in social and industrial wars, struggling for privilege, listening to lectures, practicing professions, trying the arts and wrestling with "learning," American women at large found their social economy sinking in efficiency and threatened with disintegration. This was a clear challenge to thought about ways and means of caring for life. Whether the Great Society which had been supporting them could endure and on what terms became the supreme question everywhere.

In these circumstances the National Council of Women, composed of twenty component organizations representing a total membership of five million women, issued the following Call for an International Congress of Women to assemble in Chicago in the summer of 1933 during the sessions of the Century of Progress Fair. Among those who signed the Call, in addition to the Council Chairman, Lena Madisin Phillips, was Mrs. Franklin D. Roosevelt. As we go to Press, this great women's congress prepares to assemble.

Forty years ago, the women of the world held their first International Congress during the Columbian Exposition at Chicago. It gave impetus to the development of the organized womanhood of the world. By it came the channels through which women pursued their quest for power—social, political and educational. In the Congress of 1933, we will in a realistic fashion do honor to those pioneers of 1893, by emulating their courage and foresight. The feminine quest of power wanes, but before women lie today great opportunities for the right use of that power.

The forthcoming assembly will take place at a period of world depression following a world war. So widespread is unemployment and human misery, so varied are the proposals for changes in the political and economic scene that civilization faces grave problems connected with its actual survival.

At previous assemblies of women, minor issues could be discussed with more or less urbanity. For thousands of years, men and women have been struggling with the problem of production. Now this problem is settled. We can produce all that we need.

And yet at this moment much of the world is in want. Economic distress and insecurity are the common lot of vast numbers of people everywhere. We have mastered production; we have not mastered distribution. We have not learned how to make the machine the servant, rather than the master of man. We have not lifted the burden of fear under which parents must bring up their children. We have not lifted black despair from many an aged worker. We have not learned how to attain a settled currency nor how to exchange goods from nation to nation. We have not learned to keep the peace between individuals or between nations.

And yet these problems can and must be solved. We can plan a society which will guarantee to its members a minimum security for existence and a maximum opportunity for development. We can plan a society in which there shall be security of work, of income, of health; security against the violence of war and of crime; security of government for the good of all the people. We can plan a society in which there shall be opportunity for all—of education, of vocational training, cultural life and a richer use of leisure.

In view of this situation, we summon the women thinkers throughout the world to a Congress on *Our Common Cause—Civilization*. Technology has created for us our House of Plenty. It is a challenge to the women of the world to find the keys through governmental and economic planning which will admit us to that House of Plenty.

You are invited to take part in these discussions which we believe will justify the efforts of our pioneers in their quest for power. For the justification of power is its use to wise and beneficent ends.

BIBLIOGRAPHY

ABBOTT, EDITH. *Women in Industry: a Study in American Economic History*. With an Introduction by Sophonisba Breckinridge. D. Appleton and Company, 1915.

ADAMS, CHARLES FRANCIS (Editor). *Familiar Letters of John Adams and His Wife, Abigail Adams, during the Revolution*. Houghton Mifflin Company, 1875.

ADAMS, HANNAH. *Memoir*. Boston, 1832.

ADDAMS, JANE. *Twenty Years at Hull-House*. The Macmillan Company, 1912.

ADDAMS, JANE, and Others. *Women at The Hague*. The Macmillan Company, 1915.

BALDWIN, ALICE. *New England Clergy in the American Revolution*. Duke University Press, 1928.

BLACKWELL, ALICE STONE. *Lucy Stone, Pioneer of Woman's Rights*. Little, Brown and Company, 1930.

BLATCH, HARRIOT STANTON. *A Woman's Point of View: Some Roads to Peace*. The Woman's Press, 1920.

BROWN, ALICE. *Mercy Warren*. Charles Scribner's Sons, 1896.

BROWN, HARRIET C. *Grandmother Brown's Hundred Years, 1827–1927*. Little, Brown and Company, 1929.

CARY, CONSTANCE (Mrs. Burton Harrison). *Recollections Grave and Gay*. Charles Scribner's Sons, 1911.

CATT, CARRIE CHAPMAN. With the collaboration of Nettie Rogers Shuler. *Woman Suffrage and Politics*. Charles Scribner's Sons, 1923.

CHAMPION, DEBORAH. *A Letter*. Deborah Champion Chapter, Daughters of the American Revolution, Adams, New York.

CHILD, LYDIA MARIA. *An Appeal in Favor of That Class of Americans Called Africans*. Boston, 1833.

DELAND, MARGARET. *Small Things*. D. Appleton and Company, 1919.

DEXTER, ELISABETH. *Colonial Women of Affairs*. Houghton Mifflin Company, 1924.

DOUTHIT, MARY OSBORN (Editor). *The Souvenir of Western Women*. Presses of Anderson and Duniway, Portland, Oregon, 1905. For the *Journal* of Narcissa Whitman.

Earle, Alice Morse. *Colonial Dames and Goodwives.* Houghton Mifflin Company, 1895.

Ellet, Elizabeth. *The Women of the American Revolution.* Baker and Scribner, New York, 1848.

Epler, Percy H. *Life of Clara Barton.* The Macmillan Company, 1905.

Fields, Annie (Editor). *The Letters of Sarah Orne Jewett.* Houghton Mifflin Company, 1911.

Frink, Margaret Alsip. *Original Journal of an Adventurous Trip to California in 1850.* Privately printed.

Goldmark, Josephine. *Fatigue and Efficiency.* Charities Publication Committee, New York, 1912.

Hallowell, Anna D. (Editor). *Life and Letters of James and Lucretia Mott.* Houghton Mifflin Company, 1884.

Hamilton, Alice. *Industrial Poisons in the United States.* The Macmillan Company, 1925.

Hart, Charles H. *Mary White* (Mrs. Robert Morris). Philadelphia, 1878.

Holley, Marietta. *Samantha at Saratoga; or "Racing after Fashion."* Hubbard Brothers, 1887.

Howe, Julia Ward. *Reminiscences, 1819–1899.* Houghton Mifflin Company, 1899.

Kelley, Florence. *Ethical Gains through Legislation.* The Macmillan Company, 1905.

Kellogg, Clara Louise. *Memoir of an American Prima Donna.* G. P. Putnam's Sons, 1913.

Lee, Mary. *It's a Great War.* Houghton Mifflin Company, 1929.

McIntosh, Maria J. *Woman in America: Her Work and Her Reward.* D. Appleton Company, 1850.

Meyer, Annie Nathan (Editor). *Woman's Work in America.* Henry Holt and Company, 1891.

O'Shaughnessy, Edith. *Letters of a Diplomat's Wife.* Harper & Brothers, 1916.

Ovington, Mary White. *Portraits in Color.* Viking Press, 1927.

Pringle, Elizabeth. *Patience Pennington, a Woman Rice Planter.* The Macmillan Company, 1913.

Pryor, Mrs. Roger A. *Reminiscences of Peace and War.* The Macmillan Company, 1905.

Ravenel, Harriott Horry (Editor). *Eliza Pinckney.* Charles Scribner's Sons, 1896.

Repplier, Agnes. *Under Dispute.* Houghton Mifflin Company, 1924.

Sachs, Emanie. *The Terrible Siren, Victoria Woodhull.* Harper & Brothers, 1928.

SHAW, ANNA HOWARD. With the collaboration of Elizabeth Jordan. *The Story of a Pioneer.* Harper & Brothers, 1915.

STANTON, ELIZABETH CADY, and Others (Editors). *History of Woman Suffrage,* 1881, 1922. 6 vols. Imprint varies.

TAFT, MRS. WILLIAM HOWARD. *Recollections of Full Years.* Dodd, Mead and Company, 1914.

VAN VORST, MRS. JOHN and MARIE. *The Woman Who Toils.* Doubleday, Doran and Company, 1903.

VORSE, MARY HEATON. *Men and Steel.* Boni and Liveright, 1920.

WHARTON, EDITH. *The Writing of Fiction.* Charles Scribner's Sons, 1925.

WITTENMYER, ANNIE (Editor). *History of the Woman's Temperance Crusade.* With an Introduction by Frances Willard. J. H. Earle, Boston, 1882.

WOODWARD, HELEN. *Through Many Windows.* Harper & Brothers, 1926.

MAGAZINES

Annals of the American Academy of Political and Social Sciences. Articles by Atkeson, Mary Meeks, "Women in Farm Life and Rural Economy," May, 1929; and Baker, Elizabeth F., "At the Crossroads in the Legal Protection of Women," May, 1929.

Church Intelligencer, November, 1860. Southern views of slavery.

De Bow's Review, March, 1853. Southern views of slavery.

Harper's Magazine. Article by Symes, Lillian, "The Great Fact-Finding Farce," February, 1932.

Richmond Enquirer, January, 1853. Southern views of slavery.

South Atlantic Quarterly, for article by Sherman, Caroline B., "Rural Standards of Living," 1929.

Southern Literary Messenger, February, 1853. Southern views of slavery.

The Independent Woman. Articles by Hartford, Nancy C., "Josephine Roche, Industrialist," November, 1932; Gordon, Gertrude, "Better Distribution is the Way Out," December, 1931; and Frederick, Christine, "Our American Standard," August, 1932.

The Nation. Article by Glasgow, Ellen, "What I Believe," April 12, 1933.

The New York Times Sunday Magazine. Articles by Barnard, Eunice F., "The Goddess of Our Economic Machine," June 12, 1932; and McCormick, Anne O'Hare, "The New Ordeal of Democracy," June 26, 1932.

NEWSPAPER

New York Evening Post, May 15, 1863. Comment on women's work for the emancipation of slaves.

PAMPHLET

BURSCH, ANN DENNIS. *Electric Power and the Public Welfare.* Publication of League of Women Voters.

INDEX

Abolition, 144, 148, 172 ff.
Academy of Music, 264, 268.
Adams, Abigail, 59 ff., 83, 193.
Adams, Henry, 4, 47.
Adams, James Truslow, 89.
Adams, John, 56, 59 ff., 77, 80.
Adams, Samuel, 24.
Advertising, 416 ff.
Agriculture, 33 ff., 88 ff., 91 ff., 126 ff., 232, 234 ff., 277, 397 ff., 443, 513 ff.
Aguinaldo, 289.
Aliens, 53. *See* Immigration.
American Confederation, 76.
Americanization, 323.
American Renaissance, 312.
American Revolution, 54 ff., 179 ff.
Amusements, 45, 183 f., 253 ff., 410.
Anarchism, 326, 331, 497.
Anthony, Susan B., 226 ff.
Anthropology, 8, 10.
Armaments, 532.
Armies, 203, 224, 288 ff.
Art, 43, 50, 504, 510, 514.
Autarchy, 522, 532. *See* National isolation.

Bacon's Rebellion, 19 f.
Banks and bankers, 524, 527. *See* Power, financial.
Barton, Clara, 212 ff., 462.
Birth control, 304.
Blackwell, Elizabeth, 371 ff.
Blackwell, Emily, 371 ff.
Blockade-running, 210.
Boone, Danial, 88.
Boston Tea Party, 56.
Boycotts, 54, 186, 478, 503.
Bradwell, Myra, 360.
Brent, Margaret, 21 f., 193, 359.
Brent, Mary, 21.
Brook Farm, 172.
Brown, Antoinette, 190 ff.
Brown, John, 195 ff.
Bryan, William Jennings, 290 ff.
Budgets, 506 ff.
Burns, Lucy, 359.

Business, 29 ff. *See* Commerce and Industry.

Calumet Basin, 317.
Calvinism, 46.
Capital, 126 ff., 160, 325.
Capitalism, 252 ff., 325 ff., 443 ff., 531, 540 ff. *See* Profits, Socialism, Communism, and Planning.
Carpetbaggers, 234.
Convicts, 15 f.
Coolidge, Calvin, 479, 492.
Compromise, 162, 198.
Coöperation, 172, 402, 413, 532.
Copyright, on books, 177.
Corporation, 322, 347 f., 504, 520, 526.
Corruption, 523.
Crime, 498.
Credit, 423, 511.
Crusade, the temperance, 301 ff., 380.
Cuba, 281.
Culture, 10, 43, 90 ff., 126, 172 ff., 279 ff., 443, 500, 510, 514.

Daughters of the American Revolution, 56.
Daughters of Liberty, 54.
Declaration of Independence, 55, 67, 139, 186.
Debts, 44, 161, 476, 532.
Democracy, 77, 159, 161, 328, 385 ff., 521 ff. *See* Classes, Profits, and Politics.
Depression. *See* Panic and Unemployment.
Department of Agriculture, 400, 404, 495.
Department of Commerce, 492.
Department of Interior, 492.
Department of Labor, 437, 488, 492 f., 495.
Diaz, 44 ff.
Dickinson, Anna, 197.
Diplomacy, 443 ff.
Direct primary, 528.

553

Index